A Prophet to the Peoples: Paul Farmer's Witness *and* Theological Ethics

Edited by

Jennie Weiss Block,
M. Therese Lysaught,
and
Alexandre A. Martins

PICKWICK *Publications* · Eugene, Oregon

A PROPHET TO THE PEOPLES: Paul Farmer's Witness and Theological Ethics
Theology, Ethics, and Social Justice

Copyright © 2023 Jennie Weiss Block, M. Therese Lysaught, and Alexandre A. Martins.
All rights reserved.

Except for brief quotations in critical publications or reviews, no part of this book may be reproduced in any manner without prior written permission from the publisher. Write: Permissions, Wipf and Stock Publishers, 199 W. 8th Ave., Suite 3, Eugene, OR 97401.

Pickwick Publications
An Imprint of Wipf and Stock Publishers
199 W. 8th Ave., Suite 3
Eugene, OR 97401

www.wipfandstock.com

Softcover: 978-1-6667-6503-8
Hardcover: 978-1-6667-6504-5
eBook: 978-1-6667-6505-2

DEDICATION

*Faith, hope, and love remain, these three,
but the greatest of these is love.*
1 Corinthians 13:13

In recognition of Dr. Paul Farmer's commitment to a
preferential option
for the poor in health care,
we dedicate this book to his patients,
both living and dead, for they are the first witnesses to
his vocation as a physician and a healer.

Global Theological Ethics — Book Series

Series Editors
Jason King, St. Vincent College
M. Therese Lysaught, Loyola University Chicago

The Global Theological Ethics book series focuses on works that feature authors from around the world, draw on resources from the traditions of Catholic theological ethics, and attend to concrete issues facing the world today. It advances the *Journal of Moral Theology*'s mission of fostering scholarship deeply rooted in traditions of inquiry about the moral life, engaged with contemporary issues, and exploring the interface of Catholic moral theology philosophy, economics, political philosophy, psychology, and more.

This series is sponsored in conjunction with the Catholic Theological Ethics in the World Church. The CTEWC recognizes the need to dialogue from and beyond local cultures and to interconnect within a world church. Its global network of scholars, practitioners, and activists fosters cross-cultural, interdisciplinary conversations—via conferences, symposia, and colloquia, both in-person and virtually—about critical issues in theological ethics, shaped by shared visions of hope.

Online versions of the volumes in the *Global Theological Ethics* series are available for free download as chapters at jmt.scholasticahq.com. Paper copies may be purchased from Wipf & Stock. This dual approach reflects the *Journal of Moral Theology*'s commitment to the common good as it seeks to make the scholarship of Catholic theological ethicists broadly available, especially across borders.

Series Titles

Ethical Challenges in Global Public Health: Climate Change, Pollution, and the Health of the Poor, edited by Philip J. Landrigan and Andrea Vicini, SJ (2021)

The Rising Global Cancer Pandemic: Health, Ethics, and Social Justice, edited by Andrea Vicini, SJ, Philip J. Landrigan, and Kurt Straif (2022)

Doing Theology and Theological Ethics in the Face of the Abuse Crisis, edited by Daniel J. Fleming, James F. Keenan, SJ, and Hans Zollner, SJ (2023)

A Prophet to the Peoples: Paul Farmer's Witness and Theological Ethics, edited by Jennie Weiss Block, OP, M. Therese Lysaught, and Alexandre A. Martins (2023)

Table of Contents

Acknowledgements x

Foreword
Roberto S. Goizueta xv

Artist's Statement: Unmercenary Paul, the Good Samaritan
Fr. Cristóbal Torres Iglesias, OP xxiii

Introduction
Jennie Weiss Block, OP, M. Therese Lysaught, and
   Alexandre A. Martins 1

Part 1: A Life as a Theological Text

Introduction 23

1. Towards a Realized Eschatology: Paul Farmer as Good Samaritan
Jennie Weiss Block, OP 27

2. Paul the *Anargyros*: History, God-Talk, and Ecumenism in the Healing Praxis of Dr. Paul Farmer
Susan R. Holman 58

3. Paul Farmer: A Model for the Theologian
Jorge José Ferrer, SJ 76

4. Living Witnesses and Moral Agency
Alison Lutz 94

Part 2: A Prism for Liberation Theology

Introduction 112

5. Liberation Theology and Public Health Ethics: The Tradition Behind Paul Farmer
Alexandre A. Martins 116

6. Theologians in the Field: "Dices que eres un teólogo, ¿cuál es tu practica?"
Leo Guardado 137

7. Liberating Theological Ethics from the Invisible Hand: Paul Farmer, the World's Poor, and the Quandaries of the Fortunate
M. Therese Lysaught 154

8. Confronting "Structures of Violence": Women's Empowerment and the Legacy of Paul Farmer
Suzanne Mulligan 183

Part 3: Accompaniment

Introduction 202

9. From *Amoris Laetitia* to Ebola: Accompaniment as a Model for Medical and Pastoral Care
James F. Keenan, SJ 205

10. Wasting Time with the World's Poor: Theological and Scriptural Foundations for Paul Farmer's Praxis of Accompaniment
Brian Volck 222

11. Practicing Local Listening with Village Midwives in Sudan: A Case Study for Theological Ethics
Meghan J. Clark 246

Part 4: Global Health as a Theological Locus

Introduction 271

12. Ebola and the Ravages of History in Paul Farmer: A Catholic Theological Ethical Response to Global Health Inequity in Africa
Stan Chu Ilo 275

13. The Legacy of Paul Farmer for Theological Ethics
Andrea Vicini, SJ 303

14. From Compassion to Pragmatic Solidarity: Considering the Right to Health from the Margins
Maura A. Ryan 317

---

15. 'Doctor' of the Church: Mapping the Religious Threads in Paul Farmer's Writings
D. Brendan Johnson 339

Afterword: How to Turn Preferential Option for the Poor into Active Equity
Eddy Eustache 369

Paul Farmer: Selected Works 375

Acknowledgments

It takes a village to write a book. Those in the little village that came together to write this book all share one thing in common: deep respect for the life and work of Dr. Paul Farmer and deep sadness at his unexpected death at 62 years old. As is often the case when someone dies in the prime of life, especially without warning, the grief experienced by those left behind is always mixed with shock and disbelief because, although we are constantly reminded that we do not know the day or the hour, we are again caught off guard because we always think we will have more time. The sad news that there would be no more time on this earth with Paul Farmer reverberated throughout the world. All who knew him personally were heartbroken and those who knew him by reputation were also devastated by this loss, because Paul Farmer's love for all humanity and untiring work for justice was inspiring and he modeled what was good and right in the world. In the days following his death, as the reality of his death set in, people from all walks of life across the globe, sought consolation within their own networks and communities.

Theologians around the world were among the many groups reaching out to one another to express sorrow about the magnitude of this loss and to share the ways in which their thinking, writing and teaching had been influenced by Paul's scholarship and his extraordinary success in translating theory into praxis through the work of Partners In Health. On February 22, 2022, the day after Paul's death, Therese Lysaught reached out to fellow theologians Meghan Clark, Andrea Vicini, and Alexandre Martins. She knew they would be feeling as she was—deeply saddened by Paul's passing, and reflecting about the scope and importance of his contribution the Catholic moral theology. Lacking an exact plan but searching for a way to recognize this insight, Therese proposed that perhaps they should try to pull together a symposium of short essays for the July issue of the *Journal of Moral Theology* (JMT). Their immediate and enthusiastic 'yes' affirmed that there was crucial work to do here.

Acknowledgments

The editorial staff of the *Journal*—Alexandre plus William Collinge, Mary Doyle Roche, Jason King, Chris McMahon, Mari Rapela Heidt, Kate Ward, and Jean-Pierre Fortin—wholeheartedly concurred. They helped give flesh to this nascent idea and then wisely suggested the project be expanded. They envisioned something more substantial than a symposium with the limits imposed by a three-month turnaround and suggested a book project that would give the contributors more time for scholarly development, befitting the magnitude of Farmer's life, work, and witness. The decision was made to undertake this book-length study, to be published on the first anniversary of his death. Therese invited Alexandre to co-edit the book with her, and they quickly moved ahead to develop the plans for the book as an ambitious timeline would be needed to meet the February 2023 publication date.

The very next day, an initial query was presented to the Catholic Theological Ethics in the World Church (CTEWC) planning committee about the possibility of including such a volume in the collaborative JMT/CTEWC book series; again, the idea met with a heartfelt and positive response. With a green light to pull together a proposal, we began inviting contributors. Perhaps it was providence that as Therese tuned in to the bi-weekly webinars hosted by the Duke Divinity School's Theology, Medicine, and Culture Initiative on March 4, Jennie Weiss Block, a theologian and long-time colleague and friend of Paul Farmer, was the scheduled presenter. Her own grief still fresh, she spoke movingly to a community of scholar-practitioners interested in the interface of theology and medicine about what she had learned about accompaniment from Paul Farmer. We had obviously met our third co-editor.

We are grateful to the CTEWC for accepting our proposal, making this the fourth volume in the JMT/CTEWC series. We were particularly keen to be part of this initiative as it seemed that a book on Paul Farmer and theological ethics should be open access, available to scholars and practitioners around the world, not locked behind a paywall or difficult to obtain due to shipping and supply chain constraints. We hope that the e-book version will bring the good news of Farmer's work and witness to places where he still not known. We were certain that making this book available to those with limited access would be especially pleasing to Dr. Farmer.

It indeed takes a village to write a book, especially in a one-year period with a project involving nineteen contributors along with the multiple other essential parties needed to bring a book project to fruition, and many thanks are in order. We are grateful to everyone involved in this project who added this book to their workload, rearranging busy schedules to find the time to participate—the level of commitment and cooperation speaks to the love and respect all of us have for Dr. Farmer and the joy we have taken in honoring his legacy.

We are grateful to all the scholars who immediately and enthusiastically agreed to contribute to this volume. Many of them knew Farmer well and had worked with him closely. Thus, they wrote as their grief was still fresh and raw. We are especially grateful for their willingness to meet our tight deadlines, endure our email reminders, and graciously accept our editorial suggestions. They have produced beautiful and insightful work that introduces Paul Farmer to a new and larger community of scholars and practitioners and, we hope, helps challenge and advance the field of theological ethics in important ways.

The image on the cover of our book and the accompanying artist's statement brings to life what the book hopes to communicate in ways that words cannot. We would like to express our deep appreciation to Fr. Cristóbal Torres Iglesias, OP, for so generously and freely sharing his artistic and theological gifts. Fr. Cristóbal knew Paul personally, and this image, pressed down and overflowing with meaning, was created as an act of love and gratitude to Paul.

We would like to express our appreciation to Mary Block for her invaluable editorial assistance. Her outstanding skill at organizing content and editing with care and sensitivity to intended meaning has added greatly to this book. Mary was one of Paul's former research assistants and he is her son's godfather, and it is very meaningful to her to have been asked to be a part of this book project.

Acknowledgments

We are especially grateful to the first-rate production staff at the *Journal of Moral Theology*, who proofed and typeset and formatted and corrected and proofed again and perfected the pages of this volume: JMT/CTEWC book series co-editor Jason King, senior editor William Collinge, and editorial assistant Aaron Weisel. While open access e-books meet an important need, we are also grateful to the team at Wipf and Stock, who have brought the gorgeous hard copy version of this book into print.

The unsung heroes in our village are our loving and supportive family and friends. This book would not have come to be without their patience endurance, good humor, and helpfulness. Bill, Meg, and Sam Riker knew how important Paul Farmer's work had been to Therese since 2003; she is grateful for their graciousness and good humor as this project became part of their lives as well. Jennie would like to thank her family, especially her children and their spouses, Chris and Catherine, Mary and Sean, Genevieve and Zisko for the unfailing support of her work, and her grandchildren, Sander, Annabelle, Jay and Daisy. They are her little hope givers, and she will always be sorry they will grow up without Paul's presence in their lives. And finally, Jennie would like to thank her amazingly competent assistant, Lisa Manoogian—she, too, knew Paul well and has been saddened by his death. Alexandre is very thankful for the patience, support, and hardworking of his wife Sydney caring for their twin babies, while he was working on this project.

A month from now, on Tuesday, February 21, 2023, book contributors and other friends of Paul will gather in Boston for a Memorial Mass on the first anniversary of his death. We are grateful to Fr. James Keenan, SJ, for offering this Mass and for hosting a reception at Boston College to introduce the book to the world. Jennie's long-time graphic design colleague Gayle Bordlemay brought an additional element of beauty to this event, with her expert work on the book's cover, as well as a brochure, program and holy cards for the Mass and reception.

As we pause to consider what it means to mark the first anniversary of Paul's death, we would like to extend our thanks beyond those who made the production of this book possible and recognize all those in the huge

Acknowledgments

and sprawling village where Paul lived and worked. Thank you to his many thousands of colleagues at Partners In Health sites around the world, and his academic community at Harvard Medical School, all of whom, in the midst of their own grief and deep sadness, have carried on, going forward with hope, knowing full well this is what Paul would expect. Partnership and accompaniment were the cornerstones of Paul's praxis, and he was fully aware that all he accomplished was done because he had magnificent partners and *accompagnateurs* every step of the way. No doubt many of you will see yourselves and your work in this book, and we take this opportunity to extend our sympathy and gratitude to each one of you.

Of course, no one has felt the searing and irreversible loss of this good man more acutely than his family. His mother, Ginny, his wife Didi, his children, Catherine, Elisabeth and Sebastian, and his siblings Jim, Jeff, Katie, Jennifer and Peggy have lost a loving son, a devoted husband and father, and a faithful brother. The editors, contributors, and all associated with the publication of this book, join so many others in thanking Paul's family for so generously sharing him with the world. May his legacy continue to shine brightly and bear great fruit and bring each of you consolation, peace, and hope.

Jennie Weiss Block, OP, M. Therese Lysaught, and Alexandre A. Martins

Feast of the Conversion of St. Paul
January 25, 2023

Foreword

Roberto S. Goizueta

An occupational hazard of so-called academic theologians is that our scholarship will become, indeed, merely "academic." This very real danger weighs particularly heavy on those of us who claim to be contextual or practical theologians, whose theological reflections claim to be rooted in the praxis of flesh-and-blood communities, especially marginalized communities. (Indeed, the constitutive link between theology and communal praxis is the responsibility of all theology, but that's a topic already addressed at length in many books and articles elsewhere.) Ultimately, then, our scholarship must answer to *el pueblo*, to those communities which the Gospel proclaims are the privileged bearers of God's Word in the world. This responsibility implies that, precisely as Christian scholars, we must accompany those communities in practical, everyday ways. We must also collaborate closely with those grassroots pastoral and community leaders who so often function as a bridge between *el pueblo* and academic and ecclesiastical institutions. Our first task is to listen: to the poor, to those community leaders immersed in the everyday lives of the poor, and ultimately to the living God revealed in a preferential way among the poor, in the lived faith of the poor. Dr. Paul Farmer's life and work were the embodiment of this dynamic, this preferential option for the poor. As Jorge José Ferrer argues in his chapter, Paul Farmer was the epitome of what Antonio Gramsci called an "organic intellectual."

Like so many others, I was first introduced to Paul Farmer through Tracy Kidder's bestselling book *Mountains Beyond Mountains*. However, my personal relationship with Paul began several years later in 2011. In May of that year, he gave a now-famous speech at the Harvard Kennedy School commencement entitled "Accompaniment as Policy." Unbeknownst to me at the time, he referenced my own work on accompaniment in that speech. I had no idea that Paul Farmer had ever heard of my work, much less read any of it. Needless to say, I felt incredibly honored. Most of all, I felt a sense of affirmation in the face of those ever-present fears that my scholarship would remain ensconced within the ivied walls of the academy. As it turns out, Paul had been introduced to my work by Jennie Weiss Block OP, his Chief-of-Staff, spiritual director, and herself a theologian. Since then, Jennie, Paul and I continued our conversations around the central theme of accompaniment, so fundamental to Paul's vocation. Paul and I also shared a common, long-time friendship with Fr. Gustavo Gutiérrez, who had a profound personal and intellectual impact on our lives and work.

Over the years, I observed the extraordinary influence that Paul had in the lives of so many of my own students at Boston College, several of whom went on to work at Partners In Health. In 2013, I invited him to join me at Boston College in a public conversation on the role of accompaniment in public health and theology. There was a standing-room-only crowd of over six hundred people, and hundreds of others had to be turned away. (Of course, I was under no illusions about who they were all there to see.) The entire evening was a truly moving demonstration of the power of one man's Christian witness to inspire hope in a world so often bereft of hope, especially among the young.

And yet the Paul Farmer who spoke that evening, and whom I was blessed to know, was anything but some sort of serious, pious social crusader. Oh, he was certainly a social crusader but always one who did not take himself too seriously, who—whether in the struggle against Ebola or socioeconomic devastation—had a preternatural confidence that all was indeed in God's hands. The struggle itself was not his but God's. That confidence made Paul one of the most liberated persons I've ever met. He had the indefatigable sense of humor, that "lightness of being" of someone who could joke around or laugh at the drop of a hat—not because he didn't take his work seriously (he did), not because he didn't take the persons whom he accompanied seriously (God knows, he did!), but because he didn't take himself too seriously. Indeed, he was free not to take himself seriously precisely because he took other people so very seriously; when he was with you, he was with you. He had that remarkable gift of attention that, the French philosopher Simone Weil suggested, is really the essence of love. (See Leo Guardado's chapter herein.). Paul lived the accompaniment he preached and thereby changed people's lives.

Above all, what inspired and transformed Paul was God's preferential option for the poor. His discovery of God's preferential love for the dispossessed, the unwanted, the "disposable" persons (in the words of Pope Francis) helped him rediscover his own Catholic faith and launched him in his vocation as an *accompagnateur*. As a student at Duke, he had been profoundly impacted by the murder of Archbishop Oscar Romero, which in turn led him to start reading liberation theology, especially the writings of Gustavo Gutiérrez. At the same time, he wore his faith lightly—again, because he wore his own persona lightly. He often seemed reticent, even sheepish, about talking too explicitly about his faith. When around theologians, he liked to make lighthearted, self-deprecating remarks about his supposed lack of theological sophistication despite the fact that, beneath his intellectual humility, lay a truly profound theological mind. (For a fascinating, perceptive analysis of how Paul's sophisticated knowledge of his faith undergirded so much of his thought, yet was often revealed only in seemingly innocent, spontaneous, usually humorous asides or observations, see D. Brendan Johnson's chapter in this volume.) Paul lived St. Francis's famous adage: "Preach the Gospel and, if necessary, use words." His actions themselves spoke volumes; he didn't need a lot of words.

But words he did speak, and write, for Paul was also every bit a brilliant scholar and teacher. He transformed the field of public health by transforming the very vocation of scholar-teacher-practitioner, as his friend Gustavo Gutiérrez had done in the field of theology. Inspired by Christ's preferential love for the poor, Paul entered into "pragmatic solidarity" with the dispossessed of our world. He did so to assure them that they matter, that God loves them, that they are not forgotten or abandoned, that they are indeed human beings. He accompanied the poor in their struggle for life in the face of death, for health and dignity in the face of disease and humiliation. And through it all he listened ... and learned. He learned of the incredible personal, communal, and spiritual resources the poor draw on in their everyday struggle to survive. He learned that the obstacles to that survival are not just microbes, bacteria, and viruses, but (in)human global economic and political structures that systematically keep the poor poor, the sick sick. He learned—as he repeatedly admonished us—that those microbes, bacteria, and viruses themselves have made a preferential option for the poor. And, finally, he brought those lessons back home to Harvard, to the Brigham, to anyone in our cloistered world of libraries, lecterns, and labs who would dare to listen.

Paul Farmer was a healer, in the deepest possible sense of the word. Something else he learned from the Gospel was that healing must involve the whole person: mind, body, and spirit. As a doctor, he healed his patients not only through the compassionate, expert medical care he extended to them, though he certainly did that. He healed them by listening when others were deaf, by staying (and staying and staying) when others had long left, by asking their names when others treated them as mere objects of pity, at best. He took to heart the question Gustavo Gutiérrez always asks those of us who claim to want to help the poor: "Could you please give me the names and addresses of those poor persons?" (See the chapters by Guardado and Brian Volck in this volume.) Paul could give Gustavo lots of names and addresses. That's actually a good definition of accompaniment: the ability to give names and addresses, or to say whether someone even has an address. You can't heal the whole person unless you know their names and addresses, their kids' names, their favorite jokes, their deepest sorrows, and the God they pray to. Then you can tend effectively to their physical wounds—because you now recognize whose wounds they are.

That's real contextual and practical theology! It can be practical only because it's first of all contextual—names and addresses. Finally, it can be theology at all only because it's contextual and practical. That is, if as theologians we claim to speak of the God of Jesus Christ who has privileged the poor, we cannot possibly do that so long as we still consider them underprivileged. Our theology will be little more than idolatrous wordsmithing. This is not in any way to romanticize the poor; Paul was adamant about avoiding that danger which is, in fact, simply another form of objectification. (Those pesky names and addresses are also a safeguard against romanticization.) As Gustavo Gutiérrez never tires of reminding us, the poor are privileged not because they are necessarily good but because God is good. The discarded and disposable persons of our world are accompanied by the God who is also discarded and disposable, born in a stable, murdered on the outskirts of town, and revealed in the borderlands of Galilee—always an outsider. If our theology is to have any credibility, it must be born there as well.

But it can't stay there. Jesus would not have been crucified had he just hung around with the peasants in Galilee. He had to go to Jerusalem. What he learned in Galilee, he brought back to the centers of power. He translated the language of the Galilean peasants into a language comprehensible in those centers, in order to subvert the religious and political structures of power which victimized those Galilean peasants. That's what prophets do. That's what Paul Farmer did. That's what we Christian theologians are called to do: take what we have heard on the streets, in the churches and clinics, and translate those lessons into a language comprehensible in the world of libraries, lecterns, and labs in order to call that world into question. We scholars owe the poor our very best scholarship, for only the very best scholarship will stand any chance of effectively confronting the global structures of injustice. Paul's credibility in the halls of power stemmed not only from his work as a doctor and anthropologist in Haiti and Rwanda but also from his work as a scholar, teacher, and mentor in Boston. The incredible success of Partners In Health would not have been possible without both. Nor would his transformative impact on both have been possible without his impressive ability to bridge the worlds of Haiti and Boston. That's why he spent his life on an airplane.

Paul was also a bridge between the intellectual worlds of medicine, anthropology, and theology. I was always grateful for how seriously he took theology, not only as ecclesial and pastoral reflection but also as a scholarly discipline. His work with Fr. Gustavo and myself is but one example of Paul's genuinely collaborative approach to all his work; he was not just an *accompagnateur* to his patients but also to his scholarly collaborators. As someone who has attempted to do theology in collaboration with other disciplines, especially the social sciences, I was humbled by his intellectual generosity in this regard. This was but another instance of how he served as an example to so many of us. Paul's scholarship was characterized by a generosity and humility that was but the intellectual dimension of his personal generosity and humility—which is not to say that he wasn't deeply passionate, because of course he was. Again, he was passionate about ideas only because he was first passionate about the flesh-and-blood persons with whom he worked; the latter passion drove the former, not vice versa.

Among the hundreds of personal anecdotes about Paul that have been recounted over the years, one that has always stood out for me as a prism through which to understand this many-faceted Christian disciple is a story told by Jennie Weiss Block in her beautiful book, Paul Farmer: Servant to the Poor. There she describes meeting Paul for the first time:

> Paul was sitting in the living room [of his house] reading when I arrived. As he put his book down to stand up to greet me, I glanced down and saw the title of the book he was reading: *Selected Writings by Meister Eckhart*. Eckhart (1260–1328) was a German Dominican friar, brilliant theologian, and mystic. Erudite, profound, and dense, Meister Eckhart is not an easy read ... I couldn't help but ask, "You are reading Meister Eckhart?" "Trying to, but it is not easy," was Paul's humble reply. All these years later, we both still thank Meister Eckhart for bringing us together.

As Jennie implies, if one were to ask most people which book Paul Farmer might be reading were they to encounter him sitting on his couch, the writings of a medieval theologian and mystic would hardly be the first book that would come to mind. And yet ... the more I thought about it, the more Jennie's anecdote made perfect sense, the more it reflected just who Paul Farmer really was.

Perhaps Meister Eckhart's most well-known saying is: "The eye with which I see God is the same eye with which God sees me: my eye and God's eye are one eye, one seeing, one knowing, and one love." Here Eckhart tries to convey in mere human language the fundamentally inexpressible experience of union between the human and the divine. Or, in the words of St. Augustine, "God is nearer to us than we are to ourselves." Can there be a more accurate depiction of Paul Farmer's understanding of what it means to be a human being, whose inherent dignity and rights derive not from ourselves but from the God who lives and breathes in us, especially in those who have been denied their dignity and rights?

In other words, Paul understood that, before accompaniment is a strategy it is a spirituality. To break bread with the poor is to open ourselves to the One who "became known to them in the breaking of the bread." If we reduce the praxis of accompaniment to a method or technique for delivering health care effectively (though it certainly does that), we undermine its very essence as a revelatory encounter—with other persons, of course, but even more profoundly with the God who sees us through their eyes. Indeed, the effectiveness of accompaniment as strategy will be dependent upon the authenticity of accompaniment as compassionate, revelatory encounter; the usefulness of strategies for social structural change will be dependent on the uselessness of our everyday friendships with poor persons. And another word for "uselessness" is Grace. In the end, social transformation and personal conversion can only be two sides of the same coin. Paul knew that the revolutionary and the mystic are one.

Given Paul Farmer's understanding of his own vocation, this collection of essays by prominent theologians and ethicists is a fitting tribute to his ongoing legacy. As the book's subtitle suggests, the essays all reflect Paul's vision of the integral relationship between the theological task and the prophetic demands of the Gospel. This book is also fitting because of Paul's deep interest in theology and theological ethics in particular. *A Prophet to the Peoples* makes very clear Paul's brilliance not only as doctor and anthropologist but also, indeed, as theologian. In her essay, Jennie Weiss Block recounts that "[Paul] much admired theologians and often said that if he ever got another degree, it would be in theology." Though he never had that opportunity, maybe this book represents a sort of honorary degree in theology. If Paul took theologians seriously (as he most certainly did), with this wonderful book theologians return the favor.

Roberto S. Goizueta is the Margaret O'Brien Flatley Professor Emeritus of Catholic Theology at Boston College. He received a BA in political science from Yale University and an MA and PhD in Religious Studies from Marquette University. He holds honorary degrees from Elms College and the University of San Francisco. Dr. Goizueta is a former President of both the Catholic Theological Society of America and the Academy of Catholic Hispanic Theologians of the United States. He has published six books and over a hundred scholarly articles. His book *Caminemos con Jesús: Toward a Hispanic/Latino Theology of Accompaniment* (Orbis Books, 1995) was named one of the "Fifty Foundational Books in Race, Ethnicity, and Religion" by the *Journal of Race, Ethnicity, and Religion*.

Artist's Statement: Unmercenary Paul, the Good Samaritan

Fr. Cristóbal Torres Iglesias, OP

Several months ago, Jennie Block asked if I might create an icon of Dr. Paul Farmer for the cover of this book. Jennie did not want an image intended for veneration of a Catholic saint, nor would I have created one. Paul is not a canonized saint, blessed, or "Servant of God," nor am I a formally trained writer of Byzantine icons, despite my profound debt as a Catholic artist and preacher to that sacramental art form. It was clear from the outset that what Jennie wanted was a theological image of the friend she knew and had worked so closely with for so many years, a man whose Catholic faith profoundly informed his life, poured out in imitation of Christ in service to God's poor.

Jennie first introduced me to Paul in 2013, and thanks to them both, over the years I have been blessed with opportunities to create art for Partners In Health-related projects in Haiti. As I pondered and prayed how a visual image might speak an authentic word about Paul's unique call to holiness, Jennie shared with me his special relationship with the parable of the Good Samaritan. This was an element of Paul's religious imagination with which I had been unfamiliar, but our conversation made it immediately clear to me that the Good Samaritan would provide my theological point of entry.

Before I began working, I researched the iconographical history of the Church's physician saints, and a number of elements stood out for me that I wanted to incorporate into Paul's image. One of them was the beautiful theology of the healer saint as an "unmercenary," or one who healed the poor without accepting payment. In the Byzantine iconographical tradition, physician saints like the sisters Zenaida and Philonella, or the more widely known Cosmas and Damian, are honored with the title of *anargyros*, a Greek word meaning "without silver" and usually translated as "unmercenary," owing to the gratuitous gift of their healing art to the poor.[1] These saints' icons often describe them as "The Holy Unmercenaries Cosmas and Damian," or "Holy Unmercenary Zenaida."

In the image that eventually resulted *Unmercenary Paul* approaches us, not with a flask of healing ointment or an apothecary's box—symbols traditionally associated with the holy *anargyroi*—but rather, holding up an icon of the Good Samaritan. This icon unveils the Christological form of Paul's path to sanctification. Throughout his life, Paul met the Lord as the Outsider through, with, and in whom God healed and enlightened him, to then command him to "go and do likewise." Paul is not interested in telling us about himself, but instead points us to Christ the Good Samaritan, who would heal and call us, as once he healed and called His servant Paul.

Byzantine icons of the Good Samaritan traditionally read the parable through the lens of Patristic exegesis, casting it as a typological allegory of the Incarnation. The icon visually narrates the story from beginning to end, highlighting key moments as the traveler begins his journey through the wilderness, is assaulted by robbers, left for dead by the priest and the Levite, and rescued by the mysterious Samaritan who pours healing ointment on his wounds, hoists him onto his back, and carries him to the inn, entrusting him to the innkeeper's care with two silver denarii.[2]

In this version of the story the traveler is Adam, who embodies our human nature. The robbers are demons and the damage they inflict is the wounding of our human nature by sin. Most important of all, the Samaritan is Christ the Divine Physician who, moved to visceral com-

---

[1] See, for example, Icon of the Holy "*Anárgyroi*," Sts. Cosmas and Damian, https://www.oca.org/saints/lives/2022/11/01/103133-holy-wonderworkers-and-unmercenaries-cosmas-and-damian-of-mesopo; and Icon of the Holy Unmercenaries Hermione, Philonella, and Zenaida (note the hagiographical symbols of the ointment flask and apothecary box): https://www.uncutmountainsupply.com/icons/of-saints/by-name/h-i/icon-of-the-holy-unmercenary-physicians-sts-hermione-philonella-zenaida-1up10/.

[2] For an example of a Byzantine Icon of the Good Samaritan, see https://www.reddit.com/r/OrthodoxChristianity/comments/2sc2pa/icon_of_the_good_samaritan/ and https://i.imgur.com/SnPtetZ.jpg.

passion, assumes the frailty of our human nature to heal us with the ointment of his divine nature. Christ the Good Samaritan heals us by offering us a share in his divinity, represented by the divine likeness imprinted on the silver denarii. The inn is the Church, the hospital where wounded humanity receives the life-restoring therapy of the Incarnation.

The image on the cover of this book depicts Unmercenary Paul, enlightened and healed by Christ, the divine-human Outsider and brother who restores in him the divine likeness. Paul's response is to go and do likewise, so that he becomes a sacramental sign of the divine therapy of the Incarnation. Just as Christ the Good Samaritan nourished Paul with His own Body and Blood—the medicine of immortality—so too Paul the *anargyros* humbly and lavishly offered medicine to those without silver or gold. When I finished "Unmercenary Paul, the Good Samaritan," I was surprised to learn that Susan Holman, one of the contributors to this volume, wrote a chapter titled "Paul the *Anargyros*."

I am deeply grateful to be part of a project that honors Paul and his ministry to the poor, and cannot help but see in such unexpected synergies clear evidence of the presence and activity of grace. A less surprising but equally appropriate example of creative synergy is the stethoscope draped around Paul's shoulders, an emblematic personal detail that will not be lost on those who knew him. It was Jennie who, upon seeing an earlier iteration of the image, suggested this subtle addition. Looking at it after the fact, I see a fitting if unintended twenty-first century take on the holy *anargyroi*'s traditional ointment jar and apothecary box. May Unmercenary Paul, the Good Samaritan, intercede for us, and may the example of his life awaken in us a graced awareness of Christ the Divine Physician, restoring us to his divine likeness and calling *us* to "go and do likewise."

Fr. Cristóbal Torres Iglesias, OP, is a Miami-based artist and friar of the Southern Dominican Province. His works include the painting *Dominican Last Supper* (2012); the design for the windows of St. Rose of

Lima Chapel at Zanmi Beni children's community in Port au Prince, Haiti (2013); the Cor Jesu Chapel icon cross at Barry University in Miami Shores, Florida (2016); and various works featured in private collections. He is also one of the artists featured on the Scout Comics graphic novel series *The Shepherd* (2018). Cristóbal approaches art as visual theological storytelling that bears to others the fruits of contemplation.

Paul Farmer, Miami, Florida, 2008 (Photo credit: Behna Gardner)

Introduction

Jennie Weiss Block, OP, M. Therese Lysaught, and Alexandre A. Martins

A Light that Shone in the Darkness

On February 21, 2022, a heart in Rwanda stopped beating and a gasp of grief rippled out around the world. Paul Farmer—physician, medical anthropologist, scholar, teacher, and visionary world leader who pioneered ground-breaking models for effectively delivering modern medicine to the poorest people in the world, on a large scale, with magnificent outcomes—had died, at what we now routinely consider the young age of 62. For his hundreds of colleagues, countless collaborators and partners across from every imaginable social and cultural background, thousands of patients and former patients, and the (literally) millions who had been touched and inspired by his work and witness across the forty years of his career, a light had gone out. Gone, unexpectedly and in an instant, was his indefatigable and peripatetic energy, his legendary generosity of spirit and his keen and radical moral compass that forged a social justice movement grounded in global health equity. News outlets the world over recorded the staggering loss of his life-long commitment to the lives of every poor person and noted his incisive ability to eviscerate conceptual and practical structures that work violence against the poor and endlessly diminish human life and flourishing. The loss of his physical presence, marked by his unusual ability to maintain deep relationships with a global network of colleagues and partners, while at the same time giving his full attention to the person in front of him, is searing and irreplaceable.

It was deeply fitting that Farmer died on a remote mountaintop in Butaro, in post-genocide Rwanda, where he spent his final days doing what he loved and knew he was called to do—first, serving as a physician to the poor in state-of-the-art medical facilities he had helped to build, and second, teaching the next generation of health care professionals at the University of Global Health Equity he helped to found. Dr. Farmer loved the Rwandan people and was proud of all that Partners In Health, the NGO which he co-founded, had accomplishing working in partnership with the Rwandan government. There were many other places Dr. Farmer called home amongst the world's poorest people—Haiti, Peru, Lesotho, Liberia, and Russia, just to name a few—where he could have also been found working untiringly when God called him home.

Why a Book by Theologians on Paul Farmer's Witness and Theological Ethics?

Amidst their shock and grief, within days of his death, people from all over the globe—both those who knew Dr. Farmer and those who knew of him—began to ponder how to honor his legacy of light and hope. Many claimed that keeping his vision alive was a moral imperative, believing the only authentic way to honor who he was and what he stood for was through an active commitment to continue his good works. This book is one initiative to do just that—to articulate key aspects of his vision and to reflect on how they might be continued and extended. Our collective goal has been to bring this book to fruition on the first anniversary of his death.

The essays that comprise this book—commissioned from theologians from around the world—are guided by three purposes: First, to honor the extraordinary life and the prophetic Christian witness of Dr. Paul Farmer, and second, and perhaps most significantly, to acknowledge and describe the influence and impact that his scholarly work and on-the-ground praxis have had on the field of theological ethics in general and on each of the contributors individually. As will be evident, Dr. Farmer's life, witness, and work have influenced our thinking, sometimes called into question our long-held assumptions about the moral life and the role of the theologian, and in turn, impacted our scholarly production and teaching. Beyond this, we believe, thirdly, that it holds important insights for the work of theological ethics going forward.

Introduction

We have no doubt that there will be other books written about Dr. Farmer's life and work. Some will describe the health care systems and modern hospitals that Partners In Health (PIH) built in resource-poor settings guided by his vision and leadership. Others will analyze his scholarly contributions to social medicine and anthropology. Still others will study his advocacy on international health policy which has resulted in changes in protocols that saved millions of lives. His books and eyewitness accounts of historic events, including the 2010 earthquake in Haiti and the 2014–2016 Ebola crisis in West Africa, will become classic reference books on these international events. His vision will surely live on through the thousands upon thousands of his students and colleagues working in the field around the globe. And, of course, in a world desperate for meaning, his selfless life of service and dedication to the common good will continue to inspire and console people the world over.

Farmer was a practicing Catholic who took his Christian faith seriously. Like many of us, his is the story of a questioning and sometimes irreverent young man who had to leave behind the faith of the childhood to engage the tradition as an adult so as to develop his own mature and tested faith. Within his disciplines and the largely secular world of his professional life, Farmer well understood that most of these fields tread lightly, at best, when it comes to faith, religion, and theology. It was only in the last years of his life that he began to speak a little more openly about his faith and allowed others to write about the role his faith played in his life and work. However, throughout his life, a key catalyst of Farmer's unique and powerful vision were the Scriptures related to social justice and the Catholic social tradition, particularly in its incarnation as liberation theology. By his own account, the assassination of San Oscar Romero was the birthplace of his first adult conversion experience and the witness of the lives of the likes of Gustavo Gutiérrez, who combined the scholarly life with his pastoral care for the poor that modeled for Farmer the kind of Christian life to which he aspired.

While Farmer was not trained as a theologian, he respected, studied, and engaged theological thought and read widely on many theological topics.

3

Introduction

Liberation theology—in its intellectual and pastoral dimensions—were Farmer's unfailing hermeneutic. Liberation theology provided an incisive theoretical lens by which he inverted standard assumptions within global health, medical anthropology, and international policy, and reimagined the practice of health care—both globally and in the US. He credits many of the extraordinary outcomes his work achieved to the insights and application of the principles of liberation theology and was proud to sow the seeds of liberation theology in new fields where they have produced a hundredfold.

These seeds have left a legacy which extends not only among practitioners of global health but far beyond them. His work also witnessed in critical and transformative ways to Catholic theological ethicists in the US. Farmer's work brought new visibility to a vibrant engagement between liberation theology and health care that had been developing in Latin America since the 1950s, a tradition obscured from US view by ongoing colonialist structures of thought (including language barriers). Yet, like a prism, his work augmented this tradition. It was a demonstration project, in many ways, for key elements of Catholic social thought, helping to show *in situ* what the concrete practice of concepts like accompaniment, the preferential option for the poor, *caritas*, and kenosis looked like in a specific time and place. As praxis does, his work, voice, and witness opened up new aspects of theological concepts and provided a prophetic witness to what missionary discipleship might look like both for global health, theological ethics broadly, and for the church.

Yet, while many US scholars of Catholic theological ethics, and increasingly international scholars, have drawn on Farmer's work for the past fifteen years, to our knowledge, no volume to date focuses specifically on his contributions to theological ethics. This volume proposes to fill that gap, distilling the implications, influences, and ramifications of Farmer's witness for scholars of theology and theological ethics, in both its academic and practical modalities. To do this, we have drawn together an international roster of theological ethicists, physicians, and practitioners—hailing from Haiti, Nigeria, Ireland, El Salvador, Puerto Rico, Brazil, Italy,

Introduction

and the US—to reflect on the legacy of a twenty-first century Catholic physician/scholar who has transformed the field of global health and had a significant impact on a number of theological scholars. Avoiding hagiography, these scholars and practitioners offer rigorous engagement from within their particular disciplinary locations—theological ethics, patristics, liberation theology, pastoral theology, medical practice, social medicine, global health—with the living tradition of liberation theology, the methodological contributions and implications of Farmer's work for the further advancement not only of global health but of theology and theological ethics more broadly. As theologians, it is our hope that this book will articulate the critical—and indispensable—theological dimensions of his work and his practice of the moral life for those in the secular fields.

The intended audience of this book is broad and includes those in both theological and secular spheres who are familiar with Farmer's work as well as those that might be introduced to his vision for the common good through this volume. Given the ways in which Farmer's work intentionally and thoughtfully crossed disciplines, we believe this book also has application across disciplines and might be of interest in both religious and secular circles that include theologians, pastoral ministers, and people of faith as well as secular scholars working in health care, bioethics, public health, medical anthropology, social medicine, and international policy.

Paul Edward Farmer (1959–2022)

For those not familiar with the life and work of Paul Farmer, this brief biography is intended to give the reader a snapshot of his extraordinary life. For a more in-depth and comprehensive look at his life, please see his biography *Mountains Beyond Mountains* by Tracy Kidder (Random House, 2003), or Jennie Weiss Block's *Paul Farmer: Servant to the Poor* (Liturgical Press, 2018).[1]

---

[1] As two of the co-editors worked closely with Farmer, in telling this story of his life, we refer to him informally—as he preferred—as well as formally.

Introduction

Paul Farmer was born on October 26, 1959, in North Adams, Massachusetts. His parents, Ginny and Paul, Sr. had six children, three boys and three girls. His was an unusual childhood. In the early 70's, the family relocated to Brooksville, Florida, where, for many years, Paul lived with his family in an abandoned bus (once used to treat people with tuberculosis), or an old boat in a campground. His father was a school teacher and his mother worked as a cashier at Winn-Dixie. Although there was a marginal aspect to the family's living situation, which was without any of the trappings of middle-class life (such as running water and an indoor bathroom), Paul and his siblings had a stable childhood with a lot of attention and support from their parents. His father, Paul, Sr., was strict and could be gruff and demanding (the children's nickname for him was "the Warden"). His mother, Ginny, was loving and kind, and the children were tended to with great care, and both parents took interest in their children's intellectual development and moral formation.

Paul went to Hernando High School, the local public school, where one of his teachers recognized his intellectual gifts and was instrumental in supporting his college application process. He received a scholarship to Duke University, where he took full advantage of the opportunities offered for a world-class education both in the classroom and beyond. It was during these years as an undergraduate that he was formed intellectually in the classroom, and his social consciousness was awakened while working in a nearby migrant camp. Paul knew he wanted to go to medical school but took a gap year after graduation to do his med school applications and see a little of the world. His route to Haiti was circuitous; he had hoped to go to Africa on a Fulbright and was disappointed when he did not even get an interview. He knew "someone who knew someone" at the Schweitzer hospital in Haiti, and he made his way there in hopes of getting a job at the hospital. That did not pan out either, and again he was disappointed. But one of his great attributes, which remained for all of his life, was his resilience in handling setbacks. He ended up volunteering at a hospital in Léogâne, Haiti, for a short while and was horrified to witness a medical crisis where a young pregnant woman died because she did not

Introduction

have the money to pay for the blood transfusion that would have saved her life. Filled with outrage, Paul made a promise to himself to find a way to make sure that good medical care would be available to poor people without charge.

After this both terrible and motivating experience, Paul ended up taking a job at a very modest eye clinic in Mirebalais in Haiti's Central Plateau, where he met seventeen-year-old Ophelia Dahl, who would become his life-long partner and one of the co-founders of Partners In Health. During this same year in Haiti, Paul and Ophelia met and formed a partnership with an Episcopal priest, Fr. Fritz Lafontant, and his wife, Yolande. The Lafontants lived in Cange, a small, rural, and very poor community in the Central Plateau that had been devastated by a development project that built a hydrologic dam with the unanticipated outcome of flooding the community's farmland, which effectively destroyed their livelihood. Paul's commitment to Haiti and the Haitian poor was born during this year and, in a very real sense, helped to chart the course for the rest of his life.

Farmer was accepted at Harvard Medical School and began his studies in the fall of 1984. He kept an unusual and demanding schedule, flying back and forth from Boston to Port-au-Prince and then making the long drive to Cange to continue his projects with the Lafontants, which included building a medical clinic and other support services for the community. In time, PIH would found Zanmi Lasante, its first sister organization which has grown to employ almost five thousand Haitians who staff a sprawling network of clinics and hospitals throughout the country. Over the coming years, PIH would continue to found sister organizations as part of their network in Peru, Kazakhstan, Lesotho, Liberia, Malawi, Mexico, Navajo Nation, Rwanda, and Sierra Leone, and today the organization employs over eighteen thousand people, 99 percent of whom are from within country. As the organization, grew, so too did its influence in the field of global health, where Paul and his colleagues often challenged conventional wisdom on the delivery of services in resource poor settings by developing new protocols and praxis.

Introduction

During his early years in Haiti, Paul began the lifelong practice of creating beautiful natural surroundings. In Cange, the trees had been denuded because the local community needed firewood for cooking. Paul soon initiated a replanting project and started planting hundreds of trees and landscaping the community. This would become one of his signatures, and today every hospital he has helped to found in sites around the world has trees, groves, shaded gardens, and fishponds for Paul believed that the poor deserved the same beauty in their surroundings to which the rich are accustomed and take for granted. Throughout his entire life, he was actively involved in the design of the gardens and landscaping at the PIH sites and was known to spend many happy hours outdoors doing the digging and planting himself—side by side with the local staff.

Farmer excelled in his studies, and by the time he graduated from Harvard with an MD and PhD in anthropology, he knew that he wanted to dedicate his life to accompanying the destitute sick on a journey away from premature suffering and death. During his years in medical school, as he continued to manage and build his Haiti-Harvard connection, he joined forces with Ophelia Dahl, Jim Kim (a friend from medical school), Todd McCormack (a friend from Duke), and Tom White, a successful Boston contractor, to found a non-profit organization to support their work in Haiti that they decided to call Partners In Health (PIH). Their fledgling organization was modest in every sense of the word, although their mission—to make a preferential option for the poor in health care—was expansive and ambitious. In the words of Ophelia Dahl, they "started small but dreamed big." In retrospect, given the talent and drive of the co-founders and the financial backing of the extraordinarily generous Tom White, their success was all but assured. From the beginning, the founders were determined to forge a new model for the delivery of modern medicine in some of the poorest places on the earth.

Today, thirty years later, Partners In Health is an internationally recognized NGO that successfully brings the fruits of modern medicine to over thirty-four million people in twelve countries around the world. And through the work of PIH, Farmer kept the promise he made to himself

Introduction

when, as a young man in Haiti, he watched a woman die because she did not have the funds for the treatment that would have saved her life: no PIH patient is ever charged for their medical care. The innovative PIH model has proven to even the most skeptical critics that it is possible to deliver high quality medical services in resource poor settings on a large scale. Since its founding in 1987, PIH has saved the lives of millions and millions of people with treatable diseases who otherwise would have died before their time.

The decade following Farmer's graduation from medical school was a time of professional growth and personal change. During this period, three seminal events occurred which would define his life and his career. On the professional front, he began a very productive and successful academic career. For thirty plus years, Farmer taught at both Harvard Medical School and Harvard College, and in 2010, Farmer received the highest honor and recognition Harvard offers when he was named the Kolokotrones University Professor. He was a prolific writer, authoring more than a dozen books and hundreds of scholarly papers. Several of his books have become classics in the field of global health, including *AIDS and Accusation: Haiti and the Geography of Blame* (1992), *Infections and Inequalities: The Modern Plagues* (1999), and *Pathologies of Power: Health, Human Rights and the New War on Poverty* (2003). Two of his books, *Haiti After the Earthquake* (2011) and *Fevers Feuds and Diamonds*, his last book, published in 2020, are eyewitness accounts of the 2010 earthquake that devastated Haiti in 2010 and the Ebola outbreak in West Africa in 2014. The book of his speeches at various commencements and public forums, *To Repair the World* (2013), has been a big seller with the general reader, and *In the Company of the Poor* (2013), the book he co-authored with his dear friend, Fr. Gustavo Gutiérrez, OP, is Orbis Books' best-selling book. His willingness to question the status quo on policies and practices that contribute to the oppression of the poor, and his innovative and creative thinking and proposals for meaningful change to improve the lives of the poor are captured in his writing, many of which are cited in this book.

Introduction

On the personal front, in 1996, he married Didi Bertrand, a lovely Haitian woman he met in Cange. Two years later, Paul and Didi welcomed their first child, Catherine. Didi, too, was committed to global health equity and worked side-by-side with Paul at Partners In Health. In 2005, PIH founded a sister organization in post-genocide Rwanda, and Paul, Didi, and Catherine set up housekeeping in Kigali. Didi helped to establish PIH's presence in Rwanda and Paul made the long commute between Kigali and Boston with frequent stops in other PIH sites around the world. The years in Rwanda were a happy time for the Bertrand-Farmer family as they welcomed Elisabeth Grace in 2007 and Charles Sebastien in 2008. Paul and Didi thought it best for the children to be educated in the US, and when the two younger children were in grade school, the family moved back to the States, settling in Miami. The proximity to Haiti was convenient for their work and frequent visits with Didi's family. Paul was pleased when Catherine matriculated to his alma mater, Duke University. Even with Paul's relentless travel schedule, he made every effort to spend as much time as possible with the family, although it was hard to be gone so much. And as fate would have it, he spent a year and a half at home with them during the pandemic—while he was busy on zoom teaching and working, there were family dinners every night, with movies and Scrabble games. He liked taking his daughter to her swim lessons, going to the grocery, and sitting quietly by his fishpond. And he expanded his already lush gardens with hundreds of red bromeliads.

The third life-defining event during this decade for Paul and his family was the publication of Tracy Kidder's *Mountains Beyond Mountains: The Quest of Dr. Paul Farmer, A Man Who Would Cure the World* (2003). The stunning success of this book, which has sold over a million and a half copies and been translated into nine languages, changed Paul's life in many ways, including turning him into what many refer to as a "non-profit celebrity" and a popular iconic model of a leader oriented toward the good. In the years following the publication of *Mountains Beyond Mountains*, Paul became very much in demand for speaking engagements and received significant publicity and acclaim, all of which gave him widespread

Introduction

exposure that helped to build his reputation as a global leader and visionary in the field of global health. He was also brilliant and articulate, with gracious and kind ways. These qualities, combined with his affable and friendly persona, were very appealing to others. Many found his hopeful outlook and his deep desire to serve as an "antidote to despair" inspiring and worth emulating.

An unusual aspect of Farmer's career path is that he was both a highly respected academic and a hands-on practitioner. He was a careful scholar who made pioneering academic contributions in his disciplines of medicine and anthropology while at the same time being fully engaged in the hard work of implementation. He was just as comfortable and adept in the classroom as he was in the field, proving himself a leader in very different circumstances. When Farmer was offered a top post in the Obama administration, he seriously considered the offer but, in the end, he just could not see himself giving up the two activities he most loved and valued: seeing patients and teaching students. Instead, he accepted a volunteer job as former President Bill Clinton's Deputy in the United Nations Office of the Special Envoy to Haiti—this part-time job allowed him to keep his teaching schedule and see his beloved patients along with the opportunity to work on the international stage where he focused on addressing more just policy issues around foreign aid.

The list of the honors, honorary degrees, prizes, and awards Paul Farmer received runs for multiple pages on his illustrious CV. These awards range from a Service Award from a Haitian Beauty Salon (he was given a plaque which he proudly hung in his home office) to the million-dollar Berggruen prize (all of which he promptly gave away after quipping, "I was a millionaire for a week!"). Both awards—and the many, many others too numerous to list—were received by Farmer with humility and gratitude and always on behalf of the people living in dire poverty that he so faithfully served.

As mentioned earlier in this Introduction, his death is a loss for the world. His was a life well-lived, albeit, far too short. In the months since his untimely death, he has been described as a visionary, a global health giant, a genius, a stateman, a prophet as the title of this book suggests, and even a saint in some quarters. While all these complimentary descriptors are, in large measure, accurate, Paul Farmer was much more, for his goals and his reach were way beyond the world of achievement. He possessed a humility not often found in people of his stature and had an intangible quality, which is hard to name, although many have referred to it as holiness. He will be remembered for many things; certainly, his innovative thinking on how to create durable health care systems in poor countries, and his grit for staying with the work during the arduous implementation phases. He will be known as a disciplined academic, a prolific writer, and an effective clinician who made meaningful contributions to his chosen fields and effectively built a global health equity movement. He will be revered by the students he mentored, and his grateful patients will never forget the care and attention they received. Those fortunate to be in his personal orbit—colleagues and partners—will remember him as a loyal and devoted friend, and a loving husband and father. However, in the end, it is likely he would want the narrative of his life to be told in a way that makes it clear he was a sincere man who is remembered for his faithfulness to his vocation as a physician and a healer, a flawed man who, despite his failings and shortcomings, loved God and neighbor with an open and generous heart, and finally, as a hopeful man who believed in the power of love and God's grace and tried to do good and bring hope to all those he encountered. For sure, generations to come will continue to recall and be inspired by his presence that graced the world for sixty-two short years.

Overview of the Book

This book is organized into four sections, each focused on a theme relevant to different aspects of Farmer's prophetic witness, his engagement with liberation theology, and the various ways his life and work have impacted the field of theological ethics. But first, it opens with a moving and pointed Foreword by Roberto Goizueta—one of Farmer's own theological teachers but who, as so many of Farmer's friends, equally learned from him. Goizueta presses us scholars, theologians, and readers with a central

Introduction

challenge of Farmer's work and witness: that if our work is not accountable to "*el pueblo*, to those communities which the Gospel proclaims are the privileged bearers of God's Word in the world," then our work really is simply a noisy gong, a clanging cymbal, or "little more than idolatrous wordsmithing." Such accountability looks like listening, accompanying, collaborating, loving, learning, centering, privileging, healing, and prophetically translating their realities back to the religious and political structures (civil and academic) that keep them poor and sick in order to "effectively confront the global structures of injustice." Undergirding all this for Farmer was a spirituality and deep appreciation for theology as an intellectual and lived praxis.

That spirituality is captured in the beautiful original cover image prepared for the book by Dominican friar Cristóbal Torres Iglesias, OP. Fr. Cristóbal was a friend of Paul's and has worked on several art projects in Haiti.[2] As his Artist's Statement notes, in creating the image, Fr. Cristóbal drew on one of Farmer's central spiritual images—the Good Samaritan—in conversation with the tradition of the *anargyroi* or "unmercenary saints," with whom he became acquainted through his own theological research. His resulting image crystalizes the thick theological meanings captured in the Gospel passage—picturing Paul as the one assaulted and left for dead, and Christ, Black like the poor of the world, as the Samaritan who first ministers to our wounds, heals us, and calls us to love him—and then to go minister to those on the peripheries. Fr. Cristóbal had not read the chapters before creating the image. The fact that it resonates so deeply with so many of the book's chapters—specifically with Jennie Weiss Block's and Susan's Holman's—is, we agree, "clear evidence of the presence and activity of grace."

Generative for Fr. Cristóbal and central to the discipline of theology and theological ethics are classic texts—from the scriptures to Doctors of the Church—as well as the rich panoply of Christian practices that have sustained the church across geography and history. Equally important for

---

[2] For more about Fr. Torres and his work, visit www.cristobaltorresart.com.

Introduction

theological scholarship are the concrete lives of particular people—some of whom have been named saints. Identified by their communities as exemplars of Christian practice, figures from Augustine, Perpetua, and Felicity to Teresa of Avila, Meister Eckhart, Dorothy Day, Dietrich Bonhoeffer, Thomas Merton, Simone Weil, Oscar Romero, and more, theology increasingly turns to the specifics of their witness as an important theological source.

Although he probably would have eschewed the idea, our opening section adds Farmer to this list. In Part I, we explore his "Life as Theological Text." Jennie Weiss Block opens the section with Chapter One, "Toward a Realized Eschatology: Paul Farmer as Good Samaritan." In this chapter, she reflects on Farmer as one who sought to embody the figure of the Good Samaritan. His performance of this scriptural paradigm in the face of the enormity of the suffering of the poor provides a critical source for wrestling with the challenges of theodicy and for understanding the deep, eschatological interface between the Cross and hope. In Chapter Two, "Paul the *Anargyros*: History, God-talk, and Ecumenism in the Healing Praxis of Dr. Paul Farmer," patristic scholar Susan Holman finds resonance between Farmer's life and a classic but little-known historic form of Christian discipleship—the *anargyros*, those "unmercenary" Christ-formed physicians who cared for the sick for free (captured as well in Fr. Torres's cover image). Where Block and Holman draw theological insight from Farmer's life and practice, Jorge Jose Ferrer asks in Chapter Three: "Paul Farmer: A Model for the Theologian"? Identifying him as an exemplar of Antonio Gramsci's figure of the organic intellectual, Ferrer argues that Farmer's commitment to a methodology that was at once analytical and praxical stands as a challenge and aspiration for theologians and theological ethicists. Yet for Western scholars who enter into such praxis, a danger remains: that we will unwittingly reproduce those very hierarchies of identity, knowledge, and power that have always exposed the poor to damage and death. Alison Lutz explores this challenge in Chapter Four, "Living Witnesses and Moral Agency." She finds in Farmer's decades-long practice a remedy to this danger: "Moral praxis that

Introduction

transforms iniquitous power circuits must also include—as moral agents who cross lines of power to relieve suffering—people from communities that have been historically and systematically dispossessed."

As has been mentioned, liberation theology infused Farmer's thought, work, methodology, actions, rhetoric, and writing. He drank deeply from its wells, forming friendships with Gustavo Gutiérrez, Fr. Fritz Lafontant, Fr. Gerard Jean Juste, Roberto Goizueta, Jean-Bertrand Aristide, and many other religious figures and liberation theologians. For many in the US, he was one of the first people they had seen embody a liberationist vision in health care. Indeed, the power of his witness lies in part with the fact that he was a white, American, Harvard professor who both proclaimed and thoroughly embody liberation theology, and freely and intentionally made common cause with the poor.

As such, his life and work became, as we explore in Part II, "A Prism for Liberation Theology." In this section, we explore how Farmer received and refracted the gospel light of liberation theology. In Chapter Five, "Liberation Theology and Public Health Ethics," Alexandre A. Martins details the historical tradition of liberationist health care that preceded Farmer in Latin America, as well as Farmer's own development of and contributions to that tradition. In Chapter Six, Leo Guardado's essay "Theologians in the Field: 'Dices que eres un teólogo, ¿cuál es tu practica?,'" lifts up two theological loci at the heart of the liberationist method Farmer learned from Gustavo Gutiérrez—friendship and *lo pastoral* (fieldwork as a theological practice)—to show how these ground the pedagogical and research methodology of participatory action research—a method that has only recently made headway within US academic theology. In Chapter Seven, "Liberating Theological Ethics from the Invisible Hand: Paul Farmer, the World's Poor, and the Quandaries of the Fortunate," M. Therese Lysaught focuses on Farmer's liberationist attention to economics, following his critique of the economization of the conceptual frameworks of global health care delivery to propose that neoliberalism has similarly misshapen the conceptual frameworks of medicine, bioethics, and—possibly—theology. And

Introduction

Suzanne Mulligan closes the section with Chapter Eight, "Confronting 'Structures of Violence': Women's Empowerment and the Legacy of Paul Farmer." Here she foregrounds his notion of structural violence, using Farmer's early and constant attention to the ways that structural violence particularly impacts women's health as a lens for examining theological discourse around women.

To this point in the volume, a number of essays lift up a subtle but crucial point: that solidarity and true moral praxis—be it in health care or theology—does not consist simply in the powerful entering the space of the poor. Confounding received assumptions, the vector does not simply point one way. Rather, in relentlessly foregrounding the voices of real people from dispossessed communities—from Anita and Manno in *AIDS and Accusation* (1992) to Ibrahim and Yabom in *Fevers, Feuds, and Diamonds* (2020) and the cloud of witnesses in between—a hallmark of Farmer's work has been to position the poor as equal partners in his work, to invite them across the invisible lines of power as moral and intellectual agents. A first step in his work in Cange, as Kidder narrates in *Mountains Beyond Mountains*, was to conduct a health census—asking residents what, exactly, they needed, listening to their stories.[3] Early in its work, Zanmi Lasante, designated Haitian community health workers as *accompagnateurs*, a term that was replicated in local languages as PIH expanded around the world.[4] These partners, residents of the local communities where PIH worked, proved critical both epistemologically—providing crucial knowledge for developing effective treatment modalities—and practically—indispensable for the care of millions of poor people in their communities. But both steps were more than simply instrumental—both were also practices that recognized and affirmed the dignity of each person in the local community, implemented the practice

---

[3] Kidder, *Mountains Beyond Mountains*, 82.
[4] P. Farmer, S. Robin, S.L. Ramilus, J.Y. Kim, "Tuberculosis, Poverty, and "Compliance": Lessons from Rural Haiti," *Seminars in Respiratory Infections* 6 (1991): 254–60.

Introduction

of participation, and in so doing, built community and advanced the common good in a myriad of intangible, immeasurable ways.

A product partly of his own innate instincts, this pivotal move in Farmer's witness again drew on the liberationist tradition. We explore this further in Part III, "Accompaniment." James Keenan, SJ, opens the section in Chapter Nine, "From *Amoris Laetitia* to Ebola: Accompaniment as a Model for Medical and Pastoral Care." Here he details Farmer's theoretical account of accompaniment and practice thereof and linking it to Pope Francis's advocacy for accompaniment as a key practice for both theology and ecclesial ministry. A canard lobbed against the praxis of accompaniment—be it in health care, theology, or policy—is that it is inefficient. It violates that central dogma of neoliberal economics (efficiency). It cannot be measured. It takes time. And time is, as we know, money. Brian Volck takes on these assumptions in Chapter Ten, "Wasting Time with the World's Poor: Theological and Scriptural Foundations for Paul Farmer's Praxis of Accompaniment." And in Chapter Eleven, "Practicing Local Listening with Village Midwives in Sudan: A Case Study for Theological Ethics," Meghan Clark offers an extended exemplar of a crucial component of accompaniment, the practice of local listening, drawing on her experience with the Helping Babies Breathe initiative in Sudan.

We imagine that for many readers, this volume may be an introduction to Farmer and his work, especially in the theological disciplines. In our experience, familiarity with Paul Farmer and Partners In Health is quite binary: theologians seem to either know all about them or they have never heard of either. One reason for this, we surmise, is that Farmer and his colleagues toiled in the fields of global health—a field largely unknown to many due to the deep siloes that continue to isolate our disciplines. Thus, becoming familiar with Farmer's legacy entails becoming familiar with the larger field of global health. At the same time, he makes clear for theologians that "global health," is an important locus for theological reflection, learning, analysis, and action. While the field and term "global health" is not without its own problems, Farmer's interpretation is a model

Introduction

focused on a well-developed concept of *equity* and thus, his preferred term for the field was "global health equity."

For that reason, we turn in Part IV to a set of chapters exploring "Global Health as a Theological Locus." Stan Chu Ilo opens this conversation in Chapter Twelve, "Ebola and the Ravages of History in Paul Farmer: A Catholic Theological Ethical Response to Global Health Inequity in Africa." Naming Farmer as "an African ancestor," Ilo focuses on Farmer's final book *Fevers, Feuds, and Diamonds: Ebola and the Ravages of History*, to not only highlight Farmer's work in Africa but also to raise pointed questions for Western scholars and theologians. Where Ilo helpfully zeros in on Africa, in Chapter Thirteen, "The Legacy of Paul Farmer for Theological Ethics," Andrea Vicini pulls the lens back to look at the global landscape more broadly. Synthesizing many of the themes articulated in the volume, he highlights how Farmer's theological lens helped him challenge givens and assumptions and to begin to reimagine, theoretically and practically, the field of global health. Maura Ryan ends this section with her reflections in Chapter Fourteen on moving "From Compassion to Pragmatic Solidarity: Considering the Right to Health from the Margins." Examining how Catholic social thought informs the content of a "right to health," she asks how its understanding of the relationship between health and human rights is enriched by Paul Farmer's construction of "pragmatic solidarity."

The book closes with Chapter Fifteen, entitled, "'Doctor' of the Church: Mapping the Religious Threads in Paul Farmer's Writings." Here Brendan Johnson provides an overview of Farmer's extensive body of work and highlights the specifically religious or theological aspects of his thought and rhetoric. Finally, a volume like this would not be complete without at least one voice from Haiti. Père Eddy Eustache, a Haitian priest, Director of Mental Health and Psychological Services for Zanmi Lasante, and longtime co-worker of Farmer, provides a closing reflection.

In the end, we offer this book as a starting point. One book certainly cannot capture every relevant aspect of the life, thought, and theology of a person like Paul Farmer—whose canvas was so geographically broad,

Introduction

intellectually deep, and practically radical. Our modest hope is that it will introduce Farmer and his work to scholars of theological ethics more broadly and invite those in the secular, scientific disciplines (medicine, anthropology, global health) and practitioners in the global health world to gain a better understanding of the constitutive importance of theology and Christian practice in his life, work, and innovations in global health. Farmer's work brought different people, disciplines, and realities together to dialogue and collaborate towards the common good in health care equity and justice for the poor. A charismatic leader, Farmer fostered long-term collaboration, making himself a partner who was always open to listen and learn from his patients and colleagues. The theologians who have contributed to this book have engaged with Farmer's work and offer their reflections on Farmer's contribution to theological ethics, and in turn, his legacy, which will surely expand in this and other fields in the coming years. We hope this book will serve as a starting point for the ongoing work of learning from his witness that will be carried out by other scholars and practitioners—work that starts with dialogue, critique, and response to the analyses presented here. Farmer's thought was always dynamic, growing and deepening over time through his immersion in different local cultures and realities and active engagement and accompaniment of real people, many of whom lived in lived in dire poverty. He never turned away from the emergent questions presented in these situations, real people facing different emergent questions. His efforts were not abstract. they always led back to concrete efforts to bring real change to real communities. We hope that in a small way, this book points a way forward—showing via the witness of a concrete life how the light of the gospel can transform theory, and praxis and continue to repair the world.

Part 1

A Life
as a
Theological Text

Paul Farmer and co-workers in Cange, Haiti (Photo credit: Behna Gardner)

Part 1: A Life as a Theological Text

As noted in the introduction, a key, but largely untapped, source for the work of theological ethics is the lives and witnesses of Christian exemplars—real people who boldly lived the gospel in creative faithfulness, most often among the poorest and most marginalized of God's people. This section asks: how does Farmer's life and witness serve as a theological text? In probing this question, the contributors to Part 1, "A Life as a Theological Text," raise an even more provocative question: who are we called to be as theologians? Eschatologists? *Anargyroi*? Organic intellectuals? Those who transgress received hierarchies of power/knowledge? As with other chapters in this volume, these essays challenge the regnant model of the theologian in the US, in both Catholic and broadly Christian contexts. They also raise initial questions about what we might call the intellectual infrastructure of theology and theological ethics: Farmer drew heavily on the natural and social sciences but also used theology to critique them, developing a methodology that he described as "geographically broad and historically deep." How is the work of theology informed by disciplines outside of theology and the traditional uses of philosophy—sociology, anthropology, economics, history, the natural sciences? And how do we come into a meaningful conversation with these disparate sources, all of which have the potential to add insight and depth to our thinking and inform our search for wisdom and truth?

We begin with the last things: eschatology. In Chapter One, "Toward a Realized Eschatology: Paul Farmer as Good Samaritan," Jennie Weiss Block argues that Farmer's entire corpus of writing and his life's work among the destitute were directed towards a realized eschatology, that is, the bringing about of the Kingdom of God in the here and now. This eschatology was rooted for him in the parable of the Good Samaritan coupled with Matthew 25's presentation of the corporal works of mercy. She suggests his interpretation of these seminal passages forms "the hermeneutical keys to understanding Paul Farmer's religious imagination, the day-in, day-out expression of his moral life, and in turn, the unceasing demands he freely placed on himself." They also created in him an eschatological orientation, enabling him to serve as an "antidote to despair" for those who were suffering or losing hope. She sees him as "an eschatologist, a hope-giver to everyone he met—from destitute peasant farmers to heads of state." Paul understood that "'Christian hope's statement of promise ... must stand in contradiction to the reality which can at present be experienced' ... [and that] everywhere in the New Testament, Christian hope is directed towards what is not visible." Rooted in scripture, centered on the kenotic Crucified One, Farmer's lived witness challenges theological ethics to engage more centrally the eschatological future to which the Risen Christ beckons us.

Farmer stands in a long line of physicians and others who accompanied the poor in healing. Building on Block's insights about the centrality of the Good Samaritan and Matthew 25 for Farmer, in Chapter Two, "Paul the Anargyros: History, God-Talk, and Ecumenism in the Theological Praxis of Dr. Paul Farmer," Susan R. Holman traces the line further back, beyond twentieth century Haiti to Christian antiquity, placing Farmer in the long Christian tradition of the *anargyroi*, those inexplicable and often idiosyncratic religious physicians who refused money for their medical services. As our cover artist, Fr. Cristóbal Torres, OP, also notes in his artist's statement, the word anargyroi (singular anargyros) is from the Greek, meaning those who provided health care assistance "without silver," that is, for free. Thus, these health care providers have also long been called "unmercenary saints." Holman insightfully juxtaposes Farmer's witness with that of the sixth century *anargyros* Paul of Antioch, suggesting how his life and theological ethics may offer us an exemplar of a modern anargyros. We see how in antiquity much of caring for the sick involved attention to what we now call "the social determinants of health," also a key focus for Farmer but lost on most of contemporary health care, especially in the global north. She also draws out other key themes—the role of the corporal works of mercy for health equity; ecumenicity, or non-judgmental engagement with religious diversity as well as methodological diversity; and attention to the importance of historical voices that may not otherwise be heard.

In Chapter Three, "Paul Farmer: A Model for the Theologian," we fast forward from the sixth century to the twentieth century, where Jorge Jose Ferrer, SJ, finds another possible analogue of Farmer's witness—Antonio Gramsci's notion of an "organic intellectual." For Gramsci, the organic intellectual was characterized by a two-fold methodology—one that is simultaneously analytical and praxical—actively engaged in the construction of a new society. As such, Ferrer proposes that Farmer—though not a theologian himself—challenges those who practice theology, calling us to likewise live into our vocations as organic intellectuals. Analytically, Farmer's use of social analysis to uncover the structural causes of impoverishment and exclusion provides a model for the analysis that theological ethicists are called to articulate in an acutely divided and unfair world. Yet Farmer undertook his intellectual work and social analysis within the broader context of an existential commitment to social transformation and justice as a companion to the poor. Thus, his analytical methodology is coupled to a praxical modeling: a life committed to service, advocacy, and activism at the service of the impoverished. As Ferrer notes, "Neutrality is not an option for someone who aspires to a life of authenticity in the footsteps of Jesus."

Alison Lutz closes this section, in Chapter Four, "Living Witnesses and Moral Agency." Here she says the quiet part out loud: most global health professionals—and theologians—live on the privileged side of global hierarchies of social power. Motivated by solidarity, the preferential option for the poor, and other key Christian convictions, many seek to cross the lines of social power to partner with those who suffer. But can we do so "without reproducing hierarchies of identity, knowledge, and power that have always exposed most people to danger and death in order to protect and promote the wellbeing of a small minority of others?" This is fraught terrain. To do so requires, she suggests, a moral praxis that centers people who cross the lines of power to relieve suffering from the other direction, "people from communities that have been historically and systematically dispossessed." It is here that she proposes that Farmer's life and work "provide a model for theologically-informed moral agency that transgresses the roles established by current hierarchies of being, knowledge, and power in order to relieve suffering without reproducing the iniquitous circulation of power and resources."

Chapter 1: Towards a Realized Eschatology: Paul Farmer as Good Samaritan

Jennie Weiss Block, OP

> In actual fact ... eschatology means the doctrine of the Christian hope, which embraces both the object hoped for and also the hope inspired by it. From first to last, and not merely in epilogue, Christianity is eschatology, is hope, forward looking and forward moving, and therefore also revolutionizing and transforming the present.[1]
>
> Jürgen Moltmann

> For Christians, ethical practices like the preferential "option" for the poor are *not,* in fact, optional.
> In a nutshell, no one gets into heaven without a letter of recommendation from the poor.[2]
>
> Nathan Mitchell

Introduction

I am honored to join the esteemed theologians who have written essays in this book to honor Paul Farmer's prophetic witness and contribution to theological ethics. I believe that much of what we recognize in Dr. Farmer's life and work was shaped in large measure by Christian ethics, theological thought, and, of course, his deep personal faith. My essay is perhaps less scholarly than many included in this book and takes a decidedly more personal and narrative approach, given my long-standing relationship with Dr. Farmer. I was his spiritual director for sixteen years (his "interior

---

[1] Jürgen Moltmann, *Theology of Hope: On the Ground and Implications of a Christian Eschatology,* trans. James W. Leitch (Minneapolis: Fortress Press, 1993), 16.
[2] Nathan Mitchell, *Meeting Mystery: Liturgy, Worship, Sacraments* (Maryknoll, NY: Orbis Books, 2006), 37, 42.

decorator" as he liked to joke), and he was among my closest friends. I was fortunate to work closely with him as his Chief Advisor for over a decade at the institutions where he faithfully served.[3] I also had the privilege of writing a biography about him for Liturgical Press's People of God series.[4] Thus, some of my reflections and anecdotes in this essay are personal and first-hand, and I often refer to Paul by his first name, as this seems most appropriate. The theological underpinnings of this essay are based on my observations and exposure to Paul's cosmology, if you will, and the worldview and moral framework he carefully pieced together to guide his life.

It is no mystery why Matthew 25:35–46 was selected for the Gospel reading at Paul Farmer's funeral Mass in Miami and his Memorial Service a week later in Boston.[5] In this passage, which describes the Great Judgment Day, Jesus tells the crowd exactly who is going to inherit the Kingdom of God and the reasons why this is so. He lays out the corporal works of mercy and closes with an explanation that does not lack clarity: "Whatever you did for the least of my brothers and sisters, you did for me." As I said, no great mystery there. Nor is it a great mystery why Paul's favorite Scripture passage was the parable of the Good Samaritan in Luke's Gospel (Luke 10:25–37), the equally dramatic narration in which Jesus describes what it means to show mercy and what is demanded of us to live in right relationship with our neighbors.

In this essay, I explain the ways in which the parable of the Good Samaritan, coupled with the corporal works of mercy as presented in Matthew's Gospel, are the hermeneutical keys to understanding Paul Farmer's religious imagination, the day-in, day-out expression of his moral life, and in turn, the unceasing demands he freely placed on himself. These

---

[3] These institutions include Partners In Health, Harvard Medical School, Brigham and Women's Hospital, and the United Nations Office of the Special Envoy to Haiti.

[4] Jennie Weiss Block, *Paul Farmer: Servant to the Poor* (Collegeville, MN: Liturgical Press, 2018).

[5] There were numerous memorial services for Dr. Farmer held around the world including Haiti, Rwanda, Lesotho, Sierra Leone, Liberia, Malawi, and Peru.

Towards a Realized Eschatology: Paul Farmer as Good Samaritan

two passages from the New Testament obviously imply a Christian ethic, and one can certainly make the claim that Paul Farmer's moral life was grounded in Christian ethics. However, in this essay, I wish to pursue a different line of thinking and consider how Paul's interpretation of these seminal passages—directives to living the Christian life, if you will—created in him an eschatological orientation made manifest in two particular and complementary ways. First, his entire corpus of writing and his life's work among the destitute was directed towards a realized eschatology, that is, the bringing about of the Kingdom of God in the here and now. Second, he understood his calling to serve as an "antidote to despair"[6] to those who are suffering or losing hope. He was, as I often liked to call him, an "eschatologist," that is, a hope-giver to everyone he met—from destitute peasant farmers to heads of state. Paul understood that "Christian hope's statement of promise ... must stand in contradiction to the reality which can at present be experienced."[7] Paul understood that "Everywhere in the New Testament, Christian hope is directed towards what is not visible,"[8] and he believed that hope could "prove its power," and eschatology could "formulate its statements of hope in contradiction to the present reality of suffering evil and death."[9] It was this promise of an unseen hope that gave him the motivation to move forward towards a vision of a hope-filled future and, in turn, the courage to spend his entire life working untiringly to build the Kingdom of God in the here and now.

I begin with an exegesis of the Good Samaritan parable, highlighting the ways in which this passage influenced Paul's moral and spiritual life. I then take up the topic of Paul's views on accompaniment in relation to Jesus's directive to "Go and do likewise." In the next section, I offer a few anecdotal observations and stories that describe Paul's spiritual life at the intersection of suffering and hope. The essay closes with a look at Paul's

---

[6] The expression is taken from the PIH mission statement which can be found in its entirety in footnote 16.
[7] Moltmann, *Theology of Hope*, 18.
[8] Moltmann, *Theology of Hope*, 18.
[9] Moltmann, *Theology of Hope*, 19.

Towards a Realized Eschatology: Paul Farmer as Good Samaritan

eschatology, which I argue was both, to use Moltmann's words, "revolutionizing and transforming."

Throughout my years working with Paul, I was often privileged to represent him, and at his direction, to speak for him, so I am confident in saying that he would be humbled and thrilled by this book for several reasons. He much admired theologians and often said that if he ever got another degree, it would be in theology. In the last months of his life, he had just started on a reading course in theology.[10] He had a great interest and practical concerns about the moral life and thought carefully about what he referred to as "AMC's—Areas of Moral Clarity."[11] When he heard the title of the book, his face might redden from the neck up at being called a "prophet to the peoples," as often happened when he was embarrassed, and he would have had lots of good questions about theological ethics. While he would be the first to point out that although he was not a theologian, he was drawn to theological thought and was deeply interested in gaining access to theological language. Never a week went by that he did not call to ask a theological or pastoral question across a wide range of his topics. Paul once told me, "You have shaped the latter half of my life."[12] While this lovely compliment is no doubt exaggerated, I believe he meant that his experience in spiritual direction and partnering with a theologian in the workplace gave his religious imagination a home, so to speak. It gave him access to a language and thinking that resonated with his deepest

---

[10] A few of the first books in Paul's theology reading course were *The Shape of Catholic Theology: An Introduction to Its Sources, Principles and History*, by Aidan Nichols, OP, *The Experience of God: An Invitation to Do Theology* by Dermot Lane, and *The Craft of Theology: From Symbol to System*, by Avery Dulles, along with Alister McGrath's introduction to the history of Christian thought and some spiritual reading. Paul was so funny — he kept calling me to say, "I am behind in my theology readings ... I am so sorry." To which I would reply, "You really can't be behind as there is no schedule." Although he was, in his mind, "always behind," he was very much enjoying the readings and had many good questions about the material.

[11] Tracy Kidder, *Mountains Beyond Mountains: The Quest of Dr. Paul Farmer, the Man Who Would Cure the World* (New York: Random House, 2004), 101.

[12] Paul Farmer, Text message to the author, October 26, 2021. (Sadly, this was Paul's last birthday among us.)

longing for communion with God and neighbor and acknowledged and tapped into his interior life. And while there were never any easy answers, access to religious language and theological thought was a means to engage and ponder the many profound and piercing questions—both theological and practical—with which he grappled on a daily basis.

While Paul is internationally known for his work as a physician, it is important to note that he was also an accomplished anthropologist, trained to search for meaning in all things. He was a most careful observer and interpreter of cultures, people, places, and events. Both his visual and sensory perceptions were acute; he paid careful attention to every small detail in observing others and their circumstances. Paul's search for meaning was intense and central to his identity, and, as he matured, this search for meaning was linked to the development of his religious imagination and his interior life. And, until the end, he believed that what ultimately gave his own life meaning was service to his fellow humans.

As is well-known and evident in his writings, liberation theology held a privileged place in Paul's thinking and praxis. In *Pathologies of Power: Health, Human Rights and the New War on the Poor,* he wrote an entire chapter applying the principles of liberation theology to medicine and health care. He builds a strong case, through the use of multiple case studies that show the positive impact that applying an "option-for-the-poor" model of medicine had on patient outcomes.[13] He notes, "It is my belief that liberation theologians, in advocating preferential treatment for the poor, offer those concerned with human rights a moral compass for action."[14] Throughout his entire career, he continued to rely on the work of liberation theologians, including Gutiérrez, Boff, and Sobrino, and these scholars are often cited in his books, speeches, and articles. He often expressed his gratitude for their work and its meaning to him.

---

[13] See Chapter Five of Paul Farmer, *Pathologies of Power: Health, Human Rights, and the New War on the Poor* (Berkeley: University of California Press, 2003).

[14] Farmer, *Pathologies of Power*, 138.

Towards a Realized Eschatology: Paul Farmer as Good Samaritan

> Liberation theology continues to be, for me, an inexhaustible font of inspiration. I see the spirituality associated with it as, at the very least, aspirational: any of us can aspire to be better—but only if we seek to attack contemporary poverty and to remember that we live in one world, not three. Nothing that I've seen from plague to famine to flood to quake, could persuade me otherwise.[15]

Although PIH is a secular organization, its founders[16] grounded their work in language and concepts borrowed from liberation theology, beginning with the opening line of their mission statement: "Our mission is to provide a preferential option for the poor in health care." The organization describes its mission to be both "medical and moral" and based on "solidarity, rather than charity alone." The PIH model insists that the lived experience of persons living in poverty be given priority and used to guide decision-making and planning.[17]

The influence of Fr. Gustavo Gutiérrez, OP, on Paul's intellectual and personal life cannot be overstated. As a young man, it was Fr. Gustavo's writing on poverty and structural sin that helped Paul understand what he was encountering in Haiti and, in turn, guided his methodology, praxis, and advocacy efforts. A decade later, Paul finally met the man he referred

---

[15] Paul Farmer and Gustavo Gutiérrez, *In the Company of the Poor: Conversations with Dr. Paul Farmer and Fr. Gustavo Gutierrez*, ed. Michael Griffin and Jennie Weiss Block (Maryknoll, NY: Orbis Books), 19.

[16] Paul's cofounders at Partners In Health are Ophelia Dahl, Todd McCormack, Jim Yong Kim, and the late Tom White.

[17] The PIH Mission Statement (found at www.pih.org/our-mission): "Our mission is to provide a preferential option for the poor in health care. By establishing long-term relationships with sister organizations based in settings of poverty, Partners In Health strives to achieve two overarching goals: to bring the benefits of modern medical science to those most in need of them and to serve as an antidote to despair. We draw on the resources of the world's leading medical and academic institutions and on the lived experience of the world's poorest and sickest communities. At its root, our mission is both medical and moral. It is based on solidarity, rather than charity alone. When our patients are ill and have no access to care, our team of health professionals, scholars, and activists will do whatever it takes to make them well—just as we would do if a member of our own families or we ourselves were ill."

to as his hero and mentor in Peru. Over the years, a deep friendship grounded in respect and affection developed. While Paul and Fr. Gustavo were of two entirely different worlds, they were of one mind and one heart. The book that Paul and Fr. Gustavo coauthored together, *In the Company of the Poor: Conversations with Paul Farmer and Gustavo Gutiérrez*, brought great joy to both of them. Their days together at Notre Dame working on the book was a graced time. Both men loved the quiet days with time for long conversations and meals together with friends and students. They offered a lecture together entitled "Reimaging Accompaniment: Global Health and Liberation Theology" in a packed DeBartolo Hall. Fr. Gustavo celebrated Mass on Paul's fifty-second birthday in the historic Log Chapel at Notre Dame. Everyone gathered in the little chapel knew they were experiencing something very special. Paul considered Chapter Five, "Conversion in the Time of Cholera: A Reflection on Structural Violence and Social Change," in this book to be among the best of his writings, and the interview in this book between these two great men is both historic and inspirational.

During the pandemic, Paul worried greatly about Fr. Gustavo, concerned that he was at great risk given his age and health conditions; he repeatedly asked me to check on him. In the last months of his life, Paul had several dreams about Fr. Gustavo and made me promise that we would go to Peru to see him as soon as it was possible to travel. Needless to say, Fr. Gustavo was deeply saddened by the death of his dear friend.

I will not add further comment on liberation theology, as I have written about it elsewhere and other contributors to this book have done an excellent job of describing Dr. Farmer's use of liberation theology from various perspectives; suffice it to say I know Paul would be grateful that this topic was given the attention it deserves.

Paul Farmer as Good Samaritan

With gratitude for permitting me this personal approach, I now turn to an exegesis of the parable of the Good Samaritan. This passage, and Paul's unfailing devotion to the corporal works of mercy, were, if you will, the "organizing principles" of his moral life and, in turn, his actions.[18] In a speech at Union Theological Seminary, Paul explains his commitment to the corporal works of mercy.

> Partners In Health is a secular organization but all of us believe in the corporal works of mercy, which are laid out clearly enough in the Gospels. These are not vague injunctions; they are precise. Feed the hungry. Give drink to the thirsty. Clothe the naked. Shelter the homeless. Visit the sick. Visit prisoners. Bury the dead.[19]
>
> These commands became, in fact, our guiding philosophy. ... Although we have tried to master the language of international health and sustainable development, and although we have learned much in doing so, I still believe we've learned more by returning to these first principles, laid out so long ago in the Gospel according to Matthew.[20]

The Good Samaritan parable and the corporal works of mercy captured Paul's imagination from the time he was a young man, although he was reluctant to publicly share the influence these passages and other social justice-oriented Scripture passages had on him for he feared that his faith and interest in spirituality[21] would be misconstrued or perverted. He often "felt alienated from faith as it is portrayed in this country,"[22] and he did

---

[18] This is not to suggest that these were his only organizing principles; he studied and read widely and was influenced by multiple disciplines and philosophical categories. However, justice, mercy, and equity are the consistent themes by which he evaluated any belief systems and judgments about the actions of others.

[19] Paul Farmer, "Who Stands Fast?" Union Theological Seminary, Union Medal Acceptance Speech, New York, NY, December 6, 2006, in Paul Farmer, *To Repair the World: Paul Farmer Speaks to the Next Generation*, ed. Jonathan Weigel (Berkeley: University of California Press, 2013), 187.

[20] Farmer, *To Repair the World*, 188.

[21] Paul's interest in religion was not in any way a secret; his family and friends were aware that he was a person of faith and there are numerous references to Paul's religious leanings in Kidder, *Mountains Beyond Mountains*.

[22] Paul Farmer, "Spirituality and Justice," Spirituality and Justice Award Acceptance Speech, All Saints Parish, Brookline, Massachusetts, April 27, 2008, in Paul Farmer, *To Repair the*

not want his faith to be co-opted and used by others for their own purposes. What I can say with some certainty is that the organizing principles laid out in these passages are the ones that stood the test of time, and in later years of his far-too-short-life, he openly embraced and often spoke publicly about these Gospel passages, in both secular and religious circles. This is just one example from an interview in the *Wall Street Journal* published a year before he died in an article entitled "Paul Farmer's Fight Against 'Medical Deserts' of the World:"

> For a man who spends much of his time fighting the medical status quo in slums and prisons, Dr. Farmer is unexpectedly upbeat. He says that his sense of humor runs in his family.
>
> But he is also buoyed by his faith. In his 20s, when he was shuttling between building clinics in Haiti and earning degrees in medicine and anthropology from Harvard, Dr. Farmer found inspiration in liberation theology, a sometimes-controversial Catholic movement focused on public activism to help the poor. His office at home in Miami, Fla., where he lives with his wife, Didi Bertrand (with whom he has three children), is cluttered with gifts of religious iconography. He says he feels guided by Jesus's teachings on the corporal works of mercy, which include caring for the sick, clothing the naked and burying the dead.[23]

Paul called me right after the interview to tell me that he talked about his faith with the reporter and sent the woman interviewing him a picture of the wall with his religious iconography. However, when the story ran, the *WSJ* did not use the photo, and he seemed a little disappointed that his religious art collection did not make it into the news.

World: Paul Farmer Speaks to the Next Generation, ed. Jonathan Weigel (Berkeley: University of California Press, 2013), 211.

[23] Emily Bobrow, "Paul Farmer's Fight Against the 'Medical Deserts' of the World," *Wall Street Journal,* March 5, 2021, www.wsj.com/articles/paul-farmers-fight-against-the-medical-deserts-of-the-world-11614962934.

Towards a Realized Eschatology: Paul Farmer as Good Samaritan

In a speech at Trinity Church in Boston in March of 2009, Paul referred to the Good Samaritan as "everyone's favorite parable."[24] He then proceeded to read the entire passage to his audience. After his Scripture reading, he said, "I think you can all see where I am going with this, and that's to a certain line in the Scripture: 'But, who is my neighbor?'" "Who indeed?" he asks. He spent the rest of his talk answering the question of "who is my neighbor" raised in the parable by drawing on his own global experience, and urging the audience to take "Jesus' definition of neighbor seriously."[25] In just this short speech, he named the country of Haiti as neighbor, those who are tortured at Guantanamo as neighbor, and those who have committed great crimes as neighbor, as well as those without health insurance and those living in dire poverty who have been victims of military occupations.[26] He calls for a "'tidal wave of justice' to sweep over our world,"[27] and his final words to the group were, "But when we link our desire to care for strangers, as the Samaritan did, to a knowledge of history and a commitment to truth, we can do great things."[28] He closed his talk with the poet Seamus Heaney's hopeful words:

> So hope for a great sea-change
> On the far side of revenge.
> Believe that a further shore
> Is reachable from here.
> Believe in miracles
> And cures and healing wells.[29]

In all my years with Paul, I never once saw him exact any revenge on anyone no matter the circumstances, and when he saw pettiness in others,

---

[24] Paul Farmer, "Is it Possible to Give Faith-Based Initiatives a Good Name?" Presented at Trinity Church, Boston, March 15, 2009.
[25] Farmer, "Is it Possible to Give Faith-Based Initiatives a Good Name?"
[26] Farmer, "Is it Possible to Give Faith-Based Initiatives a Good Name?"
[27] This expression is taken from Seamus Heaney's poem "The Cure at Troy," which Paul read as part of the speech.
[28] Farmer, "Is it Possible to Give Faith-Based Initiatives a Good Name?"
[29] Farmer, "Is it Possible to Give Faith-Based Initiatives a Good Name?"

he would just shake his head and then jokingly say, "Umbrage... it will be taken!" He really did live on the far side of revenge where he believed in miracles and cures and healing wells (if he heard this comment, he would insist that I add that he also believed in antibiotics and vaccines!)—all of which were part and parcel of his eschatological vision. And, while I am not sure that the Good Samaritan is "everyone's favorite scripture passage," it surely was Paul's favorite—its inspiration colored his moral life and practice, giving him the license he desired to view everyone as his neighbor.

The One Who Showed Mercy

Found only in Luke's Gospel, the storyline of this parable begins as a response to a question posed to Jesus by a lawyer. "Master, what must I do to inherit eternal life?" Jesus's reply was straightforward. "Love the Lord your God with all your heart and with all your soul and with all your strength and with all your mind and love your neighbor as yourself." The lawyer perseverates and then asks Jesus, "Who is my neighbor?" In response, Jesus tells the story of a man traveling from Jerusalem to Jericho who was attacked by robbers, badly beaten, and left "half dead." Hearers of this story in ancient times would have known that the road between Jerusalem and Jericho was a very dangerous one for travelers as it winds between limestone cliffs with numerous hidden caves, and attacks by Bedouin robbers were known to have occurred on the road.[30]

The first one to see the wounded man was a priest, who quickly passes to the other side of the road, ignoring the suffering man. Next, a Levite came by; he saw the beaten and bleeding man, and he, too, moved to the other side of the road.[31] The next person to come upon the injured man

---

[30] Taylor C. Smith, "Parable of the Samaritan," *Review and Expositor*, 47, no. 4 (1950): 427.

[31] Some scholars, such as Michel Gourgues, R.J. Karris, and J.A. Fitzmyer suggest that the priest and the Levite represent the religious leaders of Judaism; these are leading examples of law-observant people that do not aid the man for fear of being defiled. If they were on the way to or from Jerusalem for the purpose of service in the Temple, they would have been

was a man from the region of Samaria. Using a Samaritan in this situation is loaded with meaning. Samaritans and Jews had been at odds with each other from centuries of conflict, and this man would have been seen as a foreigner on the margins of society, outside of the covenant, perhaps of questionable character, and would likely have aroused some suspicion. However, Jesus surprises with yet another great reversal in the Christian narrative. Luke tells us, "But a Samaritan, as he traveled, came where the man was; and when he saw him, he took pity on him." He stopped, tended to the injured man's wounds with oil and wine, which were considered salves and antiseptics in the ancient world. He then picked the man up, put him on his own donkey, and took him to an inn to take care of him. When he had to leave, he gave the innkeeper money to take care of the suffering man while he convalesced and told him he would soon return and reimburse him for any expenses he might have incurred. Jesus then asked, "Which of these three do you think was a neighbor to the man who fell into the hands of robbers?" To which the lawyer replied, "The one who showed mercy to him." And Jesus verifies his correct response by directing him to "Go and do likewise."

I would like now to turn to explain, in some detail, my claim that this parable, coupled with the corporal works of mercy, are the hermeneutical keys to understanding Paul Farmer's religious imagination, the day-in, day-out expression of his moral life, and in turn, the unceasing demands he freely placed on himself. In this parable, Jesus introduces two contrasting archetypes: two religious leaders with high social standing in the community and an outsider, a person clearly known to be on the margins of society. For his entire adult life, Paul strongly identified with the figure of the Samaritan, that is, the ones who find themselves on the margins of society. This identification with those on the margins began when he was an undergraduate at Duke University, when he volunteered at the nearby migrant camps, working with a "social justice nun with sensible shoes," as

---

concerned about coming into contract with a corpse which would render them ritually impure for a period of twenty-four hours (Leviticus 21:1–4).

Towards a Realized Eschatology: Paul Farmer as Good Samaritan

he often fondly referred to Sr. Julianna DeWolf. Seeing firsthand the poverty and lack of personal agency that was the way of life for these good people and their children moved him deeply. These encounters opened his eyes to injustice, touched his gentle heart, troubled his conscience, and sparked his intellectual curiosity about why such circumstances exist. His identification with those on the margins was strengthened, both viscerally and intellectually, in his early years in Haiti after college and his years training as a physician and anthropologist. It was during this period of his life that he came to embrace and prioritize those on the margins as neighbor and friend.

As is well known, Paul came from very humble beginnings. He lived with his parents and five siblings in an old bus parked at a campground in central Florida. The bus did not have a bathroom or running water, and the family did not have a telephone or a television or any of the trappings of middle-class life. While Paul and his siblings were aware that their situation was unorthodox and at times quite inconvenient, theirs was not a marginal existence. Their family life was stable. Their parents were loving and intelligent, and they provided the children with moral and spiritual formation as well as the opportunity to pursue their interests and education. Paul was intellectually gifted, and thanks to full scholarships at two leading universities, he received a world-class education and enjoyed great success academically and professionally. He was named a university professor at one of the most prestigious universities in the world and authored or edited over a dozen books and hundreds of scholarly articles. He was viewed as a visionary world leader and often referred to as a "nonprofit celebrity," drawing big crowds whenever he gave lectures or presentations. He was the subject of a bestselling biography when he was only forty-five years old and was the recipient of many prestigious awards and honors. He loved and was devoted to his many friends and colleagues in this elite world, and he entered willingly into the world of accomplishments and prestige, mostly because he knew this would offer him the opportunity and ability to better serve. However, for Paul, the margins were his preferred social location or, as he would often say, his "true North." He was intent on seeing the "view from below" and felt he learned the most from listening to his many friends and colleagues socially located on the margins. In *Pathologies of Power*, Paul explains that beyond reviewing a large body of information about the distribution of disease within a population, exploring clinical characteristics and treatment regimens, he was committed to *"elicit the experience and views of poor people* and to incorporate these views into all observations, judgments, and actions."[32] He notes that failing to honor the experience and views of the poor in designing strategies to respond to disease is a terrible error.[33] When Paul expressed these views in 2005, they were radical ideas. Over time, at PIH and beyond, his "option-for-the-poor" approach has significantly and positively influenced the delivery of services in resource-poor settings.

Paul was not naïve about the cost of aligning himself with those on the margins. He once told Tracy Kidder that he knew he was "fighting the long defeat" but he was committed to "making common cause with the losers."

> I have fought the long defeat and brought others people on to fight the long defeat, and I am not going to stop because we keep losing. Now I actually think sometimes we may win. I don't dislike victory. ... You know people from our background—like you, like most PIH'ers, like me—we are used to being on a victory team, but actually what we are really trying to do in PIH is make common cause with the losers. We want to be on the winning team but at the risk of turning our back on the losers, no, it's not worth it.[34]

His strong identification with those on the margins is tied to the Good Samaritan parable in two ways. The first reason is evident; he admired the Samaritan, himself a person on the margins, for responding to the wounded man's need, and he knew that was exactly the kind of person he wanted to be. The second reason is more nuanced and significant and

---

[32] Farmer, *Pathologies of Power*, 146.
[33] Farmer, *Pathologies of Power*, 146.
[34] Kidder, *Mountains Beyond Mountains*, 288.

relates to the line in the passage that explains how the Samaritan man felt when he came upon the suffering man: "But a Samaritan, as he traveled, came where the man was; and when he saw him, he took pity on him" (Luke 10:33). The common English translations for the Greek word used in this passage are "pity" or "moved with compassion." However, this translation falls short and does not fully communicate the meaning of the Greek word, which is derived from a word that literally means "guts" or "inner organs."[35] In the ancient world, the "inner organs" were regarded as the seat of the tender affections such as kindness and tender mercies. These gradually came to denote the seat of the affections; hence, equivalent to our heartfelt emotions. The use of this word, in the original Greek, would have conveyed to those hearing it a much stronger connotation than "pity," more along the lines of a deeper, gut-wrenching reaction—a physical, visceral response that perhaps would have made one sick to their stomach.

The proper translation of this word is significant because it exactly describes the deep emotional and gut-wrenching experience Paul felt *every time* he encountered a suffering person. Even after years of exposure to too many varieties of suffering to list, he never developed any detachment. He was always overwhelmed with gut-wrenching compassion for the person in front of him. Over time, he grew experienced at hiding or just internalizing this reaction, which in many, if not most instances, was appropriate. Most of his patients, and even his students and coworkers, were likely comfortable with a sincere show of compassion, not so much with a leader who is overwhelmed, sick to his stomach, and on the verge of tears. Rather than fleeing from these harsh and disturbing feelings, Paul never turned his glance away from the suffering or lonely other, even when there was little or nothing that he could do to relieve their pain. More than anything, he wanted to "go and do likewise." More than anything, he

---

[35] The Greek noun (neuter) σπλάγχνα (*splagchna*) refers to the internal organs, especially the "nobler entrails"—the heart, lungs, liver, and kidneys. (With gratitude to Jose David Padilla, OP, and Andrew Del Valle, OP, for their assistance and insights on the Greek translation.)

wanted to be just like the Good Samaritan, the one who showed mercy. In a very real sense, this gut-wrenching compassion was a purifying fire and an ongoing source of conversion in his life.[36]

Accompaniment as Holy Interruption

This past summer, I heard a young Episcopal priest, Rev. Kellan Day, preach on the Good Samaritan parable. Of course, my thoughts turned to Paul because I knew this was his favorite passage. It helped that her preaching was beautiful and eloquent, and I found Rev. Day's insights meaningful, especially because her thinking gave me greater insight into the ways Paul practiced the art of accompaniment. Accompaniment was a central theme in Paul's life and work; he often wrote and spoke about the topic. At a commencement address at the Kennedy School of Government called "Accompaniment as Policy," he told the graduates:

> "Accompaniment" is an elastic term. It has a basic, everyday meaning. To accompany someone is to go somewhere with him or her, to break bread together, to be present on a journey with a beginning and an end. There is an element of mystery, of openness, of trust, in accompaniment. The companion, the *accompagnateur*, says, "I'll go with you and support your journey wherever it leads. I'll share your fate for a while—and by "a while." I don't mean a little while.[37]

Paul and his coworkers fashioned and extended the idea of accompaniment in multiple directions. For example, the community health workers at Partners In Health are called *accompagnateurs* and are trained to understand their work as more than distributors of medicine or record keepers. They combine good clinical care with robust accompani-

---

[36] I share this insight with a bit of trepidation for it was a frequent topic in Paul's spiritual direction; however, I believe he would be comfortable with this level of disclosure, especially if it would be helpful to the reader.

[37] Paul Farmer, "Accompaniment as Policy," Harvard Kennedy School of Government Commencement, Boston, May 25, 2011, in Paul Farmer, *To Repair the World: Paul Farmer Speaks to the Next Generation*, 234.

ment that includes complex wraparound services like food, water, housing, and transportation. When Paul served as President Clinton's Deputy in the United Nations Office of the Special Envoy to Haiti, our policy work included developing a set of "Accompaniment Principles" to influence how billions of dollars were spent for the delivery of foreign aid in resource-poor settings. Paul always advocated that accompaniment must be linked to what he called "pragmatic solidarity."

> Pragmatic solidarity is different from but nourished by solidarity, per se, the desire to make common cause with those in need. Solidarity is a precious thing: people enduring great hardship often remark that they are grateful for the prayers and good wishes of fellow human beings. But when the sentiment is accompanied by the goods and services that might diminish unjust hardship, surely it is enriched. To those in great need, solidarity without the pragmatic component can seem like so much abstract piety.[38]

Paul interpreted the closing words of the Good Samaritan passage, "Go and do likewise," in light of his vocation as a physician. To him, this made his own path to showing mercy clear, and he knew, early on, with great certainty, that his life would "be dedicated to accompanying the destitute sick on a journey away from premature suffering and death."[39]

In her homily, Rev. Day offered a quote by Dietrich Bonhoeffer from his book entitled *Life Together: The Classic Exploration of Christian Community*. Paul was a big fan of Bonhoeffer. He admired Bonhoeffer's deep faith and courage. When Paul received the Union Medal from Union Theological Seminary in 2006, Bonhoeffer's question of "Who Stands Fast?" was the theme of his acceptance speech. In *Life Together*, Bonhoeffer presents a number of ministries that he claims are important in the building of community. Several of these ministries, in my opinion, have great merit, including "the ministry of holding one's tongue" and

---

[38] Farmer, *Pathologies of Power*, 146.
[39] Farmer, *To Repair the World*, 239.

"the ministry of listening."[40] The ministry Bonhoeffer mentions that called Paul to mind is the "ministry of helpfulness." In this ministry, Bonhoeffer says,

> We must be ready to allow ourselves to be interrupted by God. God will be constantly crossing our paths and canceling our plans by sending us people with claims and petitions. We may pass them by, preoccupied with our more important tasks, as the priest passed by the man fallen among thieves.[41]

He goes on to say that often "Christians and even ministers frequently consider their work so important and urgent that they will allow nothing to disturb them. They actually think they are doing God a service in this, but actually they are disdaining God's 'crooked yet straight path.'"[42] In her homily, Rev. Day calls these encounters "holy interruptions." She told her congregation, "God's crooked yet straight path is before us every single day. God's interruptions are on our doorstep trying to cancel our plans."[43] From years of observing him in action, it strikes me that Paul's practice of accompaniment was entirely dictated by an openness to God's holy interruptions. Paul was unfailingly gracious, but this stance was more than just good manners. Sometimes his lack of self-importance was pretty spectacular and, truth be told, could be a bit aggravating to those trying to manage his extremely busy schedule, assist with his demanding workload, or help with coordination at events. He never acted like he was in a hurry. He would often stop to talk to a stranger or a student or a person that he had not seen for a while. He treated a janitor the same way he treated a prime minister. He would give whomever he was speaking with his full attention for as long as the person wanted to chat. Often the person would

---

[40] Dietrich Bonhoeffer, *Life Together: The Classic Exploration of Christian Community*, trans. John W. Doberstein (San Francisco: HarperSanFrancisco, 1954), 91, 97.
[41] Bonhoeffer, *Life Together*, 99.
[42] Bonhoeffer, *Life Together*, 99.
[43] Reverend Kellan Day, "Homily," Presented at Church of the Incarnation, Highlands, North Carolina, July 10, 2022.

ask him for one thing or another—career or personal advice, to sign a book, to write a letter of recommendation, to call their mother's doctor to confirm a diagnosis, or to come to their child's Girl Scout troop to give a talk. He always tried to accommodate their request, however large or small. This often meant that he ran late or piled up an impossible list of things to do or just did not attend to things that others deemed "important" in a timely matter

Every time Paul gave a talk or lecture, hundreds of people would wait in line for hours to have their books signed or get a picture with him. I remember one evening at a book-signing event in California. The organizers of the event came and told me that we had a "hard stop" at 7:30 p.m. because we had to leave to go to a dinner party. They told me that I should let Paul know that he would have to stop signing books at 7:30 p.m. "sharp." I was thinking to myself, "the chance of that happening is zero percent," but I just smiled and said, "I will see what I can do." We left for the dinner party at 8:55 p.m. after the last book was signed.

With his patients, the sky was the limit. I remember going to three grocery stores to find the kind of jelly he promised to bring an older lady in Haiti (we finally found it!). And everyone who ever worked for Paul will tell you about the countless cell phones, iPads, watches, Bibles, nail clippers, textbooks, and the many other requested items he cheerfully dragged in heavy suitcases all over the world. While Paul could be exacting, crisp, and focused on clinical or academic matters, he was never rushed with his patients. He sat for hours in clinics and hospitals, often quietly on the side of a bed, listening to the narratives of his patients' lives, the ears of his heart taking in their pain and their hopes and, in turn, trying to find solutions for their wants and their needs. Bonhoeffer makes the point that the reason people do not want to engage in these holy interruptions is because "They do not want a life that is crossed and balked."[44] Crossed and balked. While I probably would not have thought to use these exact words, they are indeed appropriate because they made me see that Paul willingly

---

[44] Bonhoeffer, *Life Together*, 99.

and intentionally gave himself over to a life that was "crossed and balked" because he knew that is what it takes to be a good *accompagnateur*, to be the one that shows mercy. Paul's good friend, Jesuit Jim Keenan, defines mercy as "the willingness to enter into the chaos of another person's life."[45] Paul recognized that to show mercy and to fully enter into the chaos of another person's life would mean a life that was crossed and balked, full of holy interruptions.

Rev. Day told her congregation that sometimes, a homeless woman, whom their parish had committed to help, interrupted her.

> As a young priest, I must confess to you, I often viewed them as untimely and inconvenient. I can see that every time I allowed myself to be interrupted led me to places where my heart was further cracked open. ... Those interruptions led me straight to the gaping wounds of our world and straight into the arms of an agonizing mercy. And if I had ignored those interruptions, if we, dear parish, had ignored her, we would have missed Jesus himself.[46]

Had I heard this homily when Paul was still alive, I would have asked her for a copy to send to him. We would have discussed it in detail, and her thinking would have deeply resonated with him. He would have liked the Bonhoeffer reference, but mostly it would have validated what he already knew so well—that holy interruptions are the crooked but straight path to accompaniment of the lonely other and the doorway to enter into the chaos of another's life.

The sentiments Rev. Day expressed in her preaching would have given language and explanation to Paul's own experience. He would have read her homily multiple times, probably shed some tears, and he would have treasured her closing words in his heart for a long time:

---

[45] James F. Keenan, SJ, *The Works of Mercy: The Heart of Catholicism* (Lanham, MD: Rowman and Littlefield, 2005), 3.
[46] Day, "Homily."

Towards a Realized Eschatology: Paul Farmer as Good Samaritan

So, let yourself be interrupted. Look for people making claims and petitions on your lives, look for all those in proverbial ditches. Watch for the crooked straight path to appear—and it will appear. And the next time a guttural compassion overcomes you, don't cross the road to the other side. Draw near, instead. Tend to your neighbors and their wounds. And if you do, you will find Jesus there waiting for you.[47]

Life at the Intersection of Suffering and Hope

I noted earlier that Paul was a hope giver; his sense of hope was contagious and one of the reasons so many people were drawn to him. However, he did not peddle a shallow optimism or faux sense of cheerfulness or subscribe to, in the words of Dietrich Bonhoeffer, "cheap grace."[48] Paul had a very well-developed theology of the cross. He instinctively understood that a "theology of the cross is the reverse side of the Christian theology of hope."[49] Paul knew that any authentic Christian hope begins by turning towards the Crucified One who took on the form of a slave and emptied himself with a radical outpouring of love. Moltmann makes the point that it is hope's statement of promise that stands in contradiction to the reality of the present, and thus hope does not seek to illuminate the reality which exists but the reality which is coming.[50] It was the reality of what was to come, the reign of God as described by Jesus, that motivated Paul Farmer to work tirelessly to bring about the Kingdom of God in the here and now.

Paul would often send me pictures of his patients to ask me to pray for them, to tell me how they were doing, to ask me to get something for them, or to send money to their families. Most often, these photos and messages were at the intersection of suffering and hope, where Paul radically

---

[47] Day, "Homily."
[48] Quoted in Jennie Weiss Block, OP, "Introduction," in Farmer and Gutiérrez, *In the Company of the Poor*, 9.
[49] Jürgen Moltmann, *The Crucified God: The Cross of Christ as the Foundation and Criticism of Christian Theology*, trans. R.A. Wilson and John Bowden (Minneapolis: Fortress Press, 1993), 5.
[50] Moltmann, *Theology of Hope*, 18.

experienced both sides—the cross of the Crucified One and the light of the Risen Lord—at the same time. Moltmann goes on to further explain that a theology of the cross is intended to make a theology of hope more concrete, and to add the necessary power of resistance to the power of its vision to inspire to action.[51] Two of the last communications I had with Paul about his patients in Butaro, Rwanda, in the weeks before he death well illustrate Moltmann's point.

On February 6, 2022, Paul sent me a video of a man named Faustin with the following message: "Please add Faustin to your prayer list. There is still a sliver of hope."[52] Ten days later, he wrote to me late at night to say, "We lost Faustin at midnight."[53] He sent two pictures; one of himself with Faustin's father—Paul looked so tired in this photo, standing next to Faustin's grieving father with a surgical mask under his chin. The next photo showed four men carrying Faustin's coffin draped in white. Sometimes it took a long time to take these pictures in. A day later, I asked Paul how he was doing. His response: "I know that you know. I'm okay deep down and love this work so much, but this was a real setback after weeks of slow improvement."[54] When I told him that I was grateful for his accompaniment of the family and the excellent treatment and care Faustin received, he responded, "His dad said the same thing so many times. He reminded me of you and the ministry of showing up."[55] Moltmann's view of a theology of the cross entails "comprehending the crucified Christ in the light and context of his resurrection, and therefore of freedom and hope."[56] It was to this promise of freedom and hope that Paul gravitated as he encountered again and again the crucified Christ present in the suffering of the poor people that he served. He sought to make his presence and the actions he took on their behalf a sign of hope, for "unless it

---

[51] Moltmann, *The Crucified God*, 5.
[52] Paul Farmer, message to the author, February 6, 2022.
[53] Paul Farmer, message to the author, February 16, 2022.
[54] Paul Farmer, message to the author, February 17, 2022.
[55] Paul Farmer, message to the author, February 18, 2022.
[56] Moltmann, *The Crucified God*, 4.

apprehends the pain of the negative, Christian hope cannot be realistic and liberating.[57]

On February 19, 2022, just two days before he died, Paul sent me a picture of a small girl in the children's cancer ward. She looked serious, or perhaps sad, and her beautiful little face was swollen, perhaps from her meds. He was sitting on the bed with her, and she was sitting in between his outstretched arms. He was wearing an African shirt, and he was smiling. His message to me: "Add Josiane to your prayer list."[58] In his next message, he was annoyed because Josiane had to go all the way to Kigali for a CT scan. He wrote, "She is getting staged today if she tolerates the stupid trip to Kigali. You remember our strategic priorities from years ago? Cancer care and the scanner? Well, we got the hard part done but dithered on the scanner."[59] A few hours later, he cheerfully told me that she made it back safely. A day later, another picture arrived of Paul, one of the nurses, and little Josiane. I studied the picture for a bit and then told Paul, "She is smiling—she loves you." He wrote back, "I think it's mutual. She told me she's been watching me see another young person with cancer every day and was wishing I would see her too."[60] Thirty-six hours after I got this message, Paul was dead. Amidst the chaos in the days following his death, I wondered if little Josiane was upset because her new friend had not come back to see her. A few weeks later, I asked Sheila Davis, the CEO of Partners In Health, to ask how little Josiane was doing on her upcoming trip to Rwanda. I had thought of her and looked at her picture so many times after Paul's death. Sheila wrote and told me that Josiane died just a few days after Paul and that she knew that Paul was there to greet her with open arms. I am sure this is true, but nonetheless, my first thought was that I was relieved that at least Paul was spared having to watch her die.

It so happens that these two stories in the last weeks of Paul's life were about patients that died, but I must also mention that there are just as

---

[57] Moltmann, *The Crucified God*, 5.
[58] Paul Farmer, message to the author, February 19, 2022.
[59] Paul Farmer, message to the author, February 19, 2022.
[60] Paul Farmer, message to the author, February 20, 2022.

many, if not more, stories about patients that were receiving state-of-the-art medical treatment in the poorest places in the world, many of them recovering from illnesses they would have died from before their time. Paul was especially proud of the stories that told of saving the lives of millions of mothers and fathers, all of whom were given the gifts of seeing their children grow up. Before PIH built the hospital with a cancer ward in Butaro, there was no cancer treatment available to poor people in the entire region. Paul was very proud of these extraordinary accomplishments. He loved to see his patients thrive and survive, and many patients became good friends over the years. But always, it was to those on the margins, to those who were suffering or despairing or in need to whom he first turned his attention, always trying to bring hope, healing, and help in its many forms, including the material. To so many, just his mere presence brought hope and peace.

While "friends affectionately accuse Dr. Farmer of being pathologically optimistic,"[61] his generally cheerful demeanor is not to be conflated with his understanding of the cost of believing in Christian hope nor to suggest that he did not have times of sadness or interior struggles. Paul was an extrovert; he loved the company of friends and was fun to be around. He had a quick wit and a great sense of humor, and he could be very entertaining. When I asked his friend, Fr. Jim Keenan, SJ, for a comment for Paul's obituary I was writing for the *National Catholic Reporter,* his comments captured Paul's spirit and presence perfectly. "From the very first time I met Paul some twenty years ago, I always thought of him as playful; it was that playfulness that made him so accessible. By that playfulness, he made you believe that you were fun to be with. He helped you, wherever you were, to laugh. That playfulness was infectious."[62] Jim went on to say, "I am not trying to romanticize his work or his death. To know Paul, was to know a man who faced disease and death more than anyone we knew. He was fearless and, if, for instance, you read his book

---

[61] Bobrow, "Paul Farmer's Fight Against the 'Medical Deserts' of the World."
[62] James Keenan, SJ, to the author, February 23, 2022.

on Ebola, you knew how incredibly courageous he was."[63] While Paul was playful and cheerful and so much fun to be with, he was also a very serious person with a deeply contemplative side. As he matured and grew in wisdom and grace, the need for time apart to read, to think, and to pray increased, as did his need for long periods of silence.

While I never saw Paul despair, he was no stranger to lament. He had a profound interest in theodicy, although not necessarily to seek an answer to the age-old question of why God allows suffering, especially of the innocent. He knew that this was a mystery beyond knowing but nonetheless worth pondering. His interest was somewhat academic, although not dispassionate. In *Pathologies of Power,* he notes that this book is his attempt to consider an anthropology of suffering with a "cultural inquiry into the ways that people attempt to explain the presence of pain, affliction, and evil."[64]

In an essay Paul wrote in *Via Crucis: The Way of the Cross,*[65] he reflects on the questions surrounding theodicy and suffering by asking, "How long is the way of the cross? Is it a journey with a destination?"[66] He finds looking at Bourguignon's stark and intense drawings of the stations of the cross while he is in rural Haiti between the third Sunday of Lent and Good Friday a "painful exercise." He laments, "The answer to the question—how long the way of the cross—is not at all clear, at least not to me. Here in Haiti, where the *Via Crucis* stretches out in all directions as far as the eye can see, the sorrowful dimensions of the 'good news' and of Christ's example seem more compelling than do the joyful ones." As Lent draws to

---

[63] James Keenan, SJ, to the author, February 23, 2022.

[64] Farmer, *Pathologies of Power,* 28.

[65] This publication contains a series of hauntingly beautiful paintings and drawings by Paul-Henri Bourguignon. The series was exhibited at the Pontifical College Josephinum, the Ohio governor's mansion, and in several churches. The series is owned by St. Mark's Episcopal Church in Upper Arlington, Ohio. The poems in the volume were written by Edward Lense, and the accompanying text was written by Erika Bourguignon. The foreword was written by Arthur Kleinman, and Paul's essay is a reflection at the end of the book.

[66] Paul Farmer, essay in Paul-Henri Bourguignon, *Via Crucis: The Way of the Cross* (Worthington, OH: privately printed, 2013).

a close, he asks the plaintive question, "Is Lent ever really over? Will we contemplate the *Via Crucis* and seeks its modern significance in the great and unmerited suffering of others, especially the poor? Structural violence, unwarranted suffering, misery, and premature death—most of it experienced by the poor—continues unabated.[67] His essay closes with a haunting question: "How long then is the *Via Crucis*? From this vantage point, there seems to be no end in sight. We have little left but our faith, battered and bruised, to suggest that there will be an end to the suffering that is not our own."[68] This little-known essay was not published widely, but it but was very important to Paul; every year during Holy Week, we would get it out and read it together. Throughout his writings, there are many references to theodicy and the "vast topographies of pain"[69] he witnessed in others as well as his own deep feelings. He sometimes mentioned that others did not give much notice to these topics. In many ways, this is understandable, as people looked to Paul as a hope giver, for consolation, motivation, and for inspiration.

Nonetheless, "vast topographies of pain" were never far from Paul's mind. Had *The Wall Street Journal* run the photo of his religious iconography, one would have seen multiple images of Our Lady of Sorrows for one of the ways he contemplated the "vast topographies of pain" that often surrounded him was through his great devotion to this image of Mary, the Mother of God. Our Lady of Sorrows brought him great comfort and consolation as he sought to fully enter into and manage his life at the crossroad of suffering and hope. Paul had hoped to write a book about his work that would subtly acknowledge his devotion to Our Lady of Sorrows. Taking from the prophecy in Luke 2:35 ("and a sword will pierce your own soul, too"), he planned to call this book *Swords of Sorrow*. I was saving an icon of Our Lady of Sorrows to give to him for his birthday. I will always wish I had given it to him the last time I saw him.

---

[67] Farmer, essay in *Via Crucis*.
[68] Farmer, essay in *Via Crucis*.
[69] This phrase is from Kathleen O'Connor, *Lamentations and the Tears of the World* (Maryknoll, NY: Orbis Books, 2002).

Towards a Realized Eschatology: Paul Farmer as Good Samaritan

At this juncture, it seems appropriate to add three points. First, I have greatly exceeded the suggested length of this chapter, and yet, there is so much more that I want to say. I hope I have at least scratched the surface on the topic of Paul's eschatological orientation, and that I will have further opportunity to explore this subject. Second, I regret that space does not permit me to say more about Paul's enduring dedication to the corporal works of mercy. I think this short story will explain why. A year or so after I met Paul, I went to Boston to attend a seminar with him. It was mid-November and quite chilly. When I saw him, he was shivering in the cold, as he was only wearing a suit jacket and a thin sweater vest. (I later came to find out it was his only suit!) At the lunch break, I ran over to a very nice department store and bought him a good winter coat and threw in a nice cashmere scarf for good measure. He thanked me profusely for the coat and scarf, and I was so happy that he looked nice and warm. Three weeks later, I met up with him again in New York City to attend an event where he was receiving an award. He arrived a little late, sans coat, and again was shivering in the freezing cold. I timidly asked where his coat was, and he said, "I had a cab driver a few weeks ago and he didn't have a coat or any money—so I gave him all the money I had on me and the coat." He paused for a few seconds and then earnestly said, "We're supposed to clothe the naked, right?" All I could do was nod, and think, "Yes, indeed, Paul, we are supposed to clothe the naked," knowing full well that I would probably never give my coat to a cab driver. I went and got him a new coat and scarf. It was the first of many coats that I would get him over the years, each of which, he in turn, would give away to a stranger who needed a coat. Being friends with Paul had many blessings, but experiences like this were at the top of the list. The most extraordinary thing about this little story is that I (and everyone who knew Paul) can easily narrate similar stories about him. Every single one of the corporal and spiritual works of mercy, along with his ability to articulate the theological and pastoral understanding of exactly what he was doing. Third, given that I have presented Paul in a very positive light, he would insist that I mention that he was far from perfect. Like all of us, he had quite a few faults and "issues"—to use popular parlance. He would be the first to laugh and say that his faults were "TNTC"—medical jargon he liked to use meaning "too numerous to count." To his credit, he was aware of most of his faults, and conversion of heart and habits were often on his mind. While he would be grateful to me for presenting him so generously, he would not want any of us to deny his full humanity, which surely includes his less attractive attributes.

Revolutionizing and Transforming: Towards a Realized Eschatology

In the quote that opened this essay, Moltmann tells us, "Christianity is eschatology, is hope, forward looking and forward moving, and therefore also revolutionizing and transforming the present."[70] Ultimately, Paul understood that "radical conversion to solidarity with the poor, afflicted and brokenhearted are at the heart of the Christian life"[71] and that all Christians are called to try to build the Kingdom of God in the here and now. He knew that, in the words of Nathan Mitchell, the preferential 'option' for the poor, is, in fact, not optional. He knew his calling was through his vocation as a physician and an anthropologist, and, well, he gave this life-long project his all. As Jon Weigel, one of his former students put it, "Paul is all in, all of the time."[72] Paul would be the first to say that he had many *accompagnateurs* on this holy journey for he knew that "entering into divine life is impossible unless we enter into a life of love and communion with others."[73] Catherine LaCugna claims that there are modes of relationships that reflect the truth of God's economy: "words, actions and attitudes that serve the reign of God."[74] These are the kind of relationships that Paul forged with thousands of people. With his ever-present Samaritan logic, Paul could see the reign of God preached by Jesus

---

[70] Moltmann, *Theology of Hope*, 16.
[71] Catherine Mowry LaCugna, *God for Us: The Trinity and Christian Life* (San Francisco: HarperSanFrancisco, 1991), 131.
[72] Farmer, *To Repair the World*, Introduction, xix.
[73] LaCugna, *God for Us*, 382.
[74] LaCugna, *God for Us*, 383.

as a real possibility, and he envisioned a world full of the "power of God's Holy Spirit, who rules through justice, peace, charity, love, joy, moderation, kindness, generosity, freedom, compassion, reconciliation, holiness, humility and wisdom."[75] Somehow, Paul never gave up, never despaired, and never lost hope for "our wounded but beautiful world."[76] Somehow, in spite of hardship, disappointments, setbacks, and the personal and professional struggles of a complicated life, for Paul, the light of the eschatological horizon never dimmed. In fact, I believe it grew brighter in the final decade of his life.

The journey had its ups and downs, for sure, and setbacks were to be expected. But Paul's outlook was always eschatological, that is "forward looking and forward moving," even when naysayers (and there were many) told him what he wanted to do was "not sustainable" or "too ambitious" or "too expensive" or just "plain unrealistic." He bristled when some suggested a lower standard was good enough for the poor. He was not to be deterred because his favorite parable was his constant reminder that everyone was his neighbor in need of mercy. Over on the margins with his people, he dispensed the medicine of mercy. He visited prisoners, he cared for the sick, he tended the brokenhearted, he gave food, drink, and shelter to those without, and far too often he buried the dead before their time. Moltmann tells us that "The Risen Christ calls, sends, justifies, and sanctifies men, and in doing so gathers, calls and sends them into his eschatological future for the world."[77] It was straight into this eschatological future that the Risen Christ beckoned Paul Farmer, who went with mind, eyes, and heart wide open, making his home at the

---

[75] LaCugna, *God for Us*, 384.

[76] This was an expression that Paul often used. For example, in Chapter One, "Reimagining Accompaniment: A Doctor's Tribute to Gustavo Gutiérrez," in *In the Company of the Poor*, Paul closes the chapter by saying, "As long as poverty and equality persist, as long as people are wounded and imprisoned and despised, we humans will need accompaniment—practical, spiritual, intellectual. It is for this reason, and for many others, that I am grateful for Father Gustavo's presence on this wounded but beautiful earth."

[77] Moltmann, *Theology of Hope*, 325.

intersection of the cross and hope. The outcomes of Paul's eschatological vision do not fall short of Moltmann's claim that eschatology is "revolutionizing and transforming" as evidenced by the international global health equity movement he built, which is grounded in nothing short of revolutionary models of health care delivery that have transformed the lived reality of millions and millions of the poorest people on "our wounded but beautiful earth." Paul was able to communicate and share his eschatological vision (usually without naming it as such) in a compelling and engaging manner which motivated thousands of friends and colleagues who have gone forth bravely to "go and do likewise"—with extraordinary success. Paul's abiding belief in eschatology's power to revolutionize and transform has been, and I believe will continue to be, a source of inspiration and hope to the thousands who knew him personally and for the millions who know of him by reputation.

Paul gave his life to the least among us. He took Luke's words in the Good Samaritan parable to heart. He loved God with his whole heart and mind, and he loved his neighbor as himself. Preaching at Paul's funeral Mass in Miami, Fr. Jorge Presmanes, OP, explains well the God that Paul loved with his whole heart and mind.

> The God revealed in this passage from Matthew's Gospel is the God Paul believed in and identified with. For he believed in a God of pathos. A God who feels intensely, who loves passionately, and gets angry over injustice. He believed in a God who felt hunger with the hungry and grieved with those who grieve, a God who pours out mercy, and wipes away tears. Paul believed in a God who loves all but has a preferential option for the poor—not because the poor are better than anyone else; not because the poor are necessarily good, but because God is good. Like the God of pathos, Paul felt intensely for the poor, the oppressed and the marginalized. And that sympathy with God's pathos, that divine

Towards a Realized Eschatology: Paul Farmer as Good Samaritan

compassion and outrage that he felt at the injustices of the world is what motivated his life's work.[78]

It was the God of pathos to whom Paul was drawn. It was the God of pathos that was his daily companion. It was this all-compassionate God that gave him the gift of endless compassion, and the God who favors the poor that quieted his upset stomach when he was overcome by the pain and suffering of the lonely other. It was the God of pathos that healed, again and again, his broken heart, and the God of pathos that filled him with the kind of hope that rejoices in the deepest of sorrows. It was the God of pathos that directed his path towards a realized eschatology. It is to this God of pathos that we commend our brother, Paul. May he continue to guide us and inspire us in death as he did in life, and for his years amongst us, we give praise and thanks.

Jennie Weiss Block, OP, DMin, is a Dominican laywoman and a practical theologian. She is the author of *Paul Farmer: Servant to the Poor* (Liturgical Press, 2018), and co-editor of *In the Company of the Poor: Conversations with Dr. Paul Farmer and Fr. Gustavo Gutiérrez* (Orbis Books, 2013). Her book *Copious Hosting: A Theology of Access for People with Disabilities* (Continuum, 2002) is considered a seminal text in disability theology. She served as chief adviser to Dr. Paul Farmer from 2009 to 2022 and was his chief of staff in his role as United Nations Deputy Special Envoy to Haiti under President Bill Clinton.

---

[78] Fr. Jorge Presmanes, OP, "Homily." Presented at Paul Farmer's Funeral Mass, St. Thomas Church, Miami, February 25, 2022.

Chapter 2: Paul the *Anargyros*: History, God-Talk, and Ecumenism in the Healing Praxis of Dr. Paul Farmer

Susan R. Holman

There once was a man named Paul who devoted his life to direct, hands-on care for the suffering needy. He began by doing night rounds on a team, combing the streets after dark for any "poor and old and sick." With others in this service, he cleaned bodies, mended clothes, and provided these individuals with food, money, and related health care services. Before long he was doing this 24/7. Those around him were so inspired by his example that he "organized and built up and instituted" similar services in other cities. He was constantly traveling, and his coworkers included rich and poor, men and women, ordinary people who became "fellow labourers and partners" in the work. His efforts were so effective that when he died, his body mere skin and bones, the activities he left behind "grew and increased and expanded everywhere ... to God's glory and the relief of the poor."[1]

This story clearly evokes much that readers of this volume know and love about the late Dr. Paul Farmer. But in fact, this story is about another Paul, a man who lived about 1500 years ago. Written in Syriac in the late 560s CE by a monk named John of Ephesus, this narrative, about a man from Antioch, is one of fifty-eight biographical "histories" that describe inspiring people whom John says he met and knew personally. He calls them "saints," but sainthood in his world, the fraught political borderlands of the Roman Empire during the reign of the emperor Justinian, did not require any particular process of canonization as we know it today. His purpose for writing these lives, John says, was to leave "the pattern of their

---

[1] John of Ephesus, "Life of Paul of Antioch," in *John of Ephesus: Lives of the Eastern Saints (II)*, ed. and trans. E.W. Brooks (Patrologia Orientalis; Paris: Firmin-Didot, 1924), 671–676.

likeness for posterity,"[2] to inspire in his readers an eagerness to imitate them and enter heaven hearing God say, in the words of Matthew 25:34, "Come, you who are blessed." John categorized Paul of Antioch as simply a "divine man and strenuous worker." As far as we can tell, this Paul was not a priest, monk, trained physician, nor even a miracle worker. His activities were "ministrations" or "social services,"[3] what the Catholic church today might call diaconal ministry. Insofar as Paul of Antioch's service included focused practices for healing, he models a type of healer-physicians in Christian history known as *anargyroi* (pronounced ah-NAR-gear-oi). In this essay, I summarize the characteristic nature and practices typical of *anargyroi* and then suggest how the life and theological ethics of the late Dr. Paul Farmer may offer us an exemplar of a modern *anargyros*.

Anargyroi: Unmercenary Healers

The word *anargyroi* (singular *anargyros*) is from the Greek, meaning those who provided health care assistance "without silver," that is, for free. Also called "unmercenary saints,"[4] these health care providers, typically found in texts from Mediterranean late antiquity, freely served the sick and needy in a deliberately equitable fashion—in so doing often challenging the normally corrupt social order in paradoxical ways. *Anargyroi* healing stories sometimes feel like parables missing a punchline.

Such holy healers were usually (but not always) martyrs. In life, they were said to have practiced medicine or to have been associated with skilled ascetic healers for whom social justice was part of their religious identity. God's healing power continued to work through their post-mortem remains and at their healing sites, typically Christian shrines or sometimes

---

[2] John of Ephesus, *John of Ephesus*, 2.
[3] Susan Ashbrook Harvey, *Asceticism and Society in Crisis: John of Ephesus and the* Lives of the Eastern Saints (Berkeley: University of California Press, 1990), 34 and 99.
[4] For a brief overview with more extensive bibliography, see Susan R. Holman, "Unmercenary Saints," in *The Encyclopedia of Eastern Orthodox Christianity*, Vol. 2, ed. John Anthony McGuckin (Hoboken, NJ: Wiley-Blackwell, 2010), 618–620.

extensive complexes that were part hospital, part church. Their fame drew hordes of sick supplicants who were then cared for by the *anargyroi*, who appeared in various guises. Such healing shrines were staffed by ordinary mortal volunteers, recovered patients, and attendants (sometimes church-owned slaves).[5] Treatments might include pharmaceutical recipes, physical therapies, dreams, or miraculously painless surgeries that followed certain aspects of "standard" medical care but were judged far superior to ordinary doctors for various reasons. Patients typically sought help from *anargyroi* when for-profit efforts failed or "regular" doctors gave up on them.

Money was a sensitive point in medical service ethics long before Christianity.[6] The stories from Christian healing shrines indicate both acceptance of ordinary physicians as having a valid vocation[7] and also criticism of some of them, especially medics whose beliefs, economic practices, or attitudes implied greed, pride, blind loyalty to the traditions of Galen and Hippocrates, or theological "deviance" as defined by whoever was championing the holy healer. Despite "supernatural" claims, *anargyroi* healings typically used ordinary substances—sometimes in very strange ways. In fact, the intersection between miracle and "natural" cure in the ancient world was a mesh of slippage that lacked our categorizations

---

[5] An essay that envisions one ancient Christian healing shrine based on archaeological and textual data is Béatrice Caseau, "Ordinary Objects in Christian Healing Sanctuaries," in *Objects in Context, Objects in Use: Material Spatiality in Late Antiquity*, ed. Luke Lavan, Ellen Swift, and Toon Putzeys (Leiden: Brill, 2007), 625–654. See also Ildikó Csepregi, "The Compositional History of Greek Christian Incubation Miracle Collections: Saint Thecla, Saint Cosmas and Damian, Saint Cyrus and John, Saint Artemios," PhD diss., Central European University, Budapest, 2007.

[6] On public physicians including ethics and economic ideals, the classic source is Vivian Nutton, "*Archiatri* and the Medical Profession in Antiquity," *Papers of the British School at Rome* 45 (1977): 191–226. On the development of hospitals in Late Antiquity the literature is vast, but see especially Peregrine Horden, "Poverty, Charity, and the Invention of the Hospital," *Cultures of Healing: Medieval and After* (New York: Routledge, 2019), 33–62.

[7] See, for example, Basil of Caesarea, *Asketikon,* Longer Responses (LR) 55, trans. Anna M. Silvas, *The Asketikon of St Basil the Great* (Oxford: Oxford University Press, 2005), 264–269.

of empirical "body/spirit" polarities."[8] In dream incubation stories, holy healers are often described as looking just like an ordinary doctor. Ildikó Csepregi argues that the development of early hospitals, between the fourth and eighth centuries—which eventually expanded to (sometimes) include wards, medical rounds, and recognizable clothing and equipment—likely influenced how the sick, who (also) sought out healing shrines, viewed the *anargyroi* who healed them by dreams.[9] Surviving oracle ticket fragments—answers for the patient who asked the saint for written advice or prescription—show how banal such treatment might be. One sixth/seventh century papyrus fragment from Egypt, for instance, simply reads, "Saints Kosmas and Damianos ... order your servant [..., son of] Gerontios, to bathe himself."[10]

The most popular surviving story collections about unmercenary doctors are those for the above-mentioned Cosmas and Damian,[11] Cyrus

---

[8] My purpose here is to summarize the *anargyroi* model and introduce it into discussion of Paul Farmer's medical ethics; space prohibits details here of the nuanced overlaps and differences between Christian *anargyroi* and non-Christian Asclepius healing shrines, or between *anargyroi* and the tradition of healing associated with non-medic martyrs and other "saints"; the literature is extensive. Most named *anargyroi* in Christian history are men, but the most famous woman's shrine with healing accounts is that of Thecla in Seleucia. Another "unmercenary" healing woman, Hermione, a name given to one of Philip the Deacon's daughters mentioned in Acts 21:8–9, is associated with Ephesus, is *not* a martyr, is credited with having received some medical training, and is venerated today on the Greek island of Chios.

[9] Ildikó Csepregi, "Changes in Dream Patterns between Antiquity and Byzantium: The Impact of Medical Learning on Dream Healing," in *Ritual Healing: Magic, Ritual and Medical Therapy from Antiquity until the Early Modern Period*, ed. I. Csepregi and Ch. Burnett (Firenze: SISMEL, Edizioni del Galluzzo, 2012), 131–145. On the gradual institutionalization of hospital-like facilities in this period, see Mark Alan Anderson, "Hospitals, Hospices, and Shelters for the Poor in Late Antiquity," PhD diss., Yale University, 2012.

[10] *P.Amst.* 1.22, ed. R.P. Salomons, P.J. Sijpesteijn, and K.A. Worp, trans. G. Schenke, online at Oxford University's "The Cult of Saints in Late Antiquity" database, csla.history.ox.ac.uk/record.php?recid=E06150.

[11] Ludwig Deubner, ed., *Kosmas und Damian* (Leipzig and Berlin: B.G. Teubner, 1907); and E. Rupprecht, *Cosmae et Damiani Sanctorum Medicorum Vitam et Miracula e Codice Londiniensi* (Berlin, 1935); for translation, see A. J. Festugière, trans., *Sainte Thècle, Saints*

and John,[12] and Artemios.[13] Some were specialists; Artemios attracted those with hernias, and another *anargyros* popular in Egypt, Colluthus, seemed to have specialized in eye diseases.[14] Healings did not necessarily include the full gamut of the corporal works of mercy (discussed further below). However, in the various manuscript collections of healing stories, each person healed receives whatever is appropriate to her or his disorder, which may include cures that address social factors. The stories emphasize community efforts. Care usually involved attentive accompaniment and collective teamwork—sometimes ironically forced or tricked—that engaged other patients, local merchants, or clergy. Healing partners might also include the God-guided actions of living animals such as birds, snakes, and camels, in addition to the animal, vegetable, mineral, and environmental substances that underlie ancient medicine and curative recipes based in a theory of balancing wet, dry, hot, and cold humors.

Paul the *Anargyros*?

What then does such a model offer us as we consider the theological ethics of the late Dr. Paul Farmer? How might his health care practices be seen as similar to or different from those of that other Paul who began this chapter, the ordinary man from sixth-century Antioch? Why might we consider Paul Farmer an *anargyros*?

Côme et Damien, Saints Cyr et Jean (extraits), Saint Georges (Collections grecques de miracles; Paris: Éditions A. et J. Picard, 1971).

[12] Natalio Fernández Marcos, ed., *Los "Thaumata" de Sofronio: Contribución al estudio de la Incubatio Cristiana* (Madrid: Instituto Antonio de Nebrija, 1975). The best translation of these miracles of Cyrus and John is Jean Gascou, ed. and trans., *Sophrone de Jérusalem: Miracles des Saints Cyr et Jean, BHG I 477–479* (Paris: De Boccard, 2006).

[13] For Artemios, see Virgil S. Crisafulli and John W. Nesbitt, eds. and trans., *The Miracles of St. Artemios: A Collection of Miracle Stories by an Anonymous Author of Seventh-Century Byzantium* (Leiden: E.J. Brill, 1997).

[14] On Colluthus as a physician, see especially Aaltje Hidding, *The Era of the Martyrs: Remembering the Great Persecution in Late Antique Egypt* (Berlin: DeGruyter, 2020), 67–98, doi.org/10.1515/9783110689686-003.

John's description of Paul of Antioch's work, like Farmer's, includes the core elements of the medical care of his day: typically bathing, food, and the application of various substances to, through, and around the body for restorative physical, mental, social, and spiritual balance. Also, like Farmer, Paul of Antioch, John suggests, energized a nonprofit model of accompaniment and free care, addressed social determinants of health in practical ways, and engaged enthusiastic partnerships, including savvy fiscal networking. John's readers would have understood Paul of Antioch to be doing what are popularly known as "the corporal works of mercy" based on Matthew 25:31–46, that is, serving the poor who, according to this scripture, literally manifest God's body through a moral mandate to provide basic economic, social, and cultural 'entitlements' to safe and adequate food, drink, covering, medical care, housing, and engaged, empathetic acquaintance with those sick, in prison, or dead.[15] In fact, despite this gospel text being stereotyped as acts of "mercy," it constructs these activities as ethical marching orders: a human rights mandate.[16]

The medical behaviors of both Paul of Antioch and Paul Farmer may in fact fit only some *anargyroi* characteristics. Neither man, for instance, is imaged as a super-human miracle worker. However, there are, I suggest, sufficient intersections that make the *anargyros* a reasonable (though admittedly playful) model for us to think about Paul Farmer's theological ethics today. Since I bring this image here into discussion on religious ethics, and emphatically *not* to advance sainthood or hagiography for Paul Farmer, I focus in what follows below on *anargyroi* characteristics in terms of three non-miraculous or non-supernatural themes we see in these stories: (1) the corporal works of mercy for health equity; (2) ecumenicity, or non-judgmental engagement with religious diversity; and (3) attention to the importance of historical voices that may not otherwise be heard.

---

[15] Burying the dead is not named in Matthew 25 but was soon included in the "works of mercy" and was depicted in religious art with the other "works" throughout the medieval period.

[16] Further discussed in Susan R. Holman, *Beholden: Religion, Global Health, and Human Rights* (New York: Oxford University Press, 2015), 83–122.

Corporal Works of Mercy

In working with the late Dr. Paul Farmer, between 2005 and 2018, as a writer-editor at a Harvard-affiliated hospital, school of public health, and associated academic programs and initiatives in Boston, I was constantly aware of how he seemed to consistently affirm religion and spirituality while avoiding what might be called 'god-talk.' Even when cornered on stage for a 2014 Harvard Divinity School event to discuss his book collaboration with Gustavo Gutiérrez, *In the Company of the Poor*, Paul doggedly fielded some HDS faculty's tough theological questions with answers that deftly shifted back to pragmatic measures of evidence-based health care delivery.[17] Yet, I also knew, most obviously from Chapter 5 in *Pathologies of Power*, that he could at least use the "T" word, affirming the relevance of liberation theology for both his organization Partners In Health (PIH) and for health justice writ large.[18] The Matthew 25 text is core to much of the focus on practical action in liberation theology.

Thus, when I introduce Farmer's thinking to students in my theology courses these days, I typically begin by assigning (with Paul's permission) his never-published 2007 Address to the House of Bishops in New Orleans, a talk he gave on September 21, 2007, titled "Health, Human Rights, and the Corporal Works of Mercy: Reflections on New Orleans and Haiti."[19] In this talk, he reflected on the devastation of Hurricane Katrina in August 2005 and explicitly named and defined in twenty-first century context each of the corporal works of mercy as "meaningful goals and directives" for what should have and could be changed in addressing the question, "How can faith-based and secular organizations move

---

[17] Harvey Cox, "Liberation Theology Redux?" *Harvard Divinity Bulletin* (Summer/Fall 2014), bulletin.hds.harvard.edu/liberation-theology-redux/.

[18] Paul Farmer, *Pathologies of Power: Health, Human Rights, and the New War on the Poor* (Berkeley: University of California Press, 2005), 139–159.

[19] Paul E. Farmer, "Health, Human Rights, and the Corporal Works of Mercy: Reflections on New Orleans and Haiti," Address Given at the House of Bishops, New Orleans, Louisiana, September 21, 2007, unpublished manuscript, used with permission.

forward the social justice agenda?"[20] He explained this focus on the Matthew text by noting that PIH "is a secular organization, but I'd wager that almost all of us working together—and we are 5,000 people in nine countries—believe in the corporal works of mercy."[21]

Balancing medical care with religious praxis by applying scriptural care mandates was also part of the church-driven social welfare vision of many clergy and professional physicians in Christian antiquity, who also appealed for government policy support and philanthropic health care funding. Many of them worked in cities where the sick also frequented local Christian healing shrines. The fifth-century city of Cyrrhus, for instance, at what is today the border between Syria and Turkey, was the site of the oldest known Christian healing shrine for the *anargyroi* Cosmas and Damian. Yet, during exactly this same period, we know at least the name of one ordinary physician-priest, Peter. Peter apparently moonlighted as a medic in Cyrrhus while helping the city's bishop, Theodoret. We know from Theodoret's surviving correspondence that he was a bishop with an active social conscience, since he deliberately mentions that he paid for and directed efforts to improve the city's access to adequate water.[22] It is Theodoret who first mentions Cosmas and Damian's shrine in the city,[23] and Theodoret who leaves us two brief recommendation letters for Peter. All we know from these letters is that Peter had been trained at the Harvard Medical School equivalent of his

---

[20] Farmer, "Health, Human Rights, and the Corporal Works of Mercy," 2.

[21] Farmer, "Health, Human Rights, and the Corporal Works of Mercy," 2.

[22] "From the revenues of my sees I erected public porticoes; I built two large bridges; I looked after the public baths. On finding that the city was not watered by the river running by it, I built the conduit, and supplied the dry town with water." Theodoret of Cyrrhus, *Ep.* 81, to Nomus, trans. Blomfield Jackson, in *Nicene and Post-Nicene Fathers* (*NPNF*), second series, vol. 8 (1892, repr. Grand Rapids: Eerdmans, 1983), 277; at p. 295 he mentions Peter in two recommendation letters, *Ep.* 115 (to Apella) and *Ep.* 114 (to Andiberis).

[23] For sources and the argument that the cult began in Cyrrhus, see Phil Booth, "Orthodox and Heretic in the Early Byzantine Cult(s) of Saints Cosmas and Damian," in *An Age of Saints? Power, Conflict and Dissent in Early Medieval Christianity*, ed. Peter Sarris, Matthew Dal Santo, and Phil Booth (Leuven: Brill, 2011), 114, n. 3.

day—under physician-teachers in Alexandria in Egypt—and that he needed these letters to find a new job because Theodoret was in theological trouble. These thin traces from one man's pen, that is, suggest a medical marketplace where both healing saints (Cosmas and Damian) and ordinary physicians like Peter inhabited similar clinical spaces, apparently without conflict. Both holy and ordinary doctors were also known for traveling from place to place to practice their skills. Perpetually dicey church politics had no discernible effect on the rapid spread of Cosmas and Damian's healing shrines and associated churches and monasteries across the empire over the following centuries, to Constantinople, Rome, and beyond.

We find a similar overlap of conventional Christian medics and shrines in the late sixth century Egyptian city of Antinoopolis, where a family-owned medical facility (a *xenon,* described in terms of hospital-like medical care)[24] coexisted with the large, and even today architecturally impressive, healing shrine for the *anargyros* St. Colluthus.[25] The Antinoopolis examples further hint at collaborative grouping of *anargyroi* rather than competition between them. Colluthus, Cosmas and Damian, Cyrus, John,

---

[24] The will of the public physician, Flavius Phoibammon, dated to 570 CE (*P.Cair.Masp* II 67151). For discussion, see James G. Keenan, "The Will of Flavius Phoibammon," in *Living the End of Antiquity: Individual Histories from Byzantine to Islamic Egypt*, ed. Sabine R. Huebner et al (Berlin: DeGruyter, 2020), 109–117. A translation is at Maria Nowak, *Wills in the Roman Empire: A Documentary Approach* (Warsaw: Journal of Juristic Papyrology. Supplement, 2015), 427–433.

[25] On the archaeological site, see Peter Grossmann, "Antinoopolis: The Area of St. Colluthos in the North Necropolis," in *Antinoupolis*, Vol. 2, ed. Rosario Pintaudi (Firenze: Firenze University Press, 2014), 241–300. For more on the papyrus tickets, see Lucia Papini, "Fragments of the *Sortes Sanctorum* from the Shrine of St. Colluthus," in *Pilgrimage and Holy Space in Late Antique Egypt*, ed. David Frankfurter (Religions in the Graeco-Roman World 134, 1998), 391–401; and Annemarie Luijendijk, "'If You Order That I Wash My Feet, Then Bring Me This Ticket': Encountering Saint Colluthus at Antinoë," in *Placing Ancient Texts: The Ritual and Rhetorical Use of Space*, ed. Mika Ahuvia and Alexander Kocar (Tübingen: Mohr Siebeck, 2018), 197–225.

and other *anargyroi* images line up together, life size, on several painted walls across monastic and church spaces from Egypt to Rome.[26]

To explore details of even a few of the many individual healings in the *anargyroi* collections would push well beyond the limits of this chapter. But a quick sampling of select cures from the Cosmas and Damian stories illustrates their concern for the corporal works of mercy as well as ideals present in liberation theology. For instance, we see these *anargyroi* going out of their way to listen and walk long distances with afflicted, despairing, and angry patients, even to find them suitable employment (*Mir.* 18). They slip medicinal cures under their mattresses (*Mir.* 26). They rescue and treat at least one sick monk lying alone abandoned in a prison after he had badmouthed a politician (*Mir.* 47). They help a young couple feed their new infant through consultation and gently cure the mother's inflamed breast to avoid dangerous surgery (*Mir.* 29). They force rich and poor patients into conversations where each cures the other by apparent accident or nonsense (*Mir.* 34). In each of these stories, the *anargyroi* heal by interventions that address what we today call the social determinants of health, within a framework of accompaniment. In the ancient world of tiered social class assumptions and slavery, health equity ideals do not play out as democratically as we might wish. Yet the examples above suggest *anargyroi* whose standard operating mode connected responses to sickness and extreme poverty with politics, maternal-child health, and radical, personalized health care delivery measures, with a focus on effectiveness that has from the start also characterized the heart of Paul Farmer's work and life.

Ecumenicity

The *sui generis* power of Paul Farmer's theological ethical praxis was shaped profoundly by his cultural humility, his humor, and—my second theme here—ecumenicity. By ecumenicity, I mean his ready openness to

---

[26] See images and discussion in Susan R. Holman, "Doctors in the Choir: Healing Embodiment and Ingestion in Early Church Space," *Journal of Early Christian Studies* 28, no. 2 (2020): 255–282.

welcome to the table (clinical space, mountain walk, or home visit) a wide diversity of ideological, religious, "spiritual," and secular views. As a non-profit health care delivery organization, PIH is unapologetically committed to applying the best evidence-based health care science and technology for all, but *Mountains Beyond Mountains* readers will remember how profoundly the young Farmer was shaped by a question an elderly Haitian woman asked him years ago. Cured of tuberculosis after a year of daily directly observed therapy (DOT), a year after she told him she knew that biological factors caused TB, she then admitted to believing that sorcery or voodoo [maybe also] caused her disease. When the then twenty-nine-year-old Farmer expressed his baffled confusion and asked why on earth, if she believed this, had she faithfully taken her medicines, she smiled at him as if he were a small child and asked, "Honey, are you incapable of complexity?"[27]

We find hints of similar complexity and ecumenical spirit (the latter, to be honest, only sometimes) in Christian *anargyroi* healing stories. For example, Sophronius, the seventh-century author who described Cyrus and John's healings at a shrine site now deep under water in Egypt's Aboukir Bay, was a man fixated on theological correctness. In his stories, the healers practiced heavy conversion pressure on some supplicants, withholding complete health until they admitted "right" doctrinal beliefs. However, these seventy stories of Cyrus and John's direct care for sick people, each identified by name, age, social class, hometown, and disease, also abound in rich and weirdly comic details that suggest a wider openness to cosmic forces. The children in these stories, for instance, sick as a consequence of domestic violence, eye infection causing blindness, or hunger that drove them to swallow snake's eggs or insect-infested reeds, are cured by methods that include serendipitous corrective accidents, bird

---

[27] Tracy Kidder, *Mountains Beyond Mountains: The Quest of Dr. Paul Farmer, A Man Who Would Cure the World* (New York: Random House, 2003), 35.

attacks, and one alarming entrance into the complex of a giant, keening mother serpent intent on getting her baby back.[28]

Some of the Cosmas and Damian healings recorded by various authors over about 900 years (and rarely giving patients names) are more openly broad-minded, explicitly affirming that these healers cured orthodox, heretics, and pagans alike, even when the afflicted "misunderstood" them to be not Christian saints at all but the divine Greek twin gods, Castor and Pollux.[29] This ecumenism in (or in spite of) healing therapy, argues historian Phil Booth, images "an ideology within which ... a multiplicity of doctrinal meanings ... is both acknowledged and preserved."[30] These largely pre-Islamic Christian healing narratives often include "heretics" and Jews, but Muslims would soon join the religious mix in the crowds that met in such healing places across the ancient world.[31]

In global health equity today, differing tensions over what heals and how it heals typically fall more between religious claims and non-religious secularity. There is less tendency today for arguments over the conversion-based agendas that marked certain points in antiquity as well as the medical missions of the nineteenth and early twentieth centuries. Today, the idea of "ecumenical" in health care justice might be more usefully subsumed under "solidarity." Indeed, Farmer's House of Bishops address concluded with a call to such ecumenical solidarity that it is worth repeating here for its summons to diversity and speaking truth to power:

---

[28] Discussed in Susan R. Holman, "Sick Children and Healing Saints: Medical Treatment of the Child in Christian Antiquity," in *Children in Late Ancient Christianity*, ed. Cornelia B. Horn and Robert R. Phenix (Tübingen: Mohr-Siebeck, 2009), 143–170; and Susan R. Holman, "Martyr-Saints and the Demon of Infant Mortality: Folk Healing in Early Christian Pediatric Medicine," in *Childhood and Family in Late Antiquity: Life, Death and Interaction*, ed. Christian Laes, Katariina Mustakallio, and Ville Vuolanto (Leuven: Peeters, 2014), 233–254.

[29] *Mir.* 9 (Deubner), discussed in Booth, "Orthodox and Heretic," 121ff.

[30] Booth, "Orthodox and Heretic," 114–128, 124.

[31] See, for example, Ephraim Shoham-Steiner, "Jews and Healing at Medieval Saints' Shrines: Participation, Polemics, and Shared Cultures," *Harvard Theological Review* 103, no.1 (2010): 111–129; and Adam C. Bursi, "Fluid Boundaries: Christian Sacred Space and Islamic Relics in an Early Ḥadīth," *Medieval Encounters* 27 (2021): 478–510.

To paraphrase Martin Luther King, Jr.: "the arc of the moral universe is long, but it bends toward justice." If we can all privilege acts of solidarity, as embodied in the corporal works of mercy, it will be great news for our efforts to serve the world's poor and marginalized, and to stand in solidarity with them as they fight to improve their lives.[32]

Learning from History

The third and final principle I offer to connect Farmer's theological ethics of health care with the *anargyros* model is the importance of understanding and learning from history. "Old is the new new whenever history goes down the drain," Paul wrote.[33] His focus on close readings of historical factors marked his scholarship and teaching from the start, building on his high school experience working alongside migrant farm workers and his college fascination with Rudolf Virchow's 1848 *Report on the Typhus Outbreak of Upper Silesia*.[34] Indeed, one of Paul's earliest publications in a religion-affiliated journal was an unsparing narrative of intersecting church-state travesties in the modern history of Haiti and how historical factors led to the 1989 election of Fr. Jean-Bertrand Aristide.[35] His quest to get to the root of pathologies depended on understanding history. In *Fevers, Feuds, and Diamonds* (the other Farmer reading I assign to my theology students), he considered its two hundred-plus pages of history about West Africa to be at "its heart."[36] Forgetting the past, he insisted, "is one way that structural violence is cloaked, and why it's worth

---

[32] Farmer, "Health, Human Rights, and the Corporal Works of Mercy," 7.
[33] Paul Farmer, *Fevers, Feuds, and Diamonds: Ebola and the Ravages of History* (New York: Farrar, Straus, and Giroux, 2020), 344.
[34] On which see especially Leon Eisenberg, "Rudolf Ludwig Karl Virchow, Where are you Now That We Need You?" *The American Journal of Medicine* 77 (1984): 524–532.
[35] Paul Farmer, "The Power of the Poor in Haiti," *America Magazine*, March 9, 1991, 260–267.
[36] Farmer, *Fevers, Feuds, and Diamonds*, xxvi.

Paul the Anargyros: *History, God-Talk, and Ecumenism*

looking for accounts from those unlikely to have the chance to air their views or relate their experiences."³⁷

This focus on voice and memory also threads heavily throughout the *anargyroi* healing stories. Such accounts are typically presented as the sometimes-literal narrative control of the sick poor themselves, often illiterate "little people," who may even jostle to make sure the writer gets their story in their words and even in their desired sequence related to other people's stories.³⁸ Even if we maintain an attitude of beneficent skepticism about whether what these voices say "actually happened," historicity or lack thereof is not the point. The point is: what do such stories suggest about what the narrator(s) considered important—or not—to their life and culture, experience of suffering, and quest for health?

Farmer's emphasis on learning from history was never about hagiography. It was about being aware enough to name and trace what went wrong and how it perpetuates structural violence and preventable pathologies. And sadly, the *anargyroi* tradition itself is not immune from perpetuating such wrongs. Perhaps the most troubling example of this is in the Cosmas and Damian tradition's persistent re-telling of the so-called "miracle of the black leg." This is the first image you may see if you happen to Google these two healers on a whim.

Appearing late, in the fourteenth century *Golden Legend* and illustrated in Florence by about 1370,³⁹ this story tells of a church verger with a leg cancer. Seeking cure, he experiences a dream in the Church of Saints Cosmas and Damian in Rome in which the saints surgically replace his rotting leg with the leg of a newly deceased African man who is buried in a nearby church cemetery. Waking, the (racially white) verger finds

---

³⁷ Farmer, *Fevers, Feuds, and Diamonds*, 316.

³⁸ Mention of people jostling to be heard, written down verbatim, and being included in his book before or after specific others' stories, is especially evident in Sophronius's *Miracles* of Ss. Cyrus and John.

³⁹ On its legacy in art history, see, for example, Kees Zimmerman, ed., *One Leg in the Grave Revisited: The Miracle of the Transplantation of the Black Leg by Saints Cosmas and Damian* (Eelde, Netherlands: Barkhuis, 2013).

himself with a healthy black leg, and the African's tomb, opened, verifies the switch. As this healing story was repeated and illustrated across the centuries, its implied purpose was to praise God for healing saints who do such obviously strange and wonderful things.

But confronted with the long persistence of this tale in religious healing accounts, especially considering Cosmas and Damian's global popularity still today,[40] I hear Paul in my head asking the obvious question: How is this good for the man who died? The African, buried in a churchyard, was apparently also a Christian. If the saints are so amazing that they can raid grave sites with impunity and surgically switch out legs without pain, why didn't the *anargyroi* heal the African—or maybe even bring him back to life? As Micah James Goodrich has recently charged in an eloquent critique, this tale, with its "nonconsensual seizure of a Black man's body for the benefit of a white man," is "as pseudo-historical and fantastical as it may be … a reflection of a medieval medical imaginary that deliberately relies on racial violence to effect a salvific cure."[41] Indeed, in the complex racial and locational diversities that characterize the origin debates over who Cosmas and Damian were (if they existed at all, of course), even the earliest texts that suggest them as racially Arabs seem soon hijacked into multi-institutional imperially financed sites in Constantinople and Rome, with prioritized medical care normalizing the race of whoever's voice finds the most eloquent painter and publisher. Paradoxes are not without deeply disturbing associations. Holy healer stories can be used all too easily for unholy ends; this too is history. This too Farmer constantly reminded his readers, as his books and bedside teaching parsed out stories of rights and wrongs, of places and cases of structural violence that were, as he told the

---

[40] For the intersection of these *anargyroi* with modern medicine today, see, for example, Jacalyn Duffin, *Medical Saints: Cosmas and Damian in a Postmodern World* (New York: Oxford University Press, 2013). See also Jillian Harrold, "Saintly Doctors: The Early Iconography of SS. Cosmas and Damian in Italy," PhD diss, University of Warwick, 2007.

[41] Micah James Goodrich, "Medical Violence and the Medieval 'Miracle of the Black Leg,'" *Synapsis* (2020), hmedicalhealthhumanities.com/2020/10/08/medical-violence-and-the-medieval-miracle-of-the-black-leg/.

New Orleans Bishops, "inextricably linked in history—and also in my own recent experience."[42]

Conclusion

In suggesting that theological ethics might envision the late Dr. Paul Farmer as an *anargyros*—a holy but often very strange and eccentric healer model based in the religious history of late antiquity—I purposely invite a light-hearted image into conversations about philosophical-ethical complexity and liberation theology. The *anargyros* model is by no means the only possible model for connecting these three themes in Farmer's work with pre-modern Christian, theological, or ethical history. Indeed, Farmer's health justice ethics might more logically appear to fit historic Christian texts such as Basil of Caesarea's fourth-century sermons, which preached radical divestment and material equity and condemned cancerous systemic debt bondage. Or we might think we hear Paul in Gregory of Nyssa's and Gregory of Nazianzus's sermons mandating social welfare and hands-on attention to deformed, homeless beggars on the basis of divine incarnation, philanthropic compassion, and equal human rights.[43] These are the commonly cited ancient voices in occasional papal documents that connect patristic history with liberation theology, environmental ethics, and Catholic social thought.[44] Such homiletic texts may resonate more than the *anargyroi* healings for structured theological ethics in the preferential option of health care for the poor.

I have left Basil and his contemporary homiletic family and friends out of this discussion here because they are, fundamentally, prescriptive. As useful as such writings may be for faith-based social models today, they are

---

[42] Farmer, "Health, Human Rights, and the Corporal Works of Mercy," 1.

[43] Discussed at length in Susan R. Holman, *The Hungry are Dying: Beggars and Bishops in Roman Cappadocia* (New York: Oxford University Press, 2001).

[44] See, for example, Brian Matz, *Patristics and Catholic Social Thought: Hermeneutical Models for a Dialogue* (Notre Dame: University of Notre Dame Press, 2014); and Johan Leemans, Brian J. Matz, and Johan Verstraeten, eds., *Reading Patristic Texts on Social Ethics: Issues and Challenges for Twenty-First Century Christian Social Thought* (Washington, DC: Catholic University of America Press, 2011).

texts and voices chiefly about what one *ought to do*. The *anargyroi* stories, in contrast, purport (whether we believe them or not) to carry the voices of ordinary poor, sick people and their healers and neighbors on what actually happened, however illogical, subversive, outrageous, or disturbing. Such voices matter in global medical ethics related to religion because people around the world today continue to give credit to non-rational healings, and to tell stories that may be "rational" when understood historically within particular cultural cosmologies.

Laced with humor, like a beloved trickster committed to paradoxical and subversive justice, the *anargyros*, like the late Dr. Paul Farmer, enacted healing that affirmed what it could mean to be fully human. And like the *anargyros*, it was Paul's methods, as a "divine man and strenuous worker," that often upend our assumptions about resource and energy limits (including our own) for "staff, stuff, space, and systems" in the economic logic of health care delivery. Even detached from miracles, the tradition of the ancient holy healer and their patients' narratives speaks to the theological ethics of Farmer's work and thought through the three values discussed in this essay: their practice of the corporal works of mercy, their recognition and (sometimes) affirmation of diversity, and their attention to the historical voices of those "unlikely to have the chance" to otherwise speak to efforts for health care justice. Such stories, like Paul Farmer's life and work, continue to invite us to engage in practical, creative, radical system re-thinking for the sake of what in Judaism is called *tikkun olam*, the healing of the world.[45]

---

[45] On *tikkun olam*, see for example, Gilbert S. Rosenthal, "Tikkun ha-Olam: The Metamorphosis of a Concept," *The Journal of Religion* 85, no. 2 (2005): 214–240; as it inspires modern global health efforts, see for example, Peter J. Hotez, "Science Tikkun: A Framework Embracing the Right of Access to Innovation and Translational Medicine on a Global Scale" [Editorial], *PLoS Neglected Tropical Diseases* 13, no. 6 (2019): e-0007117, doi.org/10.1371/journal.pntd.0007117. See also Paul Farmer, "Haiti's Wretched of the Earth," *Tikkun Magazine* 19, no. 3 (2004): 23–61.

Paul the Anargyros: *History, God-Talk, and Ecumenism*

Susan R. Holman is the John R. Eckrich Chair and Professor of Religion and the Healing Arts at Valparaiso University. A graduate of Tufts University's Friedman School of Nutrition Science and Policy (MS), Harvard Divinity School (MTS) and Brown University (PhD), she began research on religious responses to poverty, disease, and hunger while serving as a Registered Dietitian with low-income families in Boston. For more than twenty years she worked at Brigham and Women's Hospital and in the Harvard medical, global, and public health communities as a writer and editor. Her publications include eight books, and she is an invited speaker and writer nationally and internationally. Her book *Beholden: Religion, Global Health, and Human Rights* (Oxford, 2015) received the 2016 Grawemeyer Award in Religion. She lives in Massachusetts.

Chapter 3: Paul Farmer: A Model for the Theologian

Jorge José Ferrer, SJ

Paul Edward Farmer (1959–2022) was a physician, medical anthropologist, and social justice activist. Although interested in theology, particularly influenced by liberation theology, and spirituality, Farmer was not a professional theologian, a point that he himself would readily admit. Nonetheless, I want to present him as a model for those of us who seek to serve the world and the Church as doers of theology. Farmer presents, in my view, a dual form of modeling. I call the first one *analytical*. The second one is *existential* or *praxical*.[1] He models an *analytical methodology* that searches for the deeper structural causes of suffering and injustice. I propose that our analysis, as theological ethicists, must follow his lead without sacrificing the peculiar tools and identity of our trade. Yet, Farmer's work does not end with the publication of a paper or a book.

---

[1] I am using "existential" and "praxical" almost as interchangeable terms, although they do have different nuances. *Existential* emphasizes that it is a commitment in one's personal life. *Praxical* places the accent on the transformative dimension of the person's action. Thinking that perhaps I was coining a neologism, I did a Google search to see if "praxical" was already in use in English. It turned out two interesting websites. The first one is called *Dart Learning*. *Praxical* is defined as "a new learning initiative creating online workshops where everyone can experience science firsthand. We provide everyday people with the opportunity to be a scientist" (dartlearning.org.au/provider/praxical/). The second one is the website of the Society of Praxical Scholarship. Their definition of *praxical* is closer, although not identical to the meaning that I give to the term. They believe that students and scholars can change the world "through on the ground praxis that parses theory through empirical data, makes that abstract legible and accessible, and transforms experience into meaningful learning" (www.theoryandpraxis.institute/). In this paper, by praxical, I mean the practical dimension of intellectual work and analysis. We are reminded of the last of Marx's *Theses of Feuerbach*: *Until now, the philosophers have only interpreted the world, the point now is to change it* (Theses XI). Theory must come together with an action that transforms the world at the service of those who are impoverished because of the way we have organized the distribution of power and wealth in society. Theory and practice form a unity, one is empty without the other.

Indeed, publication plays an ancillary role in his work. The main thrust of Farmer's work is practical. He and his associates engage directly with the service of the impoverished.[2] Their work, particularly through Partners In Health, focuses, as the name suggests, on issues of health. Our focus, as theological ethicists, normally has a broader scope. I argue, however, that we cannot exonerate ourselves from a practical commitment at the service of justice.

To establish a connection between the *analytical*, what we may perhaps considered as the strictly scholarly, and the *praxical*, the dimension of service, advocacy, and activism, I use a concept borrowed from the work of the Italian Marxist thinker Antonio Gramsci (1891–1937): the *organic* as opposed to the *traditional intellectual*. Farmer was a model of the organic intellectual, and I argue that we are called to be likewise. Ultimately, as followers of Jesus of Nazareth and as theologians, we are called to conjugate the analytical and the praxical in the footsteps of Farmer, yes, but also and foremost in the footsteps of Jesus who was teacher and Good Samaritan.

The Ecclesial and Social Mission of the Theologian

On May 24, 1990, the then Congregation for the Doctrine of the Faith published an instruction on the ecclesial vocation of the theologian, known as *Donum Veritatis*. The emphasis of this document is on what we may call the strictly intellectual and religious dimension of theological work, particularly on the relationship between the Church's official teaching and the work of the theologian. According to this document, the role of the theologian is:

---

[2] I prefer to talk about the "impoverished" rather than the "poor." In my view, the term "impoverished" underlines the structural causes of much poverty. The people served by Partners In Health are not poor because of their personal limitations or faults. Structural global and national inequities have robbed them of fair equality of opportunities and, therefore, of full participation in the basic rights and goods required for a life according to human dignity.

>...to pursue in a particular way an ever deeper understanding of the Word of God found in the inspired Scriptures and handed on by the living Tradition of the Church. He does this in communion with the Magisterium which has been charged with the responsibility of preserving the deposit of faith (*Donum Veritatis*, no. 6).

Throughout the document, we find a distinct emphasis on the authority of the Church's official Magisterium. The healthy critical role of theological reflection as a contribution to the development of doctrine, in a virtuous circle with the Magisterium, is not denied, but it is not in the forefront.[3] The main concern seems to be the moderation of dissenting theologians. No one doubts that it is a legitimate concern, but if overemphasized, it runs the risk of impoverishing the understanding of the work of the theologian.

No one doubts that theological reflection is a ministry with an *ad intra* mission in the ecclesial community. As *Donum Veritatis* points out, theology is at the service of the progressive deepening of the understanding of the Christian message. It cannot be overlooked, however, that theology also has an *ad extra* mission. Theological reflection is a form of social engagement, rooted in the Gospel, with the world and its cultures. As theologians, we cannot be content with an aloof intellectual exercise, isolated in the ivory tower of academia or of the Church. This is particularly true in the work and vocation of the theological ethicist. Engagement with current social issues does not exonerate theologians

---

[3] The bibliography about the relationship of theology to the magisterium is voluminous. Looking at some recent contributions from the perspective of theological ethics, I would suggest the book recently published under the auspices of Pontifical Academy for Life: Vincenzo Paglia, ed., *Etica teologica della vita: Scrittura, tradiziones, sfide practiche* (Libreria Editrice Vaticana: Città del Vaticano, 2022), and, in that volume, Pier Davide Guenzi, "La riflessiones teologica al servizio del magistero e *sensus fidei*", 165–175. For a general overview of the volume, Roberto Dell' Oro and M. Therese Lysaught, "Theological Ethics of Life: A New Volume by the Pontifical Academy for Life," *Journal of Moral Theology* 11, no. 1 (2022): 65–77; and Jorge José Ferrer, "Rileggere l'etica teologica della vita," *Civiltà Cattolica* 4129 (2022): 60–71.

from the hard work of exegetical and historical research. It does not lighten in any way the requirements of theological scholarship. Quite on the contrary, it increases them. Besides traditional linguistic and historical learning, today the craft of theological ethics demands serious engagement with scientific contributions, particularly those from social sciences. Such an engagement has become an indispensable requirement for the theologian. Therefore, I insist that the intellectual demands are in no way diminished.

I propose that the work of Paul Farmer, his use of social analysis at the service of global health and the plight of the impoverished provide a model for a kind of theological ethics that we are called to articulate as we enter the third decade of the twenty-first century in a globalized and acutely divided world. The incorporation of the results of social analysis and a commitment to the service of the impoverished, as Farmer did, are particularly important for those of us who live and work in what Pope Francis calls the peripheries of the world. It is also a duty for those who theologize from universities and research centers located in the rich countries, perhaps even more so. Social analysis, if taken seriously, can open our eyes to our own complicities with oppression. Such unconfessed complicities may invalidate the results of a theologian's work. As a sample of Paul Farmer's intellectual work, I primarily use what probably is his most explicitly theological book: *Pathologies of Power*.[4] In this book, he engages extensively with the contributions and methods of liberation theology.

Pathologies of Power and the Analytical Component of Theological Work

Farmer presents *Pathologies of Power* as the effort of a physician and medical anthropologist to reveal the ways in which a person's most basic right—the right to survive—is trampled in an age of great affluence. He

---

[4] Paul Farmer, *Pathologies of Power: Health, Human Rights, and the New War on the Poor* (Berkeley: University of California Press, 2003).

argues that this matter should be considered as the most pressing issue of our times. Anyone who professes, argues Farmer, even a passing interest in human rights should be concerned with the tragedy of the destitute sick. He rightly points out that human rights violations are not random in distribution or effect but rather symptoms of deeper pathologies of power, intimately linked to the social conditions that so often determine who will suffer abuse and who will be shielded from harm.[5] If assaults on dignity are not random, he argues, "whose interests are served by the suggestion that they are haphazard?"[6] In other words: Who benefits from the obfuscation of reality, a particularly urgent issue in the age of post-truth and alternative facts?

Farmer worked in places, such as Haiti, Rwanda, and the Siberian prisons in Russia, marked by conditions that can only be described as violent. Those who must endure extreme conditions of deprivation, lacking access to fundamental goods required for a life according to human dignity, are the victims of real and unadulterated violence. Since the misery confronted in those places and circumstances does not necessarily involve bullets and knives, it easily eludes the analysis of those who seek to identify situations of violence. Nonetheless, Farmer points out, we are talking about a different and perhaps a more insidious type of violence: *structural violence.* He correctly argues that if someone does not have access to sufficient and adequate nutrition, decent living conditions, and access to adequate health care, among other necessities of life, that person is being denied the most basic of rights: the right to live. Among these basic rights, I would add and emphasize access to quality education and information, particularly for the younger generations. It is a fundamental requirement

---

[5] "Pathologies of power" has, in my opinion, a twofold meaning. On the one hand, oppressive power is pathological since it generates dysfunctional relationships. Oppressive power distorts the meaning and function of power. On the other hand, the pathologies suffered by the impoverished, as described by Farmer, are, to a large extent, the result of the pathologically oppressive uses of power. In other words, they are pathologies engendered by oppressive (pathological) power. When people die of preventable and easily treatable diseases, we are facing social pathologies, not only unfortunate biological infirmities.

[6] Farmer, *Pathologies of Power,* 7.

to break the cycle of impoverishment and oppression. Education gives tools for critical thinking, empowering people as agents of much needed structural change. It is striking to see that many people who declare themselves as prolife do not show much sensibility for challenges related to fundamental human rights and social justice, forgetting what the late Cardinal Bernardin taught us almost four decades ago about the seamless garment of a consistent ethic of life.[7] A prolife stance that is not committed to social justice is hollow and inconsistent.

According to Farmer, an analytical model adopted to study the phenomenon of structural violence must be both *geographically broad* and *historically deep*.[8] I propose that these two traits are also requirements for analysis developed by theological ethicists. It is interesting to notice here a virtuous circle between Farmer's methodology and liberation theology. He readily admits that the writings of liberation theologians enlightened his work as a medical anthropologist and physician at the service of the impoverished. In a similar fashion, I claim that Farmer's work can shed light on the appropriate analytical methodologies for our work in theological ethics. We can also talk about inter or transdisciplinary cross-fertilization between his anthropological reflection and our theological task. Indeed, the complexity of contemporary global ethical issues can only be fruitfully approached from an inter and transdisciplinary perspective.

In a globalized world such as ours, geographical broadness is indispensable for the analysis of most, if not all, social and ethical issues.

---

[7] This idea was promoted by the late Cardinal Joseph Bernardin (1928–1996) in several lectures in the mid-eighties. He advanced his proposal for the first time, as far as I know, in the Gannon Lecture at Fordham University in 1983. I think that the recuperation of his central idea is of the utmost importance. It would seem at times that Catholics are only interested in contraception, abortion, and euthanasia. No one doubts the relevance of those issues, but a genuine prolife stance requires much more. Commitment to human flourishing, global social justice, and ecological responsibility are essential components of a prolife commitment. It is interesting to reread a volume published in 1988 with Cardinal Bernardin's interventions and papers delivered by distinguished scholars in response to the Cardinal's proposal: Joseph Cardinal Bernardin, *A Consistent Ethic of Life* (Kansas City: Sheed & Ward, 1988).

[8] Farmer, *Pathologies of Power*, 158.

More than in any previous age, we live in one world.[9] Issues related to challenges such as pandemics or global warming can only be understood and fruitfully tackled when approached in the context of geographical broadness. The same can be said for the problem of extreme poverty in Haiti, or in the slums of Lima, or in New York. However, geographical broadness is, by itself, insufficient. Present global challenges are the result of long and complex historical processes.[10] Our analysis needs to be "deep enough to recall—for instance—that modern-day Haitians are the descendants of a people kidnapped from Africa in order to provide our forebears with sugar, coffee, and cotton."[11] It is impossible to understand the challenges of poverty and exclusion in Haiti, and in many other countries and populations, without considering the history of slavery, racism, and colonialism. These insights about analytical methodology are essential for our work in theological ethics, if we want to fully understand and to respond appropriately to the most urgent ethical issues of our time. Most of them are intimately related to the pathological uses of power that generate suffering, impoverishment, and diverse forms of violence. We certainly continue to live in a very structurally violent world.

Farmer's analytical model requires the simultaneous consideration of multiple "social axes."[12] It is important to consider factors such as gender, race or ethnicity, refugee or immigration status, sexual orientation,

---

[9] This idea recalls the title of Peter Singer's book *One World* (New Haven and London: Yale University Press, 2004).

[10] According to Henk ten Have, there are certain features that characterize global problems. A problem is global when it is not geographically located in a specific place or nation. Among other traits, global problems are systemic in character and their solution requires concerted global action. See Henk ten Have, *Global Bioethics. An Introduction* (London and New York. Routledge,2016), 55–57. The pathologies of power identified by Farmer are truly global problems requiring structural transformation on a global scale. Today, in a globalized world, social justice must be recast in *global* (or *cosmopolitan*) and not merely *political* terms. Traditionally, theories of justice, from Plato to Rawls, have been "political": the State is the locus where distributive and social justice have meaning and can be required. I am convinced that we need to move from political to global or cosmopolitan theories of justice.

[11] Farmer, *Pathologies of Power*, 158.

[12] Farmer, *Pathologies of Power*, 42–43.

religious and political beliefs, and language or educational differences.[13] We know that both during the HIV crisis in the 1980s and in the present COVID-19 pandemic, certain sociological groups have been disproportionately affected on account of some of these determinants of health and general welfare. These considerations are extremely important for the promotion of justice and the practice of medicine at the service of the impoverished. They are also essential for a lucid ethical analysis. Otherwise, we may end up blaming the victims. Farmer presents the example of recurrent tuberculosis in Haiti:

> Authorities rarely blame the recrudescence of tuberculosis on the inequalities that structure our society. Instead, we hear mostly about biological factors (the advent of HIV, the mutations that lead to drug resistance) or about cultural and psychological barriers that result in "noncompliance." Through these two sets of explanatory mechanisms, one can expediently attribute high rates of treatment failure to the organism or to uncooperative patients.[14]

This approach misses the point. Focusing on the biological tends to forget that "almost all tuberculosis deaths result from lack of access to existing effective therapy."[15] In a similar fashion, to attribute noncompliance to patients' uncooperativeness or cultural backwardness ignores the structural barriers to what we normally call "therapeutic compliance."

> Certainly, patients may be noncompliant, but how relevant is the notion of compliance in rural Haiti? Doctors may instruct their patients to eat well. But the patients will "refuse" if they have no food. They may be told to sleep in an open room and away from others, and here again they will be "noncompliant" if they do not expand and remodel their miserable huts. They may be instructed to go to a hospital. But if hospital

---

[13] These differences become barriers that marginalize people, that unfairly prevent them from reaching their full human potential, living lives according to the demands of human dignity.

[14] Farmer, *Pathologies of Power*, 147.

[15] Farmer, *Pathologies of Power*, 148.

care must be paid for in cash, as it is the case throughout Haiti, and the patients have no cash, they will be deemed "grossly negligent." ... Similar scenarios could be offered for diseases ranging from typhoid to AIDS. In each case, poor people are at higher risk of contracting the disease and are less likely to have access to care. And in each case, analysis of the problem can lead researchers to focus on patients' shortcomings (for example, failure to drink pure water, ignorance about public health and hygiene).[16]

Farmer penned these pages two decades ago. Unfortunately, we have, as already suggested, seen similar situations in the present COVID-19 crisis. In impoverished environments, citizens are advised to wash their hands frequently, but they do not have access to clean water. They are instructed to keep physical distance, but how can anyone comply living in an overcrowded refugee camp?[17] It is obvious that the structural barriers need to be removed if we want patients to be "compliant." It is necessary to engage in a form of analysis that seeks to understand the root causes of the problem.

Identifying the root causes is essential but insufficient. Once they are identified, action is required in the form of practical and timely aid to those whose very right to exist is threatened by impoverishment due to structural inequities. However, immediate aid, in the form of social services like providing food, medicines, health care, is essential but also insufficient. Engaging in the work of social transformation is required if we want to address the situation from the perspective of justice. It is important to help the person who is now in need. But it is equally important to understand and to change the pathogenic social and political structures. Social scientific analysis grounds a form of ethical reflection that inspires its practitioners to engage in transformative action, if it is going to come to

---

[16] Farmer, *Pathologies of Power*, 151.
[17] Jorge José Ferrer, "Pandemia e inequidad en América Latina", in *La humanidad puesta a prueba*, ed. R. Amo and F. de Montalvo (Madrid: Universidad Pontificia Comillas, 2020), 377–392.

fruition, reaching its proper *telos*. An ethical analysis that does not engender a social commitment is empty. It is what "traditional intellectuals" (a category to be developed in the next section of this paper) are content to do.

Before we move from the analytical to the *existential* or *praxical* dimension of our presentation of Farmer's work as a model for the theological ethicist, it is fruitful to consider his distinction between charity, development, and social justice as different approaches to the service of the impoverished. The in-depth analytical approach espoused by Farmer favors a social justice approach as the right option in the struggle against problems raised by diseases and suffering. We can and should expand the horizon beyond the medical idea of diseases to the full gamut of suffering and exclusion generated by impoverishment and structural violence.

As already suggested, the first approach is charity. Theologically, charity is the form of virtues, the very heart of Christian life and ethics. However, when Farmer talks about charity, he refers to what perhaps would be better to call beneficence or social assistance. The author is critical of the charity approach as he understands it. In his view, charity programs often tend to see those needing aid as intrinsically inferior, perhaps because poverty is seen as a result, at least in part, of the impoverished person's own shortcomings. Certainly, Farmer points out, the impoverished are largely powerless but not mainly because of their faults and shortcomings. Mere beneficence has the danger of keeping the impoverished in their situation rather than empowering them, promoting the understanding of the hidden social dynamics—such as slavery, racism, colonialism, sexism—that have generated their plight.[18]

What has been said about charity does not mean, as it has been already suggested, that social assistance should be totally dismissed. People in need require timely and appropriate help. The person who needs food or medical treatment, needs them now. Farmer admits that it is possible "to

---

[18] Farmer, *Pathologies of Power*, 153.

overstate the case against charity .... Sometimes holier-than-thou progressives dismiss charity when it is precisely the virtue demanded."[19] What is important is not to ignore the "causes of excess suffering among the poor,"[20] which obviously need to be identified and remedied through social transformation. Partners In Health seeks to do both and so should the Church. Otherwise, we may be doing a sort of a patchwork that naively perpetuates oppression.

Therefore, charity continues to be essential, but it is unacceptable to stop there. The idea is to empower, transform, and work for a world without structural violence and impoverishment. Probably, we will never be able to have a perfectly just society, but it is the horizon towards which we are called in the service of the Kingdom of God announced and realized in the life, death, and resurrection of Jesus of Nazareth. A well-known paragraph of Vatican II's *Decree on the Apostolate of the Laity* captures this:

> While every exercise of the apostolate should be motivated by charity, some works by their very nature can become especially vivid expressions of this charity. Christ the Lord wanted these works to be signs of His messianic mission. ... At the present time, with the development of more rapid facilities for communication, with the barrier of distance separating men greatly reduced, with the inhabitants of the entire globe becoming one great family, these charitable activities and works have become more urgent and universal. These charitable enterprises can and should reach out to all persons and all needs. Wherever there are people in need of food and drink, clothing, housing, medicine, employment, education; wherever men lack the facilities necessary for living a truly human life or are afflicted with serious distress or illness or suffer exile or imprisonment, there Christian charity should seek them out and find them, console them with great solicitude, and help them with appropriate relief. This obligation is imposed upon every prosperous nation and person. In order that the exercise of charity on this scale may be unexceptionable in appearance as well as in fact, it is altogether

---

[19] Farmer, *Pathologies of Power*, 154.
[20] Farmer, *Pathologies of Power*, 154.

> necessary that one should consider in one's neighbor the image of God in which he has been created, and also Christ the Lord to Whom is really offered whatever is given to a needy person... *and especially that the demands of justice be satisfied lest the giving of what is due in justice be represented as the offering of a charitable gift. Not only the effects but also the causes of these ills must be removed, and the help be given in such a way that the recipients may gradually be freed from dependence on outsiders and become self-sufficient.* (Apostolicam Actuositatem, no. 8, emphasis added)

Having examined the charity approach, the second approach is *development,* a notion that has been questioned and rejected as insufficient by liberation theology since its inception as a movement. The development approach seeks the overcoming of poverty through technological progress and increased economic productivity. The problem is this perspective preserves the power of major local and global economic interests: "Developmentalism not only erases the historical creation of poverty but also implies that development is necessarily a lineal process: progress will inevitably occur if the right steps are followed."[21] As Gustavo Gutiérrez pointed out more than half a century ago: true development must tackle the root causes of the situations of impoverishment and oppression, transforming all relations of domination both on the transnational and national levels.[22]

The third approach is the one favored by Famer: *the social justice* model. The condition of the impoverished is ethically unacceptable since it is the result of human-made structural unfairness and violence. Uniting his voice to well-known thinkers in the field of disaster studies, Farmer talks about *unnatural disasters.* Talking to the graduating class of 2008 of Tulane School of Medicine, he commented that "Katrina, surprisingly, has

---

[21] Farmer, *Pathologies of Power,* 155–156.
[22] Gustavo Gutiérrez, *Teología de la liberación. Perspectivas* (Salamanca: Sígueme, 1974), 50–52.

something in common with war: neither are 'natural disasters.'"²³ It is common in disaster literature to distinguish between the natural event and the disaster. Considering an event, such as an earthquake or hurricane, may be useful to illustrate the point. The natural event affects everyone in the impacted geographical area, but it does not affect everyone in the same way. Those who are financially and socially weaker normally are impacted in a more severe way. In "Acts of God or Human Choices?" I wrote:

> The naturalness of disasters… has been questioned or even totally rejected in much of the professional literature in the field of disaster studies. The habitual distinction between natural and anthropogenic disasters needs to be critically examined. Hazards such as hurricanes, earthquakes, droughts, volcanoes, and pandemics traditionally have been labeled as "natural disasters." On the other hand, consequences of war or an oil spill in the ocean have been labeled as anthropogenic or human-made disasters. Dónal P. O'Mathúna, Bert Gordijn, and Mike Clarke point out, however, that "such classifications can be arbitrary, especial as both natural and human-related factors are involved in most disasters." … Ben Wisner, Ilan Kelman, and J. C. Gaillard go even further. They affirm, in no uncertain terms, that there are many causes of disasters "but one clear truth: disasters are not natural."²⁴

The absoluteness of the latter affirmation in the quote goes too far. It is possible to think of situations in which the natural component is

---

[23] Paul Farmer, *To Repair the World* (Berkeley: University of California Press, 2013), 157–158.

[24] Jorge José Ferrer, "Acts of God or Human Choices? An Ethical Reflection on Natural Disasters," *Revista Iberoamericana de Bioética* 14 (2020): 5. The works cited within the quotation are: Dónal P. O'Mathúna, Bert Gordijn, and Mike Clarke, "Disaster Bioethics: An Introduction," in *Disaster Bioethics: Normative Issues When Nothing Is Normal*, ed. Dónal P. O'Mathúana, Bert Gordijn, and Mike Clarke (Dordrecht: Springer, 2014), 4; Ben Wisner, Ian Kelman, and J. C. Gaillard, "Hazard, Vulnerability, Capacity, Risk and Participation," in *Disaster Management. International Lessons in Risk Reduction, Response and Recovery*, ed. Alejandro López-Carresi, Maureen Fordham, Ben Wisner, Ilan Kelman, and J. C. Gaillard (London: Routledge, 2014), 13.

overwhelming, such as a tsunami. For the most part, however, it is true that disasters are anthropogenic. There is a direct correlation between the social vulnerability of a person or a group and their proneness to be victims of a disaster. Social vulnerability is not only related to socioeconomic status. Other factors such as race, gender, or citizenship status may enter in the equation. But the socioeconomic factors are of primary importance. Not infrequently other forms of marginalization also have a socioeconomic component. Disasters reveal in a very clear way preexisting social pathologies. At the root of disasters are structural inequities in the distribution of power and wealth in society, which are not natural.

In other words, disasters are caused, at least to a large extent, by preexisting social pathologies. Farmer's analysis uncovers those root causes of disasters and of health inequities. He carries out his analysis with the intellectual tools provided by his medical and anthropological training. It is my contention that this is also the type of analysis that we, theological ethicists, are called to adopt if our reflection is going to be at the service of a faith that does justice and promotes universal brotherhood and sisterhood. To carry out our own work we need to use both the results of qualified social scientists' work and the tools proper to theological and ethical analysis. We are called to uncover and denounce the situations of inequity and its structural roots.

Organic Intellectual

Ethical analysis of structural sin is difficult, in part, because we do not have a single identifiable person who is responsible for the situation under scrutiny. We are facing what has been called a "nonparadigmatic moral problem." [25] If A, for example, steals B's wallet, we have a responsible individual, who can be punished, as well as an identifiable victim. When we face problems such as colonialism, racism, or other forms of structural violence, the decisions that have generated the problem have been made by

---

[25] I borrow the idea of "nonparadigmatic moral problems" from Marion Hourdequin, *Environmental Ethics: From Theory to Practice* (New York: Bloomsbury Academic, 2015), 150–151.

thousands of individuals across continents and throughout centuries. No one is entirely responsible, but we all share responsibility in the situation at hand. It is important to stress that such analytical complexity does not cancel our personal and collective moral responsibilities. Quite to the contrary, both personal and collective responsibility are enhanced. It is the task of the ethicist to unravel the complexity and to clarify the responsibilities that we all share in different degrees. Farmer's books and speeches constitute masterful models for the kind of intellectual work that we are called to do as ethicists and theologians.

But it seems to me that his modeling goes beyond the methods of ethical analysis. Farmer can also be seen as a model of the kind of intellectuals that we are called to be. Intellectual work and social analysis were undertaken by him within the broader context of an existential commitment to social transformation through advocacy and sustained action at the service of the impoverished in Haiti, Peru, Rwanda, or Russia. It is my conviction that we can apply to Farmer's life and work Antonio Gramsci's category of the *organic intellectual*. I think that the essential elements of this notion have been beautifully exemplified by Farmer, and I also think that we as theologians and ethicists are called to follow suit.

To understand Gramsci's interest in the role of the intellectual, it is necessary to understand his own history. Steve Jones's observations are illuminating:

> We might ask why Gramsci was so concerned with intellectuals (indeed, his original plan was that the *Prison Notebooks* would be a history of Italian intellectuals). The answer lies in the problem of political representation: in other words, who is entitled to speak and think on behalf of a particular constituency? Like many other socialist intellectuals, Gramsci was a disaffected bourgeois who aligned himself with the working class.... The distance between middle-class intellectuals and the working class was a persistent problem for revolutionary socialism.[26]

---

[26] Steve Jones, *Antonio Gramsci* (London & New York: Routledge, 2006), 82–83.

Paul Farmer: A Model for the Theologian

Gramsci affirms that all persons are intellectuals and every human task, including manual labor, has an intellectual component. However, not all persons function as intellectuals in society. Some specialized tasks are privileged in society as intellectual while others are considered a lower status. In any case, every social group needs to produce its own intellectuals with the skills necessary to perform the intellectual tasks required not only to serve its economic interests but also for social and political identity.[27]

The Italian author distinguishes between *traditional intellectuals* and *organic intellectuals*. He favors the latter. The organic intellectual is engaged with the complexity of social life with all its difficulties and messiness. Traditional intellectuals are characterized by their apparent detachment from such matters. A man of letters or an artist who claims to be interested only in eternal truths, unconcerned about politics or the economy, is the model of the traditional intellectual, inhabiting the proverbial ivory tower.

Gramsci's devotes many pages to his reflections about intellectuals. I think, however, that the broad brushstrokes presented suffice for our purposes. The organic intellectual is engaged in ordinary life, committed to the historical struggles of her or his time. This new intellectual cannot limit herself or himself to the eloquence or the motions of the affects and the passions. He or she needs to be actively involved in the struggles of daily life as builder and organizer, as someone who is engaged in the construction of a new society. A traditional intellectual is interested, we may say, in writing his papers, getting tenured, living the comfortable life of a middle-class professional, while articulating perhaps a progressive discourse. Coffee shop or pulpit revolution is tempting; it can tranquilize one's own conscience, but it ultimately is an exercise in self-deception. These reflections about intellectual styles also apply to us, doers of theology.[28] We can very easily become classroom or pulpit revolutionaries

---

[27] Antonio Gramsci, *Quaderni del carcere,* volume III (Torino: Einaudi, 1975), 1513: Jones, *Antonio Gramsci,* 81–83.

[28] I use the term *style* in the strong technical sense that it has in the work of Maurice Merleau Ponty and in the theological work of Christoph Theobald. It is a way of interpreting and

with little existential risk or discomfort. Theology, more than any other subject, requires a praxical commitment of its practitioners. Otherwise, we are at risk of an inauthentic existence and a theological work lacking credibility beyond our close circle of likeminded colleagues.

As professional theologians, we are intellectuals. Our theological work requires long hours of study in front of our books and computers. But our work is not neutral, even when we might delude ourselves under the pretension of neutrality. We need to continuously ask: whom we serve, to whom are we committed, where are our loyalties? Farmer's legacy offers, as I have already suggested, a model of an organic intellectual. His research and writing have high academic quality, but they have no pretension of uncommitted impartiality. His work was the fruit of a profound commitment to those impoverished by structural violence and the unfair distribution of power and wealth in the world. His intellectual work was at the service of their cause. Moreover, Farmer did not limit himself to theoretical work. He was, as we all know, an actively committed physician at the service of the impoverished. His loyalties were clear, putting his own existence on the line.

Not everyone has his multifaceted talents and training, his working capacity, or his rich network of relationships. Our contribution will probably be more modest, less outstanding. Nonetheless, I am convinced that we as theologians and ethicists are called to be organic intellectuals at the service of the Kingdom proclaimed by Jesus. Such service requires a commitment to a faith that does justice. We are called to contribute to the Kingdom and the cause of the impoverished through our teaching and writing.

We cannot forget, however, that our teaching and writing are not enough. Some level of praxical commitment is required from each one of us. Neutrality is not a real option for anyone. It is even less of an option for

---

inhabiting the world. For a deeper understanding of style as a theological notion, see Luis O. Jiménez, "El concepto teológico de estilo como clave de lectura de *Laudato si'* y *Gaudete et exsultate*: una manera de encontrar a Dios en la acción transformadora del mundo," *Theologica Xaveriana* 70 (2020): doi.org/10.11144/javeriana.tx70.ctecl.

someone who aspires to a life of authenticity in the footsteps of the Lord. We are called to learn from Paul Farmer how to carry out our analysis, but, above all, we need to learn how we are to live our lives as organic intellectuals, committed to the Gospel call of universal brotherhood and sisterhood. We are also called to support each other in the quest for truth and the commitment to the Kingdom in our theological work. As I said at the beginning of this essay, Farmer was not a professional theologian, but he certainly models for us what means to be an authentic Christian intellectual in our times, committed not only to understand but also to transform a world that needs continued healing from pathological power both in our global society and in our Church.

Jorge José Ferrer, SJ, holds a doctorate in theology from Madrid's Comillas Pontifical University. He is Professor of Moral Theology and Director of the School of Theology at the Pontifical Catholic University of Puerto Rico. He has previously taught at the Gregorian University (Rome), Comillas Pontifical University (Madrid), and the University of Puerto Rico. He has held visiting appointments at Georgetown University, Seattle University, and Creighton Univesity. Jorge has authored, co-authored, or edited seven books and numerous scholarly articles in the field of bioethics. He is an academic of the Pontifical Academy for Life and a member of the of the International Theological Commission.

Chapter 4: Living Witnesses and Moral Agency

Alison Lutz

What is today called global health has shape-shifted over several centuries, with roots in colonial medicine, missionary medicine, tropical medicine, and international health.[1] Whatever the differences in name or focus, these efforts have all been directed by Western(ized) bureaucrats, technical experts, or do-gooders reporting to headquarters in Western centers of power. Resources for these transnational health interventions—regardless if they are undertaken to promote civilizing, development, or humanitarian goals—circulate along the same routes and produce the same ends established by the West for its project of global colonization: to arrange the worldwide flow of goods, services, people, opportunities, and discoveries to promote the comfort, safety, and prosperity of the Western bourgeois class, while containing the diseases and risks to which the West might be exposed through the accelerated global extraction, exploitation, and circulation of people and goods.[2] With these power dynamics at the forefront of mind, a question nags at my conscience: is it possible for today's global health professionals from or trained in the West to work across lines of social power to relieve suffering without reproducing hierarchies of identity, knowledge, and power that have always exposed most people to danger and death in order to protect and promote the wellbeing of a small minority of others?

---

[1] Paul Farmer. Arthur Kleinman, Jim Kim, and Matthew Basilico, *Reimagining Global Health: An Introduction* (Berkeley: University of California Press, 2013), 61; Joia Mukherjee, *An Introduction to Global Health Delivery: Practice, Equity, Human Rights*, Second Edition (New York: Oxford University Press, 2021), 8–9.

[2] United for Sight, "Colonial Medicine: Colonial Conceptions of Health," www.uniteforsight.org/global-health-history/module2.

Living Witnesses and Moral Agency

This question is not only academic for me. It grows out of my work as a global health professional, which began when I joined the global health organization Partners In Health (PIH) in 2008, as Haiti Program Coordinator. I worked closely with Paul Farmer in Haiti through the 2008 hurricanes, the 2010 earthquake, and the subsequent cholera outbreak. The work involved climbing mountains in rural Haiti to check on patients; hosting patients from Haiti who traveled to Boston to deliver keynote addresses at a symposium at Harvard University; and meeting with UN delegations and multilateral funders in Port au Prince and New York. As a result of what I learned working alongside Paul and attending carefully to his writings, I have come to conclude that the answer is yes. It is possible to cross lines of social power to relieve suffering without reproducing dominating power circuits, provided that such action is not the exclusive purview of Western(ized) professionals. Moral praxis that transforms iniquitous power circuits must also include—as moral agents who cross lines of power to relieve suffering—people from communities that have been historically and systematically dispossessed. I am honored to contribute to this volume dedicated to Paul's impact on theological ethics. My essay draws out insights on moral agency generated by Paul's critical reflection and action in the field of global health equity.

Paul's moral praxis was indelibly shaped by Latin American liberation theology. He brought it to bear in formulating PIH's mission "to provide a preferential option for the poor in health care."[3] Paul took seriously the insights on agency put forth by his friend and founding figure of Latin American liberation theology, Fr. Gustavo Gutiérrez: "the theology of liberation represents the right of the poor to think" and the oppressed must be "protagonists of their own liberation."[4] As a result, a "preferential option for the poor in health care" for Paul and for PIH is not only a

---

[3] Partners In Health, "Our Mission at PIH," www.pih.org/pages/our-mission.
[4] Gustavo Gutiérrez, *The Power of the Poor in History: Selected Writings* (Maryknoll, NY: Orbis Books, 1983), 90; Gustavo Gutiérrez, *Theology of Liberation: History, Politics, and Salvation*, trans., Caridad Inda and John Eagleson (Maryknoll, NY: Orbis Books, 2010), 67, 174.

preferential option for the poor to receive high quality health care from well-intentioned and well-trained professionals from communities that are better off. A preferential option for the poor in health care also means that people who face the dual burdens of poverty and disease must be preferentially engaged to design the interventions aimed at helping them. It is a preferential option for the poor to deliver health care to their own communities. PIH embraces this praxis by training and employing local community members to be providers of health care as community health workers, patient navigators, supervisors, and managers.

Paul lived out this moral praxis in contexts that appear markedly different, from rural Haiti to Harvard University to Rwanda to Sierra Leone and Liberia where the Ebola virus got a foothold in 2014. Though they might be disparate, the social conditions in these contexts are not divergent: they are generated by the same global power dynamics that channel resources to promote the life and wellbeing of some people and consign most people to struggle to survive. Paul insisted on holding together every place he worked. A slide show Paul narrated to accompany his Shattuck Lecture at the Annual Meeting of the Massachusetts Medical Society in 2013 illustrates this point:

> All accounts, especially of difficult times, are partial, and my Shattuck Lecture, which is largely about AIDS, tuberculosis, and other chronic infections, is, of course, partial. It's a view from somewhere. That somewhere is largely settings of rural poverty in Haiti and Rwanda, but also of having trained in Harvard's teaching hospitals, where I still work to this day. That contrast experience has shaped very much my views not only on AIDS, tuberculosis, and other complex pathologies but on the topic of global health equity.[5]

---

[5] Paul E. Farmer, "Chronic Infectious Disease and the Future of Health Care Delivery," *New England Journal of Medicine* 369, no. 25 (2013): 2424–2436, doi.org/10.1056/NEJMsa1310472.

Paul's life and work demonstrate that opportunities for creative and collective moral agency that aims to transform the world exist in every situation and in every place because there is, in fact, only one world.[6] All life is connected.

In Paul's analysis, pandemic diseases like AIDS and COVID-19 give lie to the illusion that people inhabit distinct and separate social worlds.[7] Since there is just one world, liberation praxis to transform it can begin where each one of us is. From anywhere, anyone can begin to make the critical connections necessary to shift perspective, change posture, and seek out the people most directly affected by social inequity by joining them where they are, or through persistent search for counternarratives authored by and with them. Every place can be the point of departure for critical reflection and action to understand the social, historical, and political forces which forged the iniquitous shape of the world and to channel energy and resources to redress what Paul has called these "steep grades of inequality."[8] To begin a lecture at Vanderbilt University School of Medicine in 2018, for example, Paul recounted his more than twenty-hour journey from Sierra Leone to Nashville. Noting that this may sound exotic to his audience, Paul put up a slide depicting a map of the transatlantic triangle trade that trafficked millions of African people into slavery. "This is not the first time the US South has been connected to West Africa," Paul pointed out. He went on to give his lecture addressing the question "How does a university engage in [global health in] an ethically sound and meaningful manner?"[9]

---

[6] Paul Farmer and Gustavo Gutiérrez, *In the Company of the Poor: Conversations with Dr. Paul Farmer and Fr. Gustavo Gutiérrez*, ed. Michael Griffin and Jennie Weiss Block (Maryknoll, NY: Orbis Books, 2013), 171–172.

[7] Farmer, "Chronic Infectious Disease and the Future of Health Care Delivery," 2426.

[8] Paul Farmer, "An Anthropology of Structural Violence," *Current Anthropology* 45, no. 3 (2004): 305–325, doi.org/10.1086/382250.

[9] Vanderbilt University, "Dr. Paul Farmer Spends Day at Vanderbilt, Sharing Perspective on Global Health and Service," medschool.vanderbilt.edu/mstp/2018/02/28/dr-paul-farmer-spends-day-at-vanderbilt-sharing-perspective-on-global-health-and-service/.

Living Witnesses and Moral Agency

For Paul, "restoring to such problems their full social complexity" is a key component of liberation moral praxis.[10] Paul's call to "resocialize the way we see ethical dilemmas" does not flatten but rather attends carefully to differences in social conditions.[11] In other words, Paul's liberative moral agency is not unconditional action but rather action under all conditions.[12] For Paul, the work of critical reflection and action is never done until there is no longer any socially structured suffering; until no one dies of a treatable disease. Any one critical insight or action is important though insufficient in itself. Yet, each helps generate necessary momentum and shifts in perspective on the way to building a world that extends care and protection to all people everywhere. To exercise critical ethical action and reflection under all conditions is moral agency that moves beyond what is currently deemed possible.

As part of his liberative moral praxis, Paul presses for ongoing critical reflection that "challenge[s] the chicanery that leads us to forget that we are part of the same world."[13] The "we" is important here. In an internal "mindfulness memo" he wrote to the PIH staff, board, partners, and supporters in 2018, Paul questions the assumptions behind the oft-repeated phrase among progressive professional-class social justice workers that "we are working ourselves out of a job":

> I doubt the aspiration of "working ourselves out of a job" is the right one for a global confederation like Partners In Health. Do we want our trainees and 17,000 co-workers to work themselves out of a job? Or is it

---

[10] Paul Farmer, *Pathologies of Power: Health, Human Rights, and the New War on the Poor* (Berkeley, CA: University of California Press, 2003), 210.
[11] Farmer, *Pathologies of Power*, 210.
[12] I owe this insight to a sermon I heard by homiletics scholar Kyle Brooks, who preached that the incarnation of God in the person of Jesus reveals not unconditional love, but the presence of love under all conditions.
[13] Farmer, *Pathologies of Power*, 211.

really a question of working more and more people into the sorts of jobs that are taken for granted in some of the places where we were born?[14]

If there is one world—riven though it is by social inequities so deep and wide they are more like gulfs separating worlds than gaps to be bridged— then where one is born ought not determine who can effectively participate in its repair.

Who Lives, Who Dies, Who Speaks, and Who Listens

PIH's commitment to heed the direction of its patients in order to understand and address together the social inequities that expose them to ill health and death is well documented in the accounts of PIH's first decades of work in the 1980s and 1990s in Haiti and Peru.[15] Listening to patients led PIH to offer treatment for multidrug-resistant tuberculosis (MDR-TB) and HIV in communities facing and fighting poverty, when the reigning global health experts said it was naive at best and irresponsible at worst, consigning millions of people to die from treatable diseases.[16] PIH ignored the Western experts and heeded its patients' aspirations for treatment. PIH's MDR-TB and HIV treatment programs were successful and changed the status quo in global health delivery. Now, even the experts advocate for MDR-TB and HIV treatment globally. But the fight is not over. With each new disease outbreak—cholera, Ebola—the reigning Western experts authorize prevention, not treatment or vaccination. And PIH fights back each time. PIH and its patients continue to expand what is possible in global health delivery, offering cancer care and surgical services to communities that had been clinical deserts. This transformation

---

[14] Paul Farmer, "On Partnership and Accompaniment: Three Questions, an Example, and Three Suggestions," November 4, 2018.

[15] Paul Farmer, *Infections and Inequalities: The Modern Plagues* (Berkeley: University of California, 2001), 45; Paul Farmer, *AIDS and Accusation: Haiti and the Geography of Blame* (Berkeley: University of California Press, 2006), 47; Farmer, *Pathologies of Power*, 149–150; Paul Farmer, *To Repair the World: Paul Farmer Speaks to the Next Generation*, ed. Jonathan Weigel (Berkeley: University of California, 2013), xxi.

[16] Farmer, *Pathologies of Power*, 201.

in health care delivery is possible because people who have been written off by the dominant circulation of resources are consulted and considered as full agents in the effort to provide a preferential option for the poor in health care. The critical reflection of the oppressed is, as Emilie Townes calls for in *Womanist Ethics and the Cultural Production of Evil,* "included into the discourse—not as additive or appendage, but as resource and co-determiner of actions and strategies."[17]

In summing up this moral praxis in conversation with Fr. Gutiérrez, Paul says "When we actually went out and did what we said we were doing, which was listening to the poor, we discovered that we weren't listening enough. Imagine even after several years of reading and thinking, there's still more you can learn about how to structure a program by actually listening to people."[18] Paul acknowledges how difficult it is to listen, "especially when the subject at hand is social suffering."[19] Despite difficulties, failures, and shortcomings, however, PIH still strives to listen and engage the people most directly affected by health care inequality as protagonists of their own liberation. They are key moral agents in the fight against the poverty that causes their suffering.

A relatively recent example is the Journey to 9 program, which began in Haiti in 2018 when the PIH team noticed that maternity patients were missing prenatal appointments, did not have clothes or blankets in which to take their newborns home, and did not return for a postnatal appointment. Haiti has the highest rate of maternal deaths in Latin America and the Caribbean, and the PIH team also wanted to increase the number of pregnant people who delivered in well-staffed and equipped health care facilities. The team asked the new parents what the barriers were for them to come to the health care center for prenatal visits, delivery, and postnatal visits. Out of those conversations, PIH designed a program which includes eight group prenatal appointments, one group postnatal

---

[17] Emilie M. Townes, *Womanist Ethics and the Cultural Production of Evil* (New York: Palgrave Macmillan, 2006), 16.
[18] Farmer and Gutiérrez, *In the Company of the Poor*, 166.
[19] Farmer and Gutiérrez, 112, 9.

appointment (hence the name Journey to 9, as in making it to all nine pre- and postnatal visits), psychosocial support and counseling, community-based care, hospital-based services, and a kit that includes onesies, a thermometer, and other hygiene supplies.[20] At a graduation ceremony, participants can share their experiences of the program. Participants have noted that the group setting makes the experience more supportive and less intimidating for women from poorer backgrounds. One participant had delivered a baby in the PIH maternity ward before the Journey to 9 program was launched. She said the Journey to 9 program made it an entirely different experience when she delivered her second child—as if it were a new facility.[21] Two thousand women have participated in the program. Since 2019, 95 percent of them have delivered in PIH health care facilities. By comparison, only 36 percent of pregnant people in Haiti give birth at a health care center. The PIH team has already expanded the program to another public hospital where PIH works in Haiti and would like to extend the program to other regions throughout Haiti. The PIH maternal health teams in Mexico and Peru expressed interest in replicating the program. In February 2020, Haiti's Journey to 9 team traveled to Chiapas to help them adapt the program for patients living in Mexico and Peru.[22]

Space to Bear Witness in the Academy

Paul and the PIH team heed the insights of people most directly affected by social inequity not only to direct the shape of clinical interventions but also make space for their participation in academic settings where the shape of the world is debated and framed. For example, Paul recounts participating in an HIV conference in rural Haiti in 2000, "attended

---

[20] Partners In Health, "Mothers and Babies Receive Long-Term Support Through J-9 Program in Haiti," www.pih.org/article/mothers-and-babies-receive-long-term-support-through-j-9-program-haiti.

[21] Conversation with the PIH Haiti research department, October 26, 2022.

[22] "Partners In Health Annual Report," 2020, 23, www.pih.org/sites/default/files/pdf/pih-annual-report-2020.pdf.

mostly by women living in poverty, several of them also living with HIV."[23] The women raised questions to challenge global health's reigning position that prevention is the best course of action in places with sparse medical infrastructure—a position supported with research conducted in low and middle-income countries by affluent Western institutions whose "ethical codes developed in affluent countries are quickly ditched as soon as affluent universities undertake research in poor countries."[24] In another salient example, a PIH symposium on global health equity held at Harvard University in 2009 featured keynote speakers Adeline Merçon and St. Coeur François, PIH staff members in Haiti who had started out as patients.[25] Paul stood with them on the stage to translate their remarks from Haitian Creole into English.

In addition to devoting space on the dais, Paul devotes much space in his books for the people on the underside of dominant power to tell their stories and analyze the structural violence that targets them most grievously. Womanist ethicist Marcia Riggs's conception of a mediating ethic helps identify one of the moral frameworks at play in Paul's approach. A mediating ethic is a move toward justice that generates momentum in the face of a moral dilemma.[26] Imperfect and insufficient though it may be, it is moral agency that moves a community enough to perceive a new possibility it could not have realized in its former position. Paul's move to include in his books the voices of the oppressed offering a critique of the socio-politico-economic structures that cause them harm is a mediating ethic that advances liberation praxis through the impasse of a moral dilemma: not hearing the perspective of the oppressed in the dominant discourse versus publishing pieces of their self-narrated stories in widely-read books written by Paul that circulate in his name.

---

[23] Farmer, *Pathologies of Power*, 198.
[24] Farmer, *Pathologies of Power*, 198–200.
[25] Partners In Health, "15th Annual Symposium Pushes Boundaries," www.pih.org/article/15th-annual-symposium-pushes-boundaries.
[26] Marcia Riggs, *Awake, Arise, & Act: A Womanist Call for Black Liberation* (Cleveland: Pilgrim, 1994), 20.

Living Witnesses and Moral Agency

In Paul's first book, *The Uses of Haiti*, Yolande Jean gets the first word. She frames and directs the book's examination of the long history of the United States' exploitative and extractive relationship with Haiti from her perspective as a refugee who qualified for political asylum in the United States because of the torture she endured under Haiti's military regime but who was detained at the Guantanamo military base and prevented from entering the United States because she was HIV positive:

> Everyone in Haiti was always criticizing the American government, and I'd say "You're not there, so how do you know they really wish us harm?" They'd say, "but look what they did to us in 1915," and I'd respond, "But that was a long time ago; things have changed." And yet I've come to see that there hasn't really been any change. My experience on Guantanamo allowed me to discover that it was true—these things are their doing. I have no idea what we are to them—their bêtes noires, or perhaps devils. We're not human to them, but I don't know what we are. It's as if they see us as a part of the world born to serve as American lackeys. And that's just what's come to pass. They use us as they see fit.[27]

Jean's critique is remarkable because too often structural violence limits the transmission of critical analysis by people on the underside of hegemonic power. "Haitian friends have commented on parts of [*The Uses of Haiti*]," Paul writes, "but all, with the exception of Yolande Jean, have asked to remain anonymous."[28] Structural violence—which Paul defines as "social arrangements that put individuals and populations in harm's way"— denies people on the underside of power public authorship of their own stories and critical analyses.[29] Paul and his Haitian friends resist in the best way they can, having Paul tell their stories under pseudonyms.

---

[27] Paul Farmer, *The Uses of Haiti* (Monroe, ME: Common Courage, 1994), 10.
[28] Farmer, *The Uses of Haiti*, 8.
[29] Paul E. Farmer, Bruce Nizeye, Sara Stulac, and Salmaan Keshavjee, "Structural Violence and Clinical Medicine," *PLoS Medicine* 3, no. 10 (2006): 1686, doi.org/10.1371/journal.pmed.0030449.

In drawing near to bear witness to his patients' stories, Paul does not instrumentalize them to justify his work and position as a Western physician-anthropologist. Rather, Paul shares the stories of individual people with their permission to indict the Western-dominated global circulation of knowledge, identity, and power that causes their local misery. Farmer makes a similar move in his latest book, *Fevers, Feuds, and Diamonds: Ebola and the Ravages of History*, as noted in Barbara King's review for NPR:

> In this grim tale, it's a relief to read about the West African survivors of Ebola who work to help others rebuild their lives. The stories of Ibrahim Kamara and Yabom Koroma, Sierra Leoneans who endured sorrowful family losses as well as terrible illness, Farmer conveys partly in their own words. It makes for two gripping chapters.[30]

In the dominant Western-centric discourse, Yolande Jean, Ibrahim Kamara, and Yabom Koroma are not viewed as moral agents or even—Jean makes plain—as human. In Paul's writing, however, they are the actors whose critical reflection and action address most effectively the major moral crises of the day: political asylees crossing oceans in rafts; HIV; Ebola. Farmer does not use the stories of Jean, Kamara, and Koroma as "local knowledge" to give authenticity to his scholarly analysis. Rather, Paul uses his position as a credentialed Western academic to make noticeable if imperfect gestures at including Jean's, Kamara's, and Koroma's critical action and reflection in the analysis of structural violence and global health.

Together, Farmer's, Jean's, Kamara's, and Koroma's liberating praxis helps shape a new moral agency. This moral agency is marked by transgression of the roles assigned by the coloniality of knowledge, power, and identity. Though the era of formal colonial governance is mostly over,

---

[30] Barbara King, "In 'Fevers, Feuds And Diamonds,' Paul Farmer Breaks Down Assumptions About Ebola," *NPR.Org*, November 17, 2020, www.npr.org/2020/11/17/935337735/in-fevers-feuds-and-diamonds-paul-farmer-breaks-down-assumptions-about-ebola.

power still flows through the colonial project's circuits: control of the knowledge and resources necessary for world-building accrue primarily to professional-class, predominantly white, cis-gendered men from Western centers of power.[31] Farmer refuses a binary construction of dominant moral agency that either takes total control of the critical knowledge and action necessary to transform the world or refuses to exercise any power to speak and act for liberation so as not to be labeled an oppressor. Instead, Paul makes the mediating ethical move to transgress the rigid bounds of the physician-scholar social position by reporting and heeding the analysis and direction of people most directly affected by the suffering he actively labors to relieve. Jean, Kamara, and Koroma boldly transgress the object-of-foreign-intervention social position by authoring a paradigm-shifting critical analysis of the global structure that placed them at risk of grievous violence and harm.

Implications for Theological Ethics and for the Current Moment

Paul's conception of moral agency—marked by Latin American liberation theology and lived out through the field of global health equity—offers theological ethics an approach for engaging positionality to open new lines of critical reflection and possibilities for action. In the communities where PIH works and within the pages of Paul's books, patients assume authorship to interpret the complex reality of their lives and the global forces that shape them. Paul and his patients exercise moral agency that troubles the roles they inhabit in the Western hierarchy of identity, power, and knowledge. Paul and his patients exercise the liberative potential of their respective social positions to relieve suffering and to shift iniquitous power imbalances together: PIH patients' use their position on the underside of power to name the social conditions and structural barriers that block their ability to exercise their rights and reach their potential;

---

[31] Nelson Maldonado-Torres, "On the Coloniality of Being," *Cultural Studies* 21, no. 2/3 (2007): 261.

Living Witnesses and Moral Agency

Paul uses his position as a credentialed Western physician and scholar to marshal resources to redress the social inequities PIH's patients and staff identify; and they do so without becoming immobilized by the reality that in a system as rife with social inequity as the current global order, any action can only be partial and imperfect. Though Paul and his patients do not suddenly escape or destroy these roles, they show that the identities defined by iniquitous social conditions do not essentially or ultimately circumscribe human critical thought and action.

As I write, Haiti is facing one of the most difficult moments in its recent history:

> a steadily deteriorating security situation over the past 15 months, which has worsened dramatically in recent weeks. Gang violence, protests, roadblocks, damaged communications infrastructure, and fuel shortages pose grave operational and logistical challenges for the team at Zanmi Lasante, as PIH is known in Haiti.[32]

In October 2022, a new cholera outbreak emerged in Haiti. I have heard people who have supported humanitarian and development projects in Haiti for decades say that they will no longer donate to projects in Haiti because of the instability. Paul's moral praxis—committed to critical reflection and action under all conditions—helps chart a way forward. The current conditions are no excuse to give up. Liberative moral praxis in this moment demands critical reflection on the historic, geopolitical, economic, social, and structural root causes of Haiti's current crisis, which are directly related to the wealth and security that Western powers enjoy. Though Haiti is only five-hundred miles from Florida, it feels like a world away from the United States. Paul would remind us that it is not.

Liberative moral praxis also demands action that heeds the direction of the people most directly affected by social misery, and that shifts resources to address the social conditions that put the majority of people in harm's

---

[32] Partners In Health, "With Instability in Haiti, Doors Remain Open at PIH Facilities," www.pih.org/article/instability-haiti-doors-remain-open-pih-facilities.

way. PIH is doing all of these things, as described in a recent article on its website. With the weight of all that the members of PIH team in Haiti are bearing, I want to quote them at length to communicate their depth of analysis, of resolve, and of spirit:

> PIH believes a solution to the current nationwide crisis must be led by Haitians, and likely with the support of the international community. But our focus remains on working with ministries of health, not politicians; looking at histories, not the news of the day; and engaging in accompaniment and strengthening of equitable, high-quality health systems.
>
> Zanmi Lasante is of course not just an organization capable of emergency response. It is a Haitian organization, led and run by Haitians. It works with and through the Ministry of Health, serving to bolster that institution's capacity to deliver quality health care to Haitians. Since 1985, it has only grown bigger and better, despite all sorts of political and environmental challenges. Its residency programs now train tomorrow's leaders. In short, it is a sterling example of how to aggressively chip away at a deep, deep problem—namely, a history of oppression that has resulted in a galling lack of modern medical care in the country—through solidarity, accompaniment, and providing a preferential option for the poor.[33]

Paul would be proud.

Paul's liberation praxis interrupts dominant assumptions about whose and which formulations of moral agency effectively diagnose, alleviate, and prevent social misery. Paul's embrace of Latin American liberation theological praxis is a mediating ethic, not a moral absolute. "A preferential option for the poor and accompaniment and structural violence," Paul writes, "are not the only good ideas out there, but rather remind us of work yet to be done."[34] Paul's life and work demonstrate that moral agency which produces movement towards social justice is possible for anyone in

---

[33] Partners In Health, "With Instability in Haiti, Doors Remain Open at PIH Facilities."
[34] Farmer and Gutiérrez, *In the Company of the Poor*, 134.

any social position. In Paul's moral calculus, there is too much ground yet to gain for anyone to make any excuse not to take part in the work to transform the world together.

Alison Lutz, PhD, is Director of Contextual Education for the global health organization Partners In Health (PIH). The Rev. Lutz earned her PhD in Religion, Ethics & Society from Vanderbilt University. Her doctoral research analyzed how liberation praxis and decolonial perspectives can change the circulation of humanitarian power, forming people who work together to relieve suffering without reproducing the dominant hierarchies that cause social misery in the first place.

Part 2

A Prism *for* Liberation Theology

Paul Farmer and Fr. Gustavo Gutiérrez, OP, Miami, Florida, 2012. (Photo credit: Jennie Weiss Block)

Part 2: A Prism for Liberation Theology

One key aspect of Paul Farmer's vision and work was the use of liberation theology which he carefully studied. Insights from "lib theo," as he liked to refer to it, informed his understanding of the problems surrounding deep poverty on a large scale. He also judiciously applied the tenets of liberation theology to his work as a physician, believing that the principles of liberation theology would improve the quality of the delivery of medical care in resource poor settings. In Part 2, "A Prism for Liberation Theology," we explore how he received and refracts the gospel light of this important theological movement. Here scholars detail the historical nexus of liberation theology and health care that preceded Farmer—a tradition still largely unknown in the US. Where Part I locates Farmer's life as a theological text, here we explore his conviction that the lives of the poor and suffering were key 'texts.' He learned from liberation theology that, as one author notes, "listening to the poor and destitute sick provides an opportunity to learn what social analysis cannot show." And to do that, one must be close enough to hear their stories. From his first major book, Farmer's work is replete with the stories of his patients and pervaded with a spirituality and theology of liberation that "invite[s] his readers to contemplate, medically and theologically, their place in the ecologies of injustice that ravage the life of the poor."

But the poor were not simply data sources nor patients to be cared for—they were brothers and sisters whose dignity confronted him and called him into the contemplative practice of loving attention, the often-silent gift of presence. His praxis of attending to story after story after story (what anthropologists call 'thick ethnographic description') pressed him deeper into theological mystery. In doing so, his work served as a prism, contributing to the ongoing development of liberation theology through his relentless attention to the realities of structural violence. This attention to the structures that created sickness among the poor—especially for poor women—was the vital means for reimagining and redesigning medical interventions that not only challenged the beliefs of the medical community in the US and Europe but transformed the practices of global health.

As Alexandre A. Martins recounts in Chapter Five, "Liberation Theology and Public Health Ethics," there is a tradition behind Paul Farmer. He was not the first person to bring a liberationist lens to health care delivery. Rather, behind the English texts he consumed, and with which US readers are largely familiar (e.g., the work of Gutiérrez, Jon Sobrino, Clodovis and Leonardo Boff) stand decades of Portuguese and Spanish language theology as yet little accessed in the US. Moreover, as Martins narrates, there is a long and robust tradition of physicians living and practicing medicine out of a liberationist framework. His stories of Adolf Serriperro, Raul Matte, and Zilda Arns stand as a witness for theologians, bishops, pastors, lay ministers—in fact, for the church as a whole. CELAM's Conference at Aparecida is clear: "In the face of the poor, we contemplate the face of the crucified Jesus." Farmer's witness asks: do we really believe this? Yet while he situates Farmer's work and witness within this tradition that preceded him, one from which he learned and to which he then contributed, Martins also articulates how Farmer's practical and scholarly work contributed to liberation theology's development and global expansion—particularly in articulating the conceptual contours of structural violence in its manifestation in the field of health care.

Farmer and others witness to what liberation theology looks like when lived as a framework for practicing medicine. In Chapter Six, "Theologians in the Field: 'Dices que eres un teólogo, ¿cuál es tu practica?'", Leo Guardado turns the tables and asks: what does liberation theology look like as a framework for the practice of theology? Where Martins challenges US theologians for their failure to engage Latin American scholarship, Guardado likewise challenges US theologians on a number of points. He critiques the false dichotomy between "academic" and "pastoral" theology—reinforced by binaries of studying/doing, theory/practice—

that plagues the US academy. He calls us to center friendship (a theological, gospel category) and fieldwork or "lo pastoral" as the foundations for generating both a theory and theology that is at the service of a suffering world. For Guardado, a contemporary mode of such a method integrating friendship and "lo pastoral" is the practice of participatory action research. What if the 'method' of theology was actually, as Gutiérrez has argued, "a lifestyle, a way of life, a way of being and becoming a disciple of Jesus" that required dwelling with Jesus by making one's home among the poor and insignificant because it is in the fractures and fissures of the world that we encounter the presence of God? Such a practice also captures Lutz's insights about the primacy of listening to what communities themselves actually want and need.

A key insight Farmer gleaned from liberation theology is another methodological plank generally obscured from academic analysis: attention to the economic dimensions of illness, death, poverty, suffering—in short, the economic dimensions of reality. In Chapter Seven, "Liberating Theological Ethics from the Invisible Hand: Paul Farmer, the World's Poor, and the Quandaries of the Fortunate," M. Therese Lysaught highlights this aspect of his work. Drawing on his twin critiques of neoliberal economics and bioethics, she foregrounds how our conceptual categories have become thoroughly economized and asks the pointed questions: whether bioethics was created as a neoliberal project and how deeply co-opted US theological discourse has been by its economic social location. What, we might ask, is the political economy of US Catholic theology? At the same time, she argues that Farmer's life and witness embody a crucial economic alternative—neither the anthropology of neoliberalism nor a distorted, reductive, economized notion of 'charity' that is the heritage of capitalism, but an anthropology of caritas. Farmer helps us see how traditional Christian practices—presence, friendship, solidarity, hospitality, and other crucial ways of embodying caritas—are at the same time deeply "economic."

This theme of economics continues in Chapter Eight, "Confronting 'Structures of Violence': Women's Empowerment and the Legacy of Paul

Part 2: A Prism for Liberation Theology

Farmer." Here Suzanne Mulligan expands on Martins's insight that develops the tradition of liberation theology, further articulating the category of structural sin into a more three-dimensional account of structural violence. Mulligan explores the relevance of this concept for helping advance Catholic theological analysis not only with regard to the poor, but equally with regard to women. Thickly displaying how structural violence plays out in health sequelae via concrete impacts on real bodies, Farmer regularly highlighted the specific impacts of structural violence on women, especially in terms of morbidity and mortality. Narrating what those structures of violence look like globally, Mulligan provides a context for asking: what would it mean concretely to advance the integral human development of women? Within a theological context, she pointedly asks: "For Farmer and others, recognizing the political, economic, and social participation of women, as well as their leadership roles in society, lies at the heart of any credible way forward. However, this needs greater affirmation by Church leadership and must find more prominence in official teaching. It remains one of Farmer's most vital contributions to global health debates."

Chapter 5: Liberation Theology and Public Health Ethics: The Tradition Behind Paul Farmer

Alexandre A. Martins

"A preferential option for the poor in health care" is part of the mission of Partners In Health (PIH), an organization co-founded by Paul Farmer.[1] Without a doubt, this motto and commitment guided Farmer during his life of service for the destitute sick around the world. The concept of the preferential option for the poor was developed by liberation theologians in Latin American. It grew out of an existential and pastoral practice of members of the Catholic Church who gathered in small communities in the 1960s to read the Bible and to lead literacy campaigns in the Brazilian Northeast. A similar practice among the poor was also developed by Catholic Action, a movement led by workers and students with a social ministry based on the method *see-judge-act*.[2] This movement gained force with the Second Vatican Council and the development of its innovations adapted for the Latin American context offered by the Conference of Latin American Bishops in Medellín (1968). The pastoral and social dynamism of these experiences offered the foundation for the systematization of a new way of doing theology, known as liberation theology. Rubem Alves, Juan Luis Segundo, Gustavo Gutiérrez, and Leonardo Boff were the first professional theologians to do theology in this new way, through which they offered a theoretical account of the preferential option for the poor.

According to his biographer Tracy Kidder, Paul Farmer's first contact with liberation theology and, therefore, with the theoretical foundation

---

[1] Partners In Health, "Mission," www.pih.org/our-mission.
[2] Ney de Souza, "Ação Católica, Militância Leiga no Brasil: Méritos e Limites" *Revista de Cultura Teológica* 14, no. 55 (2006): 39–59, doi.org/10.19176/rct.v0i55.15033.

for the option for the poor, came from his interest in the conflicts in Central America and the murder of Oscar Romero.³ Later, as he tried to understand the oppression in Haiti under the Duvalier dictatorship, liberation theology offered him resources to read this reality. In this period around 1980–1983, Farmer read Gustavo Gutiérrez's *A Theology of Liberation* and other liberation theology material.⁴ Here Farmer's love for serving the poor encountered a theoretical analysis of this service as a companion of the poor and against the structures of oppression and impoverishment.

Shortly thereafter, Farmer and a small group of friends founded Partners In Health, an organization that centered the option for the poor as the guide and lens for their service to the sick and promotion of health care as a human right. In 1995, almost ten years after the creation of PIH in 1987, he said:

> To those concerned with health, a preferential option for the poor offers both a challenge and an insight. It challenges doctors and other health providers to make an option for the poor by working on their behalf. The insight is, in a sense, an epidemiological one: most often, diseases themselves make a preferential option for the poor. That is, the poor are sicker than the non-poor. They are at heightened risk of dying prematurely, whether from increased exposure to pathogens (including pathogenic situations) or from decreased access to services or, as is most often the case, from both of these "risk factors."⁵

There is no doubt that in the context from which he came (the US) and in those where he and his partners served (several countries around the

---

³ Tracy Kidder, *Mountains Beyond Mountains: The Quest of Dr. Paul Farmer, A Man Who Would Cure the World* (New York: Random House, 2003), 61–62.
⁴ Paul Farmer and Gustavo Gutiérrez, *In the Company of the Poor: Conversations between Dr. Paul Farmer and Father Gustavo Gutiérrez*, ed. M. Griffin and J. W. Block (Maryknoll, NY: Orbis Books, 2013), 15–16; 161–162.
⁵ Paul Farmer, "Medicine and Liberation Theology" *America*, July 15, 1995, www.americamagazine.org/politics-society/1995/07/15/medicine-social-justice-149598.

world), Farmer embodied a genuine experience of a preferential option for the poor in health care. His practice made visible what many, especially in the field of theology in the US, only knew as a theory from books or had heard from pastoral experiences in Latin America. Moreover, Farmer thought that liberation theology methods, particularly the see-judge-act, and the preferential option for the poor were not only resources for theological studies and Church's pastoral and social ministry, but they were also helpful for other realms of social actions that aim to fight for justice and promote opportunities for the flourishing of the poor, such as practices of health care delivery and human rights advocacy.

As I heard from some US colleagues in theology, Farmer's account and practice of social medicine and liberation theology was the first time that one person had made this connection at the theoretical and, above all, practical levels in the context of health care. I do not remember having heard and read Farmer himself suggesting that he was an innovator in this way. I understand that certain limitations in the US (e.g., lack of fluency in Portuguese and Spanish) might have prevented US theologians from seeing beyond their own scholarship or that of their compatriots. Yet Farmer's work and novelty can be situated within a tradition that preceded him—the efforts of many—from which he learned and to which he then contributed, continuing its development and global expansion. It is inside this tradition that I read Farmer's work.

Therefore, in this chapter, I situate Paul Farmer's work within the broader lens of liberation theology in public health, particularly the activism of liberation theologians and health activists who have long advocated for universal health care coverage in Brazil, stressing health care as a human right. This liberation approach in medicine precedes Farmer's work, and also occurred simultaneous in time without one knowing the other. I argue that Farmer can be seen as part of this liberating perspective, one that he incorporated in his medical service after his reading of earlier Latin American liberation theologians. Hence, he brought to the US context (and to English readers) a liberation approach to medicine, present in his public discourse and practice around the world, through his own voice/hands and the actions of the organization he co-founded, Partners In Health. In doing so, Farmer helped to expand the liberation approach to global public health, offering a new pluralism that mediates the dialogue between the global and the local.

Liberation Theology and Health Care in Brazil

It would be ideal to examine a liberating approach to health in Latin America, but a comprehensive analysis would require more space than a book chapter.[6] Therefore, in this chapter, I focus on Brazil, the country that has, perhaps, produced more liberation theologians than any other in the region. To demonstrate this liberating approach to health care, I begin by offering three stories of liberating practices in medicine (led by health professionals) and liberation theology in health care (theologians who examine health challenges from a theological approach). They suggest that a liberating perspective in health care precedes Farmer and also occurred simultaneously without any direct or indirect connection between the practitioners in Brazil and the activism of Paul Farmer.

In 2006, I had an opportunity to work with Adolfo Serripierro, a physician who also was a Catholic priest, in Fortaleza, a northeast Brazilian city. This doctor-father, along with a religious brother and nurse, lived in a very humble house in the midst of an impoverished area, a *favela* (slum) known as Pirambú. Born in Italy where he became a priest and a physician, Serripierro came to Brazil in 1960s as a missionary. In a new country, he finished his medical education with residency in infectious-diseases and genecology. In 1989, he opened a small medical clinic in Pirambú, where he offers care for the poor, particularly for young girls who were entrapped in prostitution and victims of violence and human trafficking. Later, he founded the organization *Associação Maria Mãe da Vida* that provides education to these girls (and the children that many have) and a path for

---

[6] I think this is a work yet to be done. I do not know any comprehensive work that attempts to examine experiences of a liberating approach to health care in Latin America.

them to be reintegrated into society with opportunities to flourish away from prostitution and violence.[7]

Unlike Farmer, Serripierro is not a writer, and Farmer never heard of him. But Serripierro is clear that his work is an embodiment of the preferential option for the poor in health care. This option not only guides his work for and with the poor, but it also leads his lifestyle. He literally lives among the poor, experiencing the same insecurity and challenges the people in his *favela* experience. Serripierro was part of a movement in the early years of liberation theology called *communidades inseridas* (inserted communities), where many religious leaders were inspired by the innovations of the Vatican II and the call of the Latin American Bishops for a poor Church with the poor. A great exponent of liberation theology and of a poor, servant Church, Brazilian Bishop Hélder Câmara,[8] was one of the voices that inspired Serripiero's liberation approach in health care, going beyond offering medical services for the poor but also being a poor himself among them.

Explaining his work, Serripierro says: "Being a missionary, we proclaim the Christ, Son of God made man, who experiences the human condition in its humblest expression, guiding the prophetic actions from a preferential option for the poor."[9] He sees himself as a missionary in health care, providing care and dignity for the poor as a prophet who speaks for justice from the reality and lens of the poor.

During my time with Serripierro, I witnessed his liberation approach to health care, his use of liberating methods—above all, the preferential option for the poor guiding his work as a doctor among the poor—and his spirituality. Serripierro is a man of a great liberating spirituality. A very active man, he would stop for hours in the silence of the night to meditate on the mystery of Jesus whom he had contemplated during the day in the face of his patients. For him, the statement of the CELAM's Conference

---

[7] For information about Associação Maria Mãe da Vida, see ammv.org.br/.
[8] Hélder Câmara, *Essential Writings*, ed. F. McDonagh (Maryknoll, NY: Orbis Books, 2009).
[9] Adolfo Serripierro, "Uma Missão Camiliana" *Boletim ICAPS* 23, no. 232 (2005): 1.

at Aparecida is clear: "In the face of the poor, we contemplate the face of the crucified Jesus."[10]

Serripierro's work with the poor as a physician did not began in 1989 in Pirambú but in 1972 when he joined another physician-priest, Fr. José Raul Matte, to care for the destitute sick in one of the most remote and abandoned areas of the Brazilian Amazon, in the region around the city of Macapá, at the margins of Amazon River. Fr. Matte was a medical doctor who specialized in pediatrics. Like Serripierro, Matte embraced the liberating approach to serve the poor as a physician and a priest by delivering health care to impoverished communities at the margins of the world's largest river. With a boat named Saint John Baptist, Matte and his team travelled to the deep Amazon Forest to serve the poor. As his colleague who went to Pirambú, Matte not only served the destitute sick but also lived their life, being a poor man among the poor who cared for them and prayed with them.

Matte, who died in 2021, began to understand the liberating approach in his early twenties while in medical school. At this time of his education (1954–1959), Matte joined a student branch of Catholic Action, known as JUC (Catholic University Youth). Catholic Action was a Brazilian version of the European movement of Young Catholic Workers, which popularized the see-judge-act method that was developed by Cardinal Joseph Cardijn.[11] This method was embraced in Latin America, first by Catholic Action and then by liberation theologians and activists, becoming the most used method of liberation theology. In one of his works, Farmer discusses how he uses liberation theology's see-judge-act in his medical practice.[12] Studying medicine and engaged in the activism of

---

[10] Conferência Episcopal Latino Americana, *Documento de Aparecida* (São Paulo; Brasília: Paulus; Edições CNBB, 2007), no. 393.

[11] Movimento Cardijn, "Ver, Julgar, Agir: 50 anos de prática social Católica," *IHU online*, May 21, 2011, www.ihu.unisinos.br/noticias/43514-ver-julgar-e-agir-50-anos-de-pratica-social-catolica.

[12] Paul Farmer, *Pathologies of Power: Health, Human Rights, and the New War on the Poor* (Berkeley: University of California Press, 2003), 145–152.

JUC, Matte felt a call to be a physician to serve the poor. Later, he realized his vocation was to do that as a priest, joining the Saint Camillus Seminary in 1961 and being ordained a priest in 1967. A few years later, Matte began his medical and evangelical mission in the Amazon River, living and serving the poor until his death.

Matte was not a scholar but a servant who was aware that his mission was a humble realization of the preferential option for the poor in health care. He never wrote a scholarly work. He dedicated day and night to caring for the destitute sick and to praying with them, the *ribeirinhos*[13] and indigenous who lived at the margins of Amazon River, an area in today's Brazilian State of Amapá, sharing borders with French Guiana and Suriname. However, he liked to write reports about these medical trips throughout the river and its communities. Some of those reports were collected and published.[14] In them, we can see the simplicity of a man who was a "companion of the poor" (to use an expression often said by Farmer) with a spirituality rooted in the Christological faith of an option for the poor and committed to promote justice in health care from the lens of the communities he served. In the Foreword of this collection, Matte's religious superior stresses that Matte's service is an "experience that concretizes one of the priorities of Brazilian Conference of Consecrated People ... : 'revitalize the prophetic-missionary dimension of Religious Consecrated Life, action in new peripheries and boards, strengthening the option for the poor.'"[15]

The final person I want to spotlight is Zilda Arns Neumann and her work with the *Pastoral da Criança*. Arns was a Brazilian physician, specializing in pediatrics and public health, who founded the *Pastoral da*

---

[13] *Ribeirinhos* is a Brazilian expression to refer to humble, poor people who live at the margins of rivers in rural areas.

[14] José Raul Matte, *Missões Camilianas no Foz do Rio Amazonas: A Serviço da Vida e da Saúde dos Mais Pobres e Doentes*, ed. L. Pessini and F. Giannella Jr. (São Paulo: Centro Universitário São Camilo; Província Camiliana Brasileira, 2012).

[15] Leo Pessini, "Prefácio," in José Raul Matte, *Missões Camilianas no Foz do Rio Amazonas*, 10.

Criança in 1992 with the mission: "Promoting children's development in light of the evangelical preferential option for the poor from womb to six years old, through basic guidelines on health, nutrition, education and citizenship, based on the Christian mystique that unites faith and life, contributing to their families and communities carrying out their own transformation."[16] Arns was challenged by her brother, a Cardinal of São Paulo and great liberation theology leader Paulo Evaristo Arns, to begin a project to reduce infant mortality in Brazil. Zilda Arns accepted the challenge and launched a project that helped Brazil to reduce infant mortality by more than half; in the communities served by the *Pastoral da Criança*, infant mortality is below the national average. Today, this organization works in eleven countries, including Guinea-Bissau, Philippines, Mozambique, Bolivia, Venezuela, and Haiti (where Arns died, a victim of 2010 earthquake while caring for Haitian children).

Arns used to say that *Pastoral da Criança* was a service of the multiplication of the loaves. The biblical narrative present in the four gospels inspired her community-based method. She said: "I adapted this methodology of the miracle to the project, by organizing communities and identifying leaders who, trained and with the spirit of Christian fraternity, multiplied knowledge and generosity in neighboring families."[17]

Her project was simple, all based on the generosity and strength of humble people from their own communities. They were leaders and agents of transformation, caring for pregnant women and children. Arns understood the historical force and creativity of the poor, working to empower them to multiply actions of promoting health and life for children in impoverished communities. *Pastoral da Criança* is a concrete realization of what Gustavo Gutiérrez called the irruption of the poor in

---

[16] Pastoral da Criança, "Missão," www.pastoraldacrianca.org.br/missao.
[17] Zilda Arns Neumann, *Depoimentos Brasileiros: Zilda Arns Neumann* (Belo Horizonte: Leitura, 2003), 13.

history.[18] The success of the project had an impact on the newly created Brazilian health system, a direct result of the movement for health reform and its fight for universal health coverage as a right. Liberation theologians and community leaders in the so called *Pastorais Sociais*,[19] a social ministry of Catholic communities focused on areas such as health care, workers' rights, land reform, and environmental protection, played a significant role in the process of democratizing and developing Brazil's Unified Health System. This system has a model of community participation in decision-making in local, municipal, state, and federal levels. Community members of *Pastoral da Criança* participate in all levels of process and decision-making.

Adolf Serripierro, Raul Matte, and Zilda Arns developed community-based projects sustained and led by their own communities, with little to no external or international support from big philanthropic donations. All of them served the poor with a poor life, living in destitute communities. Arns's project gained some national and international recognition, enabling her to expand the work of *Pastoral da Criança* to other countries. Serripierro and Matte were part of the movement of *comunidades inseridas*, a liberating movement that led many religious priests, nuns, and community leaders to live among the poor, serving them with them. This occurred in many areas of social ministry where the poor were suffering. Serripierro and Matte represent those who did this in field of health care. Among those, we can include great theologians who helped to systematize liberation theology, such as Clodovis Boff—who after coming back from his doctoral studies in Europe in the 1970s, went to the state of Acre, in the Amazon region, to serve in a project caring for people with Hansen's disease[20]—and Ivone Gebara, who developed her work in advocacy for

---

[18] Gustavo Gutiérrez, "The Irruption of the Poor in Latin American and the Christian Communities of the Common People," in *The Challenge of Basic Christian Communities*, ed. S. Torres and J. Eagleson (Maryknoll, NY: Orbis Books, 1981), 107–123.

[19] Conferência Nacional dos Bispos do Brasil, *A Missão da Pastoral Social* (Brasília: Edições CNBB, 2008).

[20] Clodovis Boff, *Feet-on-the-Ground Theology* (Maryknoll, NY: Orbis Books, 1987).

women's health and reproductive rights.[21] They were not physicians or nurses, but their work had significant impact in public health, especially for those who, like myself, would shape their work for health care as a right and universal coverage in Brazil.

An Encounter: Two Experiences in Liberating Approach to Health Care

The first time I heard about Paul Farmer was in 2012 in a Global Health and Theological Bioethics class at Boston College. My professor Andrea Vicini (who has a chapter in this book) introduced me to the work of Farmer, with his texts: "Personal Efficacy and Moral Engagement in Global Health: Response to Kleinman and Hanna's Religious Values and Global Health"[22] and "Listening to Prophetic Voices: A Critique of Market-Based Medicine."[23] These texts sounded incredibly familiar to me. It seemed that I knew and had seen everything written there before, but now it was in English and not in Portuguese! The familiarity I felt reading Farmer's texts is certainly not felt by most of his readers in the US. The content did not impress me too much. I was impressed, rather, with who was developing it, a *médico estadunidense*, a professor in a secular institution (Harvard), who approached health care via liberation theology, using some liberating concepts to read the reality of impoverished communities and their health struggle.

Vicini realized that I was very excited about Farmer's writings and told me he was coming to Boston College for a public talk. I went to hear him, and after his talk, I was brave enough—with the broken English of an

---

[21] Ivone Gebara, "The Abortion Debate in Brazil: A Report from an Ecofeminist Philosopher under Siege," *Journal of Feminist Studies in Religion* 11, no. 2 (1995): 129–135.

[22] Paul Farmer, "Personal Efficacy and Moral Engagement in Global Health: Response to Kleinman and Hanna's Religious Values and Global Health," in *Ecologies of Human Flourishing*, ed. D. K. Swearer and S. L. McGarry (Cambridge, MA: Center for the Study of World Religions, distributed by Harvard University Press, 2011), 91–97.

[23] Paul Farmer, "Listening to Prophetic Voices: A Critique of Market-Based Medicine," in Paul Farmer, *Pathologies of Power: Health, Human Rights, and the New War on the Poor* (Berkeley: University of California Press, 2003), 160–178.

international student only about two months in the US—to ask a challenging question. With his empathic personality, Farmer engaged with me in a very informal and funny way to answer to the question, and we met after the event. It was the beginning of an intellectual relationship—sometimes close and often distant—between two people interested in liberation theology and health care for the poor.

When I met Farmer, I already had a strong experience and connection to liberation theology and health care in Brazil. I had served in the Brazilian northeast and Amazon with the two physicians presented above. I was part of a branch of *Pastorais Sociais* oriented to health care, the *Pastoral da Saúde*, through whom I had opportunity to develop an activism for public health and expansion of public medical services using the hermeneutical lens of the poor, and I had worked educating community leaders in impoverished areas for their agency in public health in the model of *Pastoral da Criança*'s method of community multiplication efforts. Moreover, I had a scholarly engagement with the field of bioethics and liberation theology where one can see the use of a liberating approach in health care, leading bioethical discussions in Brazil to focus on public health and to collaborate on the activism for health care as a right as part of the health reform movement that eventually created the Brazilian universal health care system.[24]

As a result, when I met Farmer in the fall of 2012, I had published in the spring of the same year a book where I addressed liberation theology, public health, and bioethical issues.[25] This book was built on the shoulders of great scholars and activists who had acted for health promotion, the development of universal public health coverage, and health care as a human right from a liberating perspective for decades, combining their

---

[24] I develop this work of liberation theologians in bioethics and their participation in the health reform movement in the article "Theological Bioethics and Public Health from the Margins: Epistemology and Latin American Liberation Theology in Bioethics," *National Catholic Bioethics Quarterly* 22, no. 2 (2022): 239–255.

[25] Alexandre A. Martins, *Bioética, Saúde, e Vulnerabilidade: em defesa da dignidade do vulneráreis* (São Paulo: Paulus, 2012).

fight for justice in health care with the struggle for democracy and social justice for the poor. They developed a liberation bioethics from the hermeneutical lens of the preferential option for the poor in health care.

Although leaders such as Arns, Matte, and Serriperro did not offer written scholarly works related to their liberating approach to health care, liberation theologians have complemented their work with the development of a liberation bioethics. Their contribution brings the cry of the poor for health to the center of health care, helping to break down the barriers of a bioethics focused on the physician-patient relationship and the use of technology, themes imported from the US, to move to the challenges that the poor were facing in their reality because of oppression, disproportional vulnerability to fall ill, lack of access to medical assistance, and premature death.

Pioneers of this social bioethics within the Catholic moral perspective were Márcio Fabri dos Anjos and Christian de Paul Barchifontaine. They developed a bioethical account that placed the problems of justice in accessing health care at the center of this discipline in Brazil, enlarging it to a practice of defending public health with universal coverage and the expansion of health services. Trained in moral theology, dos Anjos offered methodological elements for development of this social bioethics with a national character.[26] Coming from hospital practice, Barchifontaine provided a structure of militancy for justice in health care.[27] The influence

---

[26] Márcio Fabri dos Anjos, "Bioética em Perspectiva de Libertação," in *Bioética: Poder e Injustiça*, ed. V. Garrafa and L. Pessini (São Paulo: Loyola, 2003), 455–465. M. F. dos Anjos, "Rumos da Liberdade em Bioética: Uma Leitura Teológica," in *Bioética e Longevidade Humana*, ed. L. Pessini and C.P. Barchifontaine (São Paulo: Centro Universitário São Camilo Press and Loyola, 2006), 129–140.

[27] Christian de Paul Barchifontaine, *Saúde Pública, Bioética e Bíblia: Sejamos Profetas!* (São Paulo: Paulus, 2006). C.P. Barchifontaine, *Saúde Pública é Bioética?* (São Paulo: Paulus, 2005). I also highlight a book on public health ethics edited with the secular bioethicist Elma Zoboli that gathers essays from a wide range of Brazilian bioethicists from different backgrounds: C.P. Barchifontaine and E. Zoboli, eds., *Bioética, Vulnerabiliade e* Saúde (São Paulo: Centro Universitário São Camilo Press, 2007).

of these two theologians[28] went beyond Catholic theological settings, locating both them and liberation theology as disciplinary partners of secular bioethicists in the fight for universal health care coverage.[29]

Among the innovations offered by liberation theologians to bioethics, I highlight the concept of *misthanasia* suggested by dos Anjos in 1989, which became a key concept for bioethics in Brazil. This concept was first developed as a criticism of the narrow discussion of biomedical ethics regarding end-of-life and its focus on euthanasia and physician-assisted suicide. While euthanasia, meaning etymologically "good, happy death," mainly refers to bioethical discussion related to terminal patients, dos Anjos asks about "bad, unhappy deaths" because of lack of proper medical assistance, especially those deaths outside hospitals. Those deaths make us "think about slow and quiet deaths created by systems and structures."[30] Therefore, the neologism *misthanasia* incorporates these slow and quiet deaths in bioethics and end-of-life concerns: "*Misthanasia* makes us to think about those who died by hunger…makes us to think about the death of an impoverished person, embittered by the abandonment, because the lack of the most basic resources."[31]

---

[28] Dos Anjos was recognized by the US Catholic bioethicists M. Therese Lysaught and Michael McCarthy in the anthology they complied with a wide range of voices looking at bioethics from the lens of Catholic social teaching, as an influence for their work on Catholic bioethics and social justice "grounded on the insights of liberation theology, the preferential option for the poor, and a praxis-based approach," a novelty for bioethics in the US context. M. Therese Lysaught and Michael McCarthy, eds., *Catholic Bioethics and Social Justice: The Praxis of US Health Care in a Globalized World* (Collegeville, MN: Liturgical Press, 2018), 16.

[29] José E. de Siqueira, Dora Porto, and Paulo A.C. Fortes, "Linhas Temáticas da Bioética no Brasil," in *Bioética no Brasil: Tedências e Perspectivas*, ed. M.F. dos Anjos; J.E. de Siqueira (Aparecida, SP: Ideias e Letras, 2007), 163–209.

[30] Márcio Fabri dos Anjos, "Eutanásia em Chave de Libertação," *Boletim ICAPS* 7, no. 57 (1989): 6.

[31] dos Anjos, "Eutanásia em Chave de Libertação," 7.

Liberation Theology, Bioethics, and Social Medicine in Paul Farmer

Although Paul Farmer never mentioned the concept of *misthanasia*,[32] his liberating approach to medicine helped him to develop a sharp criticism of bioethics and its endless discussion related to the choices of those who have access to health care. He affirms, "In an era of globalization and increased communication, this selective attention can become absurd. The world's poor already seem to have noticed that ethicists are capable of endlessly rehashing the perils of too much care, while each year millions die what the Haitians call 'stupid deaths.'"[33]

Like liberation theologians and bioethicists in Brazil, Farmer developed this account from his encounter with the reality of the poor and the experience of listening to them. As a physician and scholar engaged with the poor in different countries and cultures, Farmer was very aware of the failure of bioethics developed in the global north to include issues related to social justice, the challenges faced by marginalized communities in accessing health care, and the manipulation of these vulnerable populations in abusive research experiments at national and international levels. He stresses that "without a social justice component, medical ethics risks becoming yet another strategy for managing inequality."[34] Bringing bioethicists out of this selective attention—shifting from managing inequality to becoming a prophetic voice against the abuses of people's integrity and stupid deaths—passes through the courage of listening to the poor, via a practice situated among them. Only this can open scholars and clinicians to see health challenges from the lens of the poor: "Within and

---

[32] Farmer knew the liberation approach to bioethics developed by Márcio Fabri do Anjos. He quotes several times dos Anjos' article, entitled "Medical Ethics in the Developing World: A Liberation Theology Perspective," published in English in the *Journal of Medicine and Philosophy* in 1996. In this article, dos Anjos did not address the concept of *misthanasia*. Farmer quoted dos Anjos at: Paul Farmer, *Partner to the Poor: A Paul Farmer Reader*, ed. Haun Saussy (Berkeley: University of California Press, 2010), 483.

[33] Farmer, *Pathologies of Power*, 205.

[34] Farmer, *Pathologies of Power*, 201.

across national boundaries, the destitute sick should be the primary judge of any code of ethics."[35]

For Farmer and liberation theologians, the best way to recognize and understand the abuses against people's human rights is from the perspective of the poor. He strongly defended the thesis "that human rights abuses are best understood (that is, most accurately and comprehensively grasped) from the point of view of the poor."[36] Poverty created by structural violence—that impoverishes, makes sick, and kills millions of people around the world—to maintain the privilege of powerful people and nations is a human rights abuse. Leonardo Boff affirms that poverty and its deaths are the scandal of humanity's failure.[37] Following this, the lack of access to health care imposed on the poor is a human right abuse and as such it must be addressed.

Farmer shows the existence of an evil relationship between structural violence, the suffering of the poor, and human rights abuses. Working in health care for the poor allows us to see this relationship. Considering liberation theology's social analysis to explain and understand human suffering,[38] Farmer develops an anthropology of suffering in which structural violence and poverty are essential to understand what he calls the "extreme suffering of the poor" and its connection to human rights abuse.[39] Therefore, structural violence must be included in the human rights debate and advocacy.[40] The human rights community and bioethicists largely fail to see this connection.

The reflection and activism of liberation theologians for universal health care coverage in Brazil in the 1980s argued that health care and opportunities to enjoy a high standard of wellbeing should be viewed as a

---

[35] Farmer, *Pathologies of Power*, 209.
[36] Farmer, *Pathologies of Power*, 17.
[37] Leonardo Boff, *Reflexões de um Velho Teólogo e Pensador* (Petrópolis: Vozes, 2018), 126–127.
[38] Farmer, *Partner to the Poor*, 336. This book is a collection of articles previously published by Farmer.
[39] Farmer, *Partner to the Poor*, 328.
[40] Farmer, *Partner to the Poor*, 343–444.

human right. This became part of the health reform movement and contributed to the health reform that included the right to health in the Brazilian constitution, followed by the creation of the Unified Health System to respond to this constitutional mandate. However, this generation of liberation theologians did not offer an account of structural violence as a risk factor for human rights abuses and the ways in which these abuses lead to the lack of health care and resulting premature deaths. They recognized direct human rights abuses committed by the oppressive dictatorship that governed Brazil for twenty-five years, but they did not read the collapse of health care services and the high rates of infant mortality, maternal mortality, and premature deaths as a direct or indirect result of structural violence understood from a human rights perspective. Farmer contributes to this liberating approach to health care by showing that there is a link between structural violence, human rights abuses, and health injustices that neither the human rights community nor bioethicists realize. It is interesting that liberation theology offered resources for Farmer to develop his account and analysis of the reality applied to the health context, while liberation theologians in bioethics and even its medical activism among the poor, such as the one mentioned above, did not realize the connections pointed out by him.

Farmer stresses—as a moral obligation, I suggest—the necessity to "discern the nature of structural violence and its contribution to human suffering" and abuses against human rights.[41] Structural violence makes people poor and vulnerable to extreme violence. For bioethicists and human rights advocates to recognize it, they must avoid reductionism in their analysis to understand the relationship between structural violence and human rights.[42] Farmer makes an incredible intellectual movement: using resources from liberation theology, he develops his critique of bioethics and human rights accounts; at the same time, he offers a contribution to the development of liberation theology in bioethics.

---

[41] Farmer, *Partner to the Poor*, 337.
[42] Farmer, *Partner to the Poor*, 338

> As an even sterner rebuke to the self-described pragmatism of those pushing for relaxed ethical practices in settings of great poverty, we once again hear the voice from liberation theology. This voice does not call for equally good treatment of the poor; it demands preferential treatment for the poor.[43]

This movement was possible because a key element of liberation theology: listening to the voices of the poor, believing that they have something to offer and that we can learn from them. Listening to the poor and the destitute sick is an opportunity to learn what social analysis cannot show. In one of his first works, Farmer already presented what he learned from the voices of the poor, saying that their "stories offer us privileged insights into what it means to be sick and poor and aware of the case of the suffering."[44] He quotes Leonardo Boff and his brother Clodovis Boff to show from where he learned the relevance of hearing the poor.[45]

Farmer's commitment to listening to the poor and to bringing their voices to global health and bioethics was clear in his work. Those who are familiar reading his books probably remember the stories of Manno, Anita, Dieudonné, Acéphie, Yolande, Jesús Valle, Julio, Tomás, Sergei, Humarr and many others. Farmer brought their voices, experiences, dramas and, most of the time, sad endings, to scholarly discussions, clinical practices, decision-making processes in public heath, and to any opportunity he had to raise a prophetic voice on behalf of the poor for justice in health.

---

[43] Farmer, *Partner to the Poor*, 447.

[44] Paul Farmer, *AIDS and Accusation: Haiti and the Geography of Blame* (Berkeley: University of California Press, 1992), 262.

[45] Farmer quotes a passage of the Boff brothers' *Introducing Liberation Theology* that says: "The oppressed are more than what social analysis—economists, sociologists, anthropologists—can tell us about them. We need to listen to the oppressed themselves. The poor, in their popular wisdom, in fact know much more about poverty than does any economist. Or rather, they know in another way, in much greater depth." Farmer, *AIDS and Accusation*, 26.

Liberation Theology and Public Health Ethics

> Listening to the afflicted is not merely moral praxis, although it is that. It affords us rich insights into the sorts of problems that we have outlined in this essay [where he rethinks bioethics from a view from below]. Because the poor quite literally embody many of the ethical dilemmas stemming from injustices within medicine and public health, they add insights that cannot be obtained through reference to philosophy, statistics, or policy papers.[46]

Paul Farmer was a man who knew how to listen to the poor and learn from them. He not only served them as a medical doctor, but he contemplated them as a brother who recognized their dignity. This is like the mystical movement of those who make the option for the poor the guide of their existence and professional practice. Recognizing the dignity of the poor leads to recognizing global public health actions when they are oriented by the hypocrisy of cost-effectiveness, something that Farmer fought against. It prevents the poor from having access to the advances of medicine, giving them only what is considered cheap, creating double standards of care and ethics, one for the rich (and people in rich countries) and another, inferior and cheap, for the poor (and people in poor counties). The dignity of the poor exhorts us that the best clinical interventions must be available for them.[47] "The notion of a preferential option for the poor challenges us by reframing the motto: the homeless poor are more deserving of good medical care than the rest of us. Whenever medicine seeks to reserve its finest services for the destitute sick, you can be sure that it is the option-for-the-poor in medicine."[48]

In his last major work, *Fevers, Feuds, and Diamonds*, Farmer reflects on the response to the Ebola epidemic in West Africa and advances his criticism of any paradigm that prevents us from offering the best medical care to treat the poor. In this case, he highlights the control-over-care

---

[46] Farmer, *Partner to the Poor*, 482.
[47] Paul Farmer, *Infections and Inequalities: The Modern Plagues* (Berkeley: University of California Press, 1999), 15.
[48] Farmer, *Pathologies of Power*, 155.

paradigm created by public health experts who do not know the reality of the poor nor listen to them. This paradigm neglects treatments for those who are infected and sick, producing a false conflict between prevention and treatment.[49] Although it does not seem that Farmer is intentionally developing a decolonial critique of certain global health practices, he certainly contributes to this critique by showing how paradigms like the control-over-care applied in former colonies follow the same structure of colonial-style inversion of clinical priorities.[50] Farmer reveals in global health practices the separation of people suggested by Cameroonian philosopher Achilles Mbembe: the division of people between those who matter—their lives must be protected and saved—and those who do not matter—they can die without proper treatment.[51]

Conclusion: Advancing a Legacy Among the Poor

As I affirmed at the beginning of this chapter, I see the work of Paul Farmer as located within a tradition of a liberating approach to health care that began in 1960s in Latin America. This tradition offered resources for Farmer to develop his clinical and scholarly work among and from the poor. At the same time, he contributed the development of the liberating approach in health. Moreover, his contribution has special relevance for the US, the global north, and English readers.

Well known in the US, both in the academic world—in several areas, including theology and anthropology—and in the medical context and in the human rights community, Farmer did not enjoy the same status in Brazil (and most Latin America, I believe). He had never visited Brazil nor had PIH established any work on Brazilian soil. In our personal encounters, he often said that I would have to help him get to Brazil. We

---

[49] Paul Farmer, *Fevers, Feuds, and Diamonds: Ebola and the Ravages of History* (New York: Farrar, Straus and Giroux, 2020), 19–33.
[50] Farmer, *Fevers, Feuds, and Diamonds*, 19.
[51] Achille Mbembe, *Necropolitics* (Durham and London: Duke University Press, 2019), 80.

took a first step in this direction with the translation of one of his main books, *Pathologies of Power*, published in 2018 in São Paulo.[52]

I did a search in the academic databases where most Brazilian journals are indexed, SciElo and CAPES Periodicos, to find out if Farmer was known by Brazilian academics, particularly in the disciplines of medical anthropology, bioethics, medicine, public health, and theology. The search confirmed my impressions: Farmer is almost unknown in Brazil. I found some articles on medical anthropology with references to some of his early works, a text translated and published as a book chapter in a volume edited by Fiocruz (a Brazilian center for public health research) and two essays on theological ethics with quotes from his works. There may be more; my search was far from being comprehensive. However, a conclusion that can be drawn is that Farmer's social and intellectual work is unknown in Brazil, even with the publication of one of his books in Portuguese.[53]

Perhaps some barriers that prevent Farmer's work from being known in Brazil are related to its similarity to many other projects that exist in Brazil or because of language or lack of presence of PIH there. The current context we are experiencing in Brazil—with the growth of anti-poor and far-right movements, the increase of poverty, and the support for neoliberal policies in health dismantling the Brazilian public health system—would benefit from Farmer's work and legacy, providing a precious contribution with his ability to navigate in secular and religious environments, always on the side of the poor. It is with this wish—that more people in Brazil and Latin America can have access to the Paul Farmer's work developed among the poor—that I conclude my chapter.

---

[52] Paul Farmer, *Patologias do Poder: Saúde, Direitos Humanos, e a Nova Guerra Contra os Pobres*, translated by Alexandre A. Martins (São Paulo: Paulus, 2018).

[53] Certainly, this book has minimal or no impact because I did not find any book review of it, four years after its publication.

Alexandre A. Martins, PhD, holds a joint position in the Theology Department and College of Nursing at Marquette University. He specializes in health care ethics and social ethics, especially in the areas of public health, global health, Catholic social teaching, and liberation theology. He is also a scholar in philosophy of religion, specializing in the work of French philosopher Simone Weil. He has engaged in ethics, theology, and health care through a dialogue with anthropology, philosophy, epidemiology, and medical science, especially engaging with marginalized voices and addressing issues from the perspective of the poor. Throughout his academic and activist life, he has acted as an advocate for universal health care coverage through grassroots and social movements as well as through his scholarship and publications. He is deeply engaged in bioethics and public health through social movements organized from marginalized communities. Widely published, he has lectured in various countries. His latest books include: *Covid-19, Política e Fé: Bioética em diálogo na realidade enlouquecida* (São Paulo, SP: O Gênio Criador, 2020), published in Brazil; and *The Cry of the Poor: Liberation Ethics and Justice in Health Care* (Lanham, MD: Lexington Books, 2020), published in the USA in English. He co-edited with MT Dávila the Special issue in Spanish of *Journal of Moral Theology* 10, no. 2 (2021): "Covid-19 y Ética Teológica en América Latina." As a health care provider and global health advocate, he has served in middle and low-income countries throughout the world, such as Brazil, Bolivia, Haiti, and Uganda. Currently he is serving as Regional Coordinator, Catholic Theological Ethics in the World Church for the Latin American and Caribbean region, and as Vice-President of the Brazilian Society of Moral Theology.

Chapter 6: Theologians in the Field: "Dices que eres un teólogo, ¿cuál es tu practica?"

Leo Guardado

A medical anthropologist and a practicing theologian who studied medicine were bound to recognize in each other their shared love and commitment for healing the wounds of humanity. The friendship between Paul Farmer and Gustavo Gutiérrez is well known, and it invites reflection on their methodologies and, more particularly, on the centrality of fieldwork or "lo pastoral" as the foundation for generating theory and theology that is at the service of a suffering world.[1] The phrase and question that is the subtitle of this chapter—"you say you are a theologian, what is your practice?"—is one of many sayings that Gutiérrez has used to spark deeper thought about the vocation of the theologian.[2] In light of this provocation, the chapter weaves together the insights of Farmer and Gutiérrez to illuminate key aspects of the path that these two friends have walked, and unto which they invite us.

I begin by centering friendship as the heart of the preferential option for the poor that has grounded Farmer's work. Then I analyze how Farmer's liberationist-infused anthropological fieldwork is a bridge for theologians who are also turning to fieldwork for theological reflection. Lastly, I gesture toward Participatory Action Research as a framework that

---

[1] See, for example, Michael Griffin and Jennie Weiss Block, eds., *In the Company of the Poor: Conversations with Dr. Paul Farmer and Fr. Gustavo Gutiérrez* (Maryknoll, NY: Orbis Books, 2013).

[2] For a longer analysis of this phrase in relation to Gutiérrez's work, see Leo Guardado, "Haciendo Teología para un Futuro de Liberación," in Andrés Gallego, Carmen Lora, and Pedro De Guchteneere, eds., *Memoria, Presencia y Futuro: A los 50 Años de Teología de la Liberación* (Lima, Perú: Centro de Estudios y Publicaciones, 2021), 502.

challenges new generations of theologians to work, like Farmer and Gutiérrez, for the healing of humanity.

Friendship is the Way

To speak of a method is to speak of a way of doing something, to examine the inner logic of how one carries out one's work. Gustavo Gutiérrez, in elaborating on the method of theology, places the accent on what he calls "a lifestyle, a way of being and of becoming a disciple of Jesus."[3] He goes on to add, making reference to the name given to the early followers of Jesus as a people of "the way,"[4] that "our methodology is our spirituality (that is, our way of being Christians)."[5] Theological work, then, is the fruit of a particular manner of living one's faith in history. To go deeper into Gutiérrez's understanding of spirituality, we must emphasize with greater precision that this way is marked not only by a preferential option for the poor—the central category at the heart of liberation theology and of the first and second testaments—but by friendship.

Friendship is at the core of a preferential option for the poor.[6] The word and concept may seem "lite," a detour from the otherwise radical calls typically associated with the struggle for historical liberation from oppression. Yet friendship is the way, the very ground that binds us together with others and with God.[7] Father Bruno Cadoré, Master of the Order of Preachers (Dominicans) from 2010–2019, writes that the

---

[3] Gustavo Gutiérrez, *The Truth Shall Make You Free* (Maryknoll, NY: Orbis Books, 1990), 5.
[4] See Acts of the Apostles 9:2; 19:9, 23; 22:4; 24:14, 22.
[5] Gutiérrez, *The Truth Shall Make You Free*, 5.
[6] Gustavo Gutiérrez, "The Option for the Poor Arises from Faith in Christ," in *In the Company of the Poor*, 157; Gustavo Gutiérrez, *A Theology of Liberation* (Maryknoll, NY: Orbis Books, 1988), xxxi.
[7] Meister Eckhart, a Dominican theologian and mystic, uses the metaphor of breaking through into the ground to speak of one's "being" and God's "being" as one. In this vein of Dominican mystical theology, we can add that friendship is that ground, that core or essence, that unites and makes one the encounter between God and others. See Meister Eckhart, sermon 52, in *Meister Eckhart: The Essential Sermons, Commentaries, Treatises, and Defense*, Classics of Western Spirituality (Mahwah, NJ: Paulist Press, 1981), 199–203. In the Gospel of John 15:12, friendship with God is the following of Jesus.

friendship between Paul and Gustavo is sealed by "an urgent concern for mutual friends. These are, first, the poor, the sick ... But the world itself is another mutual friend of these two friends ..."[8] Cadoré is pointing toward a spirituality, a way of living that affirms that the presence of the transcendent mystery of God is encountered through being present to the whole of wounded creation. The response one gives in enfleshing the urgent concern for these friends—the poor, the sick, the world—are, in Cadoré's words, "mediations of the mystery of a truth that makes free."[9] To enter into the inner logic of the preferential option for the poor is to enter into the gratuitousness of friendship, without which the preferential option for the poor loses its grounding. As Gutiérrez has emphasized, the work of Paul Farmer and the thousands with whom he worked was "propelled by friendship."[10] This is the dynamism, the spirit that energizes the way the work is worked, "the key action"[11] of a spirituality that is also the method for doing theology or medical anthropology attuned to what is simultaneously most human and divine.

Paul Farmer was not only a partner to the poor; he was a friend of the poor, a friend of God.[12] "Spirituality is always social," Farmer wrote, and in his first book we have glimpses of how he understood a spirituality grounded on friendship in the midst of geographies of suffering.[13] These glimpses are most evident in three sets of epigraphs he employs in a few chapters of *AIDS and Accusation* (1992), all of them from the book of Job and from Gutiérrez's insights into Job. Below I analyze these epigraphs in their context. The first set invites us to think of friendship as a form of witnessing.

---

[8] Bruno Cadoré, "Foreword," *In the Company of the Poor*, viii.

[9] Cadoré, "Foreword," xi.

[10] Gustavo Gutiérrez, "Saying and Showing to the Poor: 'God Loves You,'" in *In the Company of the Poor*, 34.

[11] Gutiérrez, "Saying and Showing to the Poor," 34.

[12] *Partner to the Poor* is the title of the 2010 Paul Farmer reader published by University of California Press.

[13] Paul Farmer, "Conversion in the Time of Cholera," *In the Company of the Poor*, 100.

Theologians in the Field: "Dices que eres un teólogo, ¿cuál es tu practica?"

Epigraph 1[14]

When I lie down to sleep, the hours drag; I toss all night and long for dawn. My body is full of worms; it is covered with scabs; pus runs out of my sores. My days pass by without hope, pass faster than a weaver's shuttle (Job 7:4–6).

This cry cannot be muted. Those who suffer unjustly have a right to complain and protest. Their cry expresses both their bewilderment and their faith.[15]

To witness to the cry of those who suffer one must be close enough to hear. Farmer gifted to the world his capacity to witness to the complexity of human suffering and to the agonizing search for meaning. The chapter that accompanies this first set of epigraphs tells the story of Manno, one of the first residents of the Haitian village of Do Kay to die from AIDS in 1987. Manno's own story echoes Job's own bewilderment in trying to understand not only the nature of the illness but the way that it was embedded within—and altering—the social world of his communal existence. In the midst of suffering, the search for causation is pressing. Manno sought to know whether the cause was a "microbe," or whether it was "sorcery," or whether it was a microbe that was sent through sorcery. Farmer ends the chapter by reminding the reader of the many layers of causal possibilities that, though at times in opposition across cultures and religious frameworks, are all in fact united as part of the fabric that sustains both the complaint and the faith of those in agony.[16] As a friend of Manno and of the village of Do Kay, Farmer was a close witness to their struggle for meaning.

Epigraph 2[17]

Will no one teach you to be quiet—the only wisdom that becomes you! Kindly listen to my accusation and give your attention to the way I shall plead (Job 13:5–6).

If these men were to be silent and listen, they would demonstrate the wisdom they

---

[14] Paul Farmer, *AIDS and Accusation* (Berkeley, CA: University of California Press, 1992), 61.
[15] Gustavo Gutiérrez, *On Job: God-Talk and the Suffering of the Innocent* (Maryknoll, NY: Orbis Books, 1987), 101.
[16] Farmer, *AIDS and Accusation*, 79.
[17] Farmer, *AIDS and Accusation*, 80.

Theologians in the Field: "Dices que eres un teólogo, ¿cuál es tu practica?"

claim to possess. Those who experience at close range the sufferings of the poor, or of anyone who grieves and is abandoned, will know the importance of what Job is asking for. The poor and the marginalized have a deep-rooted conviction that no one is interested in their lives and misfortunes. They also have the experience of receiving deceptive expressions of concern from persons who in the end only make their problems all the worse.[18]

The chapter that accompanies these epigraphs tells the story of Anita, who is about twenty years old and is the second person in the village of Do Kay to die from AIDS in the spring of 1988. In the epigraph, Job is responding to his friends whom he has just called "worthless physicians" (Job 13:4) in their vain attempts to distill the complexity of his situation into a single explanation. In her village, Anita is the subject of many theories that attempt to make sense of her illness, though the villagers generally agree that she is "innocent,"[19] meaning that she could not have possibly brought envy or sorcery upon herself because all of her life has been one of misfortune. In the midst of the theories and discussions, Anita's godmother, Mme. Pasquet, takes Anita into her home and cares for her, healing her unto death, incarnating the vows she made twenty years prior when Anita was born. In the words of Mme. Pasquet, "a decent death is as important as a decent life. ... The child has had a hard life; her life has always been difficult. It's important that she be washed of bitterness and regret before she dies."[20] Farmer's moving description of Mme. Pasquet tending to a dying youth speaks of a contemplative silence that cuts right through all theories, bearing with it the gift of loving attention in the midst of affliction, communicating a presence that can heal the bitterness of life.[21]

---

[18] Gutiérrez, *On Job*, 24.
[19] Farmer, *AIDS and Accusation*, 87.
[20] Farmer, *AIDS and Accusation*, 90.
[21] Simone Weil claimed that attention is the rarest of gifts: "Not only does the love of God have attention for its substance; the love of our neighbor, which we know to be the same love, is made of this same substance....The capacity to give one's attention to a sufferer is a very rare

Theologians in the Field: "Dices que eres un teólogo, ¿cuál es tu practica?"

Epigraph 3[22]

Everything you say, I have heard before. I understand it all; I know as much as you do. I'm not your inferior. But my dispute is with God, not you; I want to argue my case with him (Job 13:1–3).

Job is not a patient man, at least not in the usual sense of the word. He is rather a rebellious believer. ... Job the rebel is a witness to peace and to the hunger and thirst for justice (those who live thus will one day be called 'blessed'); he is more than simply patient, he is a peace-loving man, a peacemaker.[23]

Farmer's last set of epigraphs frame the story of Dieudonné, whose name means "given by God." Dieudonné, Farmer says, was marked by an "independence of spirit" that led him to attempt to make a living in the city, working for the wealthy in Port-au-Prince until he fell ill and was forced to return to his village of Do Kay.[24] Convinced that an illness had been sent to him in the city out of jealousy, Dieudonné entered into a cycle of accusations and sorcery that blurred the boundaries between offensive and defensive magic, which adversely affected Dieudonné's location in the geography of blame in his village. Not unlike Job's predicament, in the social landscape of Do Kay, Dieudonné was caught in a web of retributive justice that could only be transcended by directly engaging the divine in the search for the truth of his tribulation. For Dieudonné, a divination ritual confirmed what he already suspected, that the illness had been sent to him, a confirmation that also gave him the space to reflect on the need to stop the cycles of jealousy that lead to death.[25] Farmer's use of the epigraphs in relation to Dieudonné convey that some struggles can only find a re/solution with the divine. But also, that in a world of vast inequality and injustice to be a friend of life is to enter into the struggle to

---

and difficult thing; it is almost a miracle; it is a miracle." Simone Weil, *Waiting for God* (New York: Harper Perennial, 1951), 64.
[22] Farmer, *AIDS and Accusation*, 95.
[23] Gutiérrez, *On Job*, 14.
[24] Farmer, *AIDS and Accusation*, 95.
[25] Farmer, *AIDS and Accusation*, 107.

know what it is that kills people before their time and to transform it.²⁶

Thus, as early as his first major work, Farmer began to incorporate a spirituality and theology of liberation that invited his readers to contemplate, medically and theologically, their place in the ecologies of injustice that ravage the life of the poor. The epigraphs are not simply theological adornments on a book primarily informed by medical anthropology but direct challenges for the readers of his primary disciplines to think beyond their fields in order to approximate ever more the weight and density of the world of the poor. This same challenge is also for theologians.

Following Jesus into the Field

Fieldwork is a way of dwelling with Jesus, of making one's home among the poor and insignificant. Farmer's long-term commitment to dwell with particular communities around the world, from Peru to Rwanda, but especially with the people of Haiti, invites theologians to ask about their own field and about the communities with whom they work. In theology departments in the United States, however, "theology" and what could be called "pastoral" work are still separated by a barbed wire fence that in the name of scholarship creates and replicates borders in a wider fertile landscape. More recently though, some theologians have turned to ethnographic fieldwork as a means of crossing these borders.²⁷ The interest in fieldwork, especially among younger generations of theologians, points

---

²⁶ For Farmer's deeper analysis of how sorcery in Haiti has to be understood in relation to structures of inequality, see his chapter "AIDS and Sorcery," in *AIDS and Accusation,* 193–207.

²⁷ See, for example, Todd Whitmore, *Imitating Christ in Magwi: An Anthropological Theology* (London: Bloomsbury, 2019); Sara Jean Barton, *Becoming the Baptized Body: Disability and the Practice of Christian Community* (Baylor, TX: Baylor University Press, 2022); Jasiy Joseph, "The Decentered Vision of Diaspora Space: Theological Ethnography, Migration, and the Pilgrim Church," *Practical Matters* 11 (2018): 88–102; Rachelle Green, "Ethnography as Critical Pedagogy: Prisons, Pedagogy, and Theological Education," in Knut Tveitereid and Pete Ward, eds., *The Wiley Blackwell Companion to Theology and Qualitative Research* (London, UK: Wiley, 2022), 38–48.

to the hunger generated by the separation of spirituality as the methodological foundation for theology.[28] Whether we call it a way, a method, a spirituality, or *lo pastoral*, all of these signifiers point, with their own particularities, to a historical encounter with the presence of God in the fractures and fissures of the world. It is an encounter that provides an experiential taste of the divine. But as ethnographic fieldwork makes its way into theology and as theologians make their way into the field, it is helpful to reflect on what Farmer and Gutiérrez offer theologians, especially those formed in the US and in the global north.

The colonial histories of anthropology, medicine, and theology all serve as an important reminder of the fraught landscape in which theologians engaged in fieldwork are moving. After all, theology has been placed at the service of imperial desires, justifying conquest as a baptism into (Christian) civilization.[29] As theologians turn to fieldwork, we must ask about the why and wherefore of this methodological adjustment. Farmer's reflections on his own disciplines are instructive:

> Anthropologists ... have long argued that their task is to observe rather than intervene, but this claim is undermined by the arguments that anthropology's supposed neutrality was in fact perceived by others, including those studied, as a small but at times integral part of the colonial project. So, too, researchers from the modern university are invariably actors in a social field, and medical ethicists who work across steep gradients of inequality are, all objections to the contrary notwithstanding, powerful actors when compared to those they study.[30]

The classical distinction and assumption of cultural, social, or political

---

[28] For Gutiérrez's classic explanation of this bifurcation, see Gutiérrez, *A Theology of Liberation*, xxxii.

[29] The *Requerimiento* ("notification") that was used in the forced baptisms of the indigenous peoples of the Americas is but one example. See Gustavo Gutiérrez, *Las Casas: In Search of the Poor of Jesus Christ* (Maryknoll, NY: Orbis Books, 1992), 103–125.

[30] Paul Farmer, "Rethinking Medical Ethics," in *Partner to the Poor: A Paul Farmer Reader*, ed. Haun Saussy (Berkeley: University of California Press, 2010), 483.

Theologians in the Field: "Dices que eres un teólogo, ¿cuál es tu practica?"

observation rather than intervention may be tempting for theologians who either romanticize the cultures, practices, or rituals they encounter, or those who for whatever reason feel a need to live into a mythical objective neutrality. As Farmer suggests though, the place from which one sees determines what and how one sees and, of course, how one is perceived by with whom one studies or works. All (scholarly) observation already participates in a history of violence.

Farmer worked to develop ways of observation and intervention that were life-giving. As a physician, Farmer was trained to intervene, to provide treatment to the sick, which in his contexts meant treating illnesses affecting the poor, but as an anthropologist, Farmer was also committed to placing medical interventions within a wider social and cultural context that did not lose sight of the political economies that generate the diseases of the poor. As he said, "I wanted to link 'experience-near' writing to an understanding of the larger structural underpinnings of lived experience in the places where I work[ed]."[31] It was his attention to the structures that created sickness among the poor that made his ethnographic observations a vital means for designing medical interventions that challenged the beliefs of the medical community in the US and Europe.[32] Too often, these medical communities place the blame for disease, and the failure of healing, upon the poor themselves. Without a sustained focus on structural factors one may not understand how the agency of the poor is constrained,[33] leaving them with no choice but to "live sicker and die quicker," as Linda Villarosa also argues in regards to poor communities in the US.[34] All of this points to the need for theologians, and especially those

---

[31] Paul Farmer, "Introduction to Part 1," in *Partner to the Poor*, 31.

[32] Barbara Rylko-Bauer and Paul Farmer understand structures as the "social relations and arrangements—economic, political, legal, religious, or cultural—that shape how individuals and groups interact within a social system." Barbara Rylko-Bauer and Paul Farmer, "Structural Violence, Poverty, and Social Suffering," in David Brady and Linda Burton, eds., *The Oxford Handbook of the Social Science of Poverty* (Oxford, UK: Oxford University Press, 2016), 47.

[33] Paul Farmer, "Social Scientists and the New Tuberculosis," in *Partner to the Poor*, 189.

[34] Linda Villarosa, *Under the Skin: The Hidden Toll of Racism on American Lives and on the Health of our Nation* (New York: Doubleday, 2022), 2.

engaged in fieldwork, to discern the ills of observation without intervention, while nonetheless being aware of the extractive histories and legacies of colonial(ist) interventions.

A brief anecdote from Gutiérrez similarly echoes the dangers that are present in observation that does not include a commitment to eradicating structures that deal death to the poor. A few years, ago in the midst of a conversation about early moments that shaped his thinking on poverty, Gutiérrez shared with me the story of reading a book while he was finishing his studies in Europe in the late 1950s. The book he was reading sought to emphasize the spiritual value—especially for religious orders—of imitating the poverty of Jesus by essentially imitating the poverty of the poor. Thinking particularly of white European missionaries to Latin America who sought to live with the poor without working against their poverty, Gutiérrez argued that from the perspective of the poor, one possible and disastrous interpretation was that it was actually good to be poor since those who were not insignificant, or in the words of Farmer, those who "work across steep gradients of inequality," were choosing to live like them without attending to the political economies of the context.[35] For Gutiérrez, an imitation of poverty that does not seek the transformation and eradication of poverty is against the gospel of Jesus Christ. Gutiérrez's notes on the margins of that book later helped him to develop three key distinctions for understanding poverty: real poverty as an historical evil; spiritual poverty as an openness to the following of Jesus; and poverty that arises from a voluntary and incarnate commitment to struggle against real poverty in solidarity with the poor.[36] Akin to Farmer's practice of fieldwork that intervenes against diseases that have made a radical

---

[35] For a more detailed narrative of this key moment in Gutiérrez's thinking on poverty, see Leo Guardado, "From Liberation Theology to (Liberationist) Peace Studies," *The International Journal of Conflict Engagement and Resolution* 4, no. 1 (2016), 17.

[36] These distinctions were codified, with Gutiérrez's influence, in the documents that resulted from the 1968 Bishops' conference in Medellín Colombia, documents that became foundational for liberation theologians then and now.

preferential option for the poor,[37] Gutiérrez's understanding of pastoral work is always oriented toward interrelated forms of structural, intellectual, and theological/spiritual liberation, and it is this orientation that can direct how and why theologians engage in fieldwork.

It would be reductive, without qualifications, to fully identify ethnographic fieldwork with the kind of pastoral work that Gutiérrez consistently centers in his theological work. Yet, in Latin America, one can point to a convergence or affinity between "lo pastoral" and "trabajo de campo" (fieldwork) because of the social and political histories of oppression that have demanded an interdependent relationship between the creation of theory/theology and the *dwelling with* communities from whom such theory/theology arises. Gutiérrez's pastoral work and Farmer's fieldwork certainly echo each other, but it is perhaps in the wider context of what is known as Participatory Action Research (PAR) that they also become uniquely resonant for a new generation of theologians in the US who are entering or are already engaged in the field. PAR accentuates aspects of both Farmer's and Gutiérrez's contributions by highlighting the nature of collaborative research in the struggle for a more dignified future.

Theologians Working the Fields

It is well known that accompaniment is a key concept and practice for both Farmer and Gutiérrez. In this last section, I reflect on accompaniment through the tradition of Participant Action Research (PAR) in order to emphasize the need in the US for more collaborative ways of creating theology/theory in relation to communities rendered insignificant. This is a critical way of continuing to bridge the division between theology and pastoral work. Typically associated with Orlando Fals Borda's work with the campesino communities on the Caribbean coast of Colombia in the 1970s, PAR is less a strict methodology and more of an approach or set of principles and commitments that are cultivated in the research process.[38]

---

[37] Paul Farmer, "Health, Healing, and Social Justice," in *In the Company of the Poor*, 36.
[38] Joanne Rappaport, *Cowards Don't Make History: Orlando Fals Borda and the Origins of Participatory Action Research* (Durham, NC: Duke University Press, 2020), xviii.

Theologians in the Field: "Dices que eres un teólogo, ¿cuál es tu practica?"

Although PAR has its own genealogy in the history of ideas and movements, it is part of that dynamic experimentation that took place in Latin America in the late twentieth century to break down the borders dividing theory and practice, "scientific" and "popular" knowledge, and scholarship and politics.

PAR was both influenced by liberation theology and influenced liberation theology. As Joanne Rappaport states, "Participatory analysis by working-class people and peasants was undertaken in the Christian base communities that arose out of liberation theology."[39] For these communities, PAR and liberation theology went hand in hand, for both placed the poor at the heart of the struggle for historical change. Fals Borda's close friendship with Camilo Torres, and Camilo Torres's close friendship with Gustavo Gutiérrez, also point to the interconnections between PAR and liberation theology.[40] There is also an affinity between Paul Farmer's practice of medical anthropology and the commitments of PAR,[41] and both make important interventions in how theologians can accompany and collaborate across fields.

One of the key commitments of PAR, as its name implies, is the creation of participatory processes. The aim is to overcome as much as possible, "the hierarchies that even today separate researchers from researched."[42] This means even questioning the justifications that a researcher (theologian) may have for their presence among a given

---

[39] Rappaport, *Cowards Don't Make History*, 13.

[40] Lomeli Robles, Dilean Jafte, and Joanne Rappaport, "Imagining Latin American Social Science from the Global South: Orlando Fals Borda and Participatory Action Research," *Latin American Research Review* 53, no. 3 (2018): 600. Gutiérrez and Torres, both priests, were classmates at the Catholic University of Louvain. Torres studied sociology and with Fals Borda helped establish the sociology department at the Universidad Nacional de Colombia.

[41] Some scholars frame Farmer's work as a model in health care of Participatory Action Research. See, for example, Elizabeth Shannon Wheatley and Eric Hartmann, "Participatory Action Research," in *Critical Approaches to Security: An Introduction to Theories and Methods* (New York: Routledge, 2013), 152.

[42] Robles, Jafte, and Rappaport, "Imagining Latin American Social Science from the Global South," 607.

Theologians in the Field: "Dices que eres un teólogo, ¿cuál es tu practica?"

community. Lest the research become yet one more extractive enterprise among the poor, the presence of a researcher in a given community needs to further the actual needs and desires of the community. Practically, the community itself ought to participate in the questions to be researched and in the design of the research.[43] Farmer, reflecting on two decades of work, illustrates this commitment when he says:

> I was never asked, in Haiti or in any of the other places in which we work, to do much in the way of *studying* suffering. In fact, I cannot remember a single such invitation from patients or their families. Instead, we were inundated in Haiti and elsewhere with a different sort of request: to *do* something to allay the awful suffering associated with these infectious diseases and with the host of other problems—hunger, malaria, death during childbirth, mistreatment at the hands of the powerful or less impoverished—that people afflicted with the new disease, AIDS, had long faced.[44]

The contrast between "studying" and "do[ing]" to which Farmer draws our attention not only highlights the destructive separation between theory and practice but, more importantly, argues for the primacy of listening to what communities themselves actually want and need. Consistent with the approach of PAR, he points to grassroots communities participating in the creation of the research agenda and in the discernment of what actions and changes could help alleviate suffering.

For theologians working in the field, Farmer invites us to resist the temptation to simply produce a theologically-attuned ethnography (or an

---

[43] Collaboratively developing participatory research structures is an ongoing process for Partners In Health (PIH), the organization that Paul Farmer helped establish in the 1980s. PIH in Peru, known there as Socios en Salud, was established in 1996, but it was not until 2013 that they developed their first Comité Asesor Comunitario (Community Advisory Committee) for tuberculosis, which assesses, with the input of those most affected, the kinds of research and interventions that are needed. See Socios en Salud, *Reporte Anual 2020*, 99, sociosensalud.org.pe/noticias/memoria-anual/.

[44] Paul Farmer, "From Haiti to Rwanda," in *Partner to the Poor*, 138.

ethnographically-attuned theology) and instead to enter into a dialogue with the communities with whom we research to collaboratively discern what in fact would be a contribution to the community and its priorities, including political priorities.[45] In Farmer's words, this is a "pragmatic solidarity," one that "responds to the needs expressed by the people and communities who are living, and sometimes dying, on the edge."[46] Otherwise, research can easily remain a one-way path, where valued goods flow unidirectionally and where the chasm between researcher and researched expands even further rather than heals.

The point is not for theologians to imitate the work of Paul Farmer but to pay attention to how he carried out his work of healing, to learn from the knowledge and wisdom that the sick and the poor bear, and to understand what is in fact needed to heal. In reading Farmer's early work in Haiti, one is struck by how firmly he located biological disease within the experience of social ills, as well as by his profound recognition and respect of what some Participant Action Researchers call a "diálogo de saberes," a dialogue of knowledges.[47]

The haunting references to the construction of the Péligre hydroelectric dam that displaced thousands of people in the Central Plateau of Haiti in the mid-1950s is one such example of this attunement to the knowledge of the afflicted. In interviews with the residents of Do Kay in the 1980s, which given his medical work were often focused on how tuberculosis or other diseases were affecting them, the dam would appear as a source of illness and poverty. People who were forcibly displaced knew, through their lived experience and that of their families, that the dam generated not electricity for their squatter settlement but rather "malignant emotions" that were killing them.[48] Decades later, reflecting on

---

[45] Rappaport, *Cowards Don't Make History*, 7.
[46] Paul Farmer, "Rethinking Health and Human Rights," in *Partner to the Poor*, 450.
[47] Rappaport, *Cowards Don't Make History*, 221.
[48] In "Bad Blood, Spoiled Milk," in *Partner to the Poor*, 34, Farmer describes malignant emotions as "anger born of interpersonal strife, shock, grief, chronic worry, and other affects perceived as potentially harmful."

those early interviews, Farmer recognized even more clearly the vital importance not only of dialoguing with the knowledge of afflicted communities but of letting their knowledge intervene in attempts to understand disease and healing. He wrote, "Mme. Gracia was among those who chided me gently for paying attention to issues that were less pressing than the need for water, health care, and education. That was it for me. I knew Mme. Gracia was right."[49] Simply, Mme. Gracia, whose name in French means "grace," had instructed Farmer not to forget recent history—the construction of the dam, a so-called "development" project, and how it adversely impacted the poor.

Healing is never simply biological. Farmer always spoke of disease in "biosocial" terms, as "a composite event-process,"[50] and thus healing too is biosocial, a composite event-process in which theology is already implicated as communities resist all that kills. The task is to discern, in the midst of accompaniment and immersed in the ecology of knowledges that mark pastoral fieldwork,[51] which interventions will in fact contribute to healing and which will only intensify suffering. Farmer was keenly aware that his medical knowledge was simply one among other knowledges needed to begin a healing dialogue. The same disciplinary humility is demanded for theology. Yet, these and other fields are vital, and must be worked, in the company of God who is already working there, collaborating for life with a wounded humanity.

Conclusion

These brief reflections on Farmer, Gutiérrez, and the gifts and challenges of theologians in the field have sought to contemplate some aspects of their methodologies and the relevance of these approaches for scholars in the global north who seek to rebind theological reflection with

---

[49] Paul Farmer, "Introduction to Part 1," in *Partner to the Poor*, 30.
[50] Paul Farmer, "Introduction to Part 2," in *Partner to the Poor*, 153–154.
[51] For more on ecology of knowledges, see Boaventura de Sousa Santos, *The End of the Cognitive Empire: The Coming of Age of Epistemologies of the South* (Durham, NC: Duke University Press, 2018), 32.

its natural source—the following of Jesus, his witnessing unto death with the insignificant of history, and the sharing in resurrection with all who struggle for life. As theologians embrace what has been termed "the ethnographic turn in theology and ethics,"[52] the challenge facing previous generations of theologians and ethicists remains—to recognize that the political nature of all research demands an accounting for how the research in which we engage furthers the reign of life that is the orienting principle of all Christian theology. Farmer translated this principle into his medical anthropology, and his friendship with communities enduring sickness and poverty transformed and refined his practice.

Time is the essence of friendship. One could say that Farmer died too early or before his time, sentiments that certainly capture the enormous loss of Farmer's life. But the time that he did have was gifted over and over to the communities he loved, a practice that he developed early on in his studies and that continued right to his last day. In *The Little Prince*, one of Gutiérrez's favorite stories, the fox who wants to establish ties—friendship—with the little prince says to him, "People haven't time to learn anything. They buy things ready-made in stores. But since there are no stores where you can buy friends, people no longer have friends."[53] The fox's processual wisdom is an instructive reminder that friendship is built on the understanding that comes through shared time in a mutual commitment to each other's fullness of life.

For some theologians, much of the time spent in fieldwork will seem unproductive, perhaps a waste of time, but this is exactly what is needed in order to begin to imagine a different way of faith seeking understanding beyond the regulated borders of knowledge, the walls of academia, or the dominant politics of the day. For the writer of the Gospel of John, friendship is nothing less than the offering of one's life for others (John 15:12), the offering of the time one has received gratuitously, that we are

---

[52] See, for example, chapter two in Christian Scharen and Aana Marie Vigen, eds., *Ethnography as Christian Theology and Ethics* (New York: Continuum, 2011).

[53] Antoine de Saint-Exupéry, *The Little Prince,* trans. Richard Howard (New York: Harcourt, 2000), 60.

called to give away gratuitously. It is through this extravagant logic of the way of friendship that our understandings of pastoral work, or participant action research, or theology, must pass. It is then that we will have a credible and incarnate response to the question of our theological practice.

Leo Guardado, **PhD**, Salvadoran by birth, is an Assistant Professor in the Department of Theology at Fordham University. His research is focused on theological responses to the violence of forced migration, especially from Latin America. More particularly, Guardado writes on the tradition of church sanctuary, its relation to the 1980s Sanctuary Movement, and the ecclesiological implications of a church of the poor and persecuted in the US. Guardado also conducts qualitative research on the role of indigenous healing practices among migrant communities in New York City. Guardado received his BA from St. Mary's College of California, and his MTS and PhD from the University of Notre Dame.

Chapter 7: Liberating Theological Ethics from the Invisible Hand: Paul Farmer, the World's Poor, and the Quandaries of the Fortunate

M. Therese Lysaught

> Take a look at "medical ethics," a staple of medical school curricula. What is defined, these days, as an ethical issue? End-of-life decisions, medicolegal questions of brain death and organ transplantation, and medical disclosure issues dominate the published literature. In the hospital, the quandary ethics of the individual constitute most of the discussion of medical ethics....How do you make a clear distinction between life and death, between death and prolonged coma, between two technologies with near-even chances of failure? These are subtle decisions and have weighty consequences. I would be the last to trivialize them. But their formulation assumes a great many givens—a wealth of clinical alternatives, a battery of life-support mechanisms, access to potentially unlimited care. These are the quandaries of the fortunate.
>
> Paul Farmer, Pathologies of Power [1]

The "quandaries of the fortunate"—those words arced off the page like a flaming arrow, piercing the heart of my identity as a Catholic bioethicist. When I first read them in 2004, I had worked in the field of bioethics for over a dozen years. Add a heavy dose of gene therapy, genetic engineering, and stem cell research, and the above passage almost mirrored my scholarship and my syllabus. Granted, I sought to examine such issues

---

[1] Paul Farmer, *Pathologies of Power; Health, Human Rights, and the New War on the Poor* (Los Angeles: University of California Press, 2003), 175.

theologically, with some attention to their socio-economic dimensions.[2] But this phrase—the quandaries of the fortunate—crystalized for me a long-felt, nagging unease: that as trained by my discipline, I was propagating a discourse of the privileged to and for the privileged that helped them recursively reproduce structures of privilege and, correlatively and invisibly, structures of oppression.

That flaming arrow torched my *oeuvre*. I threw out my syllabus and started over from scratch. But its fire of judgement served equally as an illuminating light. Like infra-red night vision goggles, this phrase and Farmer's wider corpus made visible for me the determinative yet never-mentioned role of political economy not only for shaping illness, health, and health care delivery, but also in shaping the narrow range of what are considered "ethical issues" by mainstream US (and often, global) bioethics. In addition, I began to see how economics—particularly neoliberal economics—has shaped the conceptual apparatus of bioethics and, thereby, has subsequently reinforced neoliberal assumptions in health care and our broader social context.

Once one begins to see how neoliberalism has infused sectors not usually considered strictly economic—such as medicine and bioethics—the pervasiveness of its influence begins to come into greater focus. In this chapter, I suggest that Farmer's work—in relentlessly foregrounding the subterranean yet determinative role of neoliberalism in medicine and bioethics—presses us to ask: in what ways does it equally enthrall the disciplines of theology and theological ethics? In the first section, I briefly outline the key claims of neoliberal economics and highlight Farmer's critiques of how economic and neoliberal concepts have shaped the field of global health. I then detail how these concepts have pervaded the field

---

[2] A key early text for both my teaching and research was *Not All of Us Are Saints: A Doctor's Journey with the Poor* (New York: Random House, 1996), David Hilfiker's autobiographical account of practicing medicine among and with the homeless in Washington, DC that has deep resonances with Farmer's international counterpart. For my first encounter with Hilfiker's work see M. Therese Lysaught, "Who is My Neighbor? Commentary on David Hilfiker's Case Story," *Second Opinion* 18 (1992): 59–66, ecommons.luc.edu/ips_facpubs/10/.

of bioethics, perhaps even constituting the discipline from its inception and, perhaps, subtly positioning it as a tool for the neoliberalization of global health care. I then turn the lens to theological ethics, asking: has our discipline, too, been shaped by this invisible hand? If so, what can we do about it?

Political Economy as Root Cause Analysis

Farmer's attention to economics is just one piece of the rigorous analytical framework he developed to "discern the nature of structural violence and explore its contribution to human suffering."[3] Such a framework, which fused the insights of medical anthropology with those of liberation theology, must be, as he reiterated again and again, "geographically broad" and "historically deep," while simultaneously considering "various social 'axes' [in order to] discern a political economy of brutality."[4] A first step in his analysis was always to ask: how could the suffering of a particular patient in front of him be traced to the ways that the global neoliberal political economy had reshaped both local socio-economic contexts and health care delivery writ large? Such analyses, he maintained, provided a truer etiology for specific diseases—both in their individual manifestation and global footprints—and thereby were necessary for developing actually effective solutions.[5]

---

[3] Farmer, *Pathologies of Power*, 42.

[4] Farmer, *Pathologies of Power*, 42–43. These axes include gender, race/ethnicity, and any other social or biological construct that "can serve as a pretext for discrimination and thus as a cause of suffering," such as refugee or immigrant status, and sexual preference.

[5] In other words, Farmer's methodology moves recursively back and forth between thickly described stories of particular patients and "the larger matrix of culture, history, and political economy" (*Pathologies of Power*, 41), detailing how political economy materially manifests itself in the bodies of the poor, with ripple effects across the lives of their families, communities, and countries. We see this from his earliest analyses of AIDS (*AIDS and Accusation: Haiti and the Geography of Blame* [Berkley: University of California Press, 1992]; *Women, Poverty, and AIDS: Sex, Drugs, and Structural Violence* [Monroe, ME: Common Courage Press, 1996]) to his final book on the Ebola epidemic (*Fevers, Feuds, and Diamonds: Ebola and the Ravages of History* [New York: Farrar, Straus, and Giroux, 2020]), and at every point in between. Across his corpus, he demonstrates how, in getting to true root causes, such

Liberating Theological Ethics from the Invisible Hand

For those unfamiliar with neoliberalism, I begin with a brief history and conceptual overview. Birthed around the mid-1930s in Austria and developed over the course of the twentieth century through the work of the Chicago School of Economics and its European counterparts, neoliberalism catapulted to dominance in the global economic order around 1980 with the allied political programs of Ronald Reagan in the US and Margaret Thatcher in the United Kingdom.[6] Via the Washington Consensus, as this alliance was known, global economic policy administered through the international financial institutions established in the post-World War II era—the World Bank, the International Monetary Fund, and their satellite organizations—was radically reshaped to prioritize neoliberal philosophy and policies.

Neoliberalism has two key planks. The first is its anthropology, which imagines the human person as a radically individual chooser who must be free to maximize his preferences. I will discuss this anthropology further in the next section. The second plank is a corollary of this anthropology, namely, the radical minimization of government. Thus, neoliberalism relentlessly seeks to dismantle or delegitimate governmental structures, as well as any other robust social or community entities—such as schools, churches, unions, local economies—which might theoretically impede the freedom of the market. This anti-government ideology extends to all areas, save one: protecting the market's freedom. Neoliberal economists, as Michel Foucault notes, argue for an "active, multiple, vigilant, and

---

an economic "epidemiology" might help to generate new and effective solutions for ending endemic structural suffering.

[6] For a succinct overview of the history and conceptual outline of neoliberalism, see Jim Yong Kim, Joyce V. Millen, and Alec Irwin, *Dying for Growth: Global Inequality and the Health of the Poor* (Monroe, ME: Common Courage Press, 2002). For more in-depth analyses of neoliberalism, see Wendy Brown, *Undoing the Demos: Neoliberalism's Stealth Revolution* (Cambridge, MA: MIT Press, 2015); David Harvey, *A Brief History of Neoliberalism* (Oxford: Oxford University Press, 2008); and David Stedman Jones, *Masters of the Universe: Hayek, Friedman, and the Birth of Neoliberal Politics* (Princeton: Princeton University Press, 2013).

omnipresent" government intervention aimed at creating the possibility for a market economy.⁷

Neoliberalism seeks to limit government via three key dogmas: deregulation, liberalization, and privatization. Since the late 1970s, these commitments have shaped the internal policies of the G-20 nations and formed the heart of "structural adjustment programs," sometimes referred to as "austerity" measures, that have been imposed on countries seeking global financial assistance. Thus, neoliberal regimes focus on eliminating regulations (ranging from safety measures to minimum wage laws to financial accountability), "liberalizing" or opening borders to maximize the free and efficient flow of capital (but notably not the free movement of people), and selling government-owned public goods (such as utilities, schools, health care institutions, etc.) to private, for-profit companies.

The extractive and socially-destructive impacts of neoliberalism have devastated local communities across the globe, fueling the global rise in reactive populism.⁸ It has also undermined health and health care across the globe in three key ways: (1) it has materially impacted the structures of health care delivery and other socio-economic sectors that affect the health and well-being of the poorest and most marginal, such as agriculture, labor, education, and economies generally; (2) it has infiltrated the conceptual infrastructure of health care delivery; and (3) it has, in an allied way, transformed clinical rationality. Let me take each of these in turn, drawing where relevant on Farmer's work.

First, Farmer and his colleagues have relentlessly documented the material impact of neoliberal economic policies on the health and well-being of the poorest and most marginal via detailed studies of specific patients and communities (what anthropologists refer to as "thick description").⁹ For example, structural adjustment conditions attached to

---

⁷ Michel Foucault, *The Birth of Biopolitics* (New York: Picador Press, 2010), 160.
⁸ See, for example, Brian Elliott, *The Roots of Populism: Neoliberalism and Working-Class Lives* (Manchester, UK: Manchester University Press, 2021).
⁹ Farmer's work, as well as that of his colleagues, consistently details case studies that document the myriad of ways that complex historical and contemporary interactions between

the international financing needed by many post-colonial countries have required the dismantling—or privatizing—of public education and public health systems. "Liberalization"—requiring "open" borders and integrating "developing" or "resource poor" countries into global markets—has destroyed local agricultural economies (and therefore food self-sufficiency) and multiplied deeply oppressive, nationally-neutral "free trade zones," geographical areas within countries where transnational corporations can outsource sweatshop-like work. Deregulation has prohibited independent countries from establishing laws protecting minimum wage, benefits, or conditions for safe and humane working conditions in these zones. Dislocating workers from substantive communities of family, care, and support, such structures have exacerbated mental health issues and disease epidemics.

In addition to these macroeconomic policies, Farmer documents how neoliberal commitments have infused the conceptual infrastructure of health care delivery. He targets terms such as "cost-effective," "sustainability," "replicability," "efficiency," as well the now-ubiquitous and endless emphasis on "controlling costs." While such concepts seem reasonable or unassailable on their face, Farmer unpacks how they subtly import problematic philosophical presuppositions. "Cost-effectiveness," for example, does not function as a simple counsel of prudence; it presumes that the utility function—the central commitment of neoliberal capitalism—is ironclad, even if maximizing economic utility means that actual people will suffer or die.[10] Similarly, the efforts of Partners In Health

---

international politics, economic policies, and transnational corporation have served as an underlying etiology for individual illness and have fueled horrific disparities in morbidity and mortality across economic gradients. These case studies provide templates for the kind of thick description that should ground work in theological ethics.

[10] As Farmer notes, "The tools of my trade—again, I'm an infectious-disease doc—have been termed 'not cost-effective' in an era in which money is worshipped so ardently that it's difficult to attack market logic without being called a fool or irresponsible. Treating AIDS in a place like rural Haiti, which lacks health infrastructure, is dismissed as 'unsustainable' or not 'appropriate technology.' Each of these ideas, from cost-effectiveness to sustainability, could be a means of starting conversations or ending them. But in my experience in international

to provide medications to patients with HIV or multidrug resistant TB was criticized for being "unsustainable" due to the cost of such medications and treatment regimens.[11] Farmer himself was frequently chided for the "inefficiencies" in his approach to patient care—for spending "excessive" time with particular patients or walking seven hours to make a home visit in Haiti.[12] As his analysis makes clear, the overarching conceptual framework structuring health care delivery distills and encapsulates economic commitments which take priority over people.[13]

This transformation of the conceptual structure of health care delivery—captured in its language—is thorough-going. As Farmer notes:

> It's complex, but suffice it to say that neoliberal approaches to public health and medicine involve the commodification and privatization of our services so that they become "products" to be purchased by "consumers." Patients become "clients" or even "customers." Public service becomes private enterprise—that's the neoliberal dream. I don't

---

health, arguing that treatment is not cost-effective is largely a means of ending unwelcome conversations about the destitute sick" (*To Repair the World* [Berkley: University of California Press, 2019], 16; and similarly, 39). Again: "But this mantra was repeated without honest investigation of *why* the drugs, long off patent, were so expensive. Thus has the notion of cost-effectiveness become one of the chief means by which we manage (and perpetuate) modern inequality" (*Pathologies of Power*, 125, emphasis in original); "Certainly, distributing these developments equitably would be expensive. Certainly, excess costs must be curbed. But how can we glibly use terms like 'cost-effective' when we see how they are perverted in contemporary parlance? You want to help the poor? Then your projects must be 'self-sustaining' or 'cost-effective.' You want to erase the poor? Hey, knock yourself out. The sky's the limit!" (*Pathologies of Power*, 177).

[11] See, for example, Haun Saussy, "Introduction," *A Partner to the Poor: A Paul Farmer Reader*, ed. Haun Saussy (Berkeley and Los Angeles: University of California Press, 2010), 7, 11, and 13.

[12] Kidder, *Mountains Beyond Mountains*, 293–294. Kidder quotes Farmer: "If you say that seven hours is too long to walk for two families of patients, you're saying that their lives matter less than some others, and the idea that some lives matter less is the root of all that's wrong with the world" (294).

[13] Such conceptual commitments frame even "development" thinking, the "health transition model," and "social entrepreneurship." For Farmer's critiques of these approaches see *Pathologies of Power*, 155–157; and *To Repair the World*, 39–40.

know if the commodification of public health is bad for everyone, but I know from long years in Haiti that it's bad for those who have no purchasing power: the poor. Those with no purchasing power tend to be the very same souls who bear the greatest burden of disease.[14]

While Farmer's focus has largely been on the poorest and most marginal communities across the globe, his insights apply equally to the US context. Where the Washington Consensus drove an agenda which largely dismantled universal health systems across the Global South, it did not simply export its vision across the world. It also targeted health care in the US, catalyzing a shift toward for-profit models and practices in health care delivery (even in "non-profit" health care), starting (again) just before 1980.[15] Prior to this, as David Feldman has detailed, the US medical system was highly regulated, but through the combined agency of government and private sector forces, a new regime of deregulation, market competition, direct-to-consumer marketing, and more, radically reshaped US health care delivery within a decade.[16] The result has been the

---

[14] Farmer, *To Repair the World*, 131. Or, as he says decades earlier, rather than understanding health care as a fundamental good or human right, "commodified medicine invariably begins with the notion that health is a desirable outcome to be attained through the purchase of the right goods and services" (*Pathologies of Power*, 152).

[15] Given the decimation of health care in rural communities across the US, one could argue that the long-term outcome of the neoliberalization of health care in the US has been the same as in LIMCs—the effective dismantling of the public—and private—health care system. See, for example, Michael Ollove, "Rural America's Health Crisis Seizes States' Attention," *Pew Research Center*, January 31, 2020, www.pewtrusts.org/en/research-and-analysis/blogs/stateline/2020/01/31/rural-americas-health-crisis-seizes-states-attention. Notably, this piece was published prior to the COVID-19 pandemic, which both illustrated the problem and further exacerbated it.

[16] David Feldman, "The Emergence of Market Competition in the US Health Care System: Its Causes, Likely Structure, and Implications," *Health Policy* 6 (1996): 1–20. See also Samantha Sterba, *Neoliberal Capitalism and the Evolution of the US Healthcare System* (Doctoral Dissertation, U. Mass Amherst, December 18, 2020); and "Adam Gaffney, "The Neoliberal Turn in American Health Care," *International Journal of Health Services* 45, no. 1 (2015): 33–52. For an articulation of the relentless neoliberal agenda in health care see US Department of Health and Human Services, US Department of the Treasury, and US

transformation of every sector from mental health care, clinical trials, pharmaceuticals, to long-term care, and more with an attendant and unsurprising decline in health outcomes.[17] Even the Patient Portability and Affordable Care Act (also known as Obamacare) privileged competition and market mechanisms as the way to increase access to health insurance and, thereby, to health care.[18]

A third way that neoliberalism has negatively impacted human health and well-being is probably the most subtle: by transforming clinical reasoning. For example, as Bruce Rogers-Vaughn has helpfully illuminated, the neoliberal commitment to privatization has not only driven the dismantling of public health systems. It has also translated into shift toward "methodological individualism" in clinical practice—an approach which locates the causes, and therefore, solutions, for all illness and behaviors within individuals rather than in social structures.[19] Thus,

---

Department of Labor, *Reforming America's Healthcare System Through Choice and Competition* (2017): www.hhs.gov/sites/default/files/Reforming-Americas-Healthcare-System-Through-Choice-and-Competition.pdf.

[17] For just a sampling of the literature see: Bruce Rogers-Vaughn, *Caring for Souls in a Neoliberal Age* (New York: Palgrave-Macmillan, 2016); Jill A. Fisher, *Medical Research for Hire: The Political Economy of Pharmaceutical Clinical Trials* (New Brunswick, NJ: Rutgers University Press, 2008); Edward Nik-Khah, "Neoliberal Pharmaceutical Science and the Chicago School of Economics," *Social Studies of Science* 44, no. 4 (2014): 489–517; Vincente Navarro, "The Consequences of Neoliberalism in the Current Pandemic," *Institutional Journal of Health Services* 50, no. 3 (2020): doi.org/10.1177/0020731420925449; and Haran N. Ratna, "Medical Neoliberalism and the Decline in US Healthcare Quality," *Journal of Hospital Management and Health Policy* 4 (2020): doi.org/10.21037/jhmhp.2020.01.0.

[18] Among other targets, Farmer singles out investor-owned health insurance plans noting that: "despite much talk of 'cost effectiveness' or 'reform,' the primary feature of this transformation has been the consolidation of a major industry with the same goal as other industries: to turn a profit" (*Pathologies of Power*, 163).

[19] Rogers-Vaughn, *Caring for Souls in a Neoliberal Age*. Rogers-Vaughn examines the impact of neoliberalism on the fields of psychiatry and behavioral health, marking a shift ~1980 from approaches that emphasized social approaches to psychiatric care toward those that located the cause of the problem within the patient—in their DNA or neurotransmitters—biological loci that were then targets for market-based pharmaceutical or clinical interventions. Likewise, liberalization grounds the increased clinical focus on 'economic efficiency'—privileging technological, product-based interventions that generate profits for corporations as more

since the 1970s, scientific research and clinical medicine have sought to find causes for illness within individual bodies—within, for example, genes, neurotransmitter imbalances, perhaps now the microbiome. Such biological targets not only deflect attention from social factors; they also provide sites for profitable pharmacological interventions.[20]

This methodological individualism is at the heart of Farmer's critiques of the "immodest claims of causality" that underly global approaches to most diseases. Consider, he suggests:

> the received wisdom—and the current agenda—concerning tuberculosis. Authorities rarely blame the recrudescence of tuberculosis on the inequalities that structure our society. Instead, we hear mostly about biological factors (the advent of HIV, the mutations that lead to drug resistance) or about cultural and psychological barriers [located within individual patients] that result in 'noncompliance.' Through these two sets of explanatory mechanisms, one can expediently attribute high rates of treatment failure either to the organism or to uncooperative patients. There are costs to seeing the problem in this way. If we see the resurgence or persistence of tuberculosis as an exclusively biological phenomenon, then we will shunt available resources to basic biological research which, though needed, is not the primary solution, since almost all tuberculosis deaths result from lack of access to existing effective therapy. If we see the problem primarily as one of patient noncompliance, then we must

---

'cost-effective' than time-consuming, inefficient relationships between patients and practitioners. See also Sanah Assan, "I'm a Psychologist—and I Believe We've Been Told Devastating Lies About Mental Health," The Guardian, September 6, 2022, www.theguardian.com/commentisfree/2022/sep/06/psychologist-devastating-lies-mental-health-problems-politics. For an account of neoliberalism's effects on the related field of neuroscience, see Jeffrey P. Bishop, M. Therese Lysaught, and Andrew Michels, *Biopolitics After Neuroscience: Morality and the Economy of Virtue* (London: Bloomsbury Academic, 2022).

[20] As Alexandre A. Martins has helpfully noted, this methodological individualism also undergirds the US approach to health care, which is hospital-centered and deflects attention from other social factors or sectors.

necessarily ground our strategies in plans to change the patients rather than to change the weak tuberculosis control programs.[21]

Farmer debunked this methodological individualism in tuberculosis treatment via a simple clinical trial piloted in Haiti in 1989. One group of patients in the clinical trial received free standard TB treatment; a second group received free standard TB treatment as well as a surround of social supports—financial assistance ($30/month for three months), nutritional supplements, incentives to attend a monthly clinic (monthly reminders and travel expenses for clinic visits), and regular home visits by trained community health workers.[22] The latter approach had been recommended by community health workers but resisted by Western-trained physicians. The outcomes were statistically significant: 100 percent of the patients in the second group were cured and none died, while only 57 percent were cured and 10 percent died in the treatment-only group. For Farmer, this simple and inexpensive clinical trial confirmed that "in determining the efficacy of efforts to combat disease...many of the most important variables...are all strongly influenced by *economic* factors."[23]

In sum, a key legacy of Farmer's work is a commitment to rigorously illuminating the explicit and implicit ways that economic ideologies and policies shape both the practical and conceptual infrastructure of global health care delivery. If, per Farmer, neoliberalism has so startingly pervaded the practical and conceptual frameworks of global health delivery and has likewise transformed—or, rather—malformed—clinical rationality, could that health care-adjacent field—bioethics—have escaped unscathed? Or might it be that his critique of bioethics as "the quandaries of the fortunate" gestures toward something deeper?

---

[21] Farmer, *Pathologies of Power*, 147-148.
[22] Paul Farmer, S. Robin, S.L. Ramilus, and Jim Yong Kim, "Tuberculosis, Poverty, and 'Compliance': Lessons from Rural Haiti," *Seminar Respiratory Infections* 6, no. 4 (Dec. 1991): 254–260.
[23] Farmer, *Pathologies of Power*, 151.

The Option for the Rich: US Bioethics as a Neoliberal Project

History again provides a starting point. Bioethics, as most practitioners know, is a relatively young discipline, emerging as the discipline we now know in the US in the mid-to-late 1960s.[24] Via a series of government commissions convened during the 1970s, a normative scaffold for bioethics was developed and promulgated in the 1979 Belmont Report. As I have narrated elsewhere, this scaffold quickly—and somewhat inexplicably—morphed in 1980 into what popularly became known as the "Georgetown Mantra," an approach that spread virally to become the dominant framework for bioethics in the US and, subsequently, across the globe.[25] Although classically described as a four-principle framework, centering the principles of autonomy, beneficence, justice, and nonmaleficience, a fifth principle was present from the start: utility, a generally-unnamed partner whose elision is not insignificant.

Given the history narrated earlier, one must ask: is it simply a coincidence that the dominant conceptual framework for bioethics emerged in 1980—at the moment that neoliberalism became the dominant global economic (and eventually social) ideology? Of course, correlation does not equal causation, but this correlation presses us to examine the question further. Since a detailed analysis of this question is beyond the scope of this paper, I simply highlight three aspects of the field that suggest a need for further study.

First, the operative conceptual framework of bioethics largely distills neoliberal logic. Although theoretically five principles should be in play, over time, two have come to dominate bioethics in practice: autonomy and utility. Bioethics, as it emerged from the 1970s, conceptualized the patient as an autonomous subject, a rational agent empowered to choose amongst

---

[24] For one of those canonical histories, see Albert Jonsen, *The Birth of Bioethics* (New York: Oxford University Press, 1998).
[25] M. Therese Lysaught, "Respect: or, How Respect for Persons Became Respect for Autonomy," *Journal of Medicine and Philosophy* 29, no. 6 (2004): 665–80, doi.org/10.1080/03605310490883028.

an array of medical options (an analogy for commodities?) as a way of pursuing the good as they define it. The primary tool for decision-making—not only for the patient, but equally for physicians, ethics consultants, hospitals, and health systems—is the principle of utility, operationalized as cost-benefit analysis, a variant of "cost-effectiveness." Thus, the operative anthropology in bioethics is that of neoliberalism—a rational chooser who freely maximizes utility-based preferences.

From the start, this anthropology catalyzed bioethics as a growth-industry, seeding an endless series of quandaries and dilemmas. Why? Because, of course, many (most?) patients have lost (temporarily or permanently) or not yet attained the ability to be rational, utility-preference-maximizing choosers. Thus, from the outset, bioethics has been premised on a bifurcated anthropology, with some humans meeting the criteria for fully-functioning persons—whose rights to choose their own good is sacrosanct—and a wide-swath of others who lack that ability, and whose status as persons is correlatively called into question.[26] I return to this point shortly.

In addition, as bioethics has extended its sway as a global normative framework, the discipline has more explicitly embodied neoliberalism's three dogmas. The individualism presupposed by the anthropology of bioethics has been deepened by the neoliberal commitment to privatization. Incarnating Rogers-Vaughn's 'methodological individualism,' every decision is the patient's alone, inherently private, cut off from even family or community, except by choice (e.g., HIPAA regulations).[27] Likewise, as physicians have morphed into providers and

---

[26] See, for example, another now-canonical text in the field, H. Tristram Engelhardt's *The Foundation of Bioethics* (New York: Oxford University Press, 1996), where he actually proposes a five-tiered anthropology based on individuals' rational abilities.

[27] The flip side of this is responsibilization—a feature of neoliberal ethics where responsibility for actions previously under the aegis of social or political agents is relocated to the character or agency of the individual. For example, contemporary rhetoric might responsibilize victims of gun violence who refuse to arm themselves (Trent Steidley, "Sharing the Monopoly on Violence? Shall-Issue Concealed Handgun License Laws and Responsiblization," *Sociological Perspectives* 62, no.6 (2019): 929–947, doi.org/10.1177/073112141986), or even road safety

patients into consumers, resistance to government limits on patient preferences has increased. Thus, a key focus of secular bioethics has been the deregulation of medical practice and clinical research—e.g., from challenges to traditional prohibitions on euthanasia or physician-assisted suicide, to the ongoing challenges to regulatory oversight over practices like embryonic stem-cell research or commercial products posed by bodies such as the FDA, sometimes in the name of market efficiency and innovation, though often framed in terms of 'saving lives.'[28] And, the dogma of liberalization underlies arguments facilitating the push to open new markets for reproductive services, organs, and human research subjects.[29]

Second, an argument could be made that the neoliberal logic of bioethics is not accidental; rather, since the 1980s, it has served to facilitate the neoliberalization of medicine described earlier, in part, by masking the thorough-going economization of the sector. Since health care delivery began to shift to for-profit logics in the 1980s, the sector and its many subcomponents have experienced explosive growth. In the US, health care expenditures grew from ~$684 billion in 1980 (adjusted 2020 dollars) to

---

(Erik Hysing, "Responsiblilization: The Case of Road Safety Governance," *Regulation and Governance* 15 (2021): 356–336, doi.org/10.1111/rego.12288), and everything in between.

[28] For just a few examples from the vast literatures on these topics, see: L. Doyal, "Why Active Euthanasia and Physician Assisted Suicide Should be Legalised," *BMJ* 323, no. 7321 (2001): 1079–1080, doi.org/10.1136/bmj.323.7321.1079; Alexander M. Capron, "Stem Cell Politics: The New Shape to the Road Ahead," *AJOB* 2, no. 1 (2002): 35–37, doi.org/10.1162/152651602317267835; and. James J. Hughes, "A Defense of Limited Regulation of Human Genetic Therapies," *Cambridge Quarterly Healthcare Ethics* 28, no. 1 (2019): 112–120, doi.org/10.1017/S0963180118000440.

[29] Again for just a few examples from the significant literatures on these topics, see: Casey Humbyrd, "Fair Trade International Surrogacy," *Developing World Bioethics* 9, no. 3 (2009): 111–118, doi.org/10.1111/j.1471-8847.2009.00257.x; Charles A. Erin and John Harris, "An Ethical Market in Human Organs," *Journal of Medical Ethics* 29, no. 3 (2003): 137–138, doi.org/10.1136/jme.29.3.137; and Rosamond Rhodes, "Rethinking Research Ethics," *American Journal of Bioethics* 5, no. 1 (2005): 7–28, doi.org/10.1080/15265160590900678.

$4,124 billion in 2020—a growth of 600 percent in forty years.[30] Similarly, pharmaceutical R&D—an industry that stood at $1 billion in 1970 and $2 billion in 1980 skyrocketed to $49 billion by 2004, an increase of approximately 2,450 percent in thirty-four years.[31] Estimates suggest that the number of human subjects enrolled in clinical research trials was approximately seven million in 1992 and had increased to approximately twenty million in less than a decade (2001).[32]

Similar statistics could be cited across health care sectors. Yet, bioethics has kept the lens of ethics largely focused on "the clinical context."[33] As we

---

[30] Kaiser Family Foundation, "How Has US Spending on Healthcare Changed Over Time?" *Health System Tracker*, February 25, 2022, www.healthsystemtracker.org/chart-collection/u-s-spending-healthcare-changed-time/#Total%20national%20health%20expenditures,%20US%20$%20Billions,%201970-2020. See also Austin Frakt, "Reagan, Deregulation and America's Exceptional Rise in Health Care Costs," *New York Times*, June 4, 2018, www.nytimes.com/2018/06/04/upshot/reagan-deregulation-and-americas-exceptional-rise-in-health-care-costs.html; and John E. McDonough, "US Health Care in Our Neoliberal Era," *The Milbank Quarterly*, June 24, 2020, www.milbank.org/quarterly/opinions/us-health-care-in-our-neoliberal-era/. Importantly, over against the frequent assertions that "free" markets are self-sustaining, it is clear that in health care, as in every instantiation, neoliberalism is a deeply extractive ideology, siphoning funds from the public sector into private pockets. See, for example, Patrick P.T. Jeurissen, Florien M. Kruse, and Steffie Woolhandler, "For-Profit Hospitals Have Thrived Because of Generous Public Reimbursement Schemes, Not Greater Efficiency: A Multi-Country Case Study," *International Journal of Health Services* 51, no. 1 (2021), doi.org/10.1177/00207314 20966976.

[31] Fisher, *Medical Research for Hire*, 5.

[32] Philip Mirowski and Robert Van Horn ("The Contract Research Organization and the Commercialization of Scientific Research," *Social Studies of Science* 35 [2005]: 504–548) cite Davies that 20 million subjects were enrolled in trials run by contract research organizations (CROs) in 2001, at a point when CROs—a new entity that emerged after 1980—had garnered approximately 80 percent of the market share in clinical trials away from academic medical centers (506). See also Adriana Petryna, "Globalizing Human Subjects Research," in *Global Pharmaceuticals: Ethics, Markets, and Practices*, ed. Adriana Petryna, Andrew Lakoff, and Arthur Kleinman (Durham, NC: Duke University Press, 2007), 33–60.

[33] The COVID-19 pandemic in 2020 made this deflective role of bioethics painfully clear. As I have recounted elsewhere, as the pandemic unfolded, the discipline of bioethics focused almost exclusively on traditional questions regarding allocating scarce resources under triage conditions (to both patients and health care practitioners), end-of-life treatment issues in the

saw with clinical rationality, the methodological individualism fostered by neoliberalism restricts the parameters of "health care" to physician-mediated, biologically-focused interventions on individuals provided in a hospital or medical clinic. Bioethics has followed suit, limiting its focus almost entirely to issues and interventions in the clinical setting and to those who have the economic resources to consume clinic-based health care services. In so doing, it has assisted in keeping the powerful hand of economics largely invisible. For the most part, economic questions have been shoehorned into the narrow question of *how* to get people 'access' to the newly emerging neoliberal health care system.[34]

Even more peculiarly, amidst this explosive growth in spending across these sectors, bioethics has continued to further the presumption that the health care context is one of scarcity—and that a key task of bioethics is to assist practitioners and health care organizations to make "difficult decisions" (i.e., choose between patients' lives) in contexts of scarce resources. It is no accident that "the Trolley Problem" is foundational to

---

ICU, or questions about individual autonomy (re: mask-wearing). The same framework was deployed when the COVID-19 vaccines became available; see M. Therese Lysaught, "Sacramental Biopolitics after COVID-19," in *The Routledge Companion to Christian Ethics*, ed. D. Stephen Long and Rebekah Miles (Philadelphia: Routledge, 2022), 372–388. A few analyses did try to draw attention to global disparities in vaccine allocation, but these were in a minority. See, for example, M. Therese Lysaught, "Vatican: It's Unjust (and Dangerous) for Wealthy Nations to Hoard the Covid Vaccine," *America,* January 27, 2021, www.americamagazine.org/politics-society/2021/01/27/covid-vaccine-distribution-united-states-vatican-239797; and Christopher Ahlbach, Teresa King, and Elizabeth Dzeng, "The COVID-19 Pandemic and Ethical Challenges Posed by Neoliberal Healthcare," *Journal of General Internal Medicine* 36 (2021): 205–206.

[34] See, for example, even texts like *On Moral Medicine: Theological Perspectives in Medical Ethics*, ed. Allen Verhey and Stephen P. Lammers (Grand Rapids: William B. Eerdmans, 1998), which siloed economic questions to its nineteenth and final chapter entitled "Allocation and Distribution." In doing so, *On Moral Medicine* followed most other bioethics textbooks published to date. This was one issue specifically addressed in the third edition of *On Moral Medicine*, ed. M. Therese Lysaught and Joseph Kotva (Grand Rapids: William B. Eerdmans, 2012).

bioethics pedagogy—in fact, as one bioethicist puts it, it "should be considered of great importance in medical ethics."[35]

As Farmer notes:

> the fight over "scarce resources" involves no small amount of chicanery. There are enough resources on this planet to do the job right. These resources are far less than those required to wage wars whose justifications are never quite as good as their champions make them out to be. When you are bold in pressing for the right to health care rather than arguing how best to spend paltry sums that could never do the job, or even half the job, you advance the cause of public health.[36]

---

[35] Gabriel Andrade, "Medical Ethics and the Trolley Problem," *J Med Ethics Hist Med* 12 (2019): 3, eCollection 2019. The trolley problem is a philosophical "thought experiment" standard in medical school ethics curricula where students are posed with a choice: to allow a group of people (5–10) to be killed by an oncoming trolley or to save them by pulling a lever and diverting the trolley which will, unfortunately, kill one person. Entirely an exercise in utilitarian formation, the scenario helpfully captures many of the problematic assumptions of utilitarianism and bioethics: the omniscient, meta-perspective of the decision-maker; the constrained, emergent time frame (the decision must be made within seconds); the focus on an immediate act instead of upstream factors; the faceless nature of the people whose lives are at stake as well as the erasure of their voice; and so on. As one reviewer of an early draft of this chapter noted, "The central question in an ethics of scarcity is 'who has to die so I/we can do what we want to?'"

[36] Farmer, *To Repair the World*, 142. Or, as he notes elsewhere: "We allow not only the continuation but the entrenchment of inequalities. The justification of this sad state of affairs is usually economic: we're told that we live in a time of 'shrinking health resources.' But is this really so? Look at profits in the managed-care companies. In the mid-1990s, the Wall Street Journal described these companies as 'money machines so awash in cash that they don't know what to do with it all.'…The trend has continued unabated, as a recent Families USA report points out: 'With costs of health care coverage soaring, one aspect of health plan company expenses has kept pace: compensation packages for top executives'" (*Pathologies of Power*, 173). And: "The hypothesis that we lack sufficient means to cure all tuberculosis cases, everywhere and regardless of susceptibility patterns, is not supported by the data. There is plenty of money—even in poor countries. The degree of accumulated wealth in the world today is altogether unprecedented, but this accumulation has occurred in tandem with growing inequality" (*Pathologies of Power*, 172).

Thus, bioethics has created blinders that have prevented the conceptualization of larger structural and economic questions in the moral analysis of medicine and health care delivery. It has stood passively by as health systems have commodified health care practitioners, driving the practitioner burnout and exodus from the field that had already begun prior to the onslaught of the COVID-19 pandemic.[37] Instead of challenging this, it has often championed neoliberal values, for example, quantifying its own efficiency in "bioethics dashboards" in order to justify health system support of this non-revenue generating unit.[38]

Bioethics' ontology of scarcity returns us to neoliberalism's underlying anthropology. For not only does bioethics forward an anthropology bifurcated between those who can rationally choose and those who cannot. It also forwards the economized anthropology of capitalism, which bifurcates human persons in a different yet analogous (and often overlapping) way—namely, via the assumption the poor are not "worth" as much as the rich. As colleagues and I have detailed elsewhere, from the beginning of the history of capitalism, we hear a resonance with the anthropology of bioethics—that there are some humans who have the freedom to rationally maximize their preferences via the principle of utility and others who do not possess such a freedom.[39] More broadly, those who possess such freedom are, simply, those with means to maximize—namely, the wealthy. The poor, lacking goods to weigh via the principle of utility, have—for all practical purposes—no opportunity to exercise their

---

[37] See, for example, before the COVID-19 pandemic, Herbert L. Fred and Mark S. Scheid, "Physician Burnout: Causes, Consequences, and (?) Cures," *Texas Heart Institute Journal* 45, no. 4 (2018): 198–202, doi.org/10.14503/THIJ-18-6842; and after the COVID-19 pandemic: A. Bhardwaj, "COVID-19 Pandemic and Physician Burnout: Ramifications for Healthcare Workforce in the United States," *Journal of Healthcare Leadership* 14 (2022): 91–97, doi.org/10.2147/JHL.S360163. Similar studies trace burnout in the nursing and allied health professions.

[38] See, for example, Mark Repenshek, "Continuous Quality Improvement Initiatives in Ethics: A Proposed Communication Tool," *HCEUSA* (2012): www.chausa.org/docs/default-source/general-files/a68cc1d110cd46dea26c57c2e548751d1-pdf.pdf?sfvrsn=0.

[39] See Bishop, Lysaught, and Michels, *Biopolitics After Neuroscience*, 142–195.

autonomy, to rationally and freely choose their good. Their option—and, in fact, their responsibility—is to work in bondage as wage laborers; from David Hume in the eighteenth century forward, wage laborers—and worse, the "undeserving poor"—are described in language that approximates them as beasts, or at least less than fully human.[40]

In the history of economics, the poor—with no assets to maximize—are denied access both to the system of wealth and to full personhood. Within the ethical rhetoric surrounding neoliberal medicine, the poor—with no assets to offer—as well as those whose capacities are diminished due to circumstances or illness, are likewise often excluded both from full moral agency and from basic care. "We are urged," Farmer notes, "to avoid 'wasting' resources on groups of people who are not expected to make significant improvement."[41] "The poor," he continues, "are saddled with the greatest share of disability and disease even as they are deemed less worthy objects of health care by a medical establishment that privileges ability to pay over need."[42] Millions upon millions of poor people—both within the US and across the globe—are, in other words, "fungible," "disposable" and invisible to bioethics.[43] Farmer cites Edmund Pellegrino's "acidic commentary" to encapsulate his point:

> There is no room in the free market for the non-player, the person who can't "buy in"—the poor, the uninsured, the uninsurable. The special needs of the chronically ill, the disabled, infirm, aged, and the

---

[40] See Wendell Berry's *The Hidden Wound* (Berkeley, CA: Counterpoint, 2010) and *The Need to Be Whole: Patriotism and the History of Prejudice* (Berkeley, CA: Shoemaker and Company, 2022), among other writings, for the ways this attitude toward those who work the land is foundational in American racist and anti-rural ("white trash") stereotyping and policy. I thank Brian Volck for this connection.

[41] Farmer *To Repair the World*, 4.

[42] Farmer, *To Repair the World*, 4.

[43] Farmer, *Pathologies of Power*, 163, 167; and *To Repair the World*, 78–80. One lens throughout Farmer's work is the lens of race, though particularly mentioned in *To Repair the World*, 17–18. The relationship between US health care, bioethics, and racial capitalism merits further exploration.

emotionally distressed are no longer valid claims to special attention. Rather, they are the occasion for higher premiums, more deductibles or exclusion from enrollment. There is no economic justification for the extra time required to explain, counsel, comfort, and educate these patients and their families since these cost more than they return in revenue.[44]

Farmer poignantly summed up this insight in what now stands as one of his signature phrases: "The idea that some lives matter less is the root of all that's wrong with the world."[45]

Et tu Theological Ethics?

Farmer's relentless attention to the distortive effects of neoliberalism on health care delivery in the US and globally lays the groundwork for examining the neoliberal malformation of the very field that should have served as a stopgap against these distortive effects: bioethics. Finding its dark shadow there raises a further spectre: has it likewise infiltrated the disciplines of theology and theological bioethics? Does our theology function as an "option for the rich" discipline?

Farmer's legacy turns our attention to macro methodological issues, many of which have been raised in recent decades by scholars formed by liberationist perspectives. Does our theology and theological ethics draw primarily on *sources* produced by the economically privileged that have served (intentionally or unintentionally) to maintain social structures of privilege and oppression? If so, how do we critically complicate them? Does our discourse address primarily a privileged *audience*, focusing largely on issues of relevance to the 1 percent or 5 percent?[46] Do our

---

[44] Farmer, *Pathologies of Power*, 163, citing Edmund Pellegrino, "The Commodification of Medical and Health Care: The Moral Consequences of a Paradigm Shift from a Professional to a Market Ethic," *Journal of Medicine and Philosophy* 24, no. 3 (1999): 253.

[45] Kidder, *Mountains Beyond Mountains*, 294.

[46] Elsewhere, I have detailed how the field of Catholic theological ethics functions primarily as a racially-segregated White space, but a similar analysis would likely confirm that it largely imagines its audience as economically privileged (M. Therese Lysaught and Cory Mitchell,

theoretical frameworks prioritize abstract, theoretical *concepts* in a way that often renders invisible the social and material realities of the issues being analyzed? Does, for example, the discourse in, say, the ethics of marriage and family, mirror that in bioethics—focusing on a narrow array of issues (e.g., contraception, divorce, abortion, euthanasia) analyzed via select abstract principles (the inextricability of the unitive and procreative dimensions of the conjugal act; the conditions for annulment; the sanctity of life) applied in timeless, decontextualized ways? I hope the foregoing makes clear that a theological ethics, learning from Paul Farmer, will begin to reimagine our methodologies in ways that are geographically wide, historically deep, and take serious account of the material ways that neoliberalism has radically changed the broader socio-political realities under which actual people live.

We must also ask: what ends and larger projects do our analyses serve? Christian morality frequently positions itself as "counter-cultural," but has our work subtly been co-opted into neoliberalism's larger cultural project? How, we might ask, do we understand the growing Christian and Catholic support for homeschooling or charter schools (privatization) or against critical race theory (deregulation)? Is this, perhaps, the US version of the neoliberal priority of dismantling public education across the globe? Or what of the focus in Catholic moral theology on sexuality? As colleagues and I have traced elsewhere, part of the disciplinary apparatus aimed at controlling the "deserving" and "undeserving" poor invented by nascent capitalism in the sixteenth century has been a Christian virtue discourse hyper-focused on the sexual and labor-related vices of the poor.[47]

"Vicious Trauma: Race, Bodies, and the Confounding of Virtue Ethics," *Journal of the Society of Christian Ethics* 42, no. 1 [2022]: 75–100, doi.org/10.5840/jsce202281660, specifically 80-86). As we note, the virtue ethics literature tends to focus on a narrow range of issues, e.g., alcohol and American college life, plagiarism, premarital sex, euthanasia, homeschooling, and consumer choices—issues relevant to those with access to higher education, health care, and economic surpluses.

[47] Bishop, Lysaught, and Michel, *Biopolitics After Neuroscience*. Kelly Johnson has deftly narrated precisely such an influence in the omnipresent but theologically-troubled concept of stewardship (Kelly Johnson, *Fear of Beggars: Stewardship and Poverty in Christian Ethics*

Have—or how have—Christian accounts of sexuality contributed to this problematic construct?

Thirdly, there are troubling signs that neoliberal logic has infiltrated theology and theological ethics in ways analogous to clinical rationality and bioethics. Most benignly, the term "values"—omnipresent in the discourse of Christian ethics—is term that has been smuggled into ethics from economics.[48] More darkly, in his recent book, *Catholic Discordance: Neoconservatism vs. the Field Hospital Church of Pope Francis*, Massimo Borghesi narrates in exquisite detail the "strident Catho-capitalism" that has taken shape in the US since the 1990s, refashioning Catholicism as an apology for neoliberalism.[49] I have elsewhere suggested that a second "pillar" of this Catholic Americanism—which Borghesi describes as comprised of "neo-traditionalists" who have long "take[n] morality as their battleground"—likewise is an offshoot of the same neoliberal ideology.[50] These culture warriors forward an understanding of morality deeply infused by methodological individualism—either championing distorted notions of conscience or condemning the sick and poor for their

---

(Grand Rapids: William B. Eerdmans, 2007). See also M. Therese Lysaught, "Beyond Stewardship: Reordering the Economic Imagination of Catholic Health Care," *Christian Bioethics* 26, no. 1 (2020): 31–55, doi.org/10.1093/cb/cbaa002.

[48] See, for example, Mark Schroeder, "Value Theory," *Stanford Encyclopedia of Philosophy* (2021), plato.stanford.edu/entries/value-theory/.

[49] Massimo Borghesi, *Catholic Discordance: Neoconservatism vs. the Field Hospital Church of Pope Francis* (Collegeville, MN: Liturgical Press, 2021).

[50] It is worth noting that despite their self-claimed moniker, these neo-traditionalists spout a novel ideology, having isolated and sentimentalized certain aspects of mostly Tridentine Catholicism as "The Tradition" while ignoring everything that that narrow container does not hold. One might also suggest that since they, in good neoliberal fashion, pick and choose what constitutes "The Tradition" they reveal themselves as heretics (αἵρεσις) rather than catholic (καθ' ὅλον). I thank Brian Volck for this insight. See further, M. Therese Lysaught, "War or Peace? Toward a Better Kind of (Bio)Politics," *Vatican II, Pope Francis, and the Way Forward*, The Hank Center for the Catholic Intellectual Tradition, Loyola University Chicago, March 25, 2022, www.luc.edu/media/lucedu/ccih/formsdocumentsandpdfs/Lysaught%20Remarks.pdf. See also M. Therese Lysaught, "Reclaiming the Catholic Moral and Intellectual Tradition from the Culture Wars," *NCR*, April 7, 2022, www.ncronline.org/news/opinion/reclaiming-catholic-moral-and-intellectual-tradition-culture-wars.

own moral failings. They vociferously decry government regulation—be it of health care, public schools, workplaces, the environment, the franchise—working strenuously to undermine and dismantle these and any other substantive public goods. And what of virtue ethics—which reemerged around 1980? While Alasdair MacIntyre is decidedly not a neoliberal, his communitarian vision for ethics has been co-opted into the Ayn Randian "Benedict Option" advocated by pundits and clerics.[51]

In the end, Farmer's legacy poses critical methodological questions for our field. But as importantly, he charts a constructive way forward. He witnesses in his life and his work to what medicine looks like when grounded in and infused by an alternative (theological) economics—namely, charity. To be clear, this is not the distorted, reductive, economized notion of 'charity' that is the heritage of capitalism.[52] Farmer is rightly critical of what usually passes for charity within global health and other practices of Christian outreach: namely monetary donations and second-hand castoffs, distributed without any relationality, that do not address the root causes of problems and often create many more serious difficulties.[53] This he calls the "charity approach" to global health, a framework that he rejects.

---

[51] On MacIntyre as not a neoliberal, see M. Therese Lysaught and Daniel P. Rhodes, "Whose Revolution? Which Future? The Legacy of Alasdair MacIntyre for a Radical Pedagogy in Virtue," *Explorations: Interdisciplinary Studies in the Humanities* 14, no. 1 (2020): 97–125, expositions.journals.villanova.edu/article/view/2528/2471. On those pursuing Ayn Rand's vision, see Rod Dreher, *The Benedict Option: A Strategy for Christians in a Post-Christian Nation* (New York, NY: Sentinel, 2017); and the Texas-based Veritatis Splendor project promoted by a Catholic bishop (www.ncregister.com/news/massive-catholic-center-planned-for-east-texas, www.simchafisher.com/2021/03/03/catholic-megadevelopment-veritatis-splendor-is-long-on-rhetoric-short-on-details/) that to date has failed spectacularly (thedeaconsbench.com/what-happened-to-the-ambitious-veritatis-splendor-project-in-texas/).

[52] Johnson, *Fear of Beggars*; and Lysaught, "Beyond Stewardship."

[53] As he notes: "charity medicine too frequently consists of second-hand castoffs—leftover medicine—doled out in piecemeal fashion" (*Pathologies of Power*, 154). For an account of the problems with medical device donation, see Bruce Compton, David M. Barash, Jennifer Farrington, Cynthia Hall, Dale Herzog, Vikas Meka, Ellen Rafferty, Katherine Taylor, and Asha Varghese, "Access to Medical Devices in Low-Income Countries: Addressing

But he also challenges the tired and omnipresent contemporary dichotomy between charity and (social) justice. After identifying some serious flaws in a charity-only model of addressing global suffering, he notes,

> It is possible, however, to overstate the case against charity—it is, after all, one of the four cardinal virtues, in many traditions. Some holier-than-thou progressives dismiss charity when it is precisely the virtue demanded. In medicine, charity underpins the often-laudable goal of addressing the needs of 'underserved populations.' To the extent that medicine responds to, rather than creates, underserved populations, charity will always have its place in medicine. Unfortunately, a preferential option for the poor is all too often absent from charity medicine.[54]

Thus, for Farmer, charity and social justice necessarily work hand-in-hand.

With these caveats in place, I would argue that Farmer's legacy demonstrates at least two critically important constructive points. The first is that economics—via both traditional forms of charity as well as public investment—is a key and necessary engine of social justice and social transformation. While much of his early work in Haiti was funded via traditional methods of charity, the annals of Partners In Health are speckled with various stories of Farmer's creative approach to what he

---

Sustainability Challenges in Medical Device Donations," *National Academy of Medicine*, July 16, 2018, nam.edu/access-to-medical-devices-in-low-income-countries-addressing-sustainability-challenges-in-medical-device-donations/.

[54] Farmer, *Pathologies of Power*, 154. His criticisms of the charity-based model include that it is often premised on the bifurcated anthropology that we have discussed, namely, the "tendency—sometimes striking, sometimes subtle, and surely lurking in all of us—to regard those needing charity as intrinsically inferior" (a form of methodological individualism); a resignation to structures of injustice based on the presupposition that "there will always be those who have and those who have not"; the erasure of the twentieth century's "marked tendency toward increasing economic inequity"; and an allied form of methodological individualism which, by calling "compassionate conservatives" to address poverty through personal acts of charity absolves social agencies from responsibility to do so.

called "redistributive justice"—what has been referred to as his Robin-Hood approach to appropriating expensive resources from well-heeled Boston health care institutions to care for the poorest of the poor in Haiti and Peru.[55] "Borrowing" needed multi-drug resistant tuberculosis (MDRTB) drugs from the Brigham Women's and Children's Hospital pharmacy in 1994—to the tune of $92,000—enabled him and Jim Kim to conduct their clinical trial in Peru and develop an alternative paradigm for treating TB and MDRTB that ultimately transformed the World Health Organization's approach and subsequently has saved countless lives. These initial infusions of resources not only saved the lives of individual Peruvians; they led to longer term changes in the global pricing and production of MDRTB drugs, radically altering the economics of 'essential' pharmaceuticals.

Thus, repeatedly throughout Farmer's work, we see how initial acts of "economic" charity can be a critical seed for social transformation. This dynamic should not, however, be misconstrued as a neoliberal argument for philanthropy—a practice which, in part, justifies extreme wealth disparities by providing a path for the rich to cleanse their consciences via the (again) methodologically individualistic act of donation from their excess.[56] Rather, Farmer's witness preserves a place for the traditional Christian practice of almsgiving—a practice redescribed by Hume and the architects of capitalism from the seventeenth century forward as a vice.[57] But he pushes us to begin to reimagine what a properly Christian practice

---

[55] Kidder, *Mountains Beyond Mountains,* 90 and 149.

[56] For just a sampling of this critique, see: Michael E. Hartmann, "Philanthropy in *The Rise and Fall of the Neoliberal Order,*" *Philanthropy Daily,* May 19, 2022, www.philanthropydaily.com/philanthropy-in-the-rise-and-fall-of-the-neoliberal-order/; Juanjo Mediavilla and Jorge Garcia-Arias, "Philanthrocapitalism as a Neoliberal (Development Agenda) Artefact: Philanthropic Discourse and Hegemony in (Financing For) International Development," *Globalizations* 16 (2019) 857–875, doi.org/10.1080/14747731.2018.1560187; and Adam Saifer, "Racial Neoliberal Philanthropy and the Arts for Social Change," *Organization* (online first December 7, 2020), doi.org/10.1177/1350508420973327.

[57] See Bishop, Lysaught, and Michel, *Biopolitics After Neuroscience,* 142–195.

of charity—in concert with a broader framework committed to redistributive policies and social justice—can and should look like.

Secondly, beyond helping us reimagine what we normally understand by the word charity, Farmer more importantly *embodied an alternative anthropology*—not the anthropology of neoliberalism, but the anthropology of *caritas,* of self-gift. As captured so well in *Mountains Beyond Mountains*, as well as other narratives about his work, Farmer's story demonstrates what authentic *caritas* looks like. The initial generative step that led to Partners In Health and its transformation of global health was Farmer's decision to move to the margins, to work for no pay in the "poorest country in the Western hemisphere." This constant practice of donation characterized his life, remaining as he did "in the habit...of giving all his money away to the poor even faster than he earn[ed] it."[58]

One might ask: were these acts of charity or solidarity? Farmer might answer: that is a false construct. For he helps us see how traditional Christian practices—presence, friendship, solidarity, hospitality, and other crucial ways of embodying *caritas*—are at the same time deeply 'economic.' This is captured in one of his signature practices: walking hours to visit patients in their home. A hallmark of Farmer's work is that he *spent time* with patients, with the poor, as persons. Farmer's personal *caritas* was the seed, scattered on the unlikeliest of soil, that produced more than a hundred-fold. He did not consider himself above his patients, better than them; he resisted the subtle economization of his time and actions, refusing to consider his time "too valuable" (as many others argued) to "spend" on people who were poor. We could say, he did not consider his stature as a physician at the Brigham "something to be grasped" but rather emptied himself to meet the poor as equals—or, rather, as those to whom he deferred as more important than himself, given what they had suffered, given how Christ was present in them. Here Farmer points us to the heart of a truly theological economics—the gospel proclamation of kenotic self-

---

[58] Jennie Weiss Block, *Paul Farmer: Servant to the Poor* (Collegeville, MN: Liturgical Press, 2018), 7.

emptying. Here, "gift" is equally an act of solidarity; the practice of solidarity is equally a gift.

Conclusion

In this chapter, I have argued that Paul Farmer poses a deep—but constructive—challenge not only for global health and bioethics but equally for theology and theological ethics. I hope the foregoing account has provided a window into how Farmer's legacy presses all of us to rigorously analyze the ways that economic assumptions and ideologies—particularly the regnant neoliberal political economy in which we all live and work—have subtly shaped and deformed our own conceptual frameworks as well as those of our disciplines. Economics and political economy have shaped Christian theology since Constantine, and enmeshed with those political economies, Christian theology has too often served to bolster structures of privilege and oppression. As with bioethics, here the damage is doubly-problematic. For as our disciplines become co-opted by these frameworks, they not only fail in their mission of being a bulwark against precisely the myths and mystifications necessary to sustain structures of sin and violence; tragically—and scandalously—they imperceptibly become agents of those same myths and mystifications.

A first step forward out of this troubling history is to begin to analyze the economic infrastructure that shapes our own work. Not only do theologians need to become conversant in the histories, commitments, and practices of economics; we need to ask hard questions: is our theology an "option for the rich" theology? Do our disciplines serve as a tool for social control, or do they instead upend the discourses that create the vast amount of suffering that remains so invisible? Have we become unwitting pawns of neoliberalism, even when we appear to be 'counter-cultural'?

Engaging in such analyses is not an easy task since the invisible hand of economics likes to stay invisible. Even when it begins to come into view, as when one turns off the infra-red night vision goggles, what was seen slips back into invisibility. "Social and economic questions are," as Farmer notes, often so easily "erased."⁵⁹ Yet, it is a crucial task for at least three reasons. First, if we do not accurately understand the root causes of issues that our disciplines engage (from assisted reproduction to public policy to ecclesiology), our analyses will range from inadequate to false. Second, it is crucial to identify the ways that neoliberalism has co-opted the intellectual infrastructure of our disciplines if we are to resist and overcome the ways that it deforms our concepts and hermeneutics. Finally, it is necessary to see how neoliberalism operates in order to follow Farmer's lead in concretely reimagining alternative practices.

Farmer demonstrates that a key tool for resisting a nihilistic economics is, instead, a theological economics—the thick practice of God's kenotic grace in the world captured in an anthropology of self-gift. Thus, in his work, we find a thickly theological and embodied account of charity, one that break downs the silos separating "economics" from the ways that it is deeply interwoven into our embodied social practices and institutions. It demonstrates how the Christian tradition grounds a different "economics," one that privileges gift, that challenges narratives of 'scarcity,' and that understands that this alternative economics is a necessary key to dismantling structural violence.⁶⁰ It is hard not to see in Farmer's legacy a concrete embodiment of Pope Francis's vision of social friendship, a practical instantiation—in personal actions, social practices, and public policy—of the virtue of *caritas* (love) that catalyzes via self-gift an economy that gives life over against globalized neoliberalism, which he has so aptly named, "an economy that kills."⁶¹

---

⁵⁹ Farmer, *Pathologies of Power*, 17.
⁶⁰ "We think we've fared well in large part because we fight the violence around us not with weapons but with food, water, schools, clinics, and hospitals" (Farmer, *To Repair the World*, 185).
⁶¹ Pope Francis, *Fratelli Tutti*, 2020.

M. Therese Lysaught, **PhD**, is Professor at the Neiswanger Institute for Bioethics and Health Care Leadership at Loyola University Chicago, Stritch School of Medicine. Her scholarly work brings into conversation the fields of theology, medicine, bioethics, and global health. Her most recent book, *Biopolitics After Neuroscience: Morality and the Economy of Virtue* (Bloomsbury Academic, 2022,), co-authored with Jeffrey P. Bishop and Andrew Michel, was a 2021 recipient of an Expanded Reason Award. She has additionally co-edited *Catholic Bioethics and Social Justice: The Praxis of US Healthcare in a Globalized World* (Liturgical Press, 2019, Catholic Press Association Award) with Michael McCarthy; *On Moral Medicine: Theological Perspectives on Medical* Ethics, 3rd edition (Eerdmans, 2012) with Joseph Kotva; and *Gathered for the Journey: Moral Theology in Catholic Perspective* (Eerdmans, 2007, Catholic Press Association Award) with David Matzko McCarthy. She has also authored *Caritas in Communion: The Theological Foundations of Catholic Health Care* (Catholic Health Association, 2014). Dr. Lysaught has served as a Visiting Scholar with the Catholic Health Association and on the Editorial Board for the *Journal of the Society of Christian Ethics* and *Studies in Christian Ethics.* She is a founding member and current Editor of the *Journal of Moral Theology.* She is a member of the Pontifical Academy for Life.

Chapter 8: Confronting "Structures of Violence": Women's Empowerment and the Legacy of Paul Farmer

Suzanne Mulligan

It is sometimes said that Catholic social teaching (CST) is too vague or too general, and because of its vagueness, its documents are unlikely to have any real impact in the world. Popes are occasionally criticized for failing to offer concrete solutions to the world's problems and, as a result, for not addressing, in practical ways, the urgent concerns of our time. There is some truth to these claims. Social encyclicals can indeed be rather general; their authors avoiding the danger of getting bogged down in the minutiae of complex realities. But there is wisdom in this approach too. Popes cannot speak in detail about every global problem, nor expected to be an authority on every socio-economic reality.

Rather, CST provides us with a kind of road map, a social vision for what a more just, equitable, and inclusive world might look like. The work of implementing this vision rests with local peoples and achieving it will take different forms in different contexts. This is one of the strengths of CST since its inductive methodology makes it more universally applicable and relevant. An inductive approach facilitates the realization of CST in diverse situations, concretely manifesting the principles it articulates, specifically, participation and subsidiarity. Critically, this inductive dimension reinforces human agency, empowerment, and moral freedom as essential components of the common good.

The work of the late Dr. Paul Farmer provides a vivid example of how the Catholic social vision can find actual expression in the world. Influenced by CST, and by liberation theology in particular, Farmer understood that the liberation of the poor from oppressive economic, political, and cultural structures was key to achieving global health care and human rights. If poverty and ill health go hand in hand, then health indicators need to be analyzed alongside the marginalization, oppression, and vulnerability of the poor. If we accept this premise, then the empowerment of the world's poor, especially poor women, becomes a vital step towards securing universal human rights, including access to adequate health care.

In the Foreword to *Pathologies of Power*, Nobel Laureate Amartya Sen writes:

> The proposal to distance inequality from poverty is severely challenged by Farmer's many-sided documentation of the impact of inequality of power on the lives that the subjugated can live. This diagnosis does not, of course, yield any instant solution of the problems; but it does indicate the difficult—and often ignored—social and economic issues that must be firmly faced to eliminate preventable morbidity and escapable mortality. ... The solutions are by no means easy, but they are not beyond the reach of our informed and resolute effort.[1]

In this chapter, I seek to examine the ways in which Farmer's writings can help us reach solutions. His work provides a lens through which we can evaluate the relationship between inequality and injustice and its impact on the health of the world's poor. This chapter is structured around three themes. First, I explore the connection between injustice and disease, focusing on women in particular and their disproportionate exposure to what Farmer calls "structures of violence." Second, I argue that women's empowerment is crucial to long-term health and human rights outcomes. Finally, I consider the implications of Farmer's work for theological ethics. I draw on his writings throughout, in dialogue with various other interlocutors. His thinking, shaped by his medical experiences working among the poor, provides valuable resources for ongoing health and human rights debates.

---

[1] Amartya Sen, "Foreword," in Paul Framer, *Pathologies of Power: Health, Human Rights, and the New War on the Poor* (Berkeley: University of California Press, 2005), xvi–xvii.

Paul Farmer on Injustice and Disease

With the increased movement of peoples, disease has become more transnational than ever before. We have come to recognize the globalized nature of disease, but what is still not fully appreciated is the inequitable impact of disease globally. The poor bear the greatest burden, both in terms of infection and their inability to cope with the consequences of ill health. For this reason, Farmer coined the phrase "pathologies of power." Power, or its lack, is one of the key factors determining who becomes ill and who gains access to health care resources. Moreover, the powerful disproportionately benefit from the fruits of scientific research, as Farmer reminds us: "Although pathogens readily cross borders, the fruits of research are often delayed in customs."[2]

He goes further, denouncing a double-standard in medical ethics. The recent COVID-19 pandemic illustrates the hypocrisies to which Farmer long objected. On the one hand, the COVID-19 global emergency demonstrated an ability to develop safe, effective vaccines quickly and efficiently. On the other hand, it confirmed an absence of solidarity between the rich countries of the Global North and poorer communities in the Global South. The socio-economic re-opening of Western society, the protection of Western economies, and the profits of transnational pharmaceutical corporations took priority over the fair and equitable distribution of vaccines worldwide. Farmer questioned the extent to which the privileged take seriously the ethical claim that all human beings are made equal. He criticized the ways in which Codes of Ethics and Review Boards regularly failed the most vulnerable: they "often share an unacknowledged agreement that in fact all humans are not created equal and that this inequality accounts for both differential distribution of disease and differential standards of care."[3]

Farmer worked on a range of global health concerns and in a variety of contexts. Whether writing about TB in Russian prisons, Ebola in Central

---

[2] Farmer, *Pathologies of Power*, 199.
[3] Farmer, *Pathologies of Power*, 200.

and West Africa, or HIV/AIDS in Haiti, Harlem, or Sub-Saharan Africa, his analysis was always characterized by a deep concern for the poor and by a desire to ensure that the voices of the most vulnerable were heard. He wrote:

> In arguing that health care is a human right, one signs on to a lifetime of work dedicated to erasing double standards for rich and poor. Again, the question of social and economic rights is raised, first and loudly by the poor, and then timidly and reluctantly by the rest of us. It has taken years for the sharp critiques voiced by the poor to begin to work their way into our medical journals and ethical codes.[4]

Among the most vulnerable are women. Lacking the same social, economic, and political freedoms as men, they often find themselves at risk of violence and disease simply because they are female. They often have little say over their reproductive rights and may enjoy minimal control over their bodily well-being and integrity. They remain at higher risk of infection with STDs such as HIV/AIDS. Commenting on this situation, Farmer wrote: "One explanation is that the majority of women with AIDS had been robbed of their voices long before HIV appeared to further complicate their lives. In settings of entrenched elitism, they have been poor. In settings of entrenched sexism, they have been, of course, women."[5]

This is a consequence of what the Christian tradition calls "social" or "structural sin." But Farmer used a much stronger language, referring to it as "structures of violence." In fact, his striking language helps awaken us to the scale and gravity of the issues at hand, arguably more so than the language of "sin." In today's world, and outside a theological setting, one might ask whether the concept of "sin" carries sufficient weight in

---

[4] Farmer, *Pathologies of Power*, 201.
[5] Paul Farmer, *Infections and Inequalities: The Modern Plagues* (Berkeley: University of California Press, 1999), 62.

increasingly secular contexts. The language of "violence," on the other hand, retains a force that is less easy to ignore.

Farmer understood that women for too long have been robbed of their voices. As he notes in discussing women, poverty, and AIDS:

> Attentiveness to the life stories of women with AIDS usually reveals it to be the latest in a string of tragedies. ... Their sickness may be thought of as a result of "structural violence," because it is neither their nature nor pure individual will that is at fault, but rather historically given (and often economically driven) processes and forces that conspire to constrain individual agency. Structural violence is visited upon all those whose social status denies them access to the fruits of scientific and social advances.[6]

Thus, Farmer demonstrates throughout his work that attentiveness to women's stories must form the basis of strategies aimed at dismantling the violent structures that continue to oppress and marginalize the world's poor. How are these "structures of violence" revealed, and how do they affect women in particular?

Structures of Violence

Women across the world continue to struggle with unjust burdens arising from their lack of economic, cultural, and social equality. They remain at disproportionate risk of sexual violence and exploitation. They rarely enjoy economic parity with men: they typically work in lower paid jobs, working longer days, with fewer legal protections, while performing three-fourths of unpaid care-work.[7] At the same time, they have fewer political rights, are more likely to be reliant on a male relative for social security, and have little say over their sexual and reproductive future. And,

---

[6] Paul Farmer, "Women, Poverty, and AIDS," in *Women, Poverty, and AIDS: Sex, Drugs, and Structural Violence*, ed. Paul Farmer, Margaret Connors, and Janie Simmons (Monroe, ME: Common Courage Press, 2011), 23.

[7] Agnes Brazal, "Ethics of Care in *Laudato Si'*: A Postcolonial Ecofeminist Critique," *Feminist Theology* 29, no. 3 (2021): 223.

despite educational progress in recent decades, females make up over two-thirds of the world's 796 million illiterate people.[8]

Globally, fewer girls finish schooling than boys. Child marriage persists with approximately twelve million girls each year being forced into marriage before they reach the age of eighteen. And, shockingly, the home can be the most dangerous place for females. The UN reports that 13 percent of women and girls between the ages of fifteen and forty-nine have been subjected to intimate partner violence in the past twelve months and that one in three women will experience physical and/or sexual violence at least once in their lifetime. Approximately 47,000 women died in 2020 at the hands of a partner or family member, suggesting that poverty and lack of empowerment are forcing women to remain in abusive and dangerous situations.[9] Although much of this is fueled by economic vulnerability and social disempowerment, it is also connected to increasing levels of misogyny and sexism in society generally, something that transcends class or economic status. Where women's disempowerment and toxic masculinity combine, violence against women and girls abounds.

Assigned gender roles, therefore, and a concomitant lack of social and economic opportunities create perilous situations for women. Take, for example, the HIV/AIDS pandemic, of which Farmer wrote extensively. Considerable gains have been made in recent years, especially as regards access to antiretroviral medication and educational resources. Nevertheless, infection rates among females remain stubbornly high. In 2021, 54 percent of all people living with HIV were women and girls. Around 4,900 young women aged between fifteen and twenty-four years became infected with HIV every week. In sub-Saharan Africa, which is the poorest region in the world, six in seven new HIV infections among those aged fifteen to nineteen years are among girls. Girls and young women aged fifteen to twenty-four years are twice as likely to be HIV positive than men

---

[8] UN Women, "Facts and Figures," www.unwomen.org/en/news/in-focus/commission-on-the-status-of-women-2012/facts-and-figures.

[9] UN Women, "Facts and Figures: Ending Violence Against Women," www.unwomen.org/en/what-we-do/ending-violence-against-women/facts-and-figures.

in the same age category. In sub-Saharan Africa, women and girls accounted for 63 percent of all new HIV infections in 2021.[10] Farmer's work revealed that HIV infection among women is intimately connected to power imbalances in sexual relationships.[11] In other words, HIV and violence against women and girls are interwoven.

Importantly, the "structures of violence" that contribute to higher risk of disease and premature death among the poor are constructed and maintained by humans. Moral conversion is needed if we are to dismantle these structures, since, as Farmer provocatively put it, "structural violence requires its apologists."[12] One must ask, then, whether Catholic magisterial teaching goes far enough in naming these apologists, or can it do more to help eradicate "structures of violence" and the attitudes that underpin them? And does Farmer's work help fill any gaps in Catholic teaching? I return to these questions in the final section of the chapter.

Integral Human Development and Women's Empowerment

Church teaching on integral human development provides a potential starting point for considering women's empowerment and agency. In *Populorum Progressio*, Pope Paul VI proposed a new way of thinking about development, one that did not rely on economic indicators alone but focused on the human person in her totality. The proper goal of development, he argued, was to foster the social conditions in which human flourishing can be realized. Economic progress is important, but economic growth is not the only objective. It ought to be accompanied by an equitable distribution of resources, by the empowerment of people (especially those most marginalized), and by freedom of self-determination. Importantly for Pope Paul, development must be *inclusive*: it ought to promote the good of the whole person and of all peoples, irrespective of gender, religion, sexual orientation, and so on.

---

[10] These figures are available at UN AIDS, "Global HIV & AIDS Statistics—Fact Sheet," www.unaids.org/en/resources/fact-sheet.

[11] Farmer, "Women, Poverty, and AIDS," 24.

[12] Farmer, "Women, Poverty, and AIDS," 26.

And, critically, the advancement of peoples' empowerment, agency, and self-determination helps to act as a counterweight to the "hyper-agency" of the rich. Thus, integral human development, truly understood, ought to help create conditions in which people can realize *their own* potential. It allows people to become "artisans of their own destiny" and "architects of their own development" (*Populorum Progressio*, nos. 65 and 76). It strengthens human agency and fosters the many expressions of human freedom.

Furthermore, in *Octogesima Adveniens*, Pope Paul puts forward a methodology based on what might be called agency "from below." He understood that it was beyond the remit of any pope to provide concrete answers to all the world's social and economic problems. He also realized that responsibility for implementation of the Church's social vision rests with all people of good will, with civil society, government, and local communities all playing a vital role: "It is not enough to recall principles, state intentions, point to crying injustice and utter prophetic denunciations; these words will lack real weight unless they are accompanied for each individual by a livelier awareness of personal responsibility and by effective action" (no. 48).

For Paul VI, development and liberation were achieved through social and political action *as well as* economic improvement. The liberation of the poor required more than their economic advancement. It would be gained within and by communities empowered to work for their own well-being. Thus, we find in Pope Paul's social documents a strong endorsement of the principles of participation and subsidiarity, although, regrettably, he does not explicitly name women's role in the developmental process.

Pope John Paul II made several important statements about women, endorsing their full and equal dignity. In his 1995 *Letter to Women*, he defended the equality of women, denounced the ways in which Sacred Scripture was used to oppress and subordinate women for centuries, and acknowledges the talents and contributions of women in both the home and society. Despite his reference to the "genius" of women, he mostly failed to see beyond a singular notion of womanhood, one dependent on gender stereotypes that emphasize marriage and procreation (no. 10).

Unfortunately, we see a similar tendency in the documents of Pope Francis. For although he shows a deep concern for the injustices perpetrated against women, he too reverts to gender stereotyping. Perhaps the most obvious examples of this are found in *Fratelli Tutti* and *Querida Amazonia*. In *Querida Amazonia*, he speaks about the strength and gift of women (no. 99 ff). But the overall account suffers from inconsistencies and contradictions. British theologian Tina Beattie names problem when she notes that: "Francis' concept of 'woman' is mired in a sentimental fantasy. While in the real world, gender roles and identities are agile and malleable, he imagines 'woman' as an archetype frozen in time, its function being to 'soften' male culture with a feminine tenderness and receptivity."[13] In *Fratelli Tutti*, Francis reminds us that integral human development ought to be inclusive and equitable. He says:

> Social friendship and universal fraternity necessarily call for an acknowledgement of the worth of every human person, always and everywhere. ... Every human being has the right to live with dignity and to develop integrally; this fundamental right cannot be denied by any country (nos. 106–107).

And he goes on to say: "True wisdom demands an encounter with reality" (no. 47). But incorporating women's voices and taking seriously their lived experiences would have added greater overall weight to *Fratelli Tutti*. It is ironic that the Holy Father observes: "The organization of societies worldwide is still far from reflecting clearly that women possess the same dignity and identical rights as men. We say one thing with words, but our decisions and reality tell another story" (no. 23). This is precisely the problem. Magisterial endorsement of women's empowerment and agency remains underrepresented in, and often absent from, official

---

[13] Tina Beattie, "A 'Frozen' Idea of the Feminine," *The Tablet*, February 22, 2020, 6.

teaching. Church leadership's failure to truly hear the voices of women, and to condemn more strongly the social, economic and political vulnerability of women and girls is unacceptable, weakening the credibility of its teachings on human development, marriage, and sexuality.

Farmer's writings, on the other hand, acknowledge the importance of women's agency. He was acutely aware, however, that arguments in favor of women's agency regularly remain at an abstract level, and he advocated for the need to confront the attitudes and structures that prohibit its full realization. He named the hypocrisy that underpins so much of the discussion: "There is nothing wrong with underlining personal agency, but there is something unfair about using personal agency as a basis for assigning blame while simultaneously denying those blamed the opportunity to exert agency in their lives."[14] For Farmer and others, recognizing the political, economic, and social participation of women, as well as their leadership roles in society, lies at the heart of any credible way forward. However, this needs greater affirmation by Church leadership and must find more prominence in official teaching. It remains one of Farmer's most vital contributions to global health debates.

Implications for Theological Ethics

Undoubtedly, a major strength of Farmer's thinking was his insistence on the need for multi-dimensional, inclusive, and interconnecting strategies, based on the experiences of those most at risk. We see this continue through the cross-disciplinary work of many ethicists today. Moreover, his concern for the vulnerability of women, and in particular poorer women of color, helps highlights a weakness of CST that needs rectifying. However, progress is being made, and Farmer's work is a valuable resource for theological ethics today.

Catholic ethicists are among those who continue to investigate the correlation between injustice and disease. Michael Jaycox, for example, calls for prioritizing the needs of the oppressed, even if that means

---

[14] Farmer, "Women, Poverty, and AIDS," 29.

sacrificing the preferences of the privileged. This, he explains, is a step towards protecting the common good and promoting global health.[15] For Jaycox, political solidarity, coupled with targeted political intervention, is needed to remedy the glaring disparities within health systems, but this will require a radically new distribution of power and resources.[16]

Meghan Clark argues for a "preference for equality" in health care.[17] She tells us that the social and health costs of rising inequality in the United States are seen in reduced life expectancy and increased risk of serious illness among poorer sectors of society. "Greater equality can help us develop the public ethos and commitment to working together which we need if we are to solve the problems which threaten us all," she writes.[18] Andrea Vicini utilizes CST principles such as the common good and the option for the poor to further the global health conversation. Like Farmer, Vicini believes that an adequate understanding of global health must be diverse and inclusive, recognizing the impact of the ethnic, racial, cultural, political, and religious components of societal relationships.[19]

Others have examined the intersection between pollution, climate change, and global health, noting how poverty exacerbates the situation. Studies reveal that climate change is disproportionately affecting the health of poorer women, with some ethicists exploring the connection between women's empowerment, climate change, and health.[20] It is no surprise that

---

[15] Michael Jaycox, "The Black Lives Matter Movement: Justice and Health Equity," in *US Moral Theology from the Margins: Readings in Moral Theology No.19*, ed Charles E. Curran and Lisa A. Fullam (New York: Paulist Press, 2020), 252.
[16] Jaycox, "The Black Lives Matter Movement," 257.
[17] Meghan Clark, "Preference for Equality: How Economic Disparity Threatens our Health," *America*, October 29, 2012, www.americamagazine.org/issue/preference-equality.
[18] Clark, "Preference for Equality."
[19] Andrea Vicini, "Global Public Health and the Promotion of the Common Good," in *Ethical Challenges in Global Public Health: Climate Change, Pollution, and the Health of the Poor*, ed. Philip Landrigan and Andrea Vicini (Oregon: Pickwick Publications, 2021), 4.
[20] For an excellent account of the relationship between ecology, empowerment, and women's rights, see Brazal, "Ethics of Care in *Laudato Si'*."

pollution and environmental deterioration more severely harm the poor. Philip Landrigan explains:

> The result of this inequitable pattern is that people in low-income and lower-middle-income countries suffer disproportionately from disease, disability, and premature death caused by pollution. Nearly 92 percent of all pollution deaths occur in these countries.[21]

These are some contemporary voices that are helping to shape the global health care conversation and who, along with Farmer, inform us of the multilayered nature of the challenge.

Farmer realized that those most at risk are women, particularly women of color. He saw the need to create a space for women's voices to emerge, not just because this will accelerate more effective health care and human rights outcomes, but because he recognized the importance of women's agency *in se*. Given the lack of agency experienced by women throughout the world, Farmer's contribution to this issue was both vital and visionary.

In addition to this, one might ask how Farmer's understanding of "structures of violence" can strengthen our theology of sin, especially what is called structural or social sin. For example, Bryan Massingale has written about the absence of any serious critique of the sin of racism within CST.[22] Magisterial documents remain largely silent on this issue, and although Pope Francis does advance the question of race in *Fratelli Tutti*, this remains a largely underdeveloped area within CST. Farmer understood well how racism affects health, identifying how "poverty structured by racism" was fueling the AIDS epidemic in places like Harlem.[23]

---

[21] Philip Landrigan, "Pollution, Climate Change, and Global Public Health: Social Justice and the Common Good," in *Ethical Challenges in Global Public Health: Climate Change, Pollution, and the Health of the Poor*, ed. Philip Landrigan and Andrea Vicini (Eugene, OR: Pickwick Publications, 2021), 52.

[22] Bryan N. Massingale, *Racial Justice and the Catholic Church*, (Maryknoll, NY: Orbis Books, 2010), and "Has the Silence Been Broken? Catholic Theological Ethics and Racial Justice," *Theological Studies* 75, no. 1 (2014): 133–155.

[23] Farmer, "Women, Poverty, and AIDS," 20ff.

Confronting "Structures of Violence": Women's Empowerment

In her recent book, *Towards a Politics of Communion*, Anna Rowlands provides a robust account of structural sin, drawing from liberation theology, the work of John Paul II, and more recently the teachings of Pope Francis.[24] Structural sin is more than simply the social structures, policies, and laws that oppress people; it refers to a pervasive culture that supports formal expressions of injustice, exclusion, and intolerance. It refers to the creation of a culture, a way of seeing, that legitimizes oppression. Speaking about the plight of migrants, Rowlands argues that if we are to rectify our failure to respond adequately to those displaced, we must first come to see our "disorientation." In other words, we must acquire the ability to first identify our moral blindness before we can dismantle sinful structures and confront the attitudes that underpin them.[25]

Like Massingale, Rowlands notes several omissions within magisterial accounts of social sin, including the sin of racism.[26] But she also identifies clerical abuse within the Catholic Church as another area overlooked: "To speak of human dignity held within the framework of doctrines of sin and salvation and not to address this issue in its social and structural dimensions seems incredible. The abuse crisis is manifestly an example of social sin turned inwards, and we live as yet with an absence of a fully adequate language to address this reality."[27]

Catholic ethicists including Heyer, Rowlands, and Massingale are expanding our theology of social sin. But another concern that has yet to be properly incorporated into our theology of social sin is pervasive misogyny and sexism. Social sin is dependent on cultures and ideologies that excuse, or even encourage, violence towards others. A culture of

---

[24] See Anna Rowlands, *Towards a Politics of Communion: Catholic Social Teaching in Dark Times* (London: T&T Clark, 2021), Chapter Four in particular.

[25] Rowlands, *Towards a Politics of Communion*, 85. For an excellent account of the application of "structural sin" to the migrant crisis, see also Kristin E. Heyer, *Kinship Across Borders: A Christian Ethic of Immigration* (Washington, DC: Georgetown University Press, 2012), Chapter Two.

[26] Rowlands, *Towards a Politics of Communion*, 103ff.

[27] Rowlands, *Towards a Politics of Communion*, 109.

misogyny, including gender norms that limit women's agency, legitimizes the "structures of violence" of which Farmer spoke. Thus, his work on the empowerment of the poor, and in a particular way the empowerment of poor women of color, might help address a serious gap in Catholic teaching on social sin. Rowlands asks:

> How do we think theologically about the calcified structures in our midst, about conditioned cultural forms of thinking and knowing, from which our individual and collective minds naturally shrink? ... Why do we tend to fall silent in the face of a violent and abusive social reality—including within the Church itself—that begs for an account of failure that extends beyond individual wrongdoing? The cost of the failure to grapple with such questions is arguably (still) paid by the victims.[28]

Part of the answer lies in genuine human encounter with the other, as Kristin Heyer has argued.[29] For it is through human encounter that we become better able to look beyond simplistic stereotypes and see the human person before us. Farmer's life and writings are a vivid illustration of how encounter with, and learning from, the poor can illuminate our understanding of social exclusion, violence, and invisibility. His attention to the vulnerability of women, and by extension the importance of women's agency, points to an aspect of theological ethics that is in urgent need of magisterial development.

Given poorer women's heightened social, economic, and cultural vulnerability, some theologians have questioned whether Catholic teaching on the sanctity of marriage in fact protects women. Emily Reimer-Barry has argued that Catholic sexual teaching in fact limits women's bodily autonomy and undermines their agency. Heavily reliant on a particular theology of "woman" that places disproportionate emphasis on "motherhood," this teaching reinforces narrow, limiting

---

[28] Rowlands, *Towards a Politics of Communion*, 108.

[29] Heyer, *Kinship Across Borders*, 49: "Such metanoia, or conversion, can occur through personal encounters and relationships that provoke new perspectives and receptivity."

stereotypes.[30] In addition, I would argue that magisterial teaching does not go far enough in condemning the "toxic masculinity" which perpetuates gender-based violence and discrimination.[31] What is needed from Church leadership is strong, clear condemnation of sexism and misogyny in all its forms.

Church leaders must also denounce the violence done to women in and through marriage. One might think of practices such as child marriage, female genital mutilation, and all forms of abuse perpetrated against women within marriage. Julie Clague argues that magisterial teaching on the family is too narrow, focusing largely on divorce, remarriage, and same-sex unions. Consequently, it fails to address the complex problems facing families, and women in particular. There is an opportunity here, Clague asserts, "to broaden Catholic discourse about marriage and family life, and to mobilize Catholic action on behalf of the world's poorest families and their most vulnerable and victimised members."[32] Official teaching does not go far enough in condemning the violent structures that frequently place women at risk of serious injury and deny them their basic human rights.

It is precisely here that we see the value of Farmer's work. He reminds us that efforts to resolve complex global problems must be collaborative and inclusive; they must hear the voices of the most vulnerable and those most affected by injustice; and they need to support the empowerment and agency of women. For this reason, Farmer remains an important voice

---

[30] Paper presented at a conference in Rome, May 2022. See my account in *The Furrow*: "Receiving *Amoris Laetitia*: Learning and Listening as a Global Church," *The Furrow* 73, no.7/8 (2022): 387–394.

[31] By this I mean male stereotypes that place priority on physical strength and power, as well as views of men as dominant and dominating. At best, such stereotypes contribute to an increase in misogynistic and sexist attitudes; at worst, they contribute to rising levels of violence and abuse against women and girls, often leading to serious harm and/or death.

[32] Julie Clague, "*Amoris Laetitia* and the State of the World's Families," in Shaji George Kochuthara, ed., *Vocation and Mission of the Family: Reflections on Chavarul and* Amoris Laetitia (Bengaluru, India: Dharmaram Publications, 2020), 260.

in ongoing discussions of health and human rights, as well as within theological ethics.

Conclusion

Catholic social teaching offers a horizon of meaning and a vision for a better world, and provides us with resources to critique the injustices prevalent throughout our world. But we will always need the prophetic voice, the skeptic who refuses to let the debate die. Paul Farmer was one such voice. His work continues to be an invaluable resource in public health care debates. His thinking provides a lens through which we can better understand the complex realities that fuel injustice and disempower vulnerable populations. As Sen remarked earlier, finding solutions will be difficult, but we journey forward with courage, patience, imagination, and hope. Paul Farmer's work exemplified those virtues, and his life demonstrated vividly what can be achieved in a world that is broken yet filled with possibility.

Suzanne Mulligan, PhD, teaches Moral Theology at the Pontifical University, Maynooth, Ireland. She is a member of the Planning Committee of CTEWC; she is a member of the Editorial Board of the *Journal of Moral Theology*; she is incoming Editor of the *Irish Theological Quarterly*.

Part 3

Accompaniment

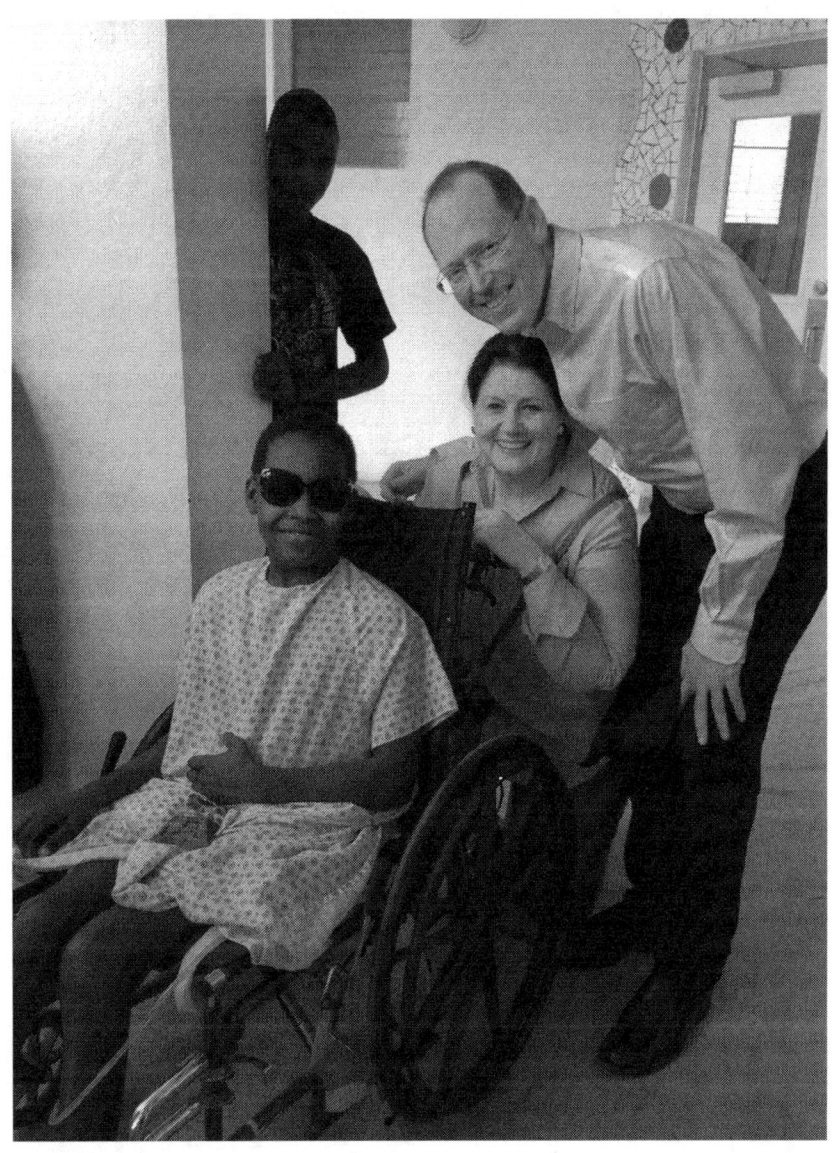

Mirebalais, Mirebalais, Haiti, 2014 (Photo credit: Behna Gardner)
Paul Farmer, Jennie Block, and patient at Hôpital Universitaire de

Part 3: Accompaniment

Foregrounding the voices of concrete people from dispossessed communities requires a preliminary methodological step: accompaniment. In many ways, this is just a different name for the practices lifted up in Part 2—practices of befriending, living with, listening to, and dwelling among the poor. As with many of Farmer's conceptual innovations, the genesis of his notion of accompaniment was simultaneously theoretical and practical. Early in its history, Partners In Health's Haitian partner, Zanmi Lasante, began naming local community health workers *accompagnateurs*. Part 3 explores the concept of accompaniment as a theoretical and praxical hallmark of Farmer's work. Closely allied to accompaniment is his concept of pragmatic solidarity. In addition to explicating the concept itself, these chapters explore key components of the practice—local listening, empowerment, and a companionship with the poor which allows us to learn from them.

The section opens with Chapter Nine, "From *Amoris Laetitia* to Ebola: Accompaniment as a Model for Medical and Pastoral Care." Here James Keenan, SJ, details both Farmer's theoretical account of accompaniment as well as his concrete practice thereof—in contexts as diverse as Boston and the Kissi Triangle (a region in West Africa). Linking it to insights in the work of Pope Francis, particularly in Amoris Laetitia, he advocates for accompaniment as a key practice for both theology and ecclesial ministry.

Among the arguments that are often leveled against the praxis of accompaniment—be it in health care, theology, or policy—is that it is hard to quantify or to measure outcomes, it is often inefficient, open-ended, and can be time consuming. And time is, as we know, money. Brian Volck takes on these assumptions in Chapter Ten, "Wasting Time with the World's Poor: Theological and Scriptural Foundations for Paul Farmer's Praxis of Accompaniment." Drawing on his own experience as a physician

Part 3: Accompaniment

working in the US, Honduras, and the Navajo Nation, Volck homes in on, again, the economic assumptions that have such a stranglehold on our lives and relationships as well as the alternative theological economics embodied in Farmer's witness. Echoing Guardado's observation that in US departments of theology, fieldwork is often considered to be "a waste of time," Farmer challenges us, Volck argues, to practically reimagine of our sense of time and value, letting it be shaped not by a "world of efficiency" but rather by a "world of love" (of charity theologically—not capitalistically—construed). And, as noted in the previous section, such a praxis of accompaniment is epistemological, teaching us (again echoing Lutz) "that the poor must be privileged partners and active participants in any work of liberation." This is not only what real solidarity looks like; it also helps relativize our own over-vaunted self-understandings—it is kenosis. And it is scriptural and sacramental. For accompaniment requires bodily presence, real presence: "For Catholics today, this discernment entails the Real Presence both in the Eucharist and in the gathered Body of Christ, particularly in the poor. Then and now, that the privileged fail to discern Christ's body arises from divisions and factions that keep rich and poor apart."

Finally, in Chapter Eleven, "Practicing Local Listening with Village Midwives in Sudan: A Case Study for Theological Ethics," Meghan Clark offers an extended exemplar of the practice of accompaniment. Drawing on her experience with Helping Babies Breathe Sudan, a training for a national program to train village midwives or traditional birth attendants in basic newborn care, Clark homes in on and details a central aspect of accompaniment already mentioned in this volume: local listening. She demonstrates what local listening, or prioritizing the voices of those excluded from access and thus from outcomes, looks like in practice. How does it look? Not always easy, sometimes hilarious, facing friction due to the social divides identified by Lutz, challenging assumptions, extraordinarily empowering, noetically essential, practically fruitful. In the end she poses a challenge to theology: what would it look like and take to center the voices of the excluded by practicing local listening as a foundation for our moral and theological analysis? It's very hard to "listen enough." Farmer acknowledges how difficult it is to listen, "especially when the subject at hand is social suffering." But he sees listening as necessary for the development of health care and for creating partnerships in which the poor are agents of transformation.

Chapter 9: From *Amoris Laetitia* to Ebola: Accompaniment as a Model for Medical and Pastoral Care

James F. Keenan, SJ

> The Church will have to initiate everyone–priests, religious and laity–into this "art of accompaniment" which teaches us to remove our sandals before the sacred ground of the other (cf. Ex 3:5). The pace of this accompaniment must be steady and reassuring, reflecting our closeness and our compassionate gaze which also heals, liberates and encourages growth in the Christian life.
>
> Pope Francis, *Amoris Laetitia*, no. 169.

> I especially ask Christians in communities throughout the world to offer a radiant and attractive witness of fraternal communion. Let everyone admire how you care for one another and how you encourage and accompany one another.
>
> *Amoris Laetitia*, no. 99.

> Someone good at such accompaniment does not give in to frustrations or fears.
>
> *Amoris Laetitia*, no. 179.

> To accompany someone is to go somewhere with him or her, to break bread together, to be present on a journey with a beginning and an end.
>
> Paul Farmer, "Accompaniment as Policy"[1]

---

[1] Paul Farmer, "Accompaniment as Policy" (commencement address, Kennedy School of Government, Harvard University, May 25, 2011), in *To Repair the World: Paul Farmer Speaks to the Next Generation* (Los Angeles: University of California Press, 2013), 233–248.

I first proposed this essay, having read and reviewed Paul Farmer's *Fevers, Feuds, and Diamonds: Ebola and the Ravages of History* for *America Magazine*, because I thought accompaniment, a word that very much belongs to Pope Francis's own magisterial legacy, very much bridges the world of Catholic theological ethics and the type of public health that Farmer unfailingly proposed.[2] This essay is the fruit of that idea, starting with the pope's proposal and the challenges it has encountered from some in the Catholic hierarchy. It then turns to Farmer's own use of the term and to witnessing his accompanying care among Ebola victims as an indictment of the sanitarians' brutal attempt to contain and not care for its victims. Believing that Farmer's legacy illuminates further the urgency of accompaniment and the way it liberates many from the shackles of colonialism, I conclude with a word about how that legacy might further Francis's campaign to reform both Church ministry and those who govern those works.

Pope Francis on Accompaniment

Much has been written about accompaniment, particularly as it appeared in Pope Francis's apostolic letter on love in the family, *Amoris Laetitia*. There he raised up the consciences of the laity, particularly those who are married, arguing that they needed to be listened to and engaged. Specifically, he called for a ministry of "accompaniment" by clergy and lay ministers who need to encounter and walk with lay people as they sought pathways of greater connection with the church and the sacraments. That ministry is captured in the first three quotations cited above. In a manner of speaking, the pope was anxious about two matters: first, that the church, and especially her priests and bishops, did not adequately appreciate the complexities and exigencies of married and family life and, more interested

---

[2] Paul Farmer, *Fevers, Feuds, and Diamonds: Ebola and the Ravages of History* (New York: Farrar, Straus and Giroux, 2020); and James F. Keenan, "Paul Farmer went to Africa to Fight Ebola. He Found a People Devastated by War and Racism," *America*, March 12, 2021, www.americamagazine.org/arts-culture/2021/03/12/paul-farmer-book-review-ebola-africa-health-240206.

in upholding church rules, they failed to reach out to laity struggling for understanding and support; and, second, at the same time, the laity took the lack of outreach ministry as a sign that they did not belong and have begun withdrawing from the church.

The type of ministry he proposed has borne fruit wherever it has been engaged. Yet, there has been an evident episcopal agnosticism in some quarters, including in the United States, wherein bishops have decidedly not received the magisterial teaching offered in *Amoris Laetitia*. Over the past five years, I have looked at both the wonderful reception and the disturbing non-reception of the ministry of accompaniment proposed by Pope Francis.[3] I have concluded that the episcopal non-reception is integrally connected to a toxic culture within the hierarchy, that I call "hierarchicalism," which generated both the sexual abuse crisis as well as its own step-child, clericalism.[4]

Moreover, the moral theologian Conor M. Kelly has argued that the ministry of accompaniment is not only a message for those in marital ministry or for those in charge of dioceses and parishes. He has charged moral theologians with the responsibility to accompany the laity so that moralists would recognize pathways for the development of both the laity in having a forum to voice their experiences and struggles *and* of the Church in having a moral tradition true to the Gospel and the needs of the People of God. In "The Role of the Moral Theologian in the Church: A Proposal in Light of *Amoris Laetitia*," Kelly responds to the papal admonition that "the teaching of moral theology should not fail to

---

[3] James F. Keenan, "Receiving *Amoris Laetitia*," *Theological Studies* 76, no. 1 (2017): 193–212; James F. Keenan, "Receiving *Amoris Laetitia* throughout the World," in *Pope Francis on the Joy of Love: Theological and Pastoral Reflections on Amoris Laetitia*, ed. Thomas Rausch and Roberto Dell'Oro (Mahwah: Paulist Press, 2018), 150–163; and James F. Keenan, "Regarding *Amoris Laetitia*: Its Language, Its Reception, Some Challenges, and the Agnosticism of Some of the Hierarchy," *Perspectiva Teológica* 53, no. 1 (2021): 41–60, www.faje.edu.br/periodicos/ index.php/perspectiva/article/view/4675/4605.

[4] James F. Keenan, "Hierarchicalism," *Theological Studies* 83, no. 1 (2022): 84–108, doi.org/10.1177/00405639211070493.

incorporate these considerations" (*AL*, no. 311).⁵ Kelly sees in the exhortation's accounts of accompaniment, conscience, and discernment the trajectory that leads to this new function for the moral theologian. He highlights Pope Francis's proposal that "individual conscience needs to be better incorporated into the Church's praxis in certain situations which do not objectively embody our understanding of marriage" (*AL*, no. 303). Kelly recognizes Pope Francis's discerning competence of conscience as resonant with conciliar theology, notably in *Gaudium et Spes*, no. 16, and writes: "By taking this conciliar idea seriously, *Amoris Laetitia* significantly advances the magisterial understanding of conscience, representing another step in an ongoing process of development and reclamation of the tradition that has been active in the church since Vatican II."⁶

Effectively, Kelly directs moral theologians to accompany the laity in developing ways that the laity can better inform the Church in her ministry *and* teaching. He contends that the pope is prompting moral theologians to see that the "magisterial understanding of conscience" requires recognizing the priority of the process of discernment over the definition and application of rules. This emphasis on discernment was routinely recognized by readers of the exhortation,⁷ and moral theologians have read the exhortation's magisterial endorsement of this discernment as a significant shift for their field. In a recent issue of *INTAMS*, I argued

---

⁵ Conor M. Kelly, "The Role of the Moral Theologian in the Church: A Proposal in Light of *Amoris Laetitia*," *Theological Studies* 77, no. 4 (2016): 922–948.

⁶ Kelly refers to David DeCosse, "The Primacy of Conscience, Vatican II, and Pope Francis: The Opportunity to Renew Tradition," in *From Vatican II to Pope Francis: Creating a Catholic Future*, ed. Paul Crowley (Maryknoll, NY: Orbis Books, 2014), 156–169.

⁷ See for instance, James Martin, "Discernment: A Key to '*Amoris Laetitia*,'" *America*, April 7, 2016, americamagazine.org/issue/discernment-key-amoris-laetitia; Nicholas Austin, "Discernment Charged with Merciful Love: Pope Francis' *Amoris Laetitia*, on Love in the Family," *Thinking Faith*, April 8, 2016, www.thinkingfaith.org/articles/discernment-charged-merciful-love-pope-francis%E2%80%99-amoris-laetitia-love-family. See also, Antonio Spadaro and Louis J. Cameli, "Watching for God: The Gift and Challenge of Discernment in 'The Joy of Love,'" *America,* August 1–8, 2016, 24 27; William L. Portier, "A Balancing Act: Reading *Amoris Laetitia*," *Commonweal*, May 20, 2016, 16-18.

that bishops and cardinals faithful to Francis stand with many contemporary moral theologians who have doubled up in interpreting and receiving the apostolic letter in promoting the need to accompany the laity as they discern in conscience their pathways forward.[8]

Paul Farmer and His Style of Accompaniment

Accompaniment is not an idea. It is a vulnerable, embodied practice where one responds to another and journeys with them. It is a very interpersonal form of engagement. The first time I met Paul Farmer, he was accompanied. In 2002, I was teaching "HIV/AIDS and Ethics" with the Jesuit AIDS physician, Jon Fuller, at Weston Jesuit School of Theology (WJST). Fuller suggested we invite Paul Farmer to speak to our graduate course. I did not know Paul at the time. He had not yet published his groundbreaking *Pathologies of Power: Health, Human Rights, and the New War on the Poor.*[9] Fuller in his work on AIDS assured me that meeting Paul would be remarkable. It was.

Paul arrived at our class along with Tracy Kidder, who was then writing *Mountains Beyond Mountains: The Quest of Dr. Paul Farmer, a Man Who Would Cure the World.*[10] Kidder wanted to see Paul in action, and he did. Paul was remarkably fluid. It was as if he had always known everyone in the class and that he and I were long-time friends. There was a playfulness and familiarity to his style that let him approach others easily. He was accompanying us. Since then, I have always thought of Paul as remarkably familiar; he slips in without any need of recognition, a bit of an approachable everyman, completely interested and accessible to the

---

[8] James F. Keenan, "Eight Ways that *Amoris Laetitia* is Being Received and Promoted around the World," *INTAMS Marriage, Families & Spirituality* 28, no. 1 (2022): 4–17.

[9] Paul Farmer, *Pathologies of Power: Health, Human Rights, and the New War on the Poor* (Berkeley: University of California Press, 2003). Paul had already coedited, with Margarete Connors and Jannie Simmons, *Women, Poverty and AIDS: Sex, Drugs and Structural Violence* (Monroe, ME: Common Courage Press, 1996).

[10] Tracy Kidder, *Mountains Beyond Mountains: The Quest of Dr. Paul Farmer, a Man Who Would Cure the World* (New York: Random House, 2003).

other. And, almost always, accompanied. The key was not people moving to him first; as I saw in the class, it was him moving to me and my class first.

Two years later, at the XV International World AIDS Conference in Bangkok, I ran into any number of people whom I knew only by their name tags and who invariably asked me, "Have you seen Paul?" I was struck by the question. I did not know these people, but I knew whom they wanted to find. I remember thinking: who is known by their first name at a meeting of 25,000 public health experts? Paul was.

For years, I have taught Paul's works in my courses, but I have also introduced any number of my undergraduate and graduate students to him, personally. Famously, I introduced Brienna Naughton to him as an undergraduate, and she ended up working at Partners In Health, including a three-year stint in Rwanda. One can say, as I do on these pages, that he accompanied others, but it still bears noting that he rarely went anywhere unaccompanied. Paul was magnetic. Whenever I brought him to speak at Boston College (BC), he came with a crowd. As in Bangkok, where Paul was, others gathered. People trusted him in uncanny ways, in part because he first trusted them.

In 2012, I arrived in Nairobi for a meeting of Catholic Theological Ethics in the World Church (CTEWC). The Jesuit theologian Agbonkhianmeghe Orobator was organizing a pan-African meeting of CTEWC there at Hekima College. A car had been sent to pick up the team from Boston College who arrived there. When we got into the car, the driver asked, "Who's Keenan?" I answered, and he slipped me a piece of paper that said, "Jim, Jennie, and I just got into Nairobi, and as he dropped us off, he remarked he was picking up another group, yours! Let's get together, Paul." The only Jennie I knew was Jennie Weiss Block; the "Paul" had to be Farmer. Five minutes into my arrival in Nairobi, I already received welcome notes from Paul.

In order to remember us, he gave us nicknames. For instance, he called me his spiritual director and Jennie Weiss Block his "interior decorator." He called me "nihil obstat" because he learned that at WJST I was hoping to receive a *nihil obstat* from the Vatican Congregation on Education, a status that means there is nothing I wrote or said that the Vatican Congregation would find objectionable. He gave me the name so as to ensure that I would be recognized as such. Like Pope Francis, he not only proposed accompaniment for the work he oversaw and participated in, he lived it.

Paul Writing on Accompaniment

Paul wrote on accompaniment before Pope Francis proposed it as a recognizable style of ministry in the Church in his apostolic letter. While there are two significant discourses that Paul gives on the term, one in 2006 and then another in 2011, after the second discourse, Paul makes the term one of his trademarks, using the rich concept extensively in three of his more cited works, *Reimagining Global Health: An Introduction*,[11] *In the Company of the Poor: Conversations with Dr. Paul Farmer and Fr. Gustavo Gutierrez*,[12] and *To Repair the World: Paul Farmer Speaks to the Next Generation*.[13]

In a significant but little-known address, "Accompaniment: The Missing Piece of the Funding Puzzle," given at *Grantmakers In Health*'s 2006 Annual Meeting on Health Philanthropy, Paul offered a description of his work in Haiti and then Rwanda with Partners In Health as literally a caring, interpersonal engagement between provider and patient. He saw this way of delivering health care as normative and brought the practice to a wider audience like philanthropists so that they could "bring a lot of people on board to support a broader movement for equity and to promote human rights."[14] Accompaniment directs us not to a disease but

---

[11] Paul Farmer, Arthur Kleinman, Jim Yong Kim, and Matthew Basilico, *Reimagining Global Health: An Introduction* (Berkeley: University of California Press, 2013). The word appears in Farmer, *Pathologies of Power*, but only as an innocent descriptive in an accompanying editorial.

[12] Paul Farmer, Michael Griffin, and Jennie Weiss Block, eds., *In the Company of the Poor: Conversations with Dr. Paul Farmer and Fr. Gustavo Gutiérrez* (Maryknoll, NY: Orbis Books, 2013).

[13] Paul Farmer, *To Repair the World: Paul Farmer Speaks to the Next Generation* (Berkeley: University of California Press, 2019).

[14] Paul Farmer, "Accompaniment: The Missing Piece of the Funding Puzzle" (plenary

to an encounter with others whose health suffers because of inequitable, unhealthy contexts.

In that lecture, Paul proposes the word less as an idea and more as a living practice, as he simply notes that their own PIH health care workers in Haiti and Rwanda are called *accompagnateurs*. These provide a patient "accompaniment—not just giving him his pills but asking how he is feeling, finding out if he needs help with anything from child care to fees for education."[15] Paul describes the experiences of their *accompagnateurs* who encounter all the precarity, challenges, and unanticipated problems that make up life in rural Haiti and Rwanda. Were health-care workers to be found in nice urban health-care centers and not in the communities where their patients lived, they would not encounter the causes of their patients' conditions. Accompaniment meant better engagement with a patient's actual well-being.

In 2011, Paul offered an address, "Accompaniment as Policy," to the graduates of the Kennedy School of Government, where he introduced them to the word as "an elastic term." He emphasized the term's Latin origins *"ad cum panis,"* which refers to a journey that requires taking bread together, noting how the parameters of the journey are unspecified, though the journey, like the bread, is shared. He then set the terms of the journey:

> There's an element of mystery, of openness, in accompaniment: I'll go with you and support you on your journey wherever it leads. I'll keep you company and share your fate for a while. And by "a while," I don't mean a little while. Accompaniment is much more often about sticking with a task until it's deemed completed by the person or people being accompanied, rather than by the *accompagnateur*.[16]

---

remarks, Washington, DC, 2006), Grantmakers In Health's 2006 Annual Meeting on Health Philanthropy, www.gih.org/publication/accompaniment-the-missing-piece-of-the-funding-puzzle/.

[15] Farmer, "Accompaniment: The Missing Piece of the Funding Puzzle," 7.
[16] Farmer, "Accompaniment as Policy," 233–234.

In this address, where one can hear how much Paul recognized the significance of the practice, he notes that leaving the terms of the journey to those being accompanied makes accompaniment "more supportive than supervisory." Clearly replacing the supervisory with the supportive is effectively the same move that Francis makes for ministers walking with the laity. Giving the decision regarding the parameters of the journey to the one being accompanied, Farmer recognizes the agency of that one, but that recognition of agency can only happen through familiar, physical proximity.

In the commencement address, Farmer quotes the theologian Roberto Goizueta: "To 'opt for the poor' is thus to place ourselves *there*, to accompany the poor person in his or her life, death, and struggle for survival."[17] He adds that Goizueta depends on one of the great liberation theologians of Latin America, Gustavo Gutiérrez, who emphasizes "the necessity of physical proximity to accompaniment."

> As a society, we are happy to help and serve the poor, as long as we don't have to walk *with* them where they walk, that is, as long as we can minister to them from our safe enclosures. The poor can then remain passive objects of our actions, rather than friends, *compañeros* and *compañeras* with whom we interact. As long as we can be sure that we will not have to live with them, and thus have interpersonal relationships with them…we will try to help "the poor"—but, again, only from a controllable, geographical distance.[18]

The journey of accompaniment is a tangible, undeniable interpersonal relationship where one walks with another in order to support the other on their journey.[19]

---

[17] Roberto Goizueta, *Christ our Companion: Toward a Theological Aesthetics of Liberation* (Maryknoll, NY: Orbis Books, 2009), 192.

[18] Goizueta, *Christ Our Companion*, 199.

[19] Two months after the commencement address, Paul reiterated many of the themes on accompaniment for a much broader audience; see Paul Farmer, "Partners in Help: Assisting

Ebola and Accompaniment

Paul's experience with Ebola taught him not only the absolute need to replace the barbaric policies of containment with caring accompaniment; it also prompted him to recognize that his patients were in danger not only from the disease and the social structures that made the disease possible but also from the medical practitioners who embodied in their containment approaches the same colonialist vices that prompted the disease in the first place.

In *Fevers, Feuds, and Diamonds: Ebola and the Ravages of History*, Paul writes the defining critique of why care and not containment must always be the only option to health care crises. In it, the story of accompaniment is the key that differentiates actual care from containment. In containment, people are not cared for; indeed, it was precisely to avoid the interpersonal dynamics of care that prompted the control model in the first place. In this monumental work, we follow Paul as he goes in October 2014 with others from Partners In Health to West Africa, specifically to Sierra Leone, Liberia, and Guinea, "the Kissi triangle" as it is known, to respond to the "longest and largest" Ebola epidemic in recorded history that was threatening to hemorrhage beyond its borders. As he writes, "To nurse the sick and to introduce supportive and critical care was what led us there in the first place."[20]

These are fighting words. In this astonishing work, Paul reveals that he and his team were fighting a public health battle against those "sanitarians," as he calls them, who were promoting a "control-over-care response" to the pandemic. As Paul notes, "there was too little *T* in the ETU" (Ebola Treatment Unit).[21] With an emphasis on quarantine and isolation, Africans were again being denied care (treatment), and Paul stood with others in realizing that without safe and effective care in the equation, the response would be a failure.

---

the Poor over the Long Term," *Foreign Affairs*, July 29, 2011, www.foreignaffairs.com/articles/haiti/2011-07-29/partners-help.

[20] Farmer, *Fevers, Feuds, and Diamonds*, xx.

[21] Farmer, *Fevers, Feuds, and Diamonds*, 13.

While history was on the sanitarians side, truth was on his. Unfortunately, control had been a key response on other occasions in the face of contagion, but Farmer did not consider it a legitimate health care response because, in his eyes, failing to provide care meant that the patient was effectively to be sacrificed. Until actual treatment was engaged, until patients were cared for, and cared for well—in other words, accompanied in the fullest sense—the Western global health regime would not be providing effective health care. Moreover, the place itself was a formative context. In the Kissi triangle, slavery, resource extraction, colonialism and warfare had left its people with both "a public health desert, which is why Ebola spread, and a clinical desert, which is why Ebola killed."[22] Into that desert, Paul went to bring care.

To help us realize what was at stake, Paul introduces us to the actors. From the start, Paul, an anthropologist as well as a physician and global health expert, wants us to appreciate that with care (treatment), every American but one survived the virus. While we see Americans and Europeans medevaced home into safety and recovery, we see in Sierra Leone physicians like Humarr Khan and surgeons like Martin Salia struggling to not only provide care but inevitably being brought low and killed by the virus in context. The difference between those who lived by being brought to their US and European homes and those who died in Sierra Leone was care. Care needed to be brought into the desert.

The decision to go to the triangle is told in the second chapter, "Tough Calls." Paul confesses how in June 2014, while attending a surgery conference in Sierra Leone's capital Freetown, a native of Sierra Leone, his student Dr. Bailor Barrie, desperately tries to draw Partners In Health into the emerging Ebola epidemic. Paul resists and leaves. In the meantime, while confronting his anxiety, Paul discovers in his eventual resolve to return that the matter of fact struggle on the horizon had no time for anxiety. Instead, he resonates with the conviction of Dr. Rieux from Albert Camus's *The Plague*: "The essential thing was to save the greatest

---

[22] Farmer, *Fevers, Feuds, and Diamonds*, 23.

From Ebola to Amoris Laetitia

possible number of persons from dying and being doomed to unending separation."[23]

And so, we enter the triangle. To help us understand the magnitude, Paul gives us not numbers, but names. While Trump tweets panic and rage in the background, Paul introduces us to Ibrahim Kamara who "by the age of twenty-six had survived Ebola and the loss of more than twenty members of his family."[24] Ibrahim is not only a victim of Ebola, but he becomes one who teaches others how to care in a time of Ebola. He becomes an *accompagnateur*. And so, Ibrahim wants Paul to hear his story, and, in listening, Paul realizes that he must write this book as a witness to Ibrahim's struggle to care, to provide as Paul later calls it, a lesson in "expert mercy."

Ibrahim's narrative of care and surviving is the story of Sierra Leone. The spectacular epiphany of his resilient compassion appears as nine year-old Mariatu, weighing only twenty-nine pounds, having watched her mother and sister die of Ebola, and having sat in hospital unable to eat in fragile silence for days, whispers into Ibrahim's ear. Once Paul lets you hear what she said, he has hooked you forever.

"The Two Ordeals of Yabom" follows "Ibrahim's Second Chance."[25] Yabom Koroma's first ordeal is confronting the Sierra Leone civil war; her second is surviving Ebola but losing her husband and sons. We see the gaunt Yabom begin her recovery, however, when the survivors program finds her the job of manager of an Interim Care Center where she mothers eighty-four orphans. Yet again, the survivors become the needed caregivers.

But it is not just the means of treatment that concerns Farmer. Earlier he asked: how could a world region boasting such abundant natural wealth have become "a public health desert ... and a clinical desert."[26] In the middle of the book, he goes down the rabbit hole of history to explain how

---

[23] Farmer, *Fevers, Feuds, and Diamonds*, 68.
[24] Farmer, *Fevers, Feuds, and Diamonds*, 96.
[25] Farmer, *Fevers, Feuds, and Diamonds*, 144-176.
[26] Farmer, *Fevers, Feuds, and Diamonds*, 28.

colonial control suffocated the natural life out of the once enormously prosperous triangle leaving it a clinical desert; slavery, resource extraction, subjugation, social theft, the breakdown of local society, and the resulting civil wars helps us see why it was there that Ebola had a chance.[27] Colonialism remains present in the land and in the sanitarians and their non-treatment.

Throughout the book, Paul narrates the pervasive colonial disinterest in the health and care of the local people. Still, he offers those who go against the grain and insist on care as part of civilization, among them, Albert Schweitzer, W.E.B. DuBois, and Graham Greene. No matter his rage, while Paul names "the good," he rarely vilifies by name the sanitarians he opposes.

There is much wisdom in this magisterial work—the riveting preface, the chapters on Ibrahim and Yabom, the epilogue on COVID as another "Black" disease—but the penultimate chapter, "How Ebola Kills" is a tour-de-force. There, in seven steps, Paul indicts the sanitarians: after taking everything away from the people of the triangle, the withholding of care in the pandemic was the last move of racist colonialism. Through the seven simple steps, Farmer shows how neglect and absence of care is integral to the spread of the virus:

> The verdict is in on the control-over-care approach. ... It didn't work during the height of the surge. During the first months of the epidemic, frightened families wanted professional and social assistance with caregiving, but what they got were martial, legal, and prejudicial approaches to Ebola, often downright disrespectful of cultural norms that could have been made safer.

But then, he immediately adds, the activism of the people of the triangle emerges: "Such approaches were not and could not be consistently applied because of brisk resistance from historically-minded and thus distrustful

---

[27] Farmer, *Fevers, Feuds, and Diamonds*, 177–189.

locals—and because of clumsy and often contradictory messages from long-resented authorities."[28]

Farmer is at war against a "therapeutic nihilism" that he rightly notes arises from colonial racist roots. The presumption that "medical intervention cannot change the outcomes," which gave the sanitarians the excuse they wanted, was a comforting fallacy. Farmer's verdict reads it differently. This is the "therapeutic nihilism again, which often leads to the dank dungeons into which black bodies, more than white ones, fall."[29]

In an interview by his landmark organization Partners In Health, Farmer provided the background of the book: "It was the night I met Ibrahim," Farmer recalled, referring to one of the survivors. "We started talking and he told me he'd lost twenty-three members of his family to Ebola. I was shocked into silence. And what he said next was: 'I'd like you to interview me about my experience.'"[30]

In the interview, Farmer noted that "writing is a solitary endeavor, right? But you can make it a bit more social. And for this book, it had to be a social process."[31] To see if he was getting the narrative right, he read parts of the book to Ibrahim and Yabom and another survivor, a young man, named Mohamed but known simply as "the Chairman" "for the efforts he made on behalf of fellow Ebola sufferers."[32] "They understood that they should interrupt me, correct me, [and] explain where I'd gone off on a false track. That was an emotionally rich if sometimes painful way to write. I learned a lot with them."[33]

---

[28] Farmer, *Fevers, Feuds, and Diamonds*, 475.
[29] Farmer, *Fevers, Feuds, and Diamonds*, 475.
[30] Partners In Health, "Q&A: Dr. Paul Farmer on His New Book: Fevers, Feuds, and Diamonds," November 17, 2020, www.pih.org/article/qa-dr-paul-farmer-his-new-book-fevers-feuds-and-diamonds/.
[31] Partners In Health, "Q&A."
[32] Farmer, *Fevers, Feuds, and Diamonds*, 99.
[33] Partners In Health, "Q&A."

From Ebola to Amoris Laetitia

Paul explained his anger at the quality and purpose of the "international response," "which replicated colonial priorities of disease control over care."[34] He notes:

> Even when I was still a medical student, I found hard-core disease control unnerving—all of your attentions are focused on stopping the spread of a pathogen without adequate attention and resources for treating people suffering from said pathogen.
>
> Where in the world was the priority most reliably placed exclusively on disease control with little interest in the care afforded the natives? This paradigm came into being during colonial rule. Year in, year out, epidemic this and epidemic that, I could find some undercurrent that said: "Good, high-quality medical care is for us—not for you, Black people and brown people. We got disease control for you."[35]

Paul's book has been received much as it was presented, by recognizing the need to replace containment with care. I found Martha Lincoln's summary insights very helpful:

> Though this volume covers an enormous amount of terrain—an *Odyssey* or *Iliad* in global public health—its core argument is simple. Farmer submits that responsibly tendered medical care and a functioning health care system would have prevented the transmission of Ebola by inspiring public trust and shifting caregiving into professional settings—and that political economic regimes that operate by limiting and withholding care thus are vectors not only of violence but also of contagion.[36]

---

[34] Farmer, *Fevers, Feuds, and Diamonds*, 99.
[35] Farmer, *Fevers, Feuds, and Diamonds*, 99.
[36] Martha Lincoln, "Global Health is Dead; Long Live Global Health! Critiques of the Field and its Future," *BMJ Global Health* 6 (2021): 4, doi:10.1136/bmjgh-2021-006648.

She concludes naming Paul's argument: "For global health to equip itself with explanatory models and situational appraisals that are humanistic, critically historicized, and focused on upstream material causes."[37]

Conclusion

At a recent conference in Rome about two hundred Catholic theologians and pastoral leaders met to discuss *Amoris Laetitia*. These theologians were among those who have labored most for its reception along with its model of ministry through accompaniment. For many of us, Francis's plea for accompaniment is so patently necessary for alienated laity that opposition to both the letter and the ministerial practice only furthers the harm that past practices prompted.[38] Had Paul been there at the conference, he would have lent support arguing that for any ministry of care, accompaniment is the only way forward.

Reading Farmer in the light of *Amoris Laetitia* yields parallels between accompaniment and care, between excommunication and containment, between sanitarians and hierarchs. They are helpful because they mutually highlight the efforts of the reformers in both contexts who see the need to go forward by a form of service that is measured by its humanity. Indeed, that is what Francis and Paul want: a more human approach to physical and spiritual well-being by drawing near to one another as we journey in support, especially of others whose own pathways have not yet been sufficiently recognized. As more take on accompaniment—physicians, ministers, moral theologians, lay persons, as well as those who carry in their

---

[37] Lincoln, "Global Health is Dead"; see also Sally Weiner, "Review of *Fevers, Feuds, and Diamonds: Ebola and the Ravages of History* by Paul Farmer," *Journal of Health Care for the Poor and Underserved* 32, no. 1 (2021): 582–583, doi.org/10.1353/hpu.2021.0042; and Priscilla Medeiros, Allyson Oliphant, Steven Farrow, and Priyanka Gill, "Anthropological Engagements with Global Health," *Medicine Anthropology Theory* 9, no. 3 (2022): 1–10, doi.org/10.17157/mat.9.3.5628.

[38] Christopher White, "Rome Conference Revisits '*Amoris Laetitia*' and Church's Call to Welcome Marginalized Catholics," *National Catholic Reporter*, May 24, 2022, www.ncronline.org/news/rome-conference-revisits-amoris-laetitia-and-churchs-call-welcome-marginalized-catholics/.

bodies the scars of centuries of colonialism, racism, hierarchicalism, clericalism—more will learn about lives long overlooked, and walking with them they will see that it is the only way to move forward.[39]

James Keenan, SJ, **STD,** is the Canisius Chair, Director of the Jesuit Institute, and Vice-Provost for Global Engagement at Boston College. A Jesuit priest since 1982, he received a licentiate and a doctorate from the Pontifical Gregorian University in Rome. He has edited or written 25 books and published over 400 essays, articles, and reviews. The founder of Catholic Theological Ethics in the World Church (www.catholicethics.com), he chaired the international conferences in Padua (2006), Trento (2010), and Sarajevo (2018). In addition to Boston College, he has taught at Fordham University, Weston Jesuit School of Theology, John Carroll University, the Ateneo de Manila, Dharmaram Vidya Kshetram in Bangalore, and at his alma mater. His most recent book, *A History of Catholic Theological Ethics*, will be published in June 2023 by Paulist Press. In 2022, he delivered The Martin D'Arcy, SJ, Memorial Lectures at Campion Hall, Oxford. The lectures, entitled *Preparing for the Moral Life*, will be published by Georgetown University Press in 2023.

---

[39] See the remarkable work, Gerard J. Ryan, *Mutual Accompaniment as Faith-Filled Living: Recognition of the Vulnerable Other* (New York: Palgrave Macmillan, 2022).

Chapter 10: Wasting Time with the World's Poor: Theological and Scriptural Foundations for Paul Farmer's Praxis of Accompaniment

Brian Volck

David Hilfiker, a physician who, like Paul Farmer, often uses theological language when critiquing the medical-industrial complex's[1] barrier-laden model of care for the poor, also shared Farmer's interest in speaking to doctors early in their career. Like Farmer, he saw how quickly the economic pressures and quotidian moral distresses of modern medical practice crush the idealism with which many enter the profession. Hilfiker recalls an address to medical students and faculty in which he described the lives of his impoverished inner-city patients and his struggles to meet their basic health needs. While his younger listeners found Hilfiker's stories inspiring, a professor of pediatric surgery publicly chided him, saying, "I can only applaud your commitment to the poor, Dr. Hilfiker, but don't you think it's a waste of your professional education?... It seems to me your job might better be done by a social worker or nurse practitioner, while you used your talents more effectively elsewhere."[2]

If most physicians would quickly brush off such pointed public criticism, Hilfiker faces it head-on. Farmer's approach to poverty medicine was more ambitious than Hilfiker's, but I suspect Farmer would have done likewise. Near the end of Tracy Kidder's *Mountains Beyond Mountains,*

---

[1] I use the term, "medical-industrial complex" to signify that conjunction of political, economic, scientific, technological, educational, and social interests, institutions, and investments that make the US health care system the most expensive in the world despite its relatively poor public health outcomes when compared to other economically developed nation-states.

[2] David Hilfiker, *Not All of Us Are Saints: A Doctor's Journey with the Poor* (New York: Ballantine Books, 1994), 213.

the author takes an arduous hike with Farmer who wants to see for himself the living conditions of one of his Haitian patients with tuberculosis. Along the way, the two Americans discuss the massive institutional barriers that prevent the world's poor from receiving appropriate medical care. Farmer describes the morally fraught triage process of choosing when, where, and to whom one allocates time, money, and other scarce resources in such unforgiving systems as "a long defeat," saying:

> You know, people from our background—like you, like most PIH-ers, like me—we're used to being on a victory team, and actually what we're trying to do is to make common cause with the *losers*. Those are two very different things. We *want* to be on the winning team, but at the *risk* of turning our backs on the losers, no, it's not worth it. So you fight the long defeat.... And most of the time when people ask about triage, most of the time they're asking not with open hostility but deep distrust of our answer.[3]

The phrase, "the long defeat," is more often associated with J.R.R. Tolkien[4], but Farmer uses it here in an apt and telling way. He reminds us that history is written by the human victors in a fallen world: the rich, the powerful, the healthy, and well-fed. In the eyes of those whose opinions are said to matter, choosing to ally with the so-called losers is a waste of time.

---

[3] Tracy Kidder, *Mountains Beyond Mountains: The Quest of Dr. Paul Farmer, A Man Who Would Cure the World*, (New York: Random House, 2003), 288–289. Emphases in the original.

[4] In *The Lord of the Rings*, Galadriel tells the surviving members of the Fellowship, "He (i.e., Celeborn) has dwelt in the West since the days of dawn, and I have dwelt with him years uncounted...and together through ages of the world we have fought the long defeat," J.R.R. Tolkien, *The Fellowship of the Ring*, Second Edition, (Boston, MA: Houghton Mifflin, 1954), 372. In a letter to Amy Ronald dated December 19, 1956, Tolkien writes, "Actually I am a Christian, and indeed a Roman Catholic, so that I do not expect 'history' to be anything but a 'long defeat'— though it contains (and in legend may contain more clearly and movingly) some samples or glimpses of final victory," Letter 195, *The Letters of J.R.R. Tolkien,* edited by Humphrey Carpenter (Boston, MA: Houghton Mifflin, 1981), 255.

Farmer, of course, used different measures of value. Never conspicuously guilty of the sin of sloth, he nonetheless cast his lot with the world's poor, spending precious time in their company when he might otherwise have been courting wealthy donors or challenging entrenched bureaucracies to modify short-sighted policies. In defending his habits and choices, Farmer was more likely to quote liberation theology and Catholic social teaching than cite scripture, yet the authors and documents he drew upon were deeply informed by biblical texts of which he was no doubt familiar. What follows is an attempt to understand Farmer's praxis of accompaniment as a theologically informed "waste of time," first through my own experience as a physician, then through the words of Paul Farmer, David Hilfiker, and selected theologians and philosophers, and finally through relevant passages from scripture. I conclude with a short coda on Paul Farmer as a doer of the word (James 1:22) whose insights on the proper use of time might inform health care professionals, theologians, and the Church.

Life Lessons from the Long Defeat

In small ways, I have skirmished in the long defeat throughout my medical career: providing hospital-based pediatric care on the Navajo Nation, helping direct an inner-city community health center, and staffing clinics in rural Honduras. I have taught medical students and residents how to adapt their care to vulnerable patient populations in challenging settings.[5] I have consulted at Indian Health Service facilities where creative colleagues provide outstanding health care with grossly inadequate resources. I have chaired international medical conferences on indigenous child health and advocated for native child health on Capitol Hill.[6]

---

[5] Tiffiny Diers, Susan Montauk, Lisa Vaughn, Corinne Lehmann, Joseph Kiesler, Charles Schubert, Douglas Smucker, and Brian Volck, "Competencies for the Adaptable Physician: Training Residents to Care for Vulnerable Populations," *The Open Medical Education Journal* 2 (2009): 26–35.

[6] See American Academy of Pediatrics Committee on Native American Child Health, www.aap.org/en/community/aap-committees/committee-on-native-american-child-

Though these have been professionally and personally rewarding for me and, I hope, of some benefit to those I claimed to serve, it would be far more telling to ask the latter rather than rely on my word.

On rare occasions—much rarer than I care to admit—I have worked *with* and *alongside* the poor: repairing roofs or weeding yards in a Hopi village and lingering afterward listening to a Hopi veteran's stories from the Korean War; digging a new outhouse or rebuilding a sheep pen alongside members of the Diné (Navajo) nation; hiking to a destitute Honduran family's one-room hut at the top of an eroded mountainside *milpa*; sharing meals, memories, and tears with parents and patients who became lifelong friends despite our many differences. While these make for great stories—details of which I am reluctant to share because they are so intimate—they largely serve as anti-credentials for anyone hoping to ascend the medical hierarchy. To what the author Wendell Berry calls medicine's "world of efficiency"—as opposed to the "world of love"—these experiences look like wasted time.[7] Once again, it would help to ask those I worked alongside if I proved anything more than a novelty in their lives, but I know these encounters have irrevocably changed me.

Changed how? Three ways come to mind. First, working *with* the poor exposed everyday realities of some who struggle to live on the wrong side of the world's savage inequalities: conditions I cannot unsee; wrongs I am obliged to remedy.

Second, I learned from good and bad examples that the poor must be privileged partners and active participants in any work of liberation. Restorative justice demands solidarity, not unidirectional charity.[8]

---

health/. My service on this committee was limited to 2009–2015. All opinions expressed here are my own and do not reflect those of the Committee on Native American Child Health, the American Academy of Pediatrics, the International Meeting on Indigenous Child Health, or the Indian Health Service.

[7] Wendell Berry, "Health is Membership," in *Another Turn of the Crank* (Washington, DC: Counterpoint, 1995), 101.

[8] Farmer wisely warns against the progressive urge "to overstate the case against charity....To the extent that medicine responds to, rather than creates, underserved populations, charity will

Third, this work encouraged me to get over myself and the pretensions of my profession. I understand now that I possess a slender skill set, the bulk of which derives from my socioeconomic privilege rather than personal merit. Anyone with my training could do what I have done *for* the poor, and many have served them far better than me. Almost nothing I have done *with* them required a medical degree though, on occasion, the impressive initials after my name helped open doors and ears that may otherwise have remained shut. My wife, who is also a physician, had a similar epiphany during her studies in public health, wondering aloud, "Why did I waste my time becoming a doctor when what really makes a difference in the lives of the poor are basics like clean water, decent sanitation, and women's education?"

Love's Grammar in a Suffering World

Perhaps "wasting time becoming a doctor" misses the mark. My wife and I have, like many other physicians, attempted to use our training and social standing for the benefit of the poor and, again like many physicians, have learned much from patients in our clinical care. Yet, our most profound lessons came when we transgressed socially constructed borders of wealth, education, nationality, race, and profession. As Paul Farmer lamented in a conversation with Gustavo Gutiérrez:

> One of the things that happens in medicine is that professionals are so busy that they limit the borders of their world to wherever they are and to whichever patients get to them in their hospitals or clinics. That's *their* world of the sick. But it's not true of the sick. There are many who never receive good medical care. The world of the sick is vast, just like the world of suffering .... The world of the sick is part of the world of suffering.[9]

---

always have its place in medicine." Paul Farmer, *Pathologies of Power: Health, Human Rights, and the New War on the Poor* (Berkeley, CA: University of California Press, 2003), 154.

[9] From "Reimagining Accompaniment: An Interview with Paul Farmer and Gustavo Gutiérrez," in *In the Company of the Poor: Conversations with Dr. Paul Farmer and Fr.*

In that same conversation, Gutiérrez—citing examples from Farmer's work—stressed the centrality of loving relationship in response to that world of suffering. "Liberation from sin is liberation from the refusal to love," Gutiérrez said, and "to accompany, to be close, and to mitigate the suffering of individuals...is an expression of love, with the intention being to show that *you* are relevant to *me*."[10] On a Christian rationale for encountering the suffering other, he added:

> Even today with the witness of Jesus, for some people, suffering is the means to save us. It is not so. It is love, not suffering. Suffering was the price to pay for announcing the Kingdom of God. Jesus accepted to pay this price, but for what? For love. We have no other reason than this.[11]

And drawing on the twentieth century Jewish philosopher, Emmanuel Levinas, Gutiérrez observed:

> The grammar book of any language will tell you that the first person is "I," "I am." I think the first person is "you are," and after we have recognized that you are, we can say, "I am." ...Levinas calls this the priority of the ethical over the epistemological. First you establish a relation with the other, and then you have a basis for choosing to pursue knowledge.... How we should be toward others, not what we can know, is the central question of philosophy.[12]

"Love" is a term rarely heard in hospital corridors and medical school classrooms. Health educators and medical ethicists typically speak of compassion rather than love, though the latter is chief among the

---

Gustavo Gutiérrez, ed. Michael Griffin and Jennie Weiss Block (Maryknoll, NY: Orbis Books, 2013), 170. Emphasis in the original.
[10] "Reimagining Accompaniment," 166. Emphasis in the original.
[11] Reimagining Accompaniment," 179.
[12] Reimagining Accompaniment," 187.

theological virtues.[13] Whenever I asked my medical team if they loved their patients, their response ranged from bewilderment to annoyance. They much preferred discussing the finer points of acid-base equilibrium to articulating reasons why we care for the unpleasant, unproductive, or unpromising patient. Yet, few questions are more relevant within the medical-industrial complex that serves as the locus of education for health care professionals and technocrats: why should anyone devote scarce time and resources on the invisible indigent, the undocumented immigrant, the intellectually disabled?[14] In a world of cost-benefit analyses, evidence-based algorithms, and corporate earnings reports, speaking of love seems a category mistake, a waste of time.

The Cost of Compassion

Even under its preferred synonym, "compassion," love is at best treated as a useful quality supplementing a far more important—and measurable—attribute: technical competence. "Time," we are told, "is money," and what truly counts in the calculus of medical value is the net total of desirable results over some predetermined interval. To be fair, I don't know anyone willing to entrust their life to an empathetic quack when a stony-faced but technically brilliant physician is available. Most prefer an affable expert to these extremes as long as the physician's compassion does not cloud her judgment. Contemporary biomedicine offers compelling reasons to discourage practitioners from becoming "overly involved" with their patients, but getting these emotional boundaries right remains a

---

[13] See Brian Volck, "What's Love Got to Do with It? Situating a Theological Virtue in the Practice of Medicine," *Journal of Moral Theology* 1, no. 2 (2012): 72–95.

[14] Calling these "far and away the most important questions in medical ethics," Farmer cites the Jesuit liberation theologian, Jon Sobrino: "The poor and impoverished of the world, in virtue of their very reality, constitute the most radical question of the truth of this world, as well as the most correct response to this question." From Jon Sobrino, *Spirituality of Liberation: Toward Political Holiness* (Maryknoll, NY: Orbis Books, 1988), 30; quoted in Farmer, *Pathologies of Power,* 202.

challenge.[15] As Hilfiker, the doctor who was told he had wasted his medical education on the poor, describes his professional experience:

> Compassion...brings me too close and threatens the wall separating us. I begin to fear that there is little essential difference between "them" and me. My own demons stir, and I must either avoid the suffering of the poor or wrestle with myself. If the impulse toward avoidance is so powerful for the individual, it becomes overwhelming for any group or organization. Institutions tend to sink to the level of the least compassionate response.[16]

As Hilfiker implies, the driving force behind compassion fatigue is not exhaustion but fear, an existential crisis of difference in which the pressing needs of the poor are sacrificed for the continued wellbeing of the privileged.[17] Farmer likewise warns that unguarded closeness to the poor risks realizing that we, the privileged, are "implicated, whether directly or indirectly, in the creation and maintenance of structural violence … [We] then feel indignation, but also humility and penitence," adding that "this posture—of penitence and indignation—is critical to effective social justice work."[18]

Having witnessed attending physicians publicly excoriate residents and medical students for trivial mistakes, I have seen the role indignation takes in medical education. Neither humility nor penitence, however, play to the medical profession's strong suit. Farmer had no language to address this lacuna until he encountered liberation theology. Having learned for

---

[15] While maintaining professional distance in medicine has deep historical roots, the Urtext of "imperturbability" in modern clinical medicine is Sir William Osler's still highly influential 1889 farewell address to the Pennsylvania School of Medicine, "Aequanimitas." See *Aequanimitas with Other Addresses to Medical Students, Nurses, and Practitioners of Medicine* (Philadelphia, PA: Blakiston, 1932).

[16] Hilfiker, *Not All of Us Are Saints*, 179.

[17] Regarding the "crisis of difference" in its original context, see René Girard, *Violence and the Sacred* (Baltimore, MD: Johns Hopkins University Press, 1972), 49–52.

[18] Farmer, *Pathologies of Power*, 157.

himself rather than in medical school that infectious disease and early death make their own preferential option for the poor, Farmer needed Gutiérrez, Jon Sobrino, and Leonardo Boff to understand why. Most physicians, Farmer discovered, invest far too much in the status quo to permit "a rejection of its comforting relativism" or to consult the suffering and exploited poor whose viewpoints "will inevitably be suppressed or neglected as long as elites control most means of communication," and, above all, "to *act* on these reflections."[19] Institutionalized inertia rather than greed or malice discourages well-intentioned health care professionals from "wasting time" with the poor. It should come as no surprise, then, that when the world's poor assess the medical-industrial complex using liberation theology's basic methodology, *"ver, juzgar, actuar"* (observe, judge, act), they find it wanting.

A Real Waste of Time

All this talk of love and wasting time with the poor brings us to the role of accompaniment as articulated by Gutiérrez, namely, "If there is no friendship with ... (the poor) and no sharing of the life of the poor, then there is no authentic commitment to liberation, because love exists only among equals."[20] Insisting that solidarity with the poor requires the privileged to make a conscious act of conversion, Gutiérrez draws on Matthew 25: 31–46 ("Whatever you did for one of these least of mine you did for me"), to assert:

> This is a work of love that implies a gift of self and is not simply a matter of fulfilling a duty. It is a work of concrete, authentic love for the poor that is not possible apart from a certain integration into their world and

---

[19] Famer, "Health, Healing, and Justice: Insights from Liberation Theology," in *In the Company of the Poor*, 41-42. Implicit in this sequence is liberation theology's basic methodology, *"ver, juzgar, actuar"* (see, judge, act).

[20] Gustavo Gutiérrez, *A Theology of Liberation* (Maryknoll, NY: Orbis Books, 1973).

not possible apart from bonds of real friendship with those who suffer despoilation and injustice.[21]

The Cuban-American theologian, Roberto Goizueta brings different emphases to the same dynamic:

> The option for the poor ... forces us to be honest about reality by forcing us to recognize the intrinsically relational or communal character of human persons and actions. In other words, the choice before us all, wealthy and poor alike, is not whether to be with the poor, but whether to do so *self-consciously* and *intentionally*; like it or not, we are already with the poor and the poor are already with us. Every day, all of us—whether poor or wealthy, underprivileged or privileged—experience the consequences of poverty and oppression. For the privileged, those consequences take many forms: a paralyzing fear of other persons, constant anxiety about protecting one's possessions against the "threat" represented by the poor, the need to enclose and seclude oneself behind increasingly high walls and expensive alarm systems, (and) the psychological problems, broken relationships, and various forms of addiction caused by this ever-present, stressful fear and anxiety. ... The need to enslave *others* inevitably produces a generalized fear and anxiety which, in the end, enslave us *all*.[22]

In Goizueta's account, the practice of accompaniment is not the heroic option of an autonomous individual but a practical response to an otherwise obscured social fact: the poor are, indeed, always with us in sickness and in health. In seeking solidarity with the world's poor, the privileged work toward a shared liberation. Health and its cognate virtues of wholeness and holiness exceed the grasp of the isolated individual. They wither when confined to gated compounds. As Wendell Berry writes,

---

[21] Gustavo Gutiérrez, "Conversion: A Requirement for Solidarity," in *In the Company of the Poor*, 81.

[22] Robert Goizueta, *Caminemos con Jesús: Toward a Hispanic/Latino Theology of Accompaniment* (Maryknoll, NY: Orbis Books, 1995), 178. Emphases in the original.

"The grace that is the health of creatures can only be held in common. In healing the scattered members are brought together."[23] A quotation usually associated with the Murri (Australian Aboriginal) activist, Lilla Watson, puts the matter more bluntly: "If you have come here to help me, you are wasting your time. But if you have come because your liberation is bound up with mine, then let us work together."[24]

Texts and Time

When Gutiérrez grounds a theology of accompaniment in scripture, he often turns to Old Testament texts including Exodus, Leviticus (especially chapter 25), Deuteronomy, Psalms, Job, and Jeremiah (especially chapter 32). Within the New Testament, he cites, among others, Matthew (especially 25:31–46), Luke-Acts, Romans, 1 Corinthians, and James.[25] While Farmer was not a scripture scholar, much of his work seems tacitly grounded in the biblical text so dear to the poor with whom he labored. As he explained to Tracy Kidder:

> The fact that any sort of religious faith was so disdained at Harvard and so important to the poor—not just in Haiti but elsewhere, too—made me even more convinced that faith was something good.... I was taken with the idea that in an ostensibly godless world that worshipped money and power *or, more seductively, a sense of efficacy and advancement,* like

---

[23] Wendell Berry, "Healing," in *What Are People For?* (New York: North Point Press), 9.

[24] Watson attributes this saying to a community of Aboriginal activists in Queensland, Australia in the 1970s. See Lilla Watson, "Keynote Address: A Contribution to Change: Cooperation Out of Conflict Conference: Celebrating Difference, Embracing Equality," *Uniting Church in Australia*, 2004, uniting.church/lilla-watson-let-us-work-together/, and "Attributing Words," *US Against Equine Slaughter*, November 3, 2008, unnecessaryevils.blogspot.com/2008/11/attributing-words.html. That Anglo-Americans reflexively assign the insight to an individual rather than a collective says a great deal about the intellectual assumptions of so-called developed nations.

[25] See, for example, Gutiérrez, *A Theology of Liberation* and *On Job: God Talk and the Suffering of the Innocent* (Maryknoll, NY: Orbis Books, 1987) as well as "Reimagining Accompaniment," in *In the Company of the Poor*. This list is in no way comprehensive and does not reflect the entirety of his profound engagement with scripture in his work.

at Duke and Harvard, there was still a place to look for God, and that was in the suffering of the poor. You want to talk crucifixion? I'll show you crucifixion, you bastards. [26]

Among the biblical texts implicitly informing Farmer's practice of accompaniment, perhaps most relevant are Matthew 25, 1 Corinthians 11–13, and James, especially chapters 2, 4, and 5. In Matthew 25:31–46, the nations standing in judgement before the throne of glory are astonished to discover that what they did or failed to do to the hungry or thirsty, the stranger, the naked, the sick, or the imprisoned was in fact rendered to the Son of Man.[27] It is deadly to misread this parable alongside Hebrews 13:2 ("Do not neglect hospitality to strangers, for by this some have entertained angels without knowing it") as if in "being nice" to those in need, a lucky few unwittingly receive a disguised and docetic Christ, thereby winning the cosmic lottery. No, the text *identifies* the Son of Man with "the least among you." In practicing the corporal acts of mercy, we encounter Christ's Real Presence by being really and corporeally present to the poor. Thoughts and prayers are inadequate responses to the God who loves and abides in the poor—a message very close to the gospel's heart.[28] Those who do not make themselves really present to the poor in embodied love cannot claim to love God for, "If someone says, 'I love God,' and yet he hates his brother or sister, he is a liar; for the one who does not love his brother and sister whom he has seen, cannot love God, whom he has not seen." (1 John 4:20)

As first century Palestinian Jews, Jesus and his hearers would have understood these practices as *mitzvot,* personal and corporate

---

[26] Kidder, *Mountains Beyond Mountains,* 85. Emphasis mine. Soon thereafter, he confides, "I'm still looking for something in the sacred text that says, 'Thou shalt not use condoms'" (86).

[27] The Greek word, ἔθνη, often translated as "nations," can also signify "people," "tribes," "gentiles," and "pagans."

[28] See, for example, Matthew 5:42, 10:42, 15:32-37, 23:14; Mark 6:30–44, 8:1-3; Luke 1:52–53, 3:10–11, 4:18, 6:20–21, 10:23–37, 14:13–14, 16:14–15 and 19–31, 19:8–9, 26:46–47; and John 6:1–14.

embodiments of Torah.[29] In the eyes of their Roman imperial occupiers, however, attending to the needs of poor, marginalized, and unproductive provincials would have seemed a misdirected effort, a colossal waste of time. Though ancient Rome numbered *liberalitas,* "generosity," among its public virtues, the practice was expected of wealthy patricians, political leaders, and emperors in conspicuous displays of largesse to the general citizenry or worthy individuals. In Judaism, the suffering other requires the attention and presence of all regardless of station in life. The observant Jew deliberately pauses to acknowledge that we are already, through a shared humanity, entailed in one another's distress. In the words of Levinas, the Jewish philosopher whom Gutiérrez quotes above, the other's face is "a trace of itself, given over to my responsibility, but to which I am wanting and faulty."[30] For Levinas, seeing the face of another person is a moment of fraught privilege, a calling to account, a summons prior to and independent of words.

Discerning Bodies

It is this disturbing privilege, rooted in scriptural tradition and sustained by embodied presence to the lives of the poor, that enabled Farmer to expose the idols of bourgeois liberalism that bury savage inequalities under a cloak of abstract procedural language. In *Pathologies of Power,* he writes:

> Liberation theologians are among the few who have dared to underline, from the left, the deficiencies of the liberal human rights movement. *The most glaring of these deficiencies emerges from intimate acquaintance with the poor* in countries that are signatory to all modern human rights agreements. When children living in poverty die of measles,

---

[29] *Pirkei Avot,* a tractate of Mishnah compiled rabbinic wisdom from the late Second Temple and early post-Temple periods. See, for example, *Pirkei Avot* 1:2, "Shimon the Righteous was among the last surviving members of the Great assembly. He would say: The world stands on three things: Torah, the service of God, and deeds of kindness," and 1:5a, "Yossei the son of Yochanan of Jerusalem would say: Let your home be wide open, and let the poor be members of your household."

[30] Emmanuel Levinas, *Otherwise than Being,* trans. A. Lingis (Dordrecht: Nijhoff, 1974), 91.

gastroenteritis, and malnutrition, and yet no party is judged guilty of a human rights violation, liberation theology finds fault with the entire notion of human rights as defined within liberal democracies. Thus, even before judgment is rendered, the "observe" part of the (liberation theology) formula reveals atrocious conditions as atrocious.[31]

Many of those ostensibly working *for* the world's poor do so from the safety of labyrinthine bureaucracies, framing their efforts within a vocabulary of rights, progress, and development. They may even know some among the poor by name yet avoid immersing themselves in the practical messiness of their lives. The world of efficiency offers compelling reasons for doing this, incentives from which I have seldom proved immune. My CV is padded with medical site visits to exotic settings and global health conferences in cosmopolitan cities. Most of these adventures were designed for brevity and efficiency, assiduously maintaining a healthy distance from the poor, the very people we claimed were our primary concern. Noted experts advised such precautions were necessary for professional functioning and personal wellbeing. Well-meaning colleagues reminded me that the poor will always be with us and warned against risking "burnout," a malady rarely diagnosed among the destitute.[32] For Farmer, however, this withholding of embodied presence leads to half solutions and sham solidarity:

> Ironically enough, some who understand, quite correctly, that the underlying causes of tuberculosis are poverty and social inequality make a terrible error in failing to honor the experience and views of the poor in designing strategies to respond to the disease. What happens if, after analysis reveals poverty as the root cause of tuberculosis, tuberculosis control strategies ignore the sick and focus on eradicating poverty? Elsewhere, I have called this the "Luddite trap," since this ostensibly progressive view would have us ignore both current distress and the tools

---

[31] Farmer, *Pathologies of Power*, 142. Emphasis mine.

[32] The poor, whose reasons for despair are legion, suffer depression and remain mired in poverty. The privileged, for whom agency is key, experience burnout and find another job.

of modern medicine that might relieve it, thereby committing a new and grave injustice. The destitute sick ardently desire the eradication of poverty, but their tuberculosis can be readily cured by drugs such as isoniazid and rifampin. The prescription for poverty is not so clear.[33]

From my own experience speaking to congressional staffers and medical organizations about social determinants of health, the difference between legislative band aids and effective therapy often turns on getting policy makers to see for themselves what's at stake. Only in the company of the poor will such momentous distinctions come to light. When the filters of bureaucracy and professional distance are removed and the suffering other is at last seen as a fellow human being in urgent need, a core component of the Partners In Health mission becomes clear: Treat the patient in front of you.

Saint Paul's First Letter to the Corinthians underscores the necessity of bodily presence to the poor. In chapters 10 through 15, Paul develops a sustained argument on the goodness of the body—both individual and corporate—in the economy of salvation. The passages most relevant to the practice of accompaniment, however, start with verses 11:17 ff., in which Paul lambastes the Corinthians for creating divisions and factions in the community so severe that some leave church sated with food and wine while others go hungry.[34] What enrages Paul is that the Corinthians do this even as they gather for Eucharist:

> Therefore, whoever eats the bread or drinks the cup of the Lord in an unworthy way, shall be guilty of the body and the blood of the Lord. But a person must examine himself, and in so doing he is to eat of the bread and drink of the cup. For the one who eats and drinks, eats and drinks judgment to himself if he does not properly recognize the body. For this

---

[33] Farmer, *Pathologies of Power*, 146.
[34] See Joel Shuman and Brian Volck, *Reclaiming the Body: Christians and the Faithful Use of Modern Medicine* (Grand Rapids, MI: Brazos Press, 2006), 55–57.

reason, many among you are weak and sick, and a number are asleep. (1 Corinthians 11:27–30)

The reason, Paul says, that some are weak, sick, or "asleep" (i.e., dead), lies in the failure of the privileged and well-fed elite to recognize (the Greek verb, διακρίνω, is often translated as "discern") the body. For Catholics today, this discernment entails the Real Presence both in the Eucharist and in the gathered Body of Christ, particularly in the poor. Then and now, that the privileged fail to discern Christ's body arises from divisions and factions that keep rich and poor apart. Those of us in the health professions too often resemble Job's alleged friends, sitting at a distance and muttering pious nonsense in answer to Job's protests of innocence. About these "comforters," Gutiérrez writes:

> If these men were to be silent and listen, they would demonstrate the wisdom they claim to possess. Those who experience at close range the sufferings of the poor, or of anyone who grieves and is abandoned, will know the importance of what Job is asking for. The poor and the marginalized have a deep-rooted conviction that no one is interested in their lives and misfortunes. They also have the experience of deceptive expressions of concern from persons who in the end only make their problems all the worse.[35]

Likewise, Farmer argues that physicians and other health care professionals should be among the poor, listening to, befriending, assisting, and advocating for those who are suffering now. Citing Rudolph Virchow, the nineteenth century pathologist and founder of social medicine, Farmer writes that the current system:

> ensures that large numbers of people, in the United States and out of it, will be simultaneously put at risk for disease and denied access to care. In fact, the spectacular successes of biomedicine have in many instances

---

[35] Gutiérrez, *On Job*, 24.

further entrenched medical inequalities. This necessarily happens whenever new and effective therapies...are not made available to those in need. Perhaps it was in anticipation of late-twentieth-century technology that Virchow argued the physicians must be the "natural attorneys of the poor."[36]

Doing the Word in God's Good Time

The Letter of James, with its emphasis on being "doers of the word," (1:22–25), the necessity to act on one's faith (2:14–26), and the imminent downfall of the unrepentant rich (5:1–6), is a textual trove for liberation theologians. I focus here on just two passages. In 2:1, the letter's author asks if those who show partiality to the rich and ignore the poor actually hold any faith in Christ. His readers, like too many of us today, take notice of the well-dressed elite and disregard the poor, thereby making problematic distinctions (2:2–4). Yet, the author continues, there are distinctions to be made:

> Listen, my beloved brothers and sisters: did God not choose the poor of this world to be rich in faith and heirs of the kingdom which He promised to those who love Him? But you have dishonored the poor man. Is it not the rich who oppress you and personally drag you into court? Do they not blaspheme the good name by which you have been called? (James 2: 5–7)

If God has made a preferential option for the poor, so must we. Of this, Gutierrez writes, "I do theology as one who come from a context of deep poverty, and thus for me, the first question of theology is *how do we say to the poor: God loves you* ... . This message—true as it is—presents a monumental challenge given the daily life of poor persons."[37] Farmer knows that

---

[36] Paul Farmer, *Infections and Inequalities: The Modern Plagues* (Berkeley, CA: University of California Press, 1999), 12.

[37] Gutiérrez, "Saying and Showing to the Poor: 'God Loves You,'" in *In the Company of the Poor*, 27. Emphasis in the original.

238

challenge, too, and behaves as if he read ahead in James's epistle to the warning, "If a brother or sister is without clothing and in need of daily food, and one of you says to them, 'Go in peace, be warmed and be filled,' yet you do not give them what is necessary for their body, what use is that?" (James 2:15–16). Farmer insists that solidarity with the poor must be pragmatic:

> Pragmatic solidarity is different from but nourished by solidarity per se, the desire to make common cause with those in need. Solidarity is a precious thing: people enduring hardship often remark that they are grateful for the prayers and good wishes from fellow human beings. But when sentiment is accompanied by the goods and services that might diminish unjust hardship, surely it is enriched. To those in great need, solidarity without the pragmatic component can seem like so much abstract piety.[38]

In James 5:14–15, the author calls on the elders of the community to anoint the sick. There is more to this text than the scriptural basis upon which Catholic tradition grounds the Sacrament of the Sick. It should be remembered that while oil was commonly used as a healing agent through much of antiquity, Jewish tradition reserved liturgical anointing for priests, kings, and prophets. In gathering the elders around the body of the sick, the sufferer becomes the privileged center of the local church. Her body is respectfully—even reverently—touched, and in this gentle and generous encounter, the community assures her that she actively contributes to the life of the gathered body.[39]

For the local church, anointing the sick is time well spent, a communal action of love, inclusion, and power. Through tactile, visual, auricular, and olfactory reminders, the community reasserts than that true healing comes only from God and no one in the gathered body suffers alone. Viewed from medicine's world of efficiency, the time wasted in gathering

---

[38] Farmer, *Pathologies of Power*, 146.
[39] See Shuman and Volck, *Reclaiming the Body*, 72–74.

nonessential personnel and conducting a dubious premodern anointing ritual might have more been profitably spent obtaining diagnostic lab data or imaging and following appropriate therapeutic algorithms. Though the two approaches need not—indeed, should not—be mutually exclusive, they are rooted in irreconcilable ways of experiencing time.

In reflecting theologically on time and cognitive disability, John Swinton draws a critical distinction between clock time and God's time which I think is relevant to all whom the world of efficiency marginalizes, including the world's poor. What Swinton calls "time of the clock" is "assumed to be linear, dynamic, and forward facing ... measurable, and controllable."[40] Accordingly, clock time is perceived as "fragmented, commodifiable, scheduled, and, above all, instrumental."[41] The resultant political economy underwrites and shapes:

> a world that adores speed, loves intellectual prowess (quickness of mind), and worships comfortably at the altar of competitiveness, productivity, efficiency, and self-sufficiency (using *your* time well on your *own* behalf). The implication is that to live humanly is to learn to live one's life effectively according to a series of culturally constructed time tracks that are laid out according to the fixed and relentless rhythm of the ... clock.[42]

God's time, by contrast, is "uncontrollable; unmanageable; simultaneously past, present, transient, and in the future; an enigmatic container; and a bridge that emerges from and leads us into God's unchanging, loving heart."[43] For God, "The purpose of time is to facilitate and sustain love."[44] God's time is slow, gentle, and punctuated with moments of rest, as the sabbath frames the seven-day week. God "takes

---

[40] John Swinton, *Becoming Friends of Time; Disability, Timefullness, and Gentle Discipleship* (London: SCM Press, 2016), 22–23. Emphases in the original.
[41] Swinton, *Becoming Friends of Time*, 23.
[42] Swinton, *Becoming Friends of Time*, 31. Emphases in the original.
[43] Swinton, *Becoming Friends of Time*, 61.
[44] Swinton, *Becoming Friends of Time*, 58.

time for the things that the world considers to be trivial. Those who follow Jesus—God incarnate—are expected to do the same."[45] Finally, Swinton writes, "Time is a gift that is intended to be given away."[46] Choosing to give away time in the company of the poor rejects the modern conviction that time really is money and its expenditure should be accounted for with utmost precision. Swinton relabels modernity's obsession with time management as "time poverty," turning the question, "Who are the poor?" on its head. What the world of medical efficiency sees as wasted time is, in fact, active participation in the life of God.

What Medicine and the Church Might Learn from Paul Farmer

The preferential option for the poor begins with recognition of the suffering other, but it does not end there. In discerning and being present to the poor, a scattered people are gathered and the body is enlarged. As Alexandre Martins writes:

> The recognition of the other is primarily seeing the faces of those who are suffering and identifying their faces with the face of the Crucified Jesus. This involves joining their lives and experience of suffering. The recognition of the other is also realizing that the poor have a knowledge originating from their experience ... . Recognition is a movement of humility and commitment to others. It creates a community of fellows who share the same human condition, history, hope, and praxis of liberation.[47]

Paul Farmer adds, "We don't live in the first world, the second world, or the third world. We live in *one* world ... . There are persons in that world.

---

[45] Swinton, *Becoming Friends of Time*, 76.
[46] Swinton, *Becoming Friends of Time*, 208.
[47] Alexandre Martins, *The Cry of the Poor: Liberation Ethics and Justice in Health Care* (Lanham, MD: Lexington Books, 2020), 59.

We need to reach across these barriers and to make genuine, authentic ties with people."[48]

Martins trained as a nurse. Farmer was a physician. Health care professionals have long been expected to provide skilled care to all who seek their assistance. That the vaunted US health care system often makes this difficult and prohibitively expensive marks a massive corporate and societal failure. Christians, as members of the Body of Christ, are obliged to transgress barriers keeping them from pragmatic solidarity with "the least." We are called not just to acknowledge the suffering other but to share in his condition. That so many of us fail to do so is a scandal. Physicians who, like me, claim to follow Jesus are thus under a double obligation to reach across illusory borders of human origin, including class, race, faith, gender, or nationality.[49] Those who, like Paul Farmer, commit themselves wholeheartedly to that vocation are rare. I am in no way exempt from the resultant shame, since my words are often better than my actions. Like too many of my colleagues, my witness runs by turns hot and cold.

I nonetheless hope that we can teach the next generation of physicians, nurses, and therapists better than we know. Any such hope should not count on cooperation from the medical-industrial complex, nor would a Christian takeover of US health care education do anything but make matters worse. What is required is not bureaucratic reform but transformed relationships. Learners entering the profession need exemplars sufficiently committed to the poor as to share in their experience and honest enough to acknowledge when and where they fail. The poor and marginalized must become full and active partners in decisions concerning their personal, communal, and environmental health. Measurements of health should take into account the entire local community, elegantly defined by Wendell Berry as "a place and *all* its

---

[48] In "Reimagining Accompaniment," in *In the Company of the Poor,* 171. Emphasis in the original.

[49] See Brian Volck, "Body Politics: Medicine, the Church, and the Scandal of Borders" in *Catholic Bioethics and Social Justice,*" ed. M. Therese Lysaught and Michael McCarthy (Collegeville, MN: Liturgical Press Academic, 2019), 301–313.

creatures."[50] Learners and teachers need to be fully present to the poor, sharing in, learning from, and responding to their suffering. Words like "love," "communion," and "pragmatic solidarity"—now rarely heard in the hallways of teaching hospitals—must become not only common parlance but everyday practice. Any artificial boundary that obscures the suffering of others—fellow creatures in whose lives we are always already entailed—should be identified and dismantled.

Farmer drank deeply from the wells of liberation theology, but he never claimed the title of theologian. His life and words suggest an unsystematic, practical, and embodied theology, an applied science much like the practice of medicine. He wrote on the intersection of health, justice, and the gospels with a passion born from experience. He spoke as a doer of the word rather than a theoretician or exegete. Yet, theology is not the exclusive province of highly credentialed academicians. For Christian scholars to treat Farmer's words and witness as somehow unworthy of serious theological reflection would be shortsighted.

That the Catholic Church—local and universal—has much to learn from Paul Farmer, I have no doubt. The number of contributors to this volume make that clear. I close, however, with one possible lesson that, while easy to say, may prove challenging to enact. Let me simply suggest, then, that Farmer's praxis of accompaniment offers a compelling model for a post-clericalist church. As a lay Catholic, I do not pretend to have a comprehensive response to massive disaffiliation of young adults and a dearth of vocations to the priesthood in the United States. I am concerned, though, when I hear neo-traditionalist Catholics propose restoring the dignity and station of the ordained to an elevated state—one that stresses their "ontological difference" from those not ordained. I do not question that Holy Orders confers a certain dignity to those called to ordination. The danger is that in elevating the priest above the laity, he is soon alienated from them as well. The everyday struggles of those entrusted to his

---

[50] Wendell Berry, "Health is Membership," in *Another Turn of the Crank* (Washington, DC: Counterpoint, 1995), 90. Emphasis mine.

spiritual care remain abstractions to be met with equally abstract theories, platitudes, and bureaucratic indifference, replicating in the Church the very dysfunction Farmer worked against in global health.

There are some, I am sure, who will say that priests who immerse themselves in the everyday lives of the laity are wasting their time, but at least one well-known priest disagrees. Pope Francis, at his first Holy Thursday Chrism Mass as Bishop of Rome, said, "A good priest can be recognized by the way his people are anointed," and urged his fellow priests "to 'go out,' then, in order to experience our own anointing, its power and its redemptive efficacy: to the 'outskirts' where there is suffering, bloodshed, blindness that longs for sight, and prisoners in thrall to many evil masters." He then made his famous call for priests to share "the smell of the sheep" (the Vatican website translates his phrase as "the odour of the sheep"), saying:

> The priest who seldom goes out of himself, who anoints little—I won't say "not at all" because, thank God, the people take the oil from us anyway—misses out on the best of our people, on what can stir the depths of his priestly heart. Those who do not go out of themselves, instead of being mediators, gradually become intermediaries, managers. We know the difference: the intermediary, the manager, "has already received his reward," and since he doesn't put his own skin and his own heart on the line, he never hears a warm, heartfelt word of thanks. This is precisely the reason for the dissatisfaction of some, who end up sad—sad priests—in some sense becoming collectors of antiques or novelties, instead of being shepherds living with "the odour of the sheep." This I ask you: be shepherds, with the "odour of the sheep," make it real, as shepherds among your flock, fishers of men.[51]

---

[51] Pope Francis, "Chrism Mass Homily, Saint Peter's Basilica," March 28, 2013, www.vatican.va/content/francesco/en/homilies/2013/documents/papa-francesco_20130328_messa-crismale.html.

I leave it to others to map out the necessary changes in priestly formation that will shape seminarians into servants who live in such intimacy with those on the "outskirts" that they share their smell. When that committee gathers, however, I sincerely hope they not only consult the laity but make lay persons from the world's neglected margins privileged partners and active participants in their deliberations. And, if they need a model for how that might be done, I recommend they examine the work of Paul Farmer, the physician who, more than anyone I know, shared the smell of those he served.

Brian Volck, **MD, MFA, MA**, is a pediatrician whose broad clinical and educational work has included the Navajo Nation, rural Honduras, an inner-city community health center, and inpatient teaching services at Cincinnati Children's Hospital Medical Center. He received his M.D. from Washington University in St. Louis, an M.F.A. in creative writing from Seattle Pacific University, and an M.A. in theology from St. Mary's Ecumenical Institute in Baltimore. He has published one volume of poetry, *Flesh Becomes Word*, and a memoir, *Attending Others: A Doctor's Education in Bodies and Words*. With Joel Shuman, he co-authored *Reclaiming the Body: Christians and the Faithful Use of Modern Medicine*. He served on the American Academy of Pediatrics' Committee for Native American Child Health and the editorial board for *The Journal of Moral Theology*. He writes and speaks on the complex intersection of health care, ethics, art, and faith. His essays, poetry, and reviews have appeared in *Ars Medica, DoubleTake, Health Affairs, IMAGE, The Journal of Moral Theology*, and *Presence: A Journal of Catholic Poetry*. He and his wife live in Baltimore.

Chapter 11: Practicing Local Listening with Village Midwives in Sudan: A Case Study for Theological Ethics

Meghan J. Clark

In April 2016, I arrived at the University of Notre Dame for the *From Aid to Accompaniment* book workshop with significant trepidation. A junior scholar and a theologian, I felt out of place in a room of public health and medical experts, but more than anything, I was nervous to meet Dr. Paul Farmer in person. From the moment I picked up *Pathologies of Power* in 2004, he inspired and influenced my approach to human rights as well as my commitment to bring theology into wider conversations about global health, human rights, and development. It was that inspiration that led me to travel to Khartoum, Sudan, in 2013 to observe an Irish/Sudanese/American medical training program for village midwives. After Khartoum, I struggled to write about the experience in a way that brought theology into conversation with global health and human rights until I was introduced to Jennie Block and eventually Paul. An earlier version of this essay was to be published in that book that was waylaid by global health crises and Paul's shocking death. Resurrecting it for this volume, I offer this case study, which benefitted from Farmer's own advice, on practicing local listening with the village midwives of Sudan.

Paul Farmer fought tirelessly for the health and human rights of those on the margins of power. The very idea "that some lives matter more than others" was for him, "the root of all that is wrong with the world."[1] In order to interrogate, spotlight, and begin to dismantle this idea, Farmer developed a holistic account of structural violence in order "to identify the forces conspiring to promote suffering, to discern the causes of extreme

---

[1] A frequently cited remark by Dr. Farmer, see the documentary *Bending the Arc: The Friendship that Changed the World*, bendingthearcfilm.com/.

suffering and also the forces that put some at risk for human rights abuses, while others are shielded from risk."[2] The concept of structural violence seeks to frame the inequity and injustice that is embedded in our social reality as violence "because they result in avoidable deaths, illness, and injury; and they reproduce violence by marginalizing people and communities, constraining their capabilities and agency, assaulting their dignity, and sustaining inequalities."[3] The first treatment for structural violence, according to Farmer, is local listening. In the documentary *Bending the Arc*, one sees a young Farmer recognize that to provide quality medical care to the people in Cange, Haiti, he needed to ask them what they need. As he recounts with humor the response of Fr. Fritz, "well OK, but they're just going to tell you they want a hospital" and a school and better road, and so on, the path to addressing structural violence is revealed.[4] For Farmer, "The experiences of those who are sick and poor remind us that inequalities of access and outcome constitute the chief drama of modern medicine."[5]

Applied outside medicine, I contend, local listening, or prioritizing the voices of those excluded from access and thus from outcomes, must also be centered in our moral and theological analysis. Local listening as a constitutive component for social, medical, and moral analysis in response to the complexities of structural violence underpins Farmer's work and his import for the practice of theological ethics. This practice of local listening must be embedded in both our analyses, programs, and implementation of health, human rights, and development programs if they are to combat underlying structural violence.

---

[2] Paul Farmer, *Pathologies of Power: Heatlh, Human Rights and the New War on the Poor* (Los Angeles: University of California Press, 2005), 50.
[3] Barbara Rylko-Bauer and Paul Farmer, "Structural Violence, Poverty, and Social Suffering," in *The Oxford Handbook of the Social Science of Poverty*, ed. David Brady and Linda M. Burton (London: Oxford Academic, 2017), 5.
[4] *Bending the Arc*.
[5] Paul Farmer, "Listening for Prophetic Voices in Medicine," *America*, July 5, 1997, 8–9.

Having the correct intellectual argument or the proper protocol is only one component of a successful medical development program. The right science or medical program on its own does nothing to dismantle the idea that some lives are worth more than others. While many development and global health programs operate with a focus on top-down structure, Paul Farmer, and Partners In Health consistently argued for local listening as the starting point. The practice of local listening is one of accompaniment, which became a foundation of PIH's own community health worker programs (called *accompagnateurs*). "Great failures of policy and governance," according to Farmer, "usually occur because of *failures of implementation*, and accompaniment is good insurance against such failures."[6] By definition, the act of accompaniment "suggests going with another on an equal basis" and, thus, "implies the transgression of discriminatory barriers," notes liberation theologian Roberto Goizueta, for "only in and through the concrete act of accompaniment do we love others as 'others, as equals, and are we, in turn, loved by them.'"[7] Accompaniment necessarily involves local listening rooted in a shared human dignity. From there, partnerships for global health, human rights, and development are able to also work to dismantle structural violence. In particular, local listening and accompaniment act as a resistance to instrumentalizing the other or dismissing the knowledge of those who experience poverty and exclusion first-hand.[8] For Christian theology, Goizueta notes, accompaniment is rooted in the narrative of Jesus of Nazareth for whom "to accompany the poor and the outcasts was to transgress the established and accepted boundaries which separate 'us' from 'them.'"[9]

---

[6] Paul Farmer, *To Repair the World: Paul Farmer Speaks to the Next Generation* (Berkeley: University of California Press, 2013), 244.

[7] Roberto Goizueta, *Caminemos Con Jesús* (Maryknoll: Orbis Books, 2005), 206.

[8] Theologically, notes Goizueta, "An essential element of God's own identification with the poor is, thus, the transgression of the spatial, geographical boundaries which separate rich and poor where they live. The violation of these physical, geographical barriers is a virtually absolute precondition for loving the poor" (*Caminemos con Jesús*, 201).

[9] Goizueta, *Caminemos con Jesús*, 203.

Practicing Local Listening with Village Midwives in Sudan

In structuring and scaling up local listening and accompaniment in dismantling structural violence and addressing urgent concerns of global health (like maternal health or newborn mortality), the next necessary component is participation. For a change in protocol or culture to occur, there must be a mutual or shared ownership of the program. Health, human rights, and development programs, if they are to be effective, must be participatory. Participation here is not completion of a medical training or treatment program but something deeper. It is an active role in the process and goals by those who are affected. If we begin with local listening, the interpretation and voices of those on the margins must have the ability to change or shape the priorities, scope, and goals of the partnership. This deeper view of participation serves as the basis for an ethics of participation and creates the capacity for accompaniment. The level of participation required for accompaniment begins with the equal dignity of all persons and therefore it requires "relationships of empathy and interdependence among the arguers."[10] A key component of full participation then is openness to the perspectives of others, even when that challenges one's own beliefs or conclusions. Local listening is an essential practice of this ethics of participation in global development. It fosters participation as mutual cooperation such that "all peoples should be able to become the principal architects of their own economic and social development,"[11] including public health.

This essay is a case study of Helping Babies Breathe Sudan, the launching training for a national program to train village midwives in basic newborn care. While different from community health workers, Sudanese village midwives or traditional birth attendants are responsible for accompanying and caring for most women and newborns in Sudan. Bringing forty-two doctors and nurses and forty-two village midwives from nineteen states across Sudan, including Darfur, the Khartoum-based

---

[10] Lisa Sowle Cahill, *Theological Bioethics: Participation, Justice, Change* (Washington, DC: Georgetown University Press, 2005), 38.

[11] World Synod of Bishops, *Justice in the World*, www.cctwincities.org/wp-content/uploads/2015/10/Justicia-in-Mundo.pdf.

initiative held two training sessions over four days. Focused on local listening and participation, this article examines lessons from this case for thinking about ethical partnerships for health and development. For theological ethics, and especially Catholic social teaching, both Farmer's own work and this case provide concrete examples that the option for the poor can be put into practice through prioritizing participation and local listening.

A Theological Ethicist in Khartoum: Helping Babies Breathe National Initiative

In January 2013, I traveled to Khartoum, Sudan, to observe the launch of the Sudan Helping Babies Breathe National Initiative, a new program for combatting newborn death developed through a unique Sudanese/Irish/American partnership. Unlike the other attendees, I was not a medical professional. I am an ethicist, a moral theologian who researches human rights and solidarity. With the permission of the organizers, I accompanied the program launch to investigate how we can structure and enact international partnerships for global health that empower local community health workers.[12] The program's successes and challenges offer important lessons about the process of developing partnerships for accompaniment. Moving from aid to accompaniment requires beginning with the personal; the success or failure of Helping Babies Breathe depended on personal relationships as much as, if not more than, on medicine.

---

[12] This ethics analysis would not have been possible without the permission and cooperation of Dr. C.A. Ryan (Ireland), Dr. Sami Ahmed (Ireland), Dr. Abdelomoniem (Sudan), and Dr. Lisa McCarthy-Clark (USA). Thank you also to Sister-Nurse Hind Waly and Abeer Hamid (Sudan) for assistance onsite and in translation. This ethics fieldwork was also made possible by a Summer Support of Research Grant from St. John's University and had IRB approval.

Newborn death[13] was and is an urgent global health crisis. In 2012, nearly three million babies died within their first twenty-eight days of life.[14] Addressing how and why these babies die is no easy task given the lack of complete birth/death records and unclear distinctions between newborn mortality and stillbirths. At the time, the World Health Organization estimated "one million babies die each year from birth asphyxia (inability to breathe immediately after delivery)"[15] and birth asphyxia or birth trauma account for 23 percent of neonatal deaths. Globally, including in developed countries, an estimated 10 percent of babies need some assistance breathing at delivery (such as clearing the airway). This percentage is higher within developing countries with severely limited resources and access to prenatal or primary preventative care. Therefore, addressing birth asphyxia or the inability of babies to breathe immediately at delivery is crucial to lowering neonatal mortality. Medically, the diagnosis is a matter of helping babies breathe.[16] Socially, it requires tackling complicated structural violence, "a rubric which includes a host of offences against human dignity: extreme and relative poverty, social inequalities ranging from racism to gender inequality,"[17] including

---

[13] Newborn death or mortality is defined as within the first twenty-eight days of birth. For more detailed definition see: World Health Organization, "Newborn Mortality," www.who.int/news-room/fact-sheets/detail/levels-and-trends-in-child-mortality-report-2021.

[14] Georgina Msemo, Augustine Massawe, Donan Mmbando, Neema Rusibamayila, Karim Manji, Hussein Lesio Kidanto, Damas Mwizamuholya, Prisca Ringia, Hege Langli Ersdal, and Jeffrey Perlman, "Newborn Mortality and Fresh Stillbirth Rates in Tanzania After Helping Babies Breathe Training," *Pediatrics* 131, no. 2 (2013): e353–e360. 10.1542/peds.2012-1795.

[15] World Health Organization, "Global Disease Burden 2004," www.who.int/whosis/whostat/EN_WHS09_Table1.pdf.

[16] John Kattwinkel, Jeffrey M. Perlman, Khalid Aziz, Christopher Colby, Karen Fairchild, John Gallagher, Mary Fran Hazinski, Louis P. Halamek, Praveen Kumar, George Little, Jane E. McGowan, Barbara Nightengale, Mildred M. Ramirez, Steven Ringer, Wendy M. Simon, Gary M. Weiner, Myra Wyckoff, and Jeanette Zaichkin "Part 15: Neonatal Resuscitation 2010: American Heart Association Guidelines for Cardiopulmonary Resuscitation and Emergency Cardiovascular Care," *Circulation* 122, no. 18, supp. 3 (2010): circ.ahajournals.org/content/122/18_suppl_3/S909.full.

[17] Paul Farmer, *Pathologies of Power*, 8.

disparities in access to preventative and emergent medical care during pregnancy and birth.

In 2010, a global alliance of partners launched Helping Babies Breathe[18] (HBB) to train community health workers in basic newborn care using a picture flip chart, simulations, and a practice doll. Its goal was to encourage birthing practices to devote the first sixty seconds after delivery, nicknamed the *Golden Minute*^{TM}[19] to helping the baby breathe, thus effectively treating the aforementioned 10 percent of all babies who simply need a bit help.[20] The program was designed for countries like Sudan in which health resources remain limited. Sudan has made significant progress on development markers over the last two decades, but in recent years, progress had slowed. In 2011, neonatal mortality was high, hovering between 31 and 41 per 1000 live births.[21] Two-thirds of the nation's 38 million citizens live outside of the urban centers and continue to rely heavily on traditional village midwives for maternal/child health.[22] Transportation around the country is hazardous, and active conflict zones remain a constant presence. The country's estimated 14,000 village midwives facilitate more than 80 percent of births. In Sudan, village

---

[18] The American Academy of Pediatrics, US AID, the World Health Organization, Save the Children, and Laerdal among others developed this evidence-based education program for low-resource settings. American Academy of Pediatrics, Helping Babies Breathe (2010), www.aap.org/en/aap-global/helping-babies-survive/our-programs/helping-babies-breathe. This program has since expanded and been rebranded as Helping Babies Survive www.aap.org/en/aap-global/helping-babies-survive/.

[19] "Saving Lives in the Golden Minute," National Institute of Health Newsroom, June 30, 2012, www.nichd.nih.gov/newsroom/resources/spotlight/062112-golden-minute.

[20] Kattwinkel et al., "Part 15: Neonatal Resuscitation 2010."

[21] According to the World Bank 2011 Development Indicators, infant mortality in Sudan remains at 57 per 1000 births and neonatal mortality at 31 per 1000 births. However, the reality on the ground in Sudan may be significantly worse. The last Sudan Household Survey (2006) approved by the government before the project placed infant mortality at 81 per 1000 births and neonatal mortality at 41 per 1000 births. See also "Sudan Household Survey" www.unicef.org/sudan/health_4284.html and "Road Map for Reducing Maternal and Newborn Mortality in Sudan."

[22] United Nations Development Program, "2014 Country Profile: Sudan," hdr.undp.org/en/countries/profiles/SDN.

midwives or traditional birth attendants are incorporated into the health care system, receiving government-sponsored medical training.[23] Effective village midwives may then later be selected for more training, promoted to Health Visitor, and function in a supervisory role over a rural area of village midwives.[24] Despite limited resources, Sudan does have several regional health services centers, known as CPD (continuing professional development) centers, which offer continuing professional development programs and coordinate ongoing training for village midwives and other health professionals.

Sudanese and Irish doctors had been engaged in an ongoing and successful partnership between the University College Cork and Ombdurman maternity hospitals since 2002.[25] However, impacting

---

[23] In general village midwives "have completed one-year midwifery course which focuses on practical trainings rather than lectures. The majority of them, however, are illiterate because they receive only primary education or even drop out of elementary school. Therefore, practical guidance is very important. On the other hand, health visitors received one-year professional training after three-years nursing course. They are assigned at midwifery schools and other government agencies as supervisors of village midwives." Japan International Cooperation Agency, "In-service Training for Village Midwives," October 2, 2011, www.jica.go.jp/project/english/sudan/005/news/general/111002.html/. For more information see The World Bank, "Rising to the Challenges: Sudan's Trained Village Midwives Contribute to Better Health for Mothers," June 11, 2012, www.worldbank.org/en/news/feature/2012/06/11/rising-to-the-challenge-sudans-trained-village-midwives-contribute-to-better-health-for-mothers.

[24] For more information on the training of Village Midwives and Health Visitors see: Kumiko Nakano, Yasuhide Nakamura, Akiko Shimizu, and Sojoud Mohamed Alamer, "Exploring Roles and Capacity Development of Village Midwives in Sudanese Communities," *Rural and Remote Health* 18 (2018): 4668.

[25] In 2002, Cork University Maternity Hospital entered into partnership with Omdurman Maternity Hospital in Khartoum, Sudan. Over the next ten years, this partnership provided Omdurman with financial, technical (equipment) and educational support. The hospital alliance as it emerged received approval for good governance from the European Union. In 2012, the Cork-Omdurman Partnership was recognized by the ESTHER alliance, which is a cooperative directed to solidarity-based hospital alliances. V.M. Carlson, M.I. Omer, S.A. Ibrahim, S.E. Ahmed, K.J. O'Byrne, L.C. Kenny, and C.A. Ryan. "Fifty Years of Sudanese Hospital-Based Obstetric Outcomes and an International Partnership," *BJOG: An International Journal of Obstetrics and Gynaecology* 118, no. 13 (2011): 1608–1616.

maternal and newborn health required thinking beyond a hospital-to-hospital partnership. Sudan's own proposal submitted in 2010 to United Nations Population Fund (UNFPA) on MDG 4 and MDG 5 points out many village midwives were not literate and did not have sufficient training in antenatal or basic newborn care to meet the United Nations definition of skilled attendance.[26] For these reasons, Helping Babies Breathe caught the attention of the Irish and Sudanese doctors. Unlike the previous collaborations, Helping Babies Breathe did not assume that practitioners had extensive education or access to many resources or a hospital at delivery, and it was easy to disseminate after an initial launch without the constant need for international personnel. It involved coordination and participation of the health infrastructure in Sudan. The Irish/Sudanese doctors developed a national plan centered on the village midwives securing the support of the Ministry for Health. Echoing the methodological approach of Farmer and PIH that health programs must be locally embedded and build up public infrastructure, this partnership brought together all segments of the Sudanese health sector—from the maternity hospital to the continuing professional development centers, to the Ministry of Health.

After two years of planning, six international medical and nursing educators from Ireland and the United States of America joined Sudanese doctors in Khartoum. International neonatal experts and master-trainers certified by Helping Babies Breathe lectured, facilitated, and supported the courses. Over the week, two sets of trainings were completed, and trainers were then sent home to begin training village midwives in their home regions. The first training was an English-speaking master trainer's course

---

[26] Republic of the Sudan, "Road Map for Reducing Maternal and Newborn Mortality in Sudan (2010–2015)," fmoh.gov.sd/Reports/ROAD-MAP-FOR-REDUCING-MATERNAL2010-2015.PDF. See also World Health Organization, "Saving the Lives of Mothers and Children: Rising to the Challenge Sudan," for more on the national strategic plan targeting expanding education for village midwives, apps.who.int/iris/handle/10665/116145.

for doctors and university-educated nurses,[27] followed by an Arabic-speaking version, which included some translation. Thirty doctors and twelve "sister" nurses were trained as master trainers to oversee ongoing trainer education; some from these top participants were selected to take the lead in the second training. Offered in Arabic, with some translation, the second course was a trainers' program for forty-two Health Visitor/Village midwives led by newly certified Sudanese master trainers with the ongoing supervision and support of the international team. It is the second training session upon which this case study focuses.

Hearing Voices from the Margins: Local Listening as Method

Over the course of the two days, my primary goal was to listen to the village midwives' experiences and reception of the program. Did they feel Helping Babies Breathe addressed their primary concerns for newborn health? Did it address the realities of giving birth in rural Sudan? Using Farmer's integrated approach, addressing newborn mortality requires examining the context of childbirth both medically and socially. Lack of access to medical resources is interwoven with the complex realities of social and gender inequalities, including poverty and lack of education. This is the complex and interdependent web which Farmer calls structural violence.[28]

When considering issues of global health and poverty, policymakers' and activists' first instinct has often been to seek a universal solution, overlooking local reality. In this case, village midwives were adept at navigating the possibilities and limits of their local reality; thus, it was necessary to listen to their counsel. Listening sounds easy and obvious. Everyone listens. You cannot have a conversation without listening. And yet, we have all fallen victim to *selective hearing* in which we only truly hear

---

[27] Obstetricians, neonatologists, pediatricians, nurse-midwives, and nurse-infection specialists made up the students in the master trainer course.
[28] Farmer, *Pathologies of Power*, 8.

that which confirms our assumptions or desires. Local listening as an ethical principle requires us to engage the participants as persons who ground us in their reality, distancing us from our abstractions or assumptions.

HBB itself is structured to be a participatory learning experience focused around simulations and practical skills. Both courses integrated specific components to enhance participation but also encountered challenges which potentially hindered this goal. From the outset, the structure was designed to move quickly from instruction by the international team to instruction by Sudanese participants. Yet power and social dynamics can often present barriers to participation by all in this kind of educational endeavor. When achieved, integrated participation during the trainings respected individual contexts and provided the necessary foundation for long term sustainability.

In the master trainer's course, the program directors took several steps to ensure maximum participation and sustainability. The atmosphere in the course was one of engagement and collaboration as doctors and nurses from Sudan interacted with the Irish, American, and Sudanese program directors. The Sudanese participants in this first group, therefore, engaged the international doctors and nurses as peer-mentors. This was clearest during both the role-play learning and the question periods. One clear example of this was the light-hearted correction by the Sudanese participants of certain assumptions within the HBB program which were incorrect for Sudanese culture. For instance, in the West and other parts of the world, fathers are commonly present for the delivery; however, it is quite rare that the father is present for home deliveries in Sudan. Village midwives rely on other female family members as the primary assistants in childbirth. Dr. Salah Ibrahim, Professor of Pediatrics at the University of Khartoum and a leading researcher in maternal/child community-based health, was invited to provide concrete descriptions of home births in Sudan. Engaged participation by noted Sudanese professionals as trainees along with their younger and less experienced colleagues lent credibility and weight to the program.

Practicing Local Listening with Village Midwives in Sudan

This level of integrated participation and collaboration demonstrated by Sudanese professionals' presentations enhanced the usefulness of the training program by providing instruction that related to the concrete available resources (an element that would be even more crucial in the second course for village midwives). All of this contributed to greater ownership of the HBB program by the Sudanese participants, and it is their adoption of the program in practice that will determine the sustainability of HBB in Sudan. By selecting participants from across Sudan, the Cork/Sudan partnership was not conducting a limited or pilot study. Instead, beginning with already established and basic newborn care, the courses sought widespread implementation across all the states of Sudan, including a participating doctor from Darfur and other conflict zones.

During the second training for Health Visitors and village midwives, it was also clear that tensions exist between rural village midwives and the mostly male doctors, as well as with female, university educated nurse-midwives. These tensions were most evident as everyone convened at the beginning of the second program. Many Sudanese doctors were highly skeptical of the village midwives' willingness to engage a new protocol and examine their practices. *They won't do it,* was a common sentiment from male doctors in the master trainer course. This suspicion was reminiscent of general compliance tropes about those living in poverty, which PIH has combatted for decades. Notably, despite the village midwives occupying a privileged position within their own local communities, the imbalance of knowledge and power between these mostly illiterate rural village midwives and the university-educated medical professionals positioned the village midwives as closely aligned with the women they served, which cast suspicion over their desire to learn a new protocol.

The Sudanese village midwives I observed were strong, confident women who clearly saw their role in childbirth as essential. In a crowded conference room, instructors and participants examined the tying off the umbilical cord. They conferred in their small groups and began to call out: *"We have cord clamps; we do not need to use string ties."* Global protocols can seem dry and abstract. The HBB protocol suggested using a bit of string to tie off the umbilical cord, as that is essentially the lowest common denominator resource. The midwives' abrupt interjection and subsequent conversation focused everyone's attention on the reality in rural Sudan. When the midwives declared "*We have cord clamps*," they asserted their participation and refocused attention on the need for the Helping Babies Breathe program to adapt to Sudan's context. Without this participation, aid programs aimed at human rights reinforce the power structures of neo-colonialism and dis-empower marginalized groups. Despite its understandable practical focus on universal applicability in low resource settings, the protocol reinforced an assumption of scarcity that did not apply to the Sudanese context. The village midwives' interjection then also represented an active resistance to what Farmer calls the socialization for scarcity by asserting their own resilience and competency. Similarly, their assertion reminds us that it is not only in assuming resource availability but also by assuming deprivation that programs can set up community health workers for failure.

The presence of non-Sudanese trainers helped to disrupt traditional power dynamics around gender, education, and class between the groups. In particular, the participation of the American women in small group role play and skill practice appeared to energize conversation. American nursing education tends to be very hands-on skills based, so the nurse practitioners easily joined small groups. Their shared gender allowed them to bond with the village midwives disrupting some tensions. The American women did not presume anything about traditional gender roles, power, or the village midwives. Despite the language barrier, the international team was actively involved in the second course through both translation and several village midwives who spoke English.

Acting out childbirth is a profoundly human and equalizing exercise. One person played the role of pregnant woman, a first-time mother in the throes of labor. Another was the village midwife and finally, the father or family member who is not quite sure what to do. The classroom erupted in laughter as they simulated labor pains and questions from the soon-to-be mother's husband. As noted above, the presence of a father at delivery is presented in the HBB flipchart caused laughter from the village midwives.[29] Fathers were of little use to the village midwives in delivery. Traditionally, a female family member will help if needed; the father, they acknowledged, could be useful in calling transport if something goes wrong. During the master trainers' class, traditional divisions of gender and power led to a few tables of male-only doctors. Here too the role playing accomplished more than the transmission of a protocols—as one of those male doctors needed to play the role of pregnant woman, and another the rural village midwife.

The role play and dialogue itself allowed the village midwives to learn, question, and adopt HBB as their own. Acting out the experience in rural Sudan created space for discussion that a sterile presentation of the steps of a protocol, albeit a medically necessary one, could not. Even though the village midwives did not have much formal education, they had significant practical knowledge and experience. Their questions showed a command of what they already knew and a desire for skills to do their job better. This was clearest when training turned to umbilical cord care, and objections immediately emerged around treatment of the umbilical cord. The Helping Babies Breathe program instituted a new WHO recommendation to wait one to three minutes before cutting the cord, to allow extra blood to flow to the baby.[30] At the time, this was a significant global change. In

---

[29] Despite a previous discussion in the master trainer course that in Sudan, fathers are not present at delivery, the father appears in the role-playing directions and chart; therefore, the newly trained Sudanese master trainers followed its prompts in the session with the midwives.

[30] For more information on the umbilical cord debate, see World Health Organization, "Care of the Cord: Review of the Evidence," 1999, apps.who.int/rht/documents/MSM98-4/MSM-98-4.htm; E. Abalos, "Effect of Timing of Umbilical Cord Clamping of Term Infants on Maternal and Neonatal Outcomes," *The WHO Reproductive Health Library* (2009), www.sciepub.com/reference/209552; Amit Upadhyay, Sunil Gothwal, Rajeshwari Parihar, Amit Garg, Abhilasha Gupta, Deepak Chawla, and Ish K. Gulati, "Effect of Umbilical Cord Milking in Term and Near Term Infants: Randomized Controlled Trial," *American Journal of Obstetrics and Gynecology* 208, no. 2 (2013): 120.e1–6; and Anup C. Katheria, "Umbilical Cord Milking: A Review," *Frontiers in Pediatrics* 6 (2018): 335.

most countries, including the US, standard practice had long been to cut the cord immediately. In 2013, many US hospitals had not fully changed to the new WHO guidelines to wait one to three minutes. In Sudan, however, the long-standing cultural practice is to "milk the cord"—rhythmically squeeze it—to send the extra blood to the baby and not immediate cutting. The HBB protocol presented asked them to stop milking the cord and just leave it for one to three minutes. The village midwives raised significant objection to changing their practice. From their perspective, they were already delivering extra blood to the baby. The dialogue quickly broke down due to both medical disagreements and power dynamics.

Evidence-based medicine is a powerful and necessary standard for establishing global guidelines for public health and human rights. Yet there are significant power dynamics involved in the assertion of evidence-based medicine as self-evidently normative, desirable, or superior in cross-cultural global partnerships. In partnerships, no partner is above question or invulnerable. Listening, participation, and accompaniment require that everyone be willing to say *I don't know*. HBB proposed waiting in contrast to immediate clamping. Sudan happens to be one of the few countries where the tradition is not to immediately clamp the cord but instead to milk it. The research on waiting versus immediate cutting is clear; however, international peer-reviewed research is vague and inconclusive with respect to waiting versus milking the cord, as it is done in this part of East Africa. The midwives raised a different concern than that which the protocol answered, and the midwives knew that simply asserting the protocol or WHO guidelines did not answer their question. They were claiming their own experience as a relevant source.

Active listening, as we saw, involves making oneself vulnerable, such that both the 'expert' and the 'student' are open to development and the need to adapt. Equality, dialogue, and encounter all seek to reduce differences of power and create mutual cooperation. The fundamental principle is that my humanity is bound up in yours. I cannot build a relationship of equal human dignity unless I begin from that starting point, and it is only from that starting point that accompaniment is possible. This is a key component of human rights, especially in situations where there are stark imbalances of power. Accompanying those on the margins involves mindfully employing equality as one's interpretive lens. With respect to the Sudanese village midwives, listening to their perspectives meant acknowledging the need to adapt, and to view the protocol as a starting framework rather than as an established canon.

While there were at times tensions between Sudanese physicians and the village midwives, vigorous participation by noted Sudanese professionals facilitated listening by all to the perspectives of the village midwives on the concrete realities in Sudan. Dr. Marwan Ibrahim Omer, Director of Omdurman Hospital and trusted advocate for the village midwives in his area, actively participated in simulations of childbirth, disarming men who did not want to "play women." Additionally, the presentations needed to accurately reflect the availability of local resources for cleaning. For example, an infection control protocol that recommends cleaning solvents that local health workers cannot access not only hinders the implementation and success of a health program; it also disempowers the community health workers. A Sudanese sister-midwife pursuing a doctorate in infection control was invited to conduct the presentation on cleaning, instructing not only her fellow Sudanese participants but also the international team on the specific infection concerns, protocols, and available resources within Sudan. During her presentation the international experts became students alongside everyone else. Prioritizing local listening and engaged participation not only ensured that the voices of all participants were respected but grounded this conceptual global health program in concrete reality.

Whenever the Helping Babies Breathe protocol seemed counterintuitive or contrary to practices believed to be effective, the midwives persistently sought explanations detailing the medical reasons for the protocol. One such area was the *Golden Minute*™ which asks midwives to focus the first sixty seconds on the newborn, then return attention to the mother. When there is only one skilled birth attendant, a delivery can quickly become precarious if anything goes wrong. Medically, devoting sixty seconds to immediately helping the baby breathe does not harm the mother, but can mean life or death for the infant. However, the testimony of the international partners alone could not replace the spoken and unspoken concerns of the village midwives. Maternal mortality is also high in Sudan, and the midwives attending the training frequently cited obstructed labor and hemorrhage as their highest concerns going into a delivery. The presence of Sudanese doctors and nurses, some of whom were from rural states, changed the conversation revealing both the concerns for obstructed labor and the limits of this one protocol at addressing those deeper concerns. The village midwives needed to be convinced that enacting the *Golden Minute*™ would not negatively affect the mother's health. This is one place where the fluidity between groups of the women nurse practitioners helped explain and alleviate anxiety. A more open and deeply participatory dialogue occurred. In the end, the practice of Helping Babies Breathe rests on the acceptance by the village midwives who will be both the primary practitioners and peer-trainers in their regions.

Participation and Empowerment: Steps Toward Solidarity and Accompaniment

Establishing participation as a fundamental ethical principle for successful development and implementation of development programs means emphasizing mutuality and agency. I may be able to take part in a development or health program for human rights, but if I have no voice, that program does not meet the standard of active participation necessary for justice. Participation is not satisfied by simple procedural assent. Agency "is central to recognizing people as responsible persons," and participation is understood as both individual and social.[31] Reflecting on the social advances made through women's empowerment, economist and philosopher Amartya Sen notes that "any practical attempt at enhancing

---

[31] Amartya Sen, *Development as Freedom* (New York: Anchor Books, 2000), 190.

the well-being of women cannot but draw on the agency of women themselves in bringing about change."[32] Focusing on participation empowered the village midwives to help babies breathe. Yet participation is challenging, as it heightens vulnerability on both sides. International health workers must share knowledge of evidence-based medicine, but they also must be prepared for elements of that knowledge to be challenged. Listening requires being open to learning from others.

An effective partnership for global health based upon participation breaks down traditional categories of teacher/student and envisions a community of learners in which everyone has knowledge and perspectives to share. Without this understanding, evidence-based medicine can easily if inadvertently strengthen the existing balance of power dynamics which disempower those in the developing world. It also creates a long-term dependency upon international experts as the authority. In the Sudan Helping Babies Breathe National Initiative, participation was a guiding principle practiced through local listening. This is the relationship sought in accompaniment, one that "requires recognition of real world complexities, acknowledging the asymmetry of power and privilege and being willing to address these while walking together."[33] Once again, mutual cooperation is the mark of a just partnership.

The challenges for lowering neonatal mortality in Sudan are great, as is the reality of structural violence faced by many of the village midwives. Lack of infrastructure, allocation of resources, communication, and the presence of conflicts are all elements of structural violence which Helping Babies Breathe does not address. However, structuring the program around participation empowered the midwives, not only by giving them knowledge but through dialogical interaction. Attacking neonatal mortality as a global health crisis requires understanding all the broader structural elements. It requires, in Farmer's catch phrase, an approach that

---

[32] Sen, *Development as Freedom*, 190.
[33] Stephen Reifenberg, "Afterward," in *In the Company of the Poor: Conversations with Dr. Paul Farmer and Fr. Gustavo Gutiérrez*, ed. Michael Griffen and Jennie Weiss Block (Maryknoll, NY: Orbis Books, 2013), 194.

is geographically broad and historically deep. Our gaze is on the people, not the particular program. In global health, this involves the dialectic of integrating both evidence-based medicine and the genuine need for global protocols, with the local reality and lived experience of community health workers. Local Listening then is a subversive tactic in combating the structural violence which is so often a lived reality for those most at risk for early death.

At the end of the course, all of the eighty-four newly certified trainers were excited about Helping Babies Breathe. In the three years following the initial launch, hundreds of trainers have been certified and thousands of village midwife providers successfully trained in all eighteen states, including hundreds in Darfur. It was a powerful start.[34] Systemic studies by the project team of skills retention one year later were positive.[35] The last ten years in Sudan have illustrated the deep complexity of addressing global health, poverty, and human rights issues. Positively, newborn mortality has steadily declined in Sudan to 27 per 1,000 live births in 2020.[36] At the same time, political turmoil continues to complicate the lives of those living in Sudan, as well as those who seek to provide medical care. Additionally, the American Academy of Pediatrics and World Health Organization have broadened and reimagined their efforts into a Helping Babies Survive initiative aiming to be more integrative by addressing newborn health beyond delivery.[37] This new version was adopted by

---

[34] See A.M.E. Arabi, S.A. Ibrahim, A.R. Manar, M.S. Abdalla, S.E. Ahmed, E.P. Dempsey, and C.A. Ryan, "Perinatal Outcomes Following Helping Babies Breathe Training and Regular Peer-Peer Skills Practice Among Village Midwives in Sudan," *Arch Dis Child* 103, no. 1(2018): 24–27, doi.org/10.1136/archdischild-2017-312809. And A.M.E. Arabi, S.A. Ibrahim, S.E. Ahmed, F. MacGinnea, G. Hawkes, E. Dempsey, and C.A. Ryan, "Skills Retention in Sudanese Village Midwives One Year Following Helping Babies Breathe Training," Archives of Disease in Childhood 101 (2016): 439–442.

[35] Arabi et al., "Skills Retention in Sudanese Village Midwives One Tear Following Helping Babies Breathe Training."

[36] The World Bank, "Morality Rate, Neonatal (per 1,000 Live Births)—Sudan," data.worldbank.org/indicator/SH.DYN.NMRT?locations=SD.

[37] Helping Babies Survive, www.aap.org/en/aap-global/helping-babies-survive/.

Sudan in 2017, and trainings of rural midwives around the country continued at least through 2020.[38]

Hope and Solidarity: Farmer's Lessons for Moral Theology

In "Rethinking Medical Ethics: A View from Below," Farmer and Nichole Gastineau Campos ask "Whose interests are [medical ethics] intended to protect? What ends do they serve?"[39] These questions should be asked of theological ethics as well. Farmer and Campos suggest, "One of the ways of rethinking medical ethics is to place the 'outcome gap' front and centre as an ethical issue."[40] A focus on equity must always be multifaceted, must build systems and not be satisfied only with low hanging fruit. This is what I saw in Sudan—an international group of doctors and nurses committed to system building via the village midwives alongside efforts to increase access to better resourced hospitals, especially obstetric and NICU care. It was done to prevent newborn death, a particularly tragic example of what Farmer calls "stupid deaths."

When reflecting on hope, Dr. Farmer noted that giving into despair by those who are not "poor, sick, or dying" is "giving up on behalf of other people."[41] It is this commitment to the dignity of the vulnerable, to a preferential option for the poor, that led Farmer to emphatically reject a lesser "cost-effective" standard of care for the poor.[42] When speaking about his own belief in a human right to health care, Paul centered his answer on the integrated problem of structural violence but also on the fact that the poor and excluded themselves believe in and call for the recognition of

---

[38] Sudanese American Medical Association, "Past Projects: Update from Sennar State 2020," sama-sd.org/past-projects/wmc/helping-babies-breathe/.

[39] Paul Farmer and Nicole Gastineau Campos, "Rethinking Medical Ethics: A View from Below," *Developing World Bioethics* 4, no. 1 (2004): 23.

[40] Farmer and Campos, "Rethinking Medical Ethics," 26.

[41] Partners In Health, "Dr. Paul Farmer On Hope," www.youtube.com/watch?v=PINxZQwde54.

[42] For more on this see *Bending the Arc*. Of note is the resistance from WHO global health experts at virtually every stage. In particular, the question of providing cancer care in Rwanda is an inflection point that draws out the division on standards of care.

their own dignity and rights.⁴³ One powerful example is the Cange Declaration by Partners In Health patients in Haiti. In the Cange Declaration, PIH patients condemned the stereotypes and lies perpetuated in order to justify denying lifesaving HIV treatment to the poor in the Global South. They stated,

> We pledge to remain steadfast in this fight and never to tire of fighting for the right of everyone to have necessary medications and adequate treatment. We also have a message for the big shots—for those from other countries as well as from Haiti, and from big organizations like the World Bank and USAID. We ask you to take consciousness of all that we continually endure. We too are human beings, we too are people.⁴⁴

Like the village midwives I met in Khartoum, lack of access to education and the reality of poverty did not mean that they were not able to stand up and claim their rights.

Catholic social teaching has long called for an integral human development approach to human rights, including for a right to health care, yet it is often critiqued or dismissed as impractical, naïve, and utopian. The concrete accomplishments of Partners In Health demonstrate that these commitments are not naïve or utopian. Instead, they require imagination, determination, and a deep abiding attention to the structural violence people endure. Catholic moral theology can and should be in a relationship of mutual learning and refinement with public health, global health, and related social science. It should be a resource for those who work on health and human rights, as it was for Farmer himself. He engaged theology directly through personal and intellectual collaborations with Gustavo Gutiérrez, OP, Roberto Goizueta, James Keenan, SJ, and others. His example then is an invitation to theological

---

⁴³ Partners In Health, "Paul Farmer, This I Believe," www.youtube.com/watch?v=xJpZnUjtorI.
⁴⁴ "Cange Declaration: PIH's First HIV Patients Advocate for Equal Access to Treatment," www.pih.org/article/cange-declaration-pihs-first-hiv-patients-advocate-for-equity-in-access-to.

ethics to be part of interdisciplinary conversations with medicine, public health, etc. It calls for Catholic moral theology to continue to engage the social and health sciences in a dialogue where we learn from each other while centering the voices of those otherwise ignored. It is perhaps only through local listening and practical collaboration and conversation that moral theology can make sure its reflections on medical ethics center the concerns of those who bear the brunt of the outcome gap and structural violence.

In Khartoum, through conversations with Sudanese doctors, nurses, village midwives, and the young women medical students who served as my translators, I learned just how much of the context never quite made it into medical, political, or the social scholarship used to drive global health and sustainable development conversations. It was their advocacy for the health of women and girls that led me to pursue more fieldwork—this time in contexts where I could more freely include religion in the conversation, as in Sudan I was there as purely as a social ethicist. In 2015 and 2018, I conducted fieldwork in Kenya, Ethiopia, and Tanzania, looking at the role of women religious on these issues of women and development.[45] For me, the impact of local listening and a crucial legacy of Farmer's work for theological ethics, is the unapologetic and continual challenge—to whom are we accountable?

This same question, framed a little differently, has been raised by Pope Francis in a call for the Catholic Church to go out of "our own comfort zone in order to reach all the "peripheries" (*Evangelii Gaudium*, no. 20) of power in the Church and society. In 2022, I was part of "Doing Theology from the Existential Peripheries" of the Migrant and Refugee Section of the Dicastery for the Promotion of Integral Human Development. "The project is built on the belief that those who have been marginalized, whether socioeconomically, socially, or in other ways, hold a wisdom capable of reopening discourse, especially where there are

---

[45] Meghan J. Clark, "Charity, Justice, and Development in Practice: A Case Study of the Daughters of Charity in East Africa," *Journal of Moral Theology* 9, no. 2 (2020): 1–14.

tensions."⁴⁶ Teams of theologians in six regional working groups sought to listen to and record the stories of faith, hope, pain, joy, and experiences of the Church of those living on the margins of power. One particularly moving witness that I interviewed was Josefa, a recycler in Brooklyn, NY. An immigrant from Mexico, Josefa makes a living by collecting cans and, as part of a workers cooperative, represents her community to the international waste pickers association. Explaining her job, she said, "We recyclers…we help to clean up the planet a little bit, in all the continents where there is a recycler, we help to clean the planet, because if we did not exist who would collect the garbage from the streets?"⁴⁷ Through local listening, Josefa's witness reveals that her strength and contribution to the community is far greater than perceptions of her economic status. Ultimately, Pope Francis and Paul Farmer both challenge theological ethics to interrogate and often recalibrate our focus, asking, whose lives and concerns are considered worthy enough to place them at the center of our questions and the inequities to which we devote our time to fighting?

Meghan J. Clark, PhD, is an associate professor of moral theology at St John's University (NY). In 2015, Dr. Clark was a Fulbright Scholar at the Hekima Institute for Peace Studies and International Relations at Hekima University College, Nairobi, Kenya. She has conducted fieldwork on human rights and solidarity in Sudan, Kenya, Ethiopia, and Tanzania. In May 2018, she was a Visiting Residential Research Fellow at the Centre for Catholic Studies at the University of Durham (UK). In 2022, she was Assistant Coordinator/Organizing Secretary for the North American

---

⁴⁶ "Doing Theology from the Existential Peripheries," Migrants & Refugee Section, Dicastery for the Promotion of Integral Human Development, migrants-refugees.va/theology-from-the-peripheries/.

⁴⁷ Stan Chu Ilo and Meghan Clark, "What We Have Seen and Heard," North American Report, "Doing Theology from the Existential Peripheries," migrants-refugees.va/wp-content/uploads/2022/10/North-America-Final-Report-FORMATTED-1.pdf.

Working Group of the "Doing Theology from the Existential Peripheries" project of the Migrant & Refugee Section of the Dicastery for the Promotion of Integral Human Development of the Holy See. She is author of *The Vision of Catholic Social Thought: The Virtue of Solidarity and the Praxis of Human Rights* (Fortress Press, 2014) as well as numerous articles and chapters. Active in public theology, she is a columnist for *US Catholic* and contributes to *NCR*, *America*, and other outlets.

Part 4

Global Health
as a
Theological Locus

Paul with Jeff at Zanmi Beni, Croix-des-Bouquets, Haiti, 2011 (Photo credit: Jennie Weiss Block)

Part 4: Global Health as a Theological Locus

Insofar as Meghan Clark focuses on a particular global health initiative in South Sudan, her essay provides a bridge to Part IV, "Global Health as a Theological Locus." While we believe that Farmer's life and work have methodological implications for the practice of theology and theological ethics, the focus of his life's work—global health—likewise remains an important locus for theological reflection, learning, analysis, and action. Caring for the sick with all its theoretical and practical correlates (suffering, embodiment, poverty, power, gift, kenosis, creation, eschatology) is inextricably central to the witness of the gospels and the historic Christian tradition, but outside of Catholic bioethics, it receives scant attention within theological methodology. What is more, on the global scale, so many lives continue to be ravaged and cut short by structural violence.

Bringing home this point, we turn to Chapter Twelve, "Ebola and the Ravages of History in Paul Farmer: A Catholic Theological Ethical Response to Global Health Inequity in Africa," by Stan Chu Ilo. Naming Farmer as "an African ancestor," Ilo focuses on Farmer's final book, *Fevers, Feuds, and Diamonds: Ebola and the Ravages of History*, to not only highlight Farmer's work in Africa but also raise pointed questions for Western scholars and theologians. Although Farmer rarely uses the terms, from his opening pages, the evils of colonialism and racism—as well as sexism, classism, and other intersectional loci—are embedded in his analyses. Ilo brings this front and center, showing how racist colonialist assumptions continue to shape the field of global health as well as the imaginations of many who work in the field. How does this history and framing continue to shape the work of theologians and churches, in our scholarship, pastoral practice, and moral analyses?

Where Ilo helpfully zeros in on Africa, in Chapter Thirteen, "The Legacy of Paul Farmer for Theological Ethics," Andrea Vicini pulls the lens back to look at the global landscape more broadly. Synthesizing many of the themes articulated in the volume, he highlights how Farmer's theological lens helped him challenge givens and assumptions and to begin to reimagine, theoretically and practically, the field of global health. Health, Farmer reminded us, is "a personal and social good that should be protected and promoted," and should be a central commitment for those embedded in the Christian tradition. Highlighting liberation theology and solidarity, the preferential option for the poor, and accompaniment, Vicini points to work that remains to be done with regard to the training of health care providers and a long list of global health priorities, and to theological ethics, Christian discipleship, ecclesial communities, and the institutional church.

Maura Ryan closes this section with her reflections in Chapter Fourteen on moving "From Compassion to Pragmatic Solidarity: Considering the Right to Health from the Margins." Examining how Catholic social thought informs the content of a "right to health," she asks how its understanding of the relationship between health and human rights is enriched by Paul Farmer's construction of "pragmatic solidarity." Examining Farmer's argument for moving from the feeling of "compassion" in the face of suffering to the action of "pragmatic solidarity" entails acknowledging that death and disease have social causes and cannot be adequately addressed without also addressing those causes. It also requires identifying and addressing the patterns of structural violence that determine how disease and death are distributed and to whom the goods of science and medicine will be available.

Chapter 12: Ebola and the Ravages of History in Paul Farmer: A Catholic Theological Ethical Response to Global Health Inequity in Africa

Stan Chu Ilo

When Paul Farmer died in Butaro, Rwanda, on February 21, 2022, many people saw it as a fitting consummation of his selfless and sacrificial commitment to Africa and people of African descent. He died in the land that he loved so much. In the last decade of his life, Farmer spent a lot of time in Africa helping to build effective, affordable, and accessible health systems; providing safe and sustainable health care delivery for the most vulnerable among us; and training a new crop of African health care workers. Paul Farmer is rightly to be called an African ancestor. This is because he worked strenuously to the point of death to promote and protect the health of Africans. Through his selfless effort, he saved the lives of many Africans, while being an agent for building the systems, staff, spaces, and stuff—as he likes to summarize health care delivery—for promoting holistic health and human and cosmic flourishing in Africa and the world. It is remarkable that the last major book of Paul Farmer, *Fever, Feuds, and Diamonds: Ebola and the Ravages of History,* was dedicated to discussing global health inequity and its devastating impact in West Africa during the Ebola outbreak of 2013–2015.[1] The message of this book, forms the central themes around which I develop this essay.

Interestingly, *Fever, Feuds, and Diamonds* offers a synthesis of the development in Farmer's thinking as he and his colleagues in Partners In Health watched the destructive effects of COVID-19 playing out because

---

[1] Paul Farmer, *Fevers, Feuds, and Diamonds: Ebola and the Ravages of History* (NY: Farrar, Straus and Giroux, 2020), 192.

the lessons learned from Ebola about the reforms of the global health systems needed to prevent and respond to the next outbreak were not heeded by the world. These lessons from the 2013 Ebola outbreak in West Africa formed the focus of a course which Paul Farmer and the current COVID-19 White House coordinator, Ashish Jha, developed at the Harvard Global Health Institute, *Lessons from Ebola: Preventing the Next Pandemic*. I participated in this course. It was there that I encountered Paul Farmer and his passion for a common humanity and especially his commitment to Africa. This course also introduced me to the work of the Independent Panel on Global Response to Ebola by Harvard Global Health Institute and the London School of Hygiene and Tropical Medicine and the ten reforms of global health systems and structures that were recommended.[2] I believe that if these reforms had been implemented globally and locally before 2019, the world would have been in a much better shape to respond effectively to the COVID-19 pandemic.

In this essay, I explore with Farmer why Ebola has persisted in Africa and why it continues to kill so many Africans as we saw in the September 2022 outbreak in Uganda with the Sudanese strain. Farmer's appeal to social medicine and social context in understanding the *remote causes of the cause* of Ebola offers an important corrective to the disease control and treatment paradigm approach in global health amidst the devastating impact of health inequity. Farmer posed an important question and offers an answer that can help us locate the central concern of this essay:

> How did West Africa become a clinical desert—a place in which the rapid human-to-human spread of Ebola was not just possible but almost inevitable? The answer begins centuries ago, when pathogens and

---

[2] Suerie Moon, Devi Sridhar, Muhammad A. Pate, Ashish K. Jha, Chelsea Clinton, Sophie Delaunay, Valnora Edwin, Mosoka Fallah, David P. Fidler, Laurie Garrett, Eric Goosby, Lawrence O. Gostin, David L. Heymann, Kelley Lee, Gabriel M. Leung, J. Stephen Morrison, Jorge Saavedra, Mercel Tanner, Jennifer A. Leigh, Benjamin Hawkins, Liana R. Woskie, and Peter Piot, "Will Ebola Change the Game? Ten Essential Reforms Before the Next Pandemic. The Report of the Harvard-LSHTM Independent Panel on the Global Response to Ebola," *The Lancet* 386, no. 10009 (2015): 2204–2221.

pathogenic forces were linked to a worldwide web of maritime commerce that bound expansionist European economies to the Americas and Africa. This web began to take shape in the mid-fifteenth century, when Portuguese explorers and traders gave Port Loko, and indeed Sierra Leone and much of the Upper Guinea Coast, their names. The result would be violent conflict, recurrent disease, and rapacious extraction—of rubber latex, timber, minerals, gold, diamonds, and human chattel.[3]

I conclude my chapter by using Farmer's analysis of the causes of global health inequity in Africa to propose how theological ethics can serve the mission of churches and African communities in designing health care systems for health improvement and health protection in solidarity with the poor and the most vulnerable. I propose some effective strategies for global health partnerships in Africa against the current preoccupation with disease control and prevention, medical mission, and crisis intervention from outside Africa.

From Congo to West Africa: How Ebola Came to West Africa[4]

Between December 2013, when the outbreak of Ebola Virus Disease (EVD) was first reported, and September 2015, more than 27,000 cases were registered with 11,000 reported deaths. It was, according to experts, the worst Ebola outbreak in history because, in less than six months after the first case was reported, it had spread to the capitals of three African countries—Conakry, Guinea; Monrovia, Liberia; and Freetown, Sierra Leone. In terms of the recorded number of affected persons, countries involved, and longest persistent transmission, the West African strain of

---

[3] Farmer, *Fevers, Feuds, and Diamonds*, 192.
[4] Some of the material from this section was taken from my essay, Stan Chu Ilo, "Where Hands Don't Touch: A Biosocial Ethical Analysis of the Ebola Outbreak and Medical Intervention in West Africa," in *Bulletin of Ecumenical Theology* 31 (2019): 34–60.

the Ebola disease was the deadliest and the most destructive. The epicenter of the disease was Liberia and Sierra Leone.[5]

According to Roca, Afolabi, Saidu, and Kampmann, the first outbreak of Ebola disease occurred in Zaire (now Democratic Republic of Congo) in 1976 and was named after the Ebola River, the area where the disease was first found. That same year, a different strain of the disease occurred in Sudan.

> Since 1976, more than 25 known outbreaks of EV have occurred in Africa, and 5 different EV species have been identified. Currently, EV hemorrhagic fever remains a plague for the population of equatorial Africa, with an increase in the number of outbreaks and causes since 2000 .... The previous largest outbreak occurred in Uganda in 2000 and involved 425 persons, less than 2% of the affected subjects in the current outbreak [2013].[6]

In past outbreaks, according to Roca et al., the disease was confined to rural and isolated areas in Central Africa, without spreading to the urban areas. In the West African outbreak, it spread more in densely populated urban areas and then to some rural communities.

Ebola is a disease which is spread through contact with bodily fluids of a symptomatic Ebola patient. It is highly contagious and kills more than 90 percent of those who are infected with this lethal virus, particularly in the absence of supportive care and therapies. The case/fatality (CFR) rate ranges from 41 percent to 89 percent depending on the strain of the Ebola virus and the setting. Five main strains have been identified—Zaire, Sudan, Bundibugyo, Tai Forest, and Reston—with the Zairean strain being the

---

[5] Anna Roca, Muhammed Afolabi, Yauda Saidu, and Beate Kampmann, "Ebola: A Holistic Approach is Required to Achieve Effective Management and Control," *The Journal of Allergy and Clinical Immunology*, 135, no. 4 (2015): 856.

[6] Roca, Afolabi, Saidu, and Kampmann, "Ebola: A Holistic Approach is Required to Achieve Effective Management and Control," 856.

deadliest in terms of the number of fatalities.[7] The West African strain—a type of the Zairean strain—was not the deadliest, but the number of deaths was higher in West Africa because of failed health care delivery in the sub-region and failed and delayed humanitarian intervention by the international community. With limited access to primary health care and the slow response of the international community, the disease spread rapidly in the West African sub-region at the pace of between four and five hundred cases per week. As Boozary, Farmer, and Jha argue:

> If the Ebola virus surfaced in Boston or Toronto, there is little doubt that their health systems, despite shortcomings, could effectively contain and then eliminate the disease with far lower case-fatality rates than those reported now in West Africa. Why the disparity when there is no proven drug or vaccine available? The answer lies not with the virus, but in the collective failure to ensure availability of adequate health care, staff, resources, and systems required for the delivery of high-quality health care. The Ebola epidemic has placed this failure into stark relief, exposing the pathology of chronic neglect amid broad global inequities.[8]

This "chronic neglect" is often the result of short-sighted local and global response to diseases like EVD in Africa. It is also caused by reactionary measures to contain the infection, while neglecting steps to provide adequate, accessible, safe, and affordable care for the sick and prioritizing health protection and improvement.

At the onset of the Ebola epidemic in Sierra Leone, Farmer observed that local doctors were working with resources similar to those that were used by American surgical teams during the American Civil War![9] Farmer decried the painful condition of the health systems and health care delivery

---

[7] Roca, Afolabi, Saidu, and Kampmann, "Ebola: A Holistic Approach is Required to Achieve Effective Management and Control," 857.

[8] Andre Boozary, Paul Farmer, and Ashish K. Jha, "The Ebola Outbreak, Fragile Health Systems and Quality as a Cure," *Journal of American Medical Association* 312, no. 18 (2014): 1859.

[9] Farmer, *Fevers, Feuds, and Diamonds*, 53.

in the most affected countries during the Ebola outbreak as medical, public health, and clinical deserts.[10] Many reasons could be attributed for this failure of humanity and health care delivery during the 2013–2015 Ebola outbreak. First, in terms of *staff*, Farmer and his colleagues argue that there was a shocking absence of trained health care workers—community health workers, nurses, and qualified physicians. A good example is Liberia, which had a broken health system before the outbreak and was recovering from over a decade of war and political and social upheavals. Statistics show that "even before the outbreak, Liberia's 4.3 million people were served by just 51 physicians—fewer than many clinical units in a typical major US teaching hospital."[11] Sierra Leone, on the other hand, had two physicians per 100,000 people and spent $96 per person a year on health, compared with 245 physicians per 100,000 people and $8895 in annual health expenditures in the United States in 2014.[12]

Second, there was the absence of health care resources—or, in Farmer's phrase, *stuff* and *systems*. Boozary, Farmer, and Jha strongly disagree with the claim that simply providing vaccines or monoclonal antibodies will help African countries fight EVD. Such success can only emerge when other systemic factors are addressed in African societies. One such factor, they argue, is the reform of the health care services and institutions. Health care services should prioritize quality of care and basic preventative measures like nutrition, water, and sanitation over the disease-control paradigm and other interventionist measures that focused on containing the epidemic rather than providing quality care. At the same time, "stuff" is not unimportant. According to the World Health Organization, "The lack of basic health care resources—such as protective gloves and gowns,

---

[10] Farmer, *Fevers, Feuds, and Diamond*, 4, 430.
[11] Boozary, Farmer, and Jha, "The Ebola Outbreak, Fragile Health Systems and Quality as a Cure," 1859.
[12] Statistics from WHO's *Global Health Observatory: Density of Physicians and Per Capita Total Expenditures on Health at the Average Exchange Rate*, in Annette Rid and Ezekiel Emanuel, "Why Should High Income Countries Help Combat Ebola" *Journal of the American Medical Association* 312, no. 13 (2014): 1297.

intravenous fluids, and straightforward protocols and guidelines—limited front-line health workers who risk their lives to care for those affected with Ebola."[13]

In addition, the absence of *spaces*, that is, good and safe health care facilities providing quality care for infected patients reduced their chances of survival. In fact, many Ebola patients who arrived in such facilities in West Africa during the outbreak

> received no intravenous rehydration and extremely limited monitoring of hematocrit and liver and kidney function. Other affected patients wait, and may die, outside the closed gates of overwhelmed facilities. Is it any wonder, then, that so many individuals are losing confidence in the ability of their health systems to care for them?[14]

As a result, there was a high case fatality rate in the isolated units of the hospitals at the peak of this outbreak. Many health care workers died from the disease because of intra-hospital transmissions. Thus, during the transmission phase of the disease, many people lost trust in the health care delivery because people feared that if the doctors and nurses could not shield or care for themselves against this disease, then it was unwise using the health care facilities under their watch.

Indeed, the pioneer Ebola doctor in Sierra Leone and Director of the Kenema hospital, Dr. Sheik Humarr Khan, who ran a special unit for treating febrile outbreaks like Lassa fever and later Ebola, died from EVD. Towards the end of his life, what worried him most was that if he died in an Ebola treatment center (ETC), it would discourage people from presenting themselves to the hospitals. In Farmer's view, Dr. Khan and thousands of West Africans who died of Ebola in the continent succumbed to the disease because "the variable virulence of pathogens is

---

[13] Boozary, Farmer, and Jha, "The Ebola Outbreak, Fragile Health Systems, and Quality as a Cure," 1859.

[14] Boozary, Farmer, and Jha, "The Ebola Outbreak, Fragile Health Systems, and Quality as a Cure," 1859.

pretty quickly swamped by the variable virulence of the world we inhabit. Giving all the credit to the virus is dubious when we humans have been the architects of the stunning inequities that characterize our shared world."[15]

Ebola is only a deadly disease if you live in Africa. Boozary and colleagues in their research show that there have been other major viral outbreaks in the world like the 1967 Marburg hemorrhagic fever, which occurred in Germany and the then Yugoslavia, or the Severe Acute Respiratory Syndrome (SARS) in Canada in 2003, or the Middle Eastern Respiratory Syndrome (MERS), the Avian influenza (H5N1), or Mad Cow disease, none of which spread like Ebola. The high fatality of Ebola disease, they argue, "is related to lack of adequate systems in which the health care staff and resources can be effectively deployed."[16] Most public health professionals know that the reason viral infections similar to Ebola that started to spread in other parts of the world before COVID-19 were contained was that "thanks to a mix of specific therapies (antibacterial, antiparasitic, antifungal, antiviral) and nonspecific therapies (supportive and critical care), we have made most formerly fatal microbial diseases eminently survivable."[17] The availability of these therapies outside Africa is the reason why American and European health workers who were infected with EVD and were flown back to the US or Europe survived the disease. They received the advanced care that Dr. Khan and his nurses and other health care workers did not receive in Sierra Leone.

However, a more comprehensive understanding of why Ebola ravaged West Africa in 2013–2015 and continues to flare up now and again in many parts of the Africa invites us to the realm of social medicine and public health. This lens can shed more light on global health inequity, helping to address why Africans and those in the global community interested in the health and wellbeing of Africans, must pay attention to

---

[15] Farmer, *Fevers, Feuds, and Diamonds*, 42–43.
[16] Boozary, Farmer, and Jha, "The Ebola Outbreak, Fragile Health Systems, and Quality as a Cure," 1860.
[17] Farmer, *Fevers, Feuds, and Diamonds*, 50.

health promotion and health improvement based on a social justice approach to addressing global health inequity.

Ebola, the Ravages of History: Why Africa?

But why is Africa home to Ebola, and why does this viral infection persist in Africa? Why do some Africans die from the disease and some live? Why do Westerners who get the disease survive from it, and Africans who get infected die? The answers to these questions have nothing to do with Africa's people, weather, climate, food, or environment. In addition, the nature of genomes of the Ebola variants circulating in West Africa between 2013 and 2015 and the hypovolemic shock that eventually killed many West Africans as a result of the disease had nothing to do with their genes or social life, as is often posited.

Rather, the answers to these questions, Farmer argues, can only be found in social medicine and in the history of the social determinants of health in the West African context. As he notes:

> If you want to explain wildly varying fatality rates among those infected with the same strains of a virus, you have to understand the social context in which care is given. The same is true of transmission: the setting determines what kind of care is available and how safely care is delivered. Similar points have been made regarding most communicable pathogens for well over a century. That century has also taught us that medical impoverishment and high fatality rates and untrammeled contagion can be radically and rapidly reduced by vigorous human countermeasures.[18]

Why are these human counter-measures not taken in Africa? This invites us to dig deeper into the history of the continent, racism, colonial medicine, and a concatenation of factors like religion, economies of scale, and past history. According to Farmer:

---

[18] Farmer, *Fevers, Feuds, and Diamonds*, 44.

West Africa's economy had long been shaped by epidemics of all-pervading fever. These, in turn, were shaped by political economy, which in these parts is always both local and translocal. There can be little doubt that slavery and its disruptive machinery triggered raids and war while unleashing epidemics across the region and in the distant lands to which its sons and daughters were dispatched. Nor is there doubt that the racism underpinning and justifying slavery was rooted in an enduring belief that some lives matter less than others.[19]

Here, Farmer called the world to pay attention to "the synergy of several factors" which contribute to bringing or threatening the conditions for abundant life and human wellbeing. These factors with regard to EVD in West Africa were undermined by:

a context of decades of civil war leading to a low level of trust in authorities, even when these are working hard to reconstruct the country; dysfunctional health services with a major scarcity of health workers, especially in Liberia and Sierra Leone; strong traditional beliefs in disease causation and even denial of the virus' existence; high-risk traditional funeral practices that amplify transmission, in addition to more recent healing practices in some churches where the bodies of patients with Ebola are touched; a slow and inadequate national and international response; and high population mobility across borders.[20]

This "synergy of several factors" can help us understand why the disease-control-and-treatment paradigm fails in public health in Africa. They also provide answers to the following questions: Why is Africa susceptible to certain kinds of diseases, and why do people who get infected with HIV/AIDS or Ebola, for instance in Africa, have less chance

---

[19] Farmer, *Fevers, Feuds, and Diamonds*, 205.
[20] Peter Piot, Jean-Jacques Muyembe, and W. John Edmunds, "Ebola in West Africa: From Disease Outbreak to Humanitarian Crisis," *The Lancet* 14 (2014): 1034.

of survival than their colleagues outside Africa?[21] What social, economic and environmental factors are at play in determining health and life outcomes for the poor in Africa which are differently aligned in other non-African settings? Why are African local knowledge and agencies still stigmatized in understanding the interaction of diseases and other non-biomedical factors in spreading infections in Africa and in the kinds of responses which Africans are making to these diseases? In the rest of this essay, I address one significant factor that has played an important role in the health of the poor and how its consequences continue even today to destroy the lives of Africans: colonial medicine and racism.

Colonial Medicine and Racism

Farmer begins chapter five of *Fevers, Feuds and Diamonds* with the question, "Why did West Africa become a clinical desert—a place in which the rapid human-to-human spread of Ebola was not just possible but almost inevitable?"[22] His answer is that "pathogens and pathogenic forces" that settled in the so-called West African "fever coasts" were linked to the worldwide web of mercantilist expeditions of the West that began the destruction and despoilation of Africa. The movement of peoples through the slave trade from Africa to the Americas and to Europe and back and forth was also accompanied with the spreading of diseases. It is significant to note that the two epicenters of Ebola disease in the 2013–2015 epidemic, Liberia and Sierra Leone, were countries that were founded by liberated slaves who were returned to the African motherland from the US, the UK, and Canada. The destruction of livelihoods, forests and fauna, and the displacement of peoples—an unintended consequence of the slave trade and after—turned West Africa into a fertile ground for the spread of

---

[21] See, for instance, Angus Deaton's analysis on "escaping death" in the African tropics and why infectious and non-infectious diseases which killed his Western ancestors in the seventeenth and eighteenth century continue to kill African babies, youth, mothers and the elderly today in *The Great Escape: Health, Wealth, and the Origins of Inequality* (Princeton: Princeton University Press, 2013), 100–106.

[22] Farmer, *Fevers, Feuds, and Diamonds*, 191.

infectious diseases. Thus, Farmer concludes that the fevers and feuds that destroyed Liberia and Sierra Leone prior to the Ebola outbreak were all linked to the slave trade in some ways. This is an important point to note because the ravages of African history that began in the slave trade all contribute to other factors that explain some of the lingering social determinants that produce sub-optimal health among a greater number of the population in these two countries.[23]

According to Quentin G. Eichbaum and his colleagues, "Colonialism directly impacted medical practice and education in Africa by using medicine as a tool for domination and control. Medicine provided a biological rationale for assigning racial superiority or inferiority. Thus, medicine was used to rationalize and justify inequities and excesses under imperial domination."[24] The argument here is that we must consider slavery, colonial medicine and its successor (global health), racism, and Western exploitation of Africa's vulnerability as some of the major factors that "*manufacture epidemics*" in Africa. It is therefore important to go back to the colonial origins of Western medicine and the Western negative framing of African bodies, spaces, and contexts in order to capture the complexity of how they combine in manufacturing epidemics and deaths in Africa. Farmer, building on the wisdom of Louis Pasteur—*le microbe n'est rien, le terrain est tout*—invites us to focus on "embodied disparities, social and economic terrains" and the desocialized and decontextualized epidemiology of disease pathogens and causality which deny history, politics, and local and structural violence of the global economy. Understanding microbial pathogenicity in people requires understanding their context and history. This understanding should take us deeper into world systems, including failed and failing democracies.[25]

---

[23] Farmer, *Fevers, Feuds, and Diamonds*, 214.
[24] Quentin G. Eichbaum, Lisa V. Adams, Jessica Evert, Ming-Jung Ho, Innocent A. Semali, and Susan C. van Schalkwyk, "Decolonizing Global Health Education: Rethinking Institutional Partnerships and Approaches," *Academic Medicine* 96, no. 3 (2021): 330.
[25] Farmer, *Fevers, Feuds, and Diamonds*, 441–444.

To understand why the deeper roots of global health inequity trace back through slavery, racism, and colonialism in Africa and why where one is born determines how the person will die, we need "a broad-scope awareness of a diversity of stories" from communities and peoples.[26] Farmer argues that for people of African descent, the story goes back to slavery and colonialism, the original twin pilots of racism for peoples of African descent. Slavery and colonial medicine in Africa gave birth to the "control-over-care" paradigm of health. During the outbreak of Ebola in West Africa, more resources were put into safe burials, contact tracing, isolation, and social distancing over treatment and care of those who were afflicted, most of whom were left to die painful deaths without any form of therapies. This was a replication of methods of allowing the sick to die to keep the colonial masters protected from contact with the *doomed Africans*. For example, the French colonial authorities responded to outbreaks of diseases during the colonial era not with caring for the sick but rather with "the destruction of housing, highly restrictive and segregationist building codes, quarantine, isolation, fines, and other penalties for infractions. Disease-control algorithms were applied in discriminatory fashion, sparing Europeans—and their businesses—in a manner that rankled Creole elites."[27] What this example among many others show is that there were no efforts to integrate preventative measures and disease control with treatment and care for the sick in the colonial period and even today in Africa. It is important to demonstrate the strong link that exists between colonial pathologies and the epidemics they foster in today's Africa.

Second, colonial medicine "paid almost exclusive attention to the unitization of people in larger aggregates."[28] This tendency to define, distort, and label the *African other* as belonging to a pathological collective

---

[26] Susan Holman, *Beholden: Religion, Global Health, and Human Rights* (NY: Oxford University Press, 2015), 43.
[27] Farmer, *Fevers, Feuds, and Diamonds*, 261.
[28] Rijk van Dijk, "Foucault and the Anti-Witchcraft Movement: A Review Article," *Critique of Anthropology* 14, no. 4 (1994): 431.

is still prevalent today. The *African other* inhabits a strange and dangerous space, and diseases like EVD only shows why that dangerous space should not be shared by the rest of humanity in order to save that humanity from contamination. The African does not belong; the African is a stranger on the global stage and his or her life really does not matter.

Third, colonial medicine reinforced stereotypes and categorization of Africans and racial prejudice by the 'othering' of blackness as a collectivized contaminating identity characterized by death, decay, and traditional cultural and religious practices which promote diseases and deaths like burial rites, eating of bush meat, and ancestral traditions. This "community linked fate" seen in the objectification of those West Africans sickened by EVD fails to pay attention to distinctions and subsequently represses the subjectivation of Africans in the African continent which undermined agency and individual and group autonomy.

Megan Vaughan's *Curing Their Ills: Colonial Power and African Illness* helps us to understand how the dynamics of global health inequity are rooted in colonial history.[29] She demonstrates how power and politics with the health of people of African descent are tied to colonial medicine and knowledge construction. According to Vaughan, "Knowledge claims and constructions that provide ideological legitimacy to hierarchical systems and social structures" create health inequalities in Africa.[30] The primary thesis of Vaughan's book is that colonial biomedicine invented an image of Africa in Western medical and social discourse from the colonial period and beyond as "a repository of evil, death, disease, and degeneration."[31] Using a social constructionist approach, she argues that British medical personnel ascribed many diseases to the racial makeup of Africans. The diseases found in Africa were projected as reflective of the social reality of Africa, just like President Trump and his ardent followers

---

[29] Megan Vaughan, *Curing Their Ills: Colonial Power and African Illness* (Stanford: Stanford University, Press, 1991).
[30] Janet K. Shim, "Bio-Power and Racial, Class, and Gender Formation in Biomedical Knowledge Production," *Research in the Sociology of Health Care* 17 (2000), 188.
[31] Vaughan, *Curing Their Ills*, 2.

referred to Coronavirus as the China virus, against the discontinuation of the health community of naming and associating a disease with the place where it was first found. Rather than looking at the scientific evidence for disease from the point of view of history and biology, colonial medicine saw the diseases in Africa as cultural; the way of life of the people, their cultural and social life and behavior were all contaminating. Colonial medicine, in this way, constructed the enduring imaginary of African society and blacks as unhealthy and pathological: "Medical discourse operated by locating difference and differences in the body, thereby not only pathologizing them but also naturalizing them."[32]

One implication of this construct, among many others, is what Farmer calls "control-over-care" paradigm.[33] This paradigm is the eternal preoccupation by Westerners with preventing the spread of diseases in the community or from the Africans to the Europeans rather than addressing the root causes of the diseases and improving the health and wellbeing of the people. Farmer gives many examples of this colonial paradigm which persists to this day in Africa. One particular example is the French approach in Africa. Two strategies were chosen by the French as external symbols of its 'civilizing mission' in Africa—public works and public health. For public works, the French built rail roads to connect its major colonial hubs in Africa like Dakar and Abidjan. For public health, the French introduced health reform through "sanitarians' grand plans."[34] The plan was to contain diseases and other forms of public health intervention on the people, which, according to Farmer, generated "fear and awe" among the people. Why? Because the plan to contain movement and control diseases was not about health improvement for Africans or improving the quality of their livelihood. Rather,

> disease control in West Africa had been linked under colonial rule to vigorous efforts to extract profits from these lands and their people. The

---

[32] Vaughan, *Curing Their Ills*, 13.
[33] Farmer, *Fevers, Feuds, and Diamonds*, 261ff.
[34] Farmer, *Fevers, Feuds, and Diamonds*, 261.

quest, which continues, always sparks conflict. Every chapter of the history of West Africa under European rule seems to include yet another cataclysmic outbreak of disease or conflict (or both) followed by ineffective or repressive measures (or both) and linked to an unbroken chain of profiteering.[35]

There is also a racial component to the colonial disease-control-over-care paradigm. African-American writer Toni Morrison decries the global project "to metaphysically void Africa" of its beauty and assets through many contaminating narratives of Africa. She also writes of what she calls "the freighted and complicated emotions" and "disdain, mythology of passivity, and traumatized Otherness" with which African history and social realities have been consigned into an "unmediated estrangement."[36] Her account describes well how contaminating narratives of Africans function. This contaminating narrative of Africanism, Morrison argues, becomes a term for the "denotative and connotative blackness that African peoples have come to signify as well as the entire range of views, assumptions, readings and misreading that accompany Eurocentric learning about these people."[37]

According to Morrison, this propensity to reify and demonize blackness, to inscribe and erase, to historicize and render timeless, to exercise power over blacks and to exclude and to assign or withdraw value to blackness is how the predominant contaminating narrative of blackness has been developed and mediated through multiple White supremacist channels.[38] This is particularly evident in the way diseases and outbreaks like EVD or HIV/AIDS have been used to construct a negative representation of African bodies, societies, institutions, social agency, and an essentialized notion of race. One of many examples that Farmer gives is

---

[35] Farmer, *Fevers, Feuds, and Diamonds*, 271
[36] Toni Morrison, *The Origin of Others* (Cambridge, MA: Harvard University Press, 2017), 101–102.
[37] Toni Morrison, *Playing in the Dark: Whiteness and the Literary Imagination* (NY: Vintage Books, 1993), 6–7.
[38] Morrison, *Playing in the Dark*, 8–9.

one tweet from then-candidate Trump who gave the impression that a total travel ban should be imposed on West Africa because of the possibility of spreading Ebola from Africa. According to Trump, "Obama won't send troops to fight jihadists, yet sends them to Liberia to contract Ebola. He is a delusional failure."[39] The truth is that for many non-Africans, the African continent is often portrayed as a repository of diseases and death with which they should not associate or from which they should escape. The African body was seen as a domain of maladies, and in many instances, African men who had protested against oppressive industrial, mining, or farm conditions were consigned to sanatoria as mental health patients.

Ebola and Global Health Inequity in Africa: A Theological Ethical Analysis

Michael Rozier argues convincingly that the Catholic Church has been less engaged in global public health discourse than one would have expected. However, the church is very active in providing health care in most parts of the world including Africa. For example, the Catholic Church has numerous health facilities in Africa. The Democratic Republic of Congo (DRC), with more than 2,185 facilities, has the highest number of Catholic health facilities in Africa. It is followed by Kenya with 1,092 and Nigeria with 524 facilities.[40] According to Rozier, the reason for this lack of engagement in public health discourse by the church is that the core motivation for Christian involvement in health care is to continue the ministry of the Lord Jesus to the sick. In Africa, this is particularly evident

---

[39] Cited in Farmer, *Fevers, Feuds, and Diamonds*, 34.

[40] For the latest statistics on Catholic health facilities in Africa, see Quentin Wodon, "Catholic Health Facilities in Africa: Achievements and Challenges," in *Handbook of African Catholicism*, ed. Stan Chu Ilo (Maryknoll, NY: Orbis Books, 2022), 540-544. See also Jill Olivier, Clarence Tsimpo, Regina Gemignani, Mari Shojo, Harold Coulombe, Frank Dimmock, Minh Cong Nguyen, Harrison Hines, Edward J. Mills, Joseph L. Dieleman, Annie Haakenstad, and Quentin Wodon, "Understanding the Roles of Faith-Based Health-Care Providers in Africa: Review of the Evidence with a Focus on Magnitude, Reach, Cost, and Satisfaction," *The Lancet* 386, no. 10005 (2015): 1765–1775.

in the fact that healing ministries are the fastest growing Christian movements in Africa.[41] As a result of this concentration on healing the sick and responding to their suffering, "the infrastructure of the Church was built largely to provide medical care to those who are ill."[42] Rozier helps us to understand why, particularly in Africa, both the local churches and their international partners focus more on providing medical supplies like drugs, diagnostic equipment, building hospitals, and sending medical workers to Africa rather than addressing health policies and public health issues like poor priority settings by local churches, failed government health programs that are reactionary, and the social determinants of health.

When Farmer invites us to pay greater attention to the multiple factors that bring about health, diseases, and death, he is inviting us to pay greater attention to the social determinants of health. These multiple factors he describes as "social drivers of epidemics," "the economic and social terrain," "therapeutic nihilism," particularly producing "differential virulence," seen everyday by "those who work in settings in which social determinants of exposure risk and access to care are thrown into relief—settings of poverty, war, or famine, or during natural or manmade disasters."[43] In order to offer hope to the sick in Africa and anywhere in the world and to build effective health systems and optimal health care delivery in Africa, one must pay attention to these social and commercial determinants of health. A good metaphor that is often used in public health to capture this point

> depicts illness as a river that people find themselves "pushed into" by adverse socio-economic conditions. They then float down the river until, if they are lucky, the health service intervenes and pulls them out. The

---

[41] See the analysis of the arguments of Paul Gifford and Bernhard Udehoven, "Searching for Healing in a Miraculous Stream," in *Wealth, Health, and Hope in African Christian Religion: The Search for Abundant Life*, ed. Stan Chu Ilo (Lexington, KY: Lexington Books, 2017), 46–55.

[42] Michael Rozier, "A Catholic Contribution to Global Public Health," *Annals of Global Health* 86, no. 1 (2020): 1.

[43] Farmer, *Fevers, Feuds, and Diamonds*, 447

health service clearly performs a vital role in this scene, but the public health response is to look further up the river and address those circumstances that make people fall in to begin with: prevention being preferred to cure.[44]

What should be the response of the church and theological ethicist to the fact that millions of Africans are being pushed into the rivers of health inequity? What are the current responses of churches in Africa and theological ethics to global health inequity as it affects Africa?[45] The response of both the church and theologians in Africa to the burden of such diseases like Ebola, HIV/AIDs, malaria, and COVID-19 in Africa has followed the following patterns:

1. A conscious attempt is made to follow the instructions from the World Health Organization or the Vatican or the funding organizations from the West who are 'partners' with Africa's church health care delivery entities;
2. African churches do not produce their own knowledge regarding the kinds of interventions needed for health care emergency or health education nor have the churches and theologians worked on identifying and addressing the barriers to optimal health in Africa. As a result, there are no strategies or ethical frameworks designed to remove these barriers nor have adaptive steps been designed to build on the African context of health and abundant life in a creative way;
3. There is a lack of interest in identifying the assets and resilience of local communities and churches in order to strengthen cultural and communal agencies through community mobilization and advocacy for the poor; and

---

[44] Matt Egan, "Health Public Policy," in *Health Promotion Practice*, 2nd Edition, ed. Will Nutland and Liza Cragg (NY: Open University Press, 2015), 71.

[45] See for instance, Jim Keenan's recent summary of the focus of Catholic theological ethics in Africa in *A History of Catholic Theological Ethics* (New York: Paulist Press, 2022), 320–327. It shows that African theological ethicists have not focused on addressing agency, the rights of the poor to universal health coverage, food and human security, and environmental health, but rather on foundational issues around liberation and inculturation theologies.

4. Ethical reflection has largely centered around the adequacy of health care services and quality and ethics of care/prevention/control; the weaknesses and threats of healing ministries; the suffering of the sick person; and end of life issues. Sadly, little attention has been paid to health protection and health promotion which address the underlying remote and proximate social determinants of health including the worldwide web of commercial interests and neo-liberal capitalism that are really the drivers of global health inequity.[46]

More than eight years before the COVID-19 pandemic, a group of international public health specialists had warned that commercial interests that had inundated the food chains of low- and middle-income countries (LMICs) and poor people in high-income countries (HICs) with cheap unhealthy food were "manufacturing epidemics" in the world.[47] Sadly, while neo-liberal capitalism and its associated false accounts of global convergence continues apace within the context of increasing public health nihilism in many parts of Africa, the accounts of health and wellbeing in Africa are being written by the WHO and other foreign agencies with a certain determinism or fixation on particular diseases that need to be contained, like HIV/AIDS, and other random epidemics that reflect Africa's history. Sadly, there is no proactive plan and strategy to improve population health by improving the quality of life of Africans and the social conditions that manufacture sickness and death. As Farmer puts

---

[46] An exception has been the works of the recently deceased Jacquineau Azétsop, ed., *HIV & AIDS in Africa: Christian Reflection, Public Health, Social Transformation* (Maryknoll, NY: Orbis Books, 2016). See also his joint study with Michael Ochieng of the rights to health improvement and promotion in public health in Chad which emphasizes some of the concerns that I address here though his focus is on public health care providers and not private entities like the church: Jacquineau Azétsop and Michael Ochieng, "The Right to Health, Health Systems Development and Public Health Policy Challenges in Chad," *Philosophy, Ethics, and Humanities in Medicine* 10, no. 1 (2015): 1–14.

[47] D. Stuckler, M. McKee, S. Ebrahim, and S. Basu, "Manufacturing Epidemics: The Role of Global Producers in Increased Consumption of Unhealthy Commodities Including Processed Foods, Alcohol, and Tobacco," *PLoS Med* 9, no. 6 (2012): e1001235, doi:10.1371/journal.pmed.1001235.

it, "The control-over-care paradigm is now caught up in a broader neoliberal one: when everything is for sale and public goods are few, both prevention and care are at risk of becoming commodities."[48] In a special commentary on *The Lancet*, Ilona Kickbusch and colleagues draw attention to how these determinants function in global health:

> Health outcomes are determined by the influence of corporate activities on the social environment in which people live and work: namely the availability, cultural desirability, and prices of unhealthy products. The environment shapes the so-called lifeworlds, lifestyles, and choices of individual consumers—ultimately determining health outcomes.[49]

Global health is a creation of colonialism. Many factors that we have identified in Farmer's work on why Ebola kills many Africans are attributable to the structure of global health today that undermine the health of the poor in the world and particularly in Africa. Global health has been generally accepted and is now a common currency circulating even in theological ethics and bioethics. However, it is a term that is fraught with many contradictions. Global health is "an artificial construct" developed in HICs to describe the kind of health care practices in LMICs and how the HICs are designing and determining the health outcomes of the poor in the erstwhile territories of the colonialists.[50] The case being made here is that population health is determined not simply by the presence of pathogens but by the presence of widespread poverty and the absence of health care delivery and health systems that are resilient, accessible, available and affordable.[51] Many West Africans died from this

---

[48] Farmer, *Fevers, Feuds, and Diamonds*, 499.
[49] Ilona Kickbusch, Luke Alle, and Christian Franz, "The Commercial Determinants of Health," *The Lancet* 4 (2016): e895–e896.
[50] Eichbaum, Adams, Evert, Ho, Semali, and Van Schalkwyk, "Decolonizing Global Health Education," 329.
[51] See, for instance, Whitelaw's theory of setting-based approaches to health promotion: S. Whitelaw, A. Baxendale, C. Bryce, L. MacHardy, I. Young, and E. Witney, "'Settings' Based

treatable disease (EVD) because they were poor and forgotten and do not seem to benefit from the advances made in global health; rather, they are victims of global neo-liberal capitalism that bolsters inequity, poverty, exploitation, props up dictatorship, and violence. This is Farmer's conclusion as well:

> Ebola and other public-health calamities strike most often in places from which human capital and raw materials have been extracted for centuries. From the rural reaches of Haiti and Rwanda, from prisons of Siberia, and from the slums of urban Peru: for thirty years, I've been pointing out how the epidemics that people have suffered in these places have arisen because of the inequities—political, economic, and medical—that such extractions invariably worsen.[52]

We can talk of global health as an ideal to be pursued. However, in reality, global health as it exists today is sustained by asymmetrical power relations that negate the assets and agency of local communities. It is also built on a racist frame about Africa, for instance, that objectifies the sick and blames the poor, while reducing them to commercial objects, consumers of medication, and burdens to local and global economies. My contention here is that there is nothing really "global" in the health of the world given the glaring inequality in health care, health systems, and health structures across the globe and in particular nations. Indeed, we should be speaking of global diseases as a counterpoint to global health. This is so because the choices humans have made and the unjust structures in the world today have made the majority of people who live in the Global South and inhabitants of slums in our big cities in North America and Europe sicker and poorer. Our collective choices have also made the planet a less habitable home. So true are the immortal words of Thomas Berry that

---

Health Promotion: A Review," *Health Promotion International* 16, no. 4, (2001): 339–353, doi.org/10.1093/heapro/16.4.339.
[52] Farmer, *Fevers, Feuds, and Diamonds*, 505.

"you cannot have healthy people in a sick planet."[53] In this kind of world, it is hard to realize the goal of "one health," a central direction for global health proposed by the US Center for Disease Control (CDC).[54]

Global health in Africa is represented through the systems of interventions from the West to Africa that Farmer calls "crisis caravans" who fly in for few hours, days, and weeks to provide medical missions, collect medical data, and provide temporary and unsustainable treatment of diseases or institute interventions for disease control. The improvement of the health of people in Africa and the courageous transformation of the medical impoverishment in Africa can only come about when the destructive chain linking the racialized global health practices and programs and virulent and persistent colonial policies that "neglected the destitute sick" are addressed. These sinful links have left intact as health orthodoxy some disastrous health policies and programs in global health today carried out by development institutions, UN agencies, and medical missions from the West to Africa, creating more crises and dislocation and worsening the health of the poor.[55] Alexandre Martins proposes a different understanding of global health from the top-down approach of international organizations, universities, and government and non-governmental agencies when he writes: "Global health is about justice in health care and incorporates the participation of individuals in the common good. A justice that fosters participation in the common good results from a collective engagement that promotes fair relationships

---

[53] Dennis Patrick O'Hara, "As Thomas Berry Concluded, It Is Not Possible to Have Healthy Humans on a Sick Planet," *The Irish News*, December 7, 2022, www.irishnews.com/lifestyle/faithmatters/2020/06/25/news/awakening-to-the-sacredness-of-creation-with-laudato-si--1982398/.

[54] 'One Health' is far from being realized. The One Health Initiative is "a collaborative, multisectoral, and transdisciplinary approach—working at the local, regional, national, and global levels—with the goal of achieving optimal health outcomes recognizing the interconnection between people, animals, plants, and their shared environment," Centers for Disease Control and Prevention, "One Health," www.cdc.gov/onehealth/index.html.

[55] Farmer, *Fevers, Feuds, and Diamonds*, 431.

among individuals."⁵⁶ Ultimately, what Martins points out is the need for community empowerment, assets, participatory practice, and self and community driven efficacy, agency and advocacy. Global health inequity and its colonial and racist roots as shown in the Ebola crisis call theology to an honest accounting of its own role in these roots as well as the ways it continues to function in colonialist and racist ways. How do the preaching in African churches and African theologies of healing, ancestral causes of diseases in Africa, and some forms of healing ministries *manufacture epidemics in Africa*?

Conclusion: Paul Farmer's Lessons for Theological Ethics

How can we think differently about the role of theological ethics in Africa going forward? Church health care agents in Africa have often provided logistic and professional support for the containment of diseases by international organizations in times of epidemic and humanitarian intervention. They have also provided health education. These agents and African theological ethicists have also raised cries for help to international community and led mission appeals and medical missions to Africa. But these efforts are not enough because they reinforce the undersides of global health—a reactionary interventionist approach that does more harm than good in the long run. Church health agents and pastoral agents in Africa have not been effective in addressing the structural violence in particular countries and designing an ethics for holistic health and a biosocial theological ethics of solidarity with the poor. There is the need for theological ethicists to pay greater attention to micro (individual), meso (national), and macro (international/global) factors in order to understand the African burden of diseases, of which EVD is only another layer in the ever-revolving cycle of disability and exposure to diseases and deaths for many poor people in Africa.

---

[56] Alexandre Martins, "Ethics and Equity in Global Health: The Preferential Option for the Poor," in *Ethical Challenges in Global Public Health: Climate Change, Pollution, and the Health of the Poor: Global Theological Ethics*, ed. Philip J. Landrigan and Andrea Vicini (Eugene, OR: Pickwick Publications, 2021), 100.

In order to do this, I propose a biosocial ethics of holistic health as an ethical framework for understanding the complexity of African history, the sinful structures on which the social and commercial determinants of health are built in Africa and in global health, and the health of the poor in Africa. A biosocial ethics that is also capable of unmasking the structures of sin and injustice and power differential in Africa can make possible solidarity and the option with the poor by courageously confronting the convergence of local and global factors that continue *to manufacture death* in Africa and sustain the deceptive and destructive global health policies and interventions in Africa.

The biosocial theological ethics of solidarity is grounded on the intrinsic goodness of all lives and provides the foundational compass for interpreting how the choices being made by individuals, systems, structures, and institutions with regard to population health, especially of the poor and vulnerable, promote and harm holistic health as well as human and cosmic flourishing. This ethics reflects on and proposes what ought to be done by individuals, societies, nations, and all men and women for health protection and health promotion by addressing the social determinants of health as they manifest in local, national, and international settings. It pays particular attention to the index of deprivation in particular societies, what factors are generating it and how they vary from one society to another. Biosocial ethics of health focuses on all the factors which interact in the procurement of abundant life—nutrition, sanitation, water, clean air, quality of one's social relationships, cultural and spiritual traditions, politics, economics, religious beliefs and practices, traditional and modern knowledge about health, sickness, diseases and healing. It examines the adequacy of human actions, health and economic policies, and value preferences—cultural, religious, social, political, etc.—in hampering or advancing the proper interaction of these integrative factors, which all must work together in bringing about human wellbeing.

Paul Farmer, through his exemplary life and writings, synthesized his wisdom in his final book, *Fevers, Feuds, and Diamonds*. Through Partners In Health, Paul Farmer tried to invent a new approach to global health equity, a partnership that places greater effort on building affordable, accessible, and available health care systems in Africa and training Africans to take care of the health of their own people. He could be said to have applied the principle of health *for* Africans *in* Africa *by* Africans. This is why he pioneered the building of the University of Global Health Equity in Rwanda, where he spent his last days here on earth.[57]

The future of global health partnership in Africa must be built on a biosocial model that aims at strengthening the capacity of local agencies, through individual and communal efficacy. Global health agents in Africa must adopt a respectful partnership with African peoples, health systems, governments, and private and religious entities. The priorities should be set by the Africans themselves, rather than by external forces and external interests; the goals should be health improvement and protection, rather than disease control and prevention.

A vital component of health systems in Africa that Farmer never addressed which is very important in concluding this essay is the role of faith-based entities. There is a growing recognition of the role of faith-based organizations in public health. In a special edition (March 2019), the *American Journal of Public Health* (AJPH) argues in an editorial that religious entities provide social capital for promoting population health particularly for vulnerable and seldom-heard communities. The editorial specifically identifies religion as a social determinant of population health, "providing leadership and capacity for service and social solidarity" in public health.[58] Joshua Williams and colleagues propose that the decisiveness of the role of faith-based entities is often seen in times of outbreak of diseases. According to them "Throughout history, faith

---

[57] The University of Global Health Equity, ughe.org/.
[58] Eileen Idler, Jeff Levin, Tyler J. VanderWeele, and Anwar Khan, "Partnerships Between Public Health Agencies and Faith Communities," *American Journal of Public Health* 109, no. 3 (2019): 346, doi.org/10.2105/AJPH.2018.304941.

communities and faith leaders have undertaken indispensable work to seek the good of their communities during contagions."[59]

Medical mission is still a very big business in Africa from faith-based agencies as well as other humanitarian organizations. Perhaps the churches with a strong sense of social justice and a new understanding of partnership that is different from tokenism, saviorism, and associated racialized thinking and acting towards Africa can be the new staging ground for a new ethical and life-giving partnership for holistic health built on the principles of social justice and option with the poor. Given the growing recognition of the importance of the leadership of faith-based health providers, Catholic ethicists could help develop some tools for measuring and assessing the effectiveness of the health care by church agencies so as to strengthen them in the service of improving and protecting the health of the population, especially the poor. Despite the significant contributions made by faith-based non-profit providers, Annabel Grieve and Jill Olivier note that "there is a distinct lack of robust evidence on their contribution, historical development, relationship with the public sector, and their contribution to UHC [universal health coverage] and to the strengthening of whole national systems."[60] In 2017, for instance, the World Council of Churches called for the mapping of faith-based health care providers in Africa in order not only to recognize their important contribution to public health but also to promote greater effectiveness and accessibility for these church hospitals.[61]

---

[59] Joshua T. B. Williams, Adrian Miller, and Abraham M. Nussbaum, "Combating Contagion and Injustice: The Shared Work for Public Health and Faith Communities During COVID-19," *Journal of Religion and Health* 60, no. 3 (2021): 1437, doi.org/10.1007/s10943-021-01243-4.

[60] Annabel Grieve, and Jill Olivier, "Towards Universal Health Coverage: A Mixed-Method Study Mapping the Development of the Faith-Based Non-Profit Sector in the Ghanaian Health System," *International Journal for Equity in Health* 17, no. 97 (2018): 2, doi.org/10.1186/s12939-018-0810-4.

[61] Jill Oliver and Quentin Wodon, "Mapping, Cost, and Reach to the Poor of Faith-Inspired Health Care Providers in Sub-Saharan Africa: A Brief Overview," in *Strengthening Faith-*

Now is the time for churches to take seriously the need to provide effective, comprehensive, safe, affordable, accessible, and timely care to the sick, especially the poor through primary health care. Ultimately, we all must become the vanguard for a new biosocial ethical approach to healing the sick, improving health, and promoting the conditions for human and cosmic flourishing so that God's people may have abundant life. In this much needed movement, we are glad that we have Dr. Paul Farmer as our model and guide speaking to us from the communion of saints.

Stan Chu Ilo, **MPH**, **EEd**, **PhD**, is research professor of World Christianity, Ecclesiology and African Studies at the Center for World Catholicism and Intercultural Theology, DePaul University, Chicago; the Coordinating Servant of the Pan-African Catholic Theology and Pastoral Network (PACTPAN); the North American Regional Coordinator of "Doing Theology from the Existential Peripheries," a project of the Migrant and Refugee Section, Dicastery for Integral Human Development; and editor of the *Handbook of African Catholicism* (2022). He is also one of the editors of *Concilium* International Catholic Journal.

Inspired Health Engagement, vol 3, ed. Jill Olivier and Quentin Wodon (Washington, DC: The World Bank, HNP Discussion Papers; 2012).

Chapter 13: The Legacy of Paul Farmer for Theological Ethics

Andrea Vicini, SJ

Reflecting on Paul Farmer's legacy for theological ethics unveils what might surprise many. Theological approaches, with the practices that inform them, are neither marginal nor reserved to theologically closed circles. On the contrary, they can inspire, animate, and transform ways of being and acting that reach out to diverse moral agents in complex disciplinary contexts and influence social environments beyond theological circles. Moreover, these modes in which theological approaches are embodied influence theology in comprehensive ways by contributing to the shaping of ideas and by enriching theology and theologians.

In discrete but significant ways, theology inspired and enriched Farmer's life and guided some of the choices that he made to advance global health. At the same time, his life and work contributed to a deeper understanding of theology and showed how theological discourse and practices can make a difference in society and culture by addressing what concerns the lives of people, their well-being, and their personal and social flourishing. However, because of structural violence, flourishing cannot happen "if there is hunger, unfair political arrangements, ongoing assaults on the environment, and no safety net to protect the sick, the unemployed, and the frail."[1] This chapter discusses Paul Farmer's legacy by highlighting how his work, with the theological insights that inspired his commitments, contributes to inform a renewed theological ethics that aims at promoting justice and the well-being of populations.

---

[1] Paul Farmer, "Sacred Medicine: How Liberation Theology Can Inform Public Health," *Sojourners* 43, no. 1 (2014): 9.

A Committed Theology and Its Fruits

Liberation theology, together with the key elements that characterize Catholic social thought, are expressions of theological developments that aim at embodying Jesus's transformative announcement of God's kingdom. Following the Gospels, theological discourse believes and reaffirms that such a divine kingdom is already here and now, at least in some initial stages of its manifestations but, at the same time, is neither fully realized nor realizable in its entirety. Each disciple of Jesus is invited to experience how the Good News of God's love and justice is not solely the expression of a pious longing, but it is a historical reality—at least to some extent. Care, mercy, love, and justice—which contribute to characterizing God's kingdom and how Jesus's disciples live—can be experienced in the challenging situations that populations face.

In its longing and struggle for justice, liberation theology shows how what concerns the divine, and what is at the core of experiencing God in human life, history, and creation, are inseparable from embracing everything that is human. The mystery of the Incarnation never stops surprising humankind. A critical awareness of unjust systems, oppressive structures, and inhuman power dynamics should lead to a resolute commitment to promote greater justice and to empower individuals and communities. Reflecting on structures demands a critical assessment of structural violence by emphasizing that

> Violence is done to some people in this world by poverty, racism, gender inequality, homophobia, and xenophobia. Just as this violence, which Gutiérrez and others term structural violence or 'structural sin,' can be institutionalized through unjust social arrangements, so too can it be undone with the help of more just ones.[2]

Theological discourse, and in particular Catholic social thought, by stressing the sinful dimensions of these structural arrangements, with the

---

[2] Farmer, "Sacred Medicine," 9.

violence that they embody, empowers to recognize, identify, and name what oppresses and dehumanizes while, at the same time, strives for transformative actions.³ Such an engagement with people's lives and stories, joining them in a shared struggle for justice, well-being, and flourishing is integral to living Christian discipleship. Embracing and living the Gospel expresses one's humanity and supports efforts to humanize the world.

During his studies and training and throughout his career, one can recognize how the awareness of systemic and structural conditions of injustice, which affect the personal and social development and health of people and communities, shaped and formed Paul Farmer.⁴ In reflecting on his life, one notices how the needed attention he gave to social, cultural, religious, and political determinants of health became inseparable from his more traditional approach to health that focuses on patients, their

---

³ See, for example, Margaret Pfeil, "Doctrinal Implications of Magisterial Use of the Language of Social Sin," *Louvain Studies* 27 (2002): 132–152; Daniel K. Finn, "What Is a Sinful Social Structure?," *Theological Studies* 77, no. 1 (2016): 136–164; Christine Firer Hinze, "The Drama of Social Sin and the (Im)Possibility of Solidarity: Reinhold Niebuhr and Modern Catholic Social Teaching," *Studies in Christian Ethics* 22, no. 4 (2009): 442–460; James F. Keenan, SJ, "Raising Expectations on Sin," *Theological Studies* 77, no. 1 (2016): 165–180; James F. Keenan, SJ, *Moral Wisdom: Lessons and Texts from the Catholic Tradition*, 3rd ed. (Lanham, MD: Rowman & Littlefield, 2017), 46–50; Conor M. Kelly, "The Nature and Operation of Structural Sin: Additional Insights from Theology and Moral Psychology," *Theological Studies* 80, no. 2 (2019): 293–327; Conor M. Kelly, "Everyday Solidarity: A Framework for Integrating Theological Ethics and Ordinary Life," *Theological Studies* 81, no. 2 (2020): 414–437. See also the chapter "Structures of Sin" in Josef Fuchs, SJ, *Moral Demands and Personal Obligations* (Washington, DC: Georgetown University Press, 1993), 63–73.
⁴ See Paul Farmer, *Pathologies of Power: Health, Human Rights, and the New War on the Poor* (Berkeley, CA: University of California Press, 2003), 139–159. Together with the exemplar of Archbishop Oscar Romero, among the volumes that inspired him Paul Farmer mentions two works of Gustavo Gutiérrez, OP: Gustavo Gutiérrez, *The Power of the Poor in History: Selected Writings*, trans. R.R. Barr (Maryknoll, NY: Orbis Books, 1983); and Gustavo Gutiérrez, *We Drink from Our Own Wells: The Spiritual Journey of a People*, trans. M. J. O'Connell (Maryknoll, NY: Orbis Books, 1984). See Farmer, "Sacred Medicine," 8.

symptoms, their disease, and their compliance with the proposed therapies.[5]

Liberation theology empowers health care professionals by shaping their awareness of the contexts in which patients live, work, and suffer. It also provides them with the needed critical approach to criticize unjust social situations and arrangements in constructive ways, aiming at overcoming troubling dynamics and fostering human and social liberation, with the health benefits that these transformations will entail in terms of preventive care, acute and long-term care, as well as social services (from education to infrastructures and to environmentally safe living and working conditions) and a quality of life that promotes peace and flourishing. Finally, liberation theology helps health care professionals in their efforts to join other agents in the social fabric who strive to care for the common good[6] and for the well-being of people and communities (from social workers to political activists, from religious communities and their leaders to grassroots organizations) by critically examining the process of health care delivery and what it demands to address the needs of vulnerable people and communities.[7] In what follows, I note liberation theology's key lessons for health care.

Solidarity

In diverse social contexts across the planet, those who experience multiple challenges, disadvantages, and difficulties that hinder their existence, well-being, and flourishing—those that society labels as "the poor"—demand help, care, peace, and justice. The structural conditions that contribute to create poverty should be addressed and changed. The Gospels call for a

---

[5] See Tracy Kidder, *Mountains Beyond Mountains: The Quest of Dr. Paul Farmer, A Man Who Would Cure the World* (New York: Random House, 2003).

[6] See Lisa Sowle Cahill, "Social Justice and the Common Good: Improving the Catholic Social Teaching Framework," in *Ethical Challenges in Global Public Health: Climate Change, Pollution, and the Health of the Poor*, ed. Philip J. Landrigan and Andrea Vicini, SJ (Eugene, OR: Pickwick Publications, 2021), 106–117.

[7] See Paul E. Farmer, "Shattuck Lecture: Chronic Infectious Disease and the Future of Health Care Delivery," *New England Journal of Medicine* 369, no. 25 (2013): 2424–2436.

resolute commitment for effective transformative praxes. The whole history of Christianity tried to embody compassion and love in concrete ways. However, in too many instances people who are struggling with poverty have been considered passive recipients of what the givers and caretakers estimated they needed. The agency of the poor was curtailed as if they could not be considered interlocutors and partners, involved in challenging and removing the systemic injustices that oppress them and that inhibit their personal and social flourishing. At the same time, the contributions of liberation theologians, which were informed not only by academic reasoning but by the struggle of peoples and communities in the Latin American continent, led to a more explicit theological commitment and practical engagement with those who suffer because of poverty, at the service of their well-being.

Despite its commitment to be for the poor and with the poor, the historical reception of liberation theology's insights and methodological approaches is marked by resistance and misunderstandings and followed by recognition and ongoing incorporation. Initially, the Catholic magisterium resisted acknowledging the urgency of liberation in the Latin American continent, not even when liberation was framed in light of the biblical liberation of God's people from slavery and oppression featured in the book of Exodus. Such a resistance mostly depended on misunderstandings regarding the sources of liberation theology's social critique and its liberationist praxes. Gradually, Catholic theological thought on social matters recognized and named the inequities that affect the poor, began to appreciate the evangelical call to personal and systemic conversion that characterizes liberation theology, and centered itself on making a preferential option for the poor as essential to promoting just societies.[8] This option is now a constitutive element of official Catholic social teaching, and Pope Francis is further contributing to its

---

[8] See Stephen J. Pope, "Proper and Improper Partiality and the Preferential Option for the Poor," *Theological Studies* 54, no. 2 (1993): 242–271; and Stephen J. Pope, "Christian Love for the Poor: Almsgiving and the 'Preferential Option,'" *Horizons* 21, no. 2 (1994): 288–312.

implementation by stressing how the promotion of social justice is integral to announcing God's kingdom and living the Gospel and how solidarity demands concrete actions and practices. As Pope John Paul II famously stressed, solidarity "is not a feeling of vague compassion or shallow distress at the misfortunes of so many people, both near and far. On the contrary, it is a firm and persevering determination to commit oneself to the common good; that is to say, to the good of all and of each individual, because we are all really responsible for all" (*Sollicitudo Rei Socialis*, no. 38).

The Preferential Option for the Poor

As Alexandre Martins writes in this volume, in the field of health, numerous are the shining examples of committed health care professionals who embodied the preferential option for the poor as the core of their efforts to promote health. Paul Farmer joins these exemplars, while he inspired others to make similar commitments and collaborated with many to institutionalize projects and initiatives to serve the poor and promote their health. Partners In Health—the international nonprofit public health organization founded in 1987 by Paul Farmer, Ophelia Dahl, Thomas J. White, Todd McCormack, and Jim Yong Kim to provide health care services in the poorest areas of developing countries—exemplifies this collaborative effort and commitment.[9]

The work of both Paul Farmer and Partners In Health aims at concrete achievements promoting health in some of the world peripheries. In particular, Partners In Health strives to "make 'a preferential option for the poor in health care' in settings ranging from rural Latin America (Haiti, Guatemala, Mexico) and Africa (Rwanda, Malawi, Lesotho) to areas of urban poverty (Peru, the United States) and even into the prisons

---

[9] See Partners In Health, "Together, We Can Repair the World," 2022, www.pih.org/our-impact. See also Daniel Palazuelos, Paul E. Farmer, and Joia Mukherjee, "Community Health and Equity of Outcomes: The Partners in Health Experience," *Lancet Global Health* 6, no. 5 (2018): e491–e493.

of Siberia."[10] At the same time, it is urgent to continue learning from those who are poor, appreciating the value of their experiences, their tested wisdom, and their struggles, needs, and longings. One should avoid any romantic understanding of people who are poor that disconnects them from the unjust and oppressive contexts in which they live and that betrays their hurt human condition.[11] On the contrary, a profound sense of justice, informed by concrete relationships and stories is essential to what it means to be human and to strive for health.[12] Hence, health care professionals, civil servants, and theologians should continue to learn from those who are marginalized, excluded, and considered irrelevant.[13] Within Christianity, relationality is constitutive of theological discourse and shapes praxes. It manifests the Incarnational nature of theology and expresses the condition of humankind, how the divine is discovered and encountered in people, in their life stories, their struggles, their challenges, and their achievements.

Ecclesially, "Go out to the peripheries" has been at the core of Pope Francis's call addressed to people of good will.[14] As Cathleen Kaveny stresses, Francis's call has epistemological relevance by centering on those

---

[10] Farmer, "Sacred Medicine," 9. On multidrug-resistant tuberculosis in prisons in the US and Russia, see Farmer, *Pathologies of Power: Health, Human Rights, and the New War on the Poor*, 179–195.

[11] See Miguel Cerón Becerra, SJ, "Health Care in US Detention Centers: Ethical Analysis from the Preferential Option for the Poor," *Journal of Catholic Social Thought* 18, no. 1 (2021): 35–63. See also David Becerra, Stephanie Lechuga-Pena, Jason Castillo, Raquel Perez Gonzalez, Nicole Ciriello, Fabiola Cervantes, and Francisca Porchas, "'Esto No Se Lo Deseo a Nadie': The Impact of Immigration Detention on Latina/o Immigrants," *Journal of Human Rights and Social Work* (2022): doi.org/10.1007/s41134-022-00210-7.

[12] See Alexandre Andrade Martins, *The Cry of the Poor: Liberation Ethics and Justice in Health Care* (Lanham, MD: Lexington Books, 2020), 123–127; Paul Farmer, "Ebola, the Spanish Flu, and the Memory of Disease," *Critical Inquiry* 46, no. 1 (2019): 56–70; Paul Farmer, *Fevers, Feuds, and Diamonds: Ebola and the Ravages of History* (New York: Farrar, Straus and Giroux, 2020); and Farmer, *Pathologies of Power*, 160–178.

[13] See Martins, *The Cry of the Poor*, 143–161.

[14] See Francis, *Evangelii Gaudium*, no. 20; Francis, "To the Group of the 'Lazare' Association from France," 2021, www.vatican.va/content/francesco/en/speeches/2021/august/docume nts/20210828-associazione-lazare.html.

excluded,[15] recognizes the marginalized as having social priority, and invites people and believers to walk together with the poor by accompanying one another.[16] The pope urges humankind to listen to the cry of the poor and of the whole planet, responding with committed actions informed by love and justice,[17] and aimed at fostering global fraternity. Hence, what one recognizes in Paul Farmer's reasoning and praxis is also informing the papal teaching and engagement.

As Paul Farmer never stopped stressing, the preferential option for the poor is not only a theological choice or a choice made by people of good will. Diseases too make a preferential option for the poor. As he wrote, "Any serious examination of epidemic disease has always shown that microbes also make a preferential option for the poor. But medicine and its practitioners, even in public health, do so all too rarely. Imagine how much unnecessary suffering we might collectively avert if our health care and educational systems, foundations, and nongovernmental organizations genuinely made a preferential option for the poor?"[18] Striving to promote health should lead them to address the social and political determinants that affect those who suffer from poverty, increasing their vulnerability to disease and, ultimately, affecting the whole society.[19]

---

[15] See Cathleen Kaveny, "Pope Francis and Catholic Healthcare Ethics," *Theological Studies* 80, no. 1 (2019): 192.

[16] See Kaveny, "Pope Francis and Catholic Healthcare Ethics," 192.

[17] See Leonardo Boff, *Cry of the Earth, Cry of the Poor*, trans. P. Berryman, Ecology and Justice (Maryknoll, NY: Orbis Books, 1997); Leonardo Boff and Virgilio P. Elizondo, eds., *Concilium: Ecology and Poverty: Cry of the Earth, Cry of the Poor* (London: SCM Press; Maryknoll, NY: Orbis Books, 1995); Alexandre Andrade Martins, "Preferential Option for the Poor and Equity in Health," *Camillianum* 14, no. 40 (2014): 31–48; Alexandre Andrade Martins, "Healthy Justice: A Liberation Approach to Justice in Health Care," *Health Care USA* 22, no. 3 (2014): 1–14; and Martins, *The Cry of the Poor*.

[18] Farmer, "Sacred Medicine, 9." Quoted in: Anne Pollock, *Sickening: Anti-Black Racism and Health Disparities in the United States* (Minneapolis, MN: University of Minnesota Press, 2021), 177.

[19] See Alexandre Andrade Martins, "*Laudato Si'*: Integral Ecology and Preferential Option for the Poor," *Journal of Religious Ethics* 46, no. 3 (2018): 410–424.

The commitment of health care professionals joining theologians in making a preferential option for the poor implies avoiding any paternalistic and patronizing attitude, recognizing the explicit or lurking Western colonial presumptions of having figured out all the questions and knowing all the answers because of the assumed supremacy and privilege of Western cultures, histories, social arrangements, and religions. On the contrary, the preferential option for the poor embodies equality, reciprocity, mutuality, and humility, joining in a shared search for what is truthful and authentic. The lives of people, with their strengths, needs, and limitations should be at the forefront of theological concerns, as well as of care providers and of civil servants.

Embodying this commitment, Partners In Health strives to provide care in the world's peripheries and, at the same time, to create opportunities for forming health care providers. Among the many personal stories of community health workers Mabel Koroma, from Sierra Leone, exemplifies this commitment.[20] Sierra Leone has the highest maternal mortality rate in the world (1 in 17 women has a lifetime risk of dying in pregnancy or childbirth). After a pregnancy check-up, Mabel discovered she was HIV-positive. Helped by Partners In Health, Mabel started her antiretroviral treatment, gave birth, succeeding in having a child who was HIV negative. In light of this experience, because of the help that she received, and after targeted training, she became a community health worker, helping other women to care for their health, accompanying them in their struggle for health.

Accompaniment

Accompaniment is neither a vague word nor a fashionable and catchy slogan. On the contrary, it is a concrete manifestation of solidarity, of being with the people and for them.[21] Accompaniment implies conversion

---

[20] See Partners In Health, "Reducing Maternal Mortality (Mabel)," 2019, www.pih.org/reducing-maternal-mortality.

[21] See Paul Farmer, "Partners in Help: Assisting the Poor over the Long Term," *Foreign Affairs*, July 29, 2011, www.foreignaffairs.com/articles/haiti/2011-07-29/partners-help; and

of hearts, leads to seeing reality anew, and fosters personal change and social transformation. Moreover, accompaniment characterizes prophetic witnesses.[22] For Paul Farmer, accompaniment is "a staple in liberation theology."[23] Moreover, in his practice, he recognized what happened to "patients facing both poverty and chronic disease."[24] As he writes, "They missed appointments, didn't fill prescriptions, didn't 'comply' with our [professional] counsel. And this was true in every country in which I've worked. But when we began working with community-health workers to take care to [*sic*] patients, the outcomes we all sought were much more likely to happen. Instead of asking 'why don't patients comply with our treatments?' we began to ask, 'How can we accompany our patients on the road to cure or wellness or a life with less suffering due to disease?'"[25]

Accompaniment is both a personal and social virtue and, as every virtue, it depends on virtuous dynamics of virtuous moral agents (from health care professionals to community health workers and citizens alike) within their social contexts, while each one contributes to make the social fabric more virtuous. For Farmer and Partners In Health, working with the local authorities is part of this process of accompaniment. Reconstructing in innovative ways the Rwandan health care system exemplifies a concrete form of accompaniment that empowered local agents, organizations, and structures and led them to articulate proposals and realize projects that are targeted to the country's reality and are feasible. In Rwanda, a further example of a targeted project is the University of Global Health Equity, which was planned, built, and launched in a rural area of the country to "advance global health delivery

---

Michael P. Griffin and Jennie Weiss Block, eds., *In the Company of the Poor: Conversations between Dr. Paul Farmer and Fr. Gustavo Gutiérrez* (Maryknoll, NY: Orbis Books, 2013). See also Stephen J. Pope, "Integral Human Development: From Paternalism to Accompaniment," *Theological Studies* 80, no. 1 (2019): 123–147.

[22] See Farmer, *Pathologies of Power*, 160–178.
[23] Farmer, "Sacred Medicine," 9.
[24] Farmer, "Sacred Medicine," 9.
[25] Farmer, "Sacred Medicine," 9.

by training a new generation of global health leaders who are equipped in not just building, but sustaining effective and equitable health systems."[26]

Conclusion

Training the current and future generations of health care providers within one of the world's peripheries, with a privileged attention given to global public health and to the need of fostering equity, reveals how, in Paul Farmer's vision of global health, education is integral to promoting health and social justice with a preferential option for the poor. Certainly, education also is at the heart of theological endeavors. Farmer's vision of how education should foster personal and social flourishing is both a reminder and a renewal of the enduring engagement of theology, with its discourses and the practices that they inspire, in promoting education in many concrete ways, striving for justice, and accompanying disadvantaged, marginalized, and oppressed people.

Focusing on global health, together with education, other priorities should also be mentioned. As a result of their ongoing global work in four continents and twelve countries—including Russia, the Navajo Nation, and the US—in 2013, Paul Farmer and colleagues stressed the urgency of fostering maternal and child health; advancing vaccination campaigns; reducing the incidence of the "big three" global diseases (i.e., AIDS, tuberculosis, and malaria); addressing the challenges of neglected tropical diseases that, despite affecting large populations in the Global South, still receive insufficient attention from researchers and drug companies; tackling noncommunicable diseases and, among them, cancer;[27] promoting surgical services and opportunities in the Global South; offering better primary care services in the US; and, across the globe,

---

[26] University of Global Health Equity, "Our Story," 2022, ughe.org/the-story-behind-the-university.

[27] See Andrea Vicini, SJ, Philip J. Landrigan, and Kurt Straif, eds., *The Rising Global Cancer Pandemic: Health, Ethics, and Social Justice* (Eugene, OR: Pickwick Publications, 2022).

313

expanding the presence of and access to health care services.[28] This list of global health priorities is far from being addressed. After a decade, its increased urgency is confirmed. Internationally, the Sustainable Development Goals (2015–2030),[29] which followed the Millennium Development Goals (2000–2015),[30] include these priorities. The partial success of the Millennium Development Goals is a reminder that there should be no further delays in caring for vulnerable populations and in strengthening health care systems across the planet and, particularly, in the Global South.[31]

Furthermore, the global COVID-19 pandemic showed how even what were considered the most advanced health care structures and services on the planet were insufficiently prepared and unable to respond to the challenges of this pandemic. This pandemic further slowed the progress toward achieving the Sustainable Development Goals, calling for a renewed commitment now that COVID-19 has become endemic.

---

[28] See Paul Farmer, Matthew Basilico, Vanessa Kerry, Madeleine Ballard, Anne Becker, Gene Bukhman, Ophelia Dahl, Andy Ellner, Louise Ivers, David Jones, John Meara, Joia Mukherjee, Amy Sievers, and Alyssa Yamamoto, "Global Health Priorities for the Early Twenty-First Century," in *Reimagining Global Health: An Introduction*, ed. Paul Farmer, Arthur Kleinman, and Jim Kim (Berkeley, CA: University of California Press, 2013), 302–339.

[29] See United Nations Development Programme, "What Are the Sustainable Development Goals?," 2022, www.undp.org/sustainable-development-goals.

[30] See World Health Organization, "Millennium Development Goals (Mdgs)," February 19, 2018, www.who.int/news-room/fact-sheets/detail/millennium-development-goals-(mdgs).

[31] See Madisen Fuller and Puneet Dwivedi, "Assessing Changes in Inequality for Millennium Development Goals among Countries: Lessons for the Sustainable Development Goals," *Social Sciences (Basel)* 8, no. 7 (2019), doi.org/10.3390/socsci8070207; Dora Benedek, Edward R. Gemayel, Abdelhak S. Senhadji, and Alexander F. Tieman, "A Post-Pandemic Assessment of the Sustainable Development Goals," April 27, 2021, www.imf.org/en/Publications/Staff-Discussion-Notes/Issues/2021/04/27/A-Post-Pandemic-Assessment-of-the-Sustainable-Development-Goals-460076; Eduardo Cuenca-García, Angeles Sánchez, and Margarita Navarro-Pabsdorf, "Assessing the Performance of the Least Developed Countries in Terms of the Millennium Development Goals," *Evaluation and Program Planning* 72 (2019): 54–66; and James O'Sullivan, "Millennium Development Goals and Catholic Social Teaching: Ongoing Responsibility and Response," *Lumen et Vita* (2011): 1–20.

More recently, Paul Farmer's agenda for the future highlighted the urgency of identifying the multiple and diverse ways in which those who experience poverty suffer disproportionately–whether one considers historic examples of the colonial past or ongoing inequities which depend on racial discrimination and marginalization.[32] What affects people depends in great part on social factors. The critical assessment of oppression, discrimination, gender, race, social status, and wealth should lead civil society to respond by making anew a preferential option for the poor. This is also an ongoing challenge for theological ethics, for Christian discipleship, for ecclesial communities, and for the institutional Church.

Farmer's contributions and vision both enrich and provoke theological ethics by inviting theologians to critically examine their vision, priorities, and methodologies. In terms of vision, since the Second Vatican Council, "the duty of scrutinizing the signs of the times and of interpreting them in the light of the Gospel" (*Gaudium et Spes*, no. 4) should inform and guide theological reasoning and teaching, as well as ecclesial praxes. Such a duty should continue to be resolutely embraced in new ways by recognizing and addressing any form of exclusion and discrimination. Moreover, for Pope Francis, to promote "a sustainable and integral development" (*Laudato Si'*, no. 13) is an urgent global priority. This form of development requires that the poor "be acknowledged and valued in their dignity, respected in their identity and culture, and thus truly integrated into society" (*Fratelli Tutti*, no. 187). Those who struggled with poverty because of systemic inequities are not passive recipients of opportunities for change and equity; they should be empowered and engaged participants and contributors. Finally, concrete forms of solidarity and the preferential option for the poor and with the poor should shape theological engagements and ecclesial contributions. This commitment should pervasively inform theological ethics as an academic discipline that strives

---

[32] See Paul Farmer and Andrea Vicini, SJ, "An Ethical Agenda for Global Public Health," in *Ethical Challenges in Global Public Health: Climate Change, Pollution, and the Health of the Poor*, ed. Phillip J. Landrigan and Andrea Vicini, SJ (Eugene, OR: Pickwick Publications, 2021), 193–198.

to educate and contribute to personal and social flourishing in diverse social contexts.

Theological discourse joins the efforts spearheaded by Paul Farmer by reaffirming health as a personal and social good that should be protected and promoted and by inspiring civil servants, health care professionals, and people of good will to embrace, in the whole social fabric, an inclusive vision of social justice that fosters solidarity and that empowers people of good will and those excluded and on the margins. In such a way, Paul Farmer's legacy will be greater global health and a more just world.

Andrea Vicini, SJ, is Chairperson, Michael P. Walsh Professor of Bioethics, and Professor of Theological Ethics in the Theology Department and an affiliate member of the Ecclesiastical Faculty at the School of Theology and Ministry at Boston College. MD and pediatrician (University of Bologna), he is an alumnus of Boston College (STL and PhD) and holds an STD from the Pontifical Faculty of Theology of Southern Italy in Naples. He taught in Italy, Albania, Mexico, Chad, and France. He is co-chair of the international network *Catholic Theological Ethics in the World Church*, as well as lecturer and member of associations of moral theologians and bioethicists in Italy, Europe, and the US. His research interests and publications include theological bioethics, global public health, new biotechnologies, environmental issues, and fundamental theological ethics. During the academic year 2015–2016, he had a research fellowship at the Center of Theological Inquiry in Princeton, NJ, on the Societal Implications of Astrobiology. Since 2021 he has been a Fellow of the Collegium Ramazzini. Recent publications include three co-edited volumes: *Reimagining the Moral Life: On Lisa Sowle Cahill's Contrib-utions to Christian Ethics* (2020), *Ethics of Global Public Health: Climate Change, Pollution, and the Health of the Poor* (2021), and *The Rising Global Cancer Pandemic: Health, Ethics, and Social Justice* (2022).

Chapter 14: From Compassion to Pragmatic Solidarity: Considering the Right to Health from the Margins

Maura A. Ryan

Paul Farmer has been among the most influential figures in the growing movement to understand and underscore the relationship between health and human rights. Drawing from his experience as a physician to the poor and the marginalized in Haiti, Latin America, Russia, Africa, and the US, Farmer joined Jonathan Mann and others in exposing the necessary connections between poverty, inequality, and disease and between differential vulnerability to disease and systemic violations of human rights.[1] Arguing for a "right to health" grounded in advocacy for the protection and promotion of those social, political, economic, and cultural conditions that allow individuals and communities to flourish as human beings, Farmer challenged conventional human rights discourses as excessively legalistic and narrowly focused on theory over practice. Drawing from liberation theology, Farmer argued that it is not enough to acknowledge the reality of global health inequities or to assert a human right to health or health care; recognizing the interrelated social, political, economic, and cultural conditions that affect health and well-being and constrain access to care, particularly for the most marginalized, must be

---

[1] Jonathan Mann was an American physician who is widely considered a pioneer in the movement to recognize the relationship between health and human rights. He oversaw the World Health Organization's Global Programme for AIDS and was a founding member of Project SIDA (devoted to understanding and addressing AIDS in Africa) and HealthRight (a research and advocacy organization for promoting global health and human rights). Mann was among the first to develop the implications of recognizing health as a human right for the field of global health and to articulate the connections between disease and the violation of human rights. For a helpful overview of developments in the field of health and human rights, see George J. Annas, Jonathan M. Mann, Michael A. Grodin, and Sofia Gruskin, eds., *Health and Human Rights: A Reader* (New York and London: Routledge, 1999).

linked to action in the struggle for social and economic rights. It is not enough merely to treat the diseases of the destitute poor; rather, respect for human dignity requires a lived commitment to improving the conditions that result in too many people around the world dying of preventable diseases. In his argument for "pragmatic solidarity" in the face of global health inequities, Farmer reminds us that caring for the poor is not just about exercising compassion. The willingness to "suffer with others" becomes pragmatic solidarity when it is joined with action to reduce their suffering. Pragmatic solidarity is about asking the question: "how much of this suffering is premature or even unnecessary and what might we do collectively to lessen it?"[2]

This essay explores the ways in which Catholic social thought informs the content of a "right to health" and asks how its understanding of the relationship between health and human rights is enriched by Farmer's construction of "pragmatic solidarity." What would it mean to incorporate attention to the patterns of structural violence that determine how disease and death are distributed and to whom the goods of science and medicine will be available? What would it mean, in other words, to acknowledge that death and disease have social causes and cannot be adequately addressed without also addressing those causes? What does it look like to join the affirmation of a right to health with action in the struggle for social, economic, and cultural rights?

Farmer's influence on our understanding of the relationship between health and human rights has been most profound in the arena of global health and in the context of diseases that have long disproportionately affected the poor and marginalized, like AIDS and tuberculosis. He was also a strong voice for equitable access to vaccines as COVID-19 raged world-wide. Although the pandemic and its impact in the United States are not yet fully understood, it is impossible to ignore the differential course of the virus according to race, age, and economic status. It is

---

[2] See Paul Farmer, "Pragmatic Solidarity," *The Center for Compassion and Global Health*, ccagh.org/conversations/editorials/paul-farmer.

instructive, even in a preliminary way, to bring the lens of pragmatic solidarity to bear on our experience of COVID-19, to ask what we might learn about existing patterns of structural violence, of socially constructed risk and resilience, that resulted in deaths both tragic and avoidable.

Interrogating Health and Human Rights

In his book *Pathologies of Power*, Farmer observed: "When children living in poverty die of measles, gastroenteritis, and malnutrition, and yet no party is judged guilty of a human rights violation, liberation theology finds fault with the entire notion of human rights as defined within liberal democracies."[3] This observation captures several key themes in Farmer's analysis of the relationship between health and human rights. First, it raises up the focus on protections for civil and political rights in contemporary liberal discourses to the exclusion of social, economic, and cultural rights. Although Article 25 of the 1948 Universal Declaration of Human Rights holds that "everyone has the right to a standard of living adequate for the health and well-being of himself and of his family, including food, clothing, housing and medical care," human rights protections, even in countries where a right to health care is constitutionally recognized, tend to take the form of freedom from interference and explicit discrimination.

Western bioethics maps on to this emphasis with human rights violations in medicine typically characterized as violations of individual liberty (as in undermining protections against unwanted medical treatment) or privacy (as in denying the right to determine the time and manner of one's death). In the mainstream bioethics literature, human rights "dilemmas" almost exclusively focus on questions related to the state's treatment of individuals, e.g., whether physicians may ethically participate in torturing prisoners of war. However, as Farmer argues, the children who die "stupid deaths," that is, deaths that can be prevented by use of available therapeutic remedies, bear witness to the hardly visible

---

[3] Paul Farmer, *Pathologies of Power: Health, Human Rights and the New War on the Poor* (Berkeley and Los Angeles: University of California Press, 2005), 142.

structures of violence (global as well as local) perpetrated by the powerful on the weak and marginalized. "Structural violence," those deeply ingrained patterns of distributing power and resources, constrains not only what kinds of treatment will be required and available to those in need, but who has access to the conditions conducive to health and well-being: safe drinking water, sanitation, education, nutrition, and adequate housing.

As Farmer correctly argues, structural violence escapes analysis in human rights discourses because, unlike the protection of civil and political rights, achieving a "standard of living adequate for the health and well-being" of everyone requires substantive governmental investments. Although human rights are articulated as "universal," they are broadly assumed to be protected by states. Thus, both the definition and the achievement of "an adequate standard of living" occur within a discrete context. Moreover, to a large extent, the promotion of human rights, in particular social, economic and cultural rights, requires good faith commitments. When those in power refuse to accept the responsibilities of stewardship, resulting in deep divisions between the haves and the have nots that threaten health and well-being, politicians and policy-makers may be subject to criticism but are seldom held accountable. Even international human rights organizations tend to treat poverty and inequality as "simply distracting background considerations" rather than as human rights violations, further undermining the protection of social and economic rights.[4]

When we acknowledge that the powers at work behind the unequal and multiple worlds of health and health care across the globe are not only political but economic, we see other interrelated manifestations of structural violence that often elude naming in debates over health and human rights. We cannot understand the course of the HIV/AIDS

---

[4] See Paul Farmer, *Never Again? Reflections on Human Values and Human Rights*, delivered as The Tanner Lectures on Human Values, University of Utah, March 30, 2005, tannerlectures.utah.edu/_resources/documents/a-to-z/f/Farmer_2006.pdf.

epidemic, for example, without also exposing the reach of multinational pharmaceutical corporations and their impact on access to treatment, availability of testing, standards of care, and even the training of physicians. We cannot understand why some children in the Global South disproportionately die "stupid deaths" without acknowledging the impact of multinational corporations on the flow of money, technologies, goods and services, and, ultimately, on local economies and patterns of cultivation and distribution of resources.

Farmer's observation that diseases make a "preferential option for the poor," demanding a response from those who claim to be concerned about health and equity, points to his impatience with theory divorced from action. Admitting the often overwhelming character of global health challenges even for those charged with responding, he argued nonetheless: "Those who formulate health policy in Geneva, Washington, New York, or Paris do not really labor to transform the social conditions of the wretched of the earth. Instead, the actions of technocrats—and what physician is not a technocrat?—are most often tantamount to managing social inequality, to keeping the problem under control."[5]

Given his commitment not only to providing the best possible care to the poor but transforming their social conditions, it is not surprising that Farmer was deeply attracted to liberation theology, a movement that arose within small Christian communities in Latin America. Liberation theology takes as its starting point the real situation of the most destitute. Citing influential Peruvian theologian Gustavo Gutiérrez's critique of liberal human rights discourses, Farmer insisted that a commitment to human rights must be a commitment to the "rights of the poor," to standing with the poor in the struggle to meet their basic human needs; otherwise, it is merely a defense of laissez-faire doctrine that pretends that one's society enjoys an equality that it does not.[6]

---

[5] Farmer, *Pathologies of Power*, 140.
[6] Farmer, *Pathologies of Power*, 142; Gustavo Gutiérrez, *The Power of the Poor in History* (Maryknoll, NY: Orbis Books, 1983), 87.

Pathologies of Power follows liberation theology's "observe, judge, act" method.[7] Farmer's analysis is rooted in the concrete struggles of the destitute poor for survival, challenges a status quo that is fundamentally unperturbed by their suffering, and calls for action by the powerful in response to the demands of the poor to meet their basic human needs. Farmer often began with a story, an introduction to a patient who led him not only to treat the presenting illness but to observe the circumstances of his patients' lives and the shape of their suffering and from there to question the structures of violence at work. His critique of international efforts to address multi-drug resistant tuberculosis (MDRTB), for example, starts with Sergei, who contracted tuberculosis while enduring more than a year in pretrial detention in Russia. After transfer to a penal TB colony, Sergei received erratic treatment and faced chronic shortages of basic medical supplies, overcrowded living conditions, and inadequate nutrition. Farmer meets Sergei as he is preparing to be released, most likely carrying infectious, multidrug resistant TB home to his family and his community.[8] In Farmer's hands, Sergei's story is a window into seeing clearly how the failure to invest in effective, comprehensive second-line drug treatment, along with failure to address the conditions under which prisoners are detained in unsafe conditions, feeds a widespread TB epidemic that results in an undeclared death penalty extending beyond the prison walls.

In the method of liberation theology, observation leads to judgment: "We look at the lives of the poor and are sure, just as they are, that something is terribly wrong."[9] Farmer's analysis of what exactly is terribly wrong has several levels. At the root is the willingness to accept the proposition that some lives are worth more than others. To the extent that we allow the policies and practices by which life-saving therapies are not available to the poor in many parts of the world to go unchallenged, we

---

[7] See Leonardo and Clodovis Boff, *Introducing Liberation Theology* (Maryknoll, NY: Orbis Books, 1987), for a helpful treatment of this method.
[8] Farmer, *Pathologies of Power*, 113–121.
[9] Farmer, *Pathologies of Power*, 142.

Considering the Right to Health from the Margins

have made a commitment to an ideology of fundamental inequality. In Sergei's case, and the case of the thousands of other Russian prisoners and staff infected with MDRTB, decisions to provide only standard, short-course therapy are declarations that their lives are worth less than the lives of those who are not imprisoned or who are able to access effective drugs, adequate nutrition, and supportive care. In addition, when we treat health care as a commodity to be distributed on the market, we are ratifying the belief that those who have resources are entitled to protection against physical vulnerabilities not available to others with the same vulnerabilities but insufficient resources. The high cost of comprehensive treatment for MDRTB is a result of pricing decisions made by drug companies along with the unwillingness of international public health authorities to use moral pressure to bring down drug prices as proved effective in facing other emergencies such as HIV/AIDS.

Farmer acknowledges that the process of observation and judgment is difficult in the arena of global health, both because the voices of the poor seldom enter into discussions regarding policies and practices in development or international health and also because vested interests "have an obvious stake in shaping observations about causality and in attenuating harsh judgments of harsh conditions."[10] He cites as examples of the latter the prevailing wisdom in international development circles that AIDS could not be successfully treated in very low resource areas even after effective and affordable drugs became available. His work with Partners In Health in Haiti directly challenged powerful, unquestioned assumptions that the destitute poor in countries such as Haiti could not comply with medication protocols that involved multiple, carefully spaced daily doses taken with meals (assumptions that, not surprisingly, shore up arguments for "cost-effective treatment" that is inferior to the standard of care in resource-rich countries). Farmer's patients did well when offered an approach that combined individual assistance from community health workers in taking medications with financial and nutritional support. A

---

[10] Farmer, *Pathologies of Power*, 144.

similar approach to treating TB outbreaks in Haiti and Peru called into question a simple reliance either on biological factors (e.g., the inability to overcome mutations that create drug resistance) or psychological factors leading to patients' discontinuing treatment (e.g., confidence in sorcery). Rather, Farmer's work demonstrated that removing structural barriers to compliance with drug regimens, by addressing economic factors that affect initial exposure, stage at diagnosis, access to therapy and length of convalescence, resulted in greatly improved outcomes.[11] In both cases, the act of judgment exposes what is invisible in a focus on patient behavior (e.g., when the course of an infection is blamed on ignorance about hygiene) that becomes visible when the lens widens to the conditions that structure patients' risk (e.g., lack of access to adequate nutrition and clean water, economic opportunities and safe shelter).[12]

Just as observation leads to judgment, observation and judgment lead to action. As Farmer argues, the goal of reflecting, studying, and gaining the local knowledge borne of listening deeply to the poor is not to produce more books or articles or reports or even witness to standing with the poor. Rather, the point of joining the poor in understanding their experience is to change the world, to act with them for their liberation. Thus, for Farmer, liberation theology demands "yok[ing] all of its reflection to the service of the poor."[13]

Farmer's liberation ethic is most compelling for health care here, as observation and judgment turn to action in the form of what he calls "pragmatic solidarity." He describes "pragmatic solidarity" in various ways. It is first a way of practicing medicine: "Medicine becomes pragmatic solidarity when it is delivered with dignity to the destitute poor."[14] At its most basic level, this involves insisting that goods and services reach those who need them the most, not only those who can afford to pay. This commitment is visible throughout his work, in finding innovative ways to

---

[11] Farmer, *Pathologies of Power*, 151.
[12] Farmer, *Pathologies of Power*, 121–122; 151.
[13] Farmer, *Pathologies of Power*, 138; 144–145.
[14] Farmer, *Pathologies of Power*, 138.

treat HIV/AIDS or MDRTB in areas of the world and in certain populations in which it was widely argued that it could not be done. As we have seen, however, once the connections between vulnerability to disease and death and the failure to protect social and economic rights are acknowledged, tending to the medical needs of the poor also involves acting to address the impact of structural violence. It is not only medical care that expresses solidarity but the "rapid deployment of our tools and resources to improve the health and wellbeing" of the poor.[15]

Pragmatic solidarity also describes the turn from compassion as sentiment to joining the poor in their struggle for liberation. This involves recognizing, as Gutiérrez expressed it, that "the poverty of the poor is not a call to generous relief action, but a demand that we go and build a different social order."[16] In the context of global health, Farmer interprets this sense of pragmatic solidarity as a challenge to question the strong, if unstated, belief that charity is the answer to the problems of poverty and access to care.[17] Reliance on the generosity of those of means to address the longstanding needs of the destitute poor is dangerous insofar as it assumes that poverty and disease are random or happen to certain people and not to others because of some combination of personal choices. Quoting theologian Jon Sobrino, he argues that poverty is not the inevitable result of history or geography or personal behavior; rather, poverty and other forms of structural violence result from the actions of other human beings, and the poor are victims of these actions.[18] Charitable relief efforts are often tinged with an assumed superiority on the part of those bestowing their charity; moreover, medical missions tend to be sporadic or piecemeal and offer care that would not be offered to those with means, e.g., expired

---

[15] Farmer, *Pathologies of Power*, 220.

[16] Gutiérrez, *The Power of the Poor in History*, 45.

[17] Farmer acknowledges that charity can be a powerful expression of love of neighbor for religious believers. His critique is leveled at the type of charitable response that substitutes either money or "helicopter treatment" for accompaniment.

[18] Farmer, *Pathologies of Power*, 143; Jon Sobrino, *Spirituality of Liberation: Toward Political Holiness* (Maryknoll, NY: Orbis Books, 1988), 31.

drugs or cast-off medical goods. Not only is this a failure to respect the human dignity of the poor; it ignores or attempts to erase the history of inequality and unequal opportunity that have led to current conditions. Charitable relief efforts often assume as well that the structures of inequity are fixed or inevitable. In its most pernicious form, those in power choose charity so as to protect their self-interest while commending themselves for their efforts to mitigate the suffering of the least well-off.

The challenge to build a different social order extends to asking difficult questions of the prevailing models of international development. Farmer is critical of development models that measure overall gains in health, income, or national productivity and declare success while ignoring persistent gaps in income levels. Farmer recognizes that there have been wonderous advances in science and technology, advances that have great potential for addressing the suffering and death of millions of people, and that the lives of many poor people have been improved. But advances in knowledge or skill alone do not guarantee equitable development without redistribution of goods and services, nor is development necessarily either linear or inevitable. Although he does not use the language of integral human development as found in contemporary Catholic social thought, he argues that genuine development depends upon guaranteeing the conditions for the dignified participation of all members of a society. When the dominant values in development discourses are "cost effectiveness" and "market responsiveness" and development efforts accept gross income gaps as temporary or culturally specific, development efforts will not lead to a different social order.

Sobrino insisted that "the only correct way to love the poor will be to struggle for their liberation. This liberation will consist, first and foremost, in their liberation at the most elementary level—that of their simple, physical life, which is at stake in the present situation."[19] It is fair to say that, for Farmer, the only correct way to care for the poor is to join them in the struggle for their dignity against all that threatens their survival and

---

[19] Sobrino, *Spirituality of Liberation: Toward Political Holiness*, 32.

well-being. "Caring for the poor" takes many forms in Farmer's work, from making medical goods and services available to the destitute poor, to challenging political, economic, and social dogma that justifies the present world order, to reorienting research to include the social and economic determinants of health, to changing the way medical students are taught to think about medicine. In all these forms, pragmatic solidarity becomes possible (and necessary) when the conviction that "the world is not as it should be" leads to accepting responsibility for one's own role in maintaining the structures of violence and committing to the path of liberation.

Pragmatic Solidarity, Catholic Social Thought, and the Challenge of COVID-19

The clearest defense of a right to health care and the related importance of social, economic, and political rights in Catholic social thought is found in Pope John XXIII's encyclical *Pacem in Terris*. There he argues: "Every man (*sic*) has the right to life, to bodily integrity, and to the means which are necessary and suitable for the proper development of life"; these means, he goes on to state, "are primarily food, clothing, shelter, rest, medical care, and finally the necessary social services" (no. 11).[20] Pope John XXIII praised the United Nations' *Universal Declaration of Human Rights* for its attention to the full range of subsidiary rights—and responsibilities—invoked in the right to a dignified life. He recognized, as Farmer does, that articulating a "right to health" is an empty gesture if not accompanied by the will to promote and safeguard access to the range of goods and services that protect individuals and communities from the conditions that impede human development. The biblical mandate to care for the poor and the most vulnerable foregrounds the needs and longings of the least well-off or the most marginalized in what has come to be called the "preferential option for the poor."

---

[20] See also, Louis F. Buckley, "Catholic Social Thought Concerning the Right to Health and to Health Care," *Linacre Quarterly* 87, no. 2 (2020): 138–146.

The *Ethical and Religious Directives for Catholic Health Care Services* (ERD), issued periodically by the United States Catholic bishops to provide guidance for care in Catholic health care institutions and health care systems, also assert a universal right to health care grounded in four central values: respect for human dignity, the preferential option for the poor, concern for the common good, and the responsible stewardship of resources.[21] As was the case for Pope John XXIII, the ERDs presume not only that suffering people should be cared for as a dimension of Christian discipleship but also that all human beings have a right to health care by virtue of being human. To acknowledge the fundamental and universal equality and dignity of all persons is to recognize both their equal potential for human flourishing and their shared vulnerability before the threat of illness, disability, and death. Drawing from Catholic social thought, access to health care is held to be important in a just society for the same reason that access to a range of political and economic goods is important. They are conditions, or in some cases, avenues for social participation, self-determination, and the pursuit of opportunity.[22]

The ERDs value health care as a contribution to the common good: "Catholic health care ministry seeks to contribute to the common good. The common good is realized when economic, political, and social conditions ensure protection for the fundamental rights of all individuals and enable all to fulfill their common purpose and reach their common goals."[23] It is presupposed that health care is a social or public good rather than a private good, in part because science and medicine are maintained by social investments. But it is also public in the sense of being necessary for realizing the opportunities and obligations of the common good, e.g.,

---

[21] United States Conference of Catholic Bishops, *Ethical and Religious Directives for Catholic Health Care Services*, 6th edition, www.usccb.org/about/doctrine/ethical-and-religious-directives/upload/ethical-religious-directives-catholic-health-service-sixth-edition-2016-06.pdf.

[22] For a fuller discussion of the implications of a right to heath care in Catholic social thought in the context of COVID-19, see Maura A. Ryan, "Tragic Choices, Revisited: COVID-19 and the Hidden Ethics of Rationing" *Christian Bioethics* 28, no. 1 (2022): 58–75.

[23] *Ethical and Religious Directives*, Introduction to Part One.

governance, work and leisure, family life, and intellectual development. Health care should be available to all in need without regard to the ability to pay.

Despite the longstanding defense of a "right to health and health care" in Catholic social thought and its incorporation in the ERDs, Catholic bioethics has been slow to make the connections between access to health care and structural violence or to engage directly the implications of social, economic, and political inequality for health and well-being. Indeed, as M. Therese Lysaught and Michael McCarthy argue in the introduction to their volume, *Catholic Bioethics and Social Justice*, despite the long tradition of Catholic social thought as a resource for reflection on the conditions for human flourishing, Catholic bioethics and Catholic social thought have remained largely siloed. Moreover, "Catholic bioethics has remained virtually silent—with a few notable exceptions around inequalities in accessing health care services and HIV/AIDS—with respect to social determinants of health, environmental effects on health, and broader questions in global health."[24]

As Lysaught and McCarthy note, the near-blindness of Catholic bioethics to the social construction of health and illness can be attributed to several factors including a preoccupation—visible in the ERDs—with moral issues in clinical medicine, particularly with bedside decision-making at the beginning and end of life. Also in the background is the persistent gap between theory and practice in human rights discourses described by Pope John Paul II in *Evangelium Vitae*, a gap he linked to false accounts of human freedom: "The roots of the contradiction between the solemn affirmation of human rights and their tragic denial in practice lies in a notion of freedom which exalts the isolated individual in an absolute way, and gives no place to solidarity, to openness to others and service of them" (no. 19).

---

[24] M. Therese Lysaught and Michael McCarthy, eds., *Catholic Bioethics & Social Justice* (Collegeville, MN: Liturgical Press Academic, 2019), 4.

John Paul II shared Farmer's critique of notions of "solidarity" that fail to move beyond "feeling(s) of vague compassion or shallow distress at the misfortunes of so many people, both near and far." Rather, solidarity is a "firm and persevering determination to commit oneself to the common good; that is to say, to the good of all and of each individual, because we are all really responsible for all" (*Sollicitudo Rei Socialis*, no. 38). But it is precisely as the challenge of solidarity moves from feelings of vague compassion to the assumption of responsibility that Farmer's development of pragmatic solidarity is most compelling. The Catholic Church has a long tradition of delivering health care to the poor. However, as Farmer repeatedly argued, delivering health care to the poor is a necessary but not sufficient practice of solidarity. If we are unwilling to address the patterns of structural violence that account for differential vulnerability to disease and death, if we fail to put human and financial resources to bear on the social causes of disease, if we do not call powerful actors to accountability, whether local or global, we are simply managing inequality. We are not working toward a new social order on behalf of the poor and marginalized.

Recent experience with COVID-19 provides an opportunity to ask what pragmatic solidarity might look like in the context of health care in the United States. It is not possible in this space to explore all the ethical dimensions of the pandemic. Nor is it possible to acknowledge all of the factors—political, religious, social, economic—that turned a public health emergency into a public health disaster. However, it is possible, even in a preliminary way, to bring the lens of pragmatic solidarity to bear and to ask what we might learn from COVID-19 about the role of structural violence in risk and resilience.

Pope Francis called the COVID-19 pandemic "the moment to see the poor."[25] In an editorial published in the journal *Science* in April 2020,

---

[25] Inés San Martin, "Pope Says Pandemic a Chance to 'See' the Poor and Rethink Production, Consumption," *Crux*, April 8, 2020, cruxnow.com/covid-19/2020/04/pope-says-pandemic-a-chance-to-see-the-poor-and-rethink-production-consumption.

leaders of the Pontifical Academies of Science and Social Science pleaded for acknowledgment of the ways in which COVID-19 both revealed and exacerbated long-standing inequalities in access to information, medical care, safe employment, and decent housing.[26] COVID-19 drew attention to the acute vulnerability of some people on both a global and a national scale. In the United States, COVID-19 had a disproportionate impact on older Americans and communities of color, especially in the early stages. While the higher incidence of death and disability can be explained in part by the higher likelihood of co-morbidities in people over the age of 65 and among African-Americans, unequal vulnerability to infection, serious illness, and death from COVID-19 is the product of a complex set of social, political, and economic choices made and reaffirmed for decades.

An article in the *New England Journal of Medicine* described nursing homes in the United States in March 2020 as "tinderboxes, ready to go up with just a spark" and attributed the then unfolding tragedy in nursing homes to "decades of neglect of long-term care policy."[27] By May 2020, COVID-19 had claimed the lives of twenty-eight thousand nursing home residents, accounting for 35 percent of the nation's deaths. In February of 2022, the Centers for Disease Control reported that more than two hundred thousand long-term care facility residents and staff had died due to COVID since the start of the pandemic. According to the authors, both in-home and institutional long-term care is underfunded by Medicaid and insufficiently monitored. In the height of the COVID-19 crisis in urban areas such as New York City, nursing homes faced critical shortages in PPE, respiratory support and equipment, medications, and staff. Low wages for nursing home staff meant many held more than one job, spreading the virus from one facility to another.

---

[26] Joachim von Braun, Stefano Zamagni, and Marcelo Sánchez Sorondo, "The Moment to See the Poor," *Science* 368, no. 6488 (2020): 214.

[27] Rachel M. Werner, Allison K. Hoffman, and Norma B. Coe, "Long-Term Care Policy after Covid-19—Solving the Nursing Home Crisis," *New England Journal of Medicine* 383, no. 30 (2020): 903–905.

As compared to White Americans, especially in the early stages of the pandemic in the fall of 2020, Black Americans were 2.6 times more likely to contract COVID-19, 4.7 times more likely to require hospitalization, and 2.1 times more likely to die; American Indian or Alaskan Native Americans were 2.8 percent more likely to contract COVID-19, 5.3 times more likely to require hospitalization, and 1.4 times more likely to die; Hispanic or Latinx Americans were 2.8 times more likely to contract COVID-19, 4.6 times more likely to require hospitalization, and 1.1 times more likely to die. [28]

In testimony before the US House of Representatives Committee on Education and Labor, labor economist Valerie Wilson explained the disparate racial impact from COVID-19 as rooted in deeper, longstanding disparities in health status, access to health care, wealth, employment, wages, housing, and income.[29] In the COVID-19 economy, there were three main groups: those who had lost their jobs; those who were essential workers and faced health insecurity as a result; and those who could continue working safely from home. As Wilson notes, Black, Latinx, Native Americans, and low-income workers were the most likely to be in the first two groups. Moreover, access to high quality health care, including preventative care for comorbid conditions such as hypertension and diabetes, differs significantly by geography and ability to pay.

Although a more substantive analysis is necessary to understand fully the differential path of the virus, it is possible to glimpse the patterns of structural violence that determine how disease and death are distributed in a pandemic. We can see, for example, how overinvestment in end-stage

---

[28] See Centers for Disease Control and Prevention, "Risk for COVID-19 Infection, Hospitalization, and Death by Race/Ethnicity," www.cdc.gov/coronavirus/2019-ncov/covid-data/investigations-discovery/hospitalization-death-by-race-ethnicity.html. The demographics of COVID-19 morbidity and mortality shifted over time as vaccine resistance accounted for more White Americans becoming ill or dying.

[29] Valerie Wilson, "Inequities Exposed: How COVID-19 Widened Racial Inequities in Education, Health, and the Workforce: Testimony Before the US House of Representatives Committee on Education and Labor," *Economic Policy Institute*, June 22, 2020, www.epi.org/publication/covid-19-inequities-wilson-testimony/.

rescue care undermines preventative care and how decisions to fund hospitals versus community clinics determines what kind and quality of care is available in particular communities. As Farmer often observed in his work in under-resourced areas of the world, those who are already at risk of poor health due to their living conditions and inadequate access to health care are more likely to have a bad outcome from exposure to a highly transmissible virus. We can also see, in the toll COVID-19 took on nursing home patients, the consequences of a longstanding failure to invest in long-term care in the United States. At the most fundamental level, practicing pragmatic solidarity involves addressing the disparities that underlie differential vulnerability under pandemic conditions and making a genuine commitment to treat health care as a human right rather than a commodity. We practice pragmatic solidarity when we turn commitments to the common good into investments in guaranteeing equity in employment, education, and housing.

Paul Farmer's Legacy for Theological Ethics

Much could and will be said about the impact of Farmer's work for theological ethics. Here I will highlight three features that are particularly significant for theological bioethics. First, very few have articulated what Lysaught and McCarthy called "bioethics in a liberationist key" as powerfully as Paul Farmer.[30] Not only was Latin American liberation theology deeply woven into his scholarship, but he lived his commitment to standing with the poor in his medical practice and challenged the powerful to see and actively respond to the social, economic, and political conditions that rendered his patients subject to unnecessary suffering, whether in a Russian prison or a rural Haitian village. Not only did he care for the bodies of the poor, he struggled with them for their liberation.

Second, in foregrounding the promotion of social, economic, and cultural rights in the context of global health, Farmer breaks out of the focus on the individual and on rights of non-interference that has

---

[30] Lysaught and McCarthy, *Catholic Bioethics & Social Justice*, 16.

dominated both international human rights discourses and debates within contemporary bioethics. He effectively shifts the subject and context for theological bioethics—from the individual patient in the clinical setting to the communities and conditions within which health and disease are experienced—and in so doing expands what counts as a moral question. It is not only decisions about when to stop treatment that should capture our theological and moral imaginations but the many-layered choices that explain why no treatment or inferior treatment is available for some people in some places. In the process, he suggests what shape a rapprochement between Catholic bioethics and Catholic social thought might take.

Finally, Farmer's challenge to practice pragmatic solidarity lends explicit content to the movement from compassion to solidarity. His call to uproot those patterns of structural violence that render some individuals and communities disproportionately vulnerable to disease and death, to unnecessary suffering, traces the path from "vague compassion" to a genuine "commitment to the common good," from managing inequality to advancing a new social order. He shows us what it looks like to practice works of mercy that are also works of justice.

Conclusion

Paul Farmer dedicated his professional life to advocating for a universal right to health grounded in the protection and promotion of those social, political, economic, and cultural conditions that allow individuals and communities to flourish as human beings. Committed not just to the care of the destitute poor but to honoring their full human dignity, he made it impossible for proponents of human rights to ignore the realities of structural violence and the connections between poverty, inequality, and disease and between differential vulnerability to disease and systemic violations of human rights. Deeply indebted to liberation theology, his development of pragmatic solidarity resonates with and expands the call to solidarity in the Catholic social tradition. He leaves contemporary theological bioethics with both a challenge and a roadmap: to see clearly what connects poverty, inequality, and disease and to go beyond by bringing all our resources (moral, theological, financial, intellectual, medical) to the creation of a new social order.

Maura A. Ryan, **PhD**, is the John Cardinal O'Hara, CSC, Associate Professor of Christian Ethics, and vice president and associate provost for faculty affairs at the University of Notre Dame. She holds a bachelor's degree in philosophy from St. Bonaventure University, a master's in theology from Boston College, and both a master's and a doctorate in religious studies from Yale University. A fellow of Notre Dame's Kroc Institute for International Peace Studies and the Ansari Institute for Global Engagement with Religion, Ryan specializes in the study of bioethics and health policy, feminist ethics, and fundamental moral theology. She is the author of the book *Ethics and Economics of Assisted Reproduction: The Cost of Longing*, and she co-edited *The Challenge of Global Stewardship: Roman Catholic Responses* with fellow Notre Dame theologian Todd Whitmore. She was also the co-editor of *A Just & True Love: Feminism at the Frontiers of Theological Ethics*.

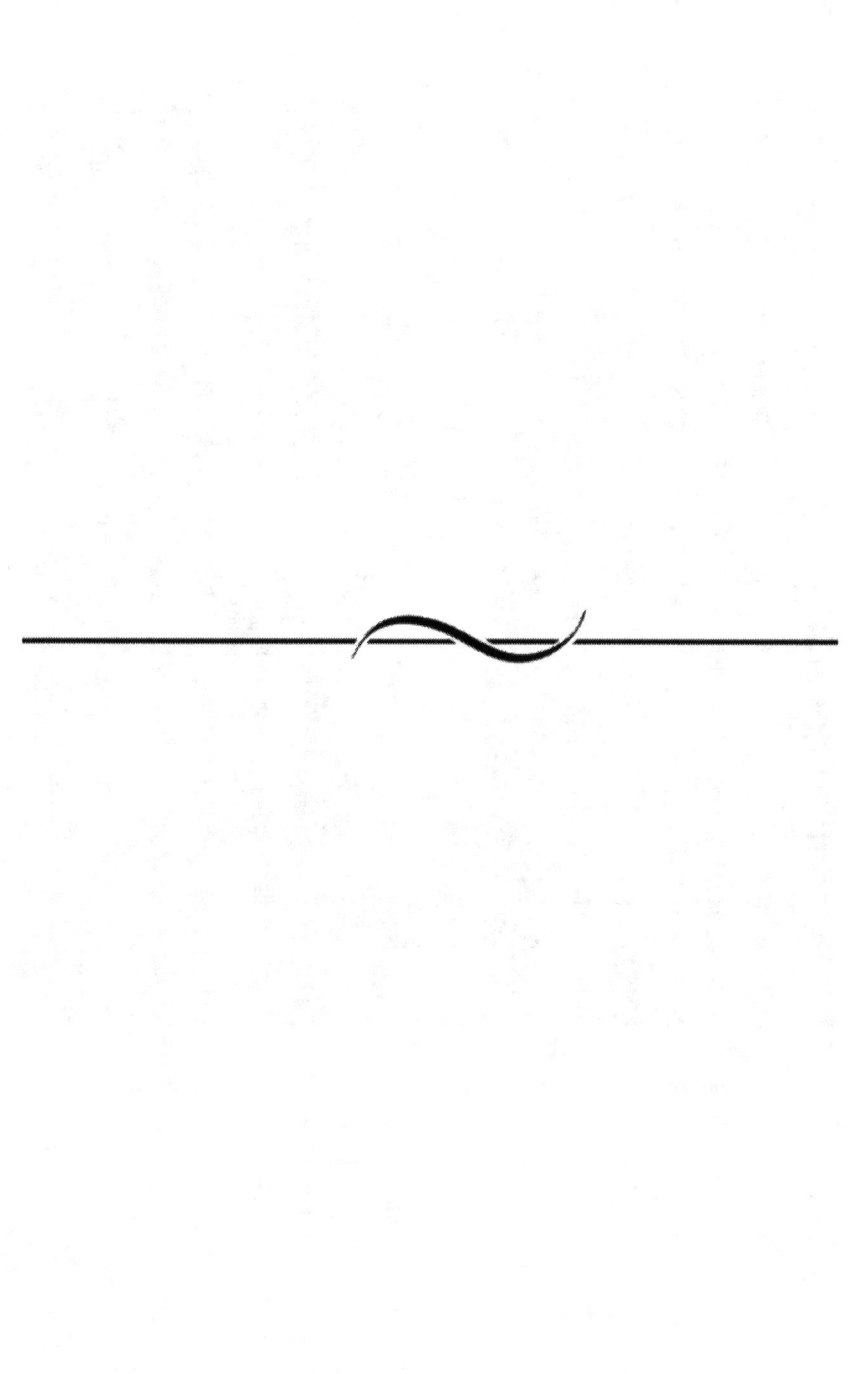

Paul Farmer with the $1 million dollar Berggruen Prize for Philosophy and Culture, May 18, 2021, Miami, Florida (Silver, black marble and amethyst sculpture designed by Cai Guo-Qiang) (Photo credit: Jennie Weiss Block)

Chapter 15: 'Doctor' of the Church: Mapping the Religious Threads in Paul Farmer's Writings

D. Brendan Johnson

> Place your whole human heart before the reality of a crucified world.
>
> Fr. Ignacio Ellacuría[1]

The late Paul Farmer, famous for his work as a physician, medical anthropologist, and founder of the non-profit Partners in Health (PIH), is not primarily known as a religious thinker. The purpose of this review essay is to overturn that view. Reading his works with a religious eye reveals a man who lived religiously in its deepest sense. According to John Caputo, a religious ethicist Farmer cites approvingly, "religion" (*re-ligare*) means binding ourselves to something other than—greater than—ourselves.[2] Farmer indeed lived a life of deep commitment: bound to justice, to his patients, to the poor, to Haiti, and to his students, friends, and co-laborers.

This review essay provides an annotated bibliography of Farmer's corpus for readers more familiar with ecclesiology than ethambutol. As other authors in this volume describe in more depth, Farmer was a social medicine physician who spent his career between the poorest places of the work and Harvard, creating a substantive corpus of written work. Most of

---

[1] Ignacio Ellacuría, "Discurso de graduación en la Universidad de Santa Clara," *Escritos Universitarios* (San Salvador: UCA Editores, 1999), 226.

[2] John D. Caputo, *On Religion* (London; New York: Routledge, 2001), 31. Farmer cites Caputo in an epigraph to a chapter critiquing mainstream (bio)ethics: Paul Farmer, "The New Malaise: Medical Ethics and Social Rights in the Global Era," in *Pathologies of Power: Health, Human Rights, and the New War on the Poor* (Berkeley: University of California Press, 2005 [2003]), 197.

his writing focused on medicine, global health, or medical anthropology, the 'ore' from which this essay tries to concentrate his theological 'gold.' Until roughly the last decade of his life, Farmer did not speak or write much about his relationship with faith or his religious tradition. Before then, when he did, he spoke of it askance—either in relatively out-of-the-way publications where he spoke more personally, or as the intellectual fire behind his medical and public health writing. But his theological motivations have been there since the beginning, as even his secular biographers notice.[3] Because Farmer was often reluctant to lead with explicitly religious language to mainstream audiences, especially early in his life, the task of situating him theologically—via his various influences and reoccurring themes—becomes all the more important.

As a US medical student whose vocational trajectory, personal religiosity, life choices, and decision to pursue a graduate degree in theology were all deeply influenced by my discovery of Paul Farmer and Fr. Gustavo Gutiérrez, I have long been deeply interested in this topic. The methodology behind this chapter—reading his books in chronological order, finding the most important non-book publications, and speaking to religiously-literate members of his circle to make sure nothing was missed—was in its own way a formalized version of what I have been doing in an ad hoc way for years. In the following, I lay out a map of his writings in roughly reverse-chronological order, piece-by-piece, rather than thematically.[4] A reverse-chronological structure allows us to begin where most people meet him, already doing his famous work and with a fully matured point of view, and follow these threads to his earlier days. Similarly, a piece-by-piece approach is chosen to help the reader get a sense

---

[3] Mark Klempner, "A Conversation with Tracy Kidder About Mountains Beyond Mountains," *HuffPost*, March 17, 2008, www.huffpost.com/entry/a-conversation-with-tracy_b_91799: "His personal history vis-à-vis religion struck me as really important. It took me a while to realize that, and to begin to try to get at it."

[4] In a forthcoming work, I hope to analyze Farmer's spirituality in more detail, as well as describing him and his work in the language of the church.

of the landscape and his development, and to find the appropriate Farmer texts for their own uses.

Fevers, Feuds, and Diamonds: Ebola and the Ravages of History (2020)

While Farmer became less reticent about religious language and concepts in the last decade of his life, the main focus of his work from his first book to his last was medicine and the field now known as global health. His final book, *Fever, Feuds, and Diamonds: Ebola and the Ravages of History*, analyzes the 2014 outbreak of Ebola in West Africa, its response by the local and global community, and the context in which it occurred.[5] In his characteristic style, he shows that these communities—far from being a "clinical desert" in a poor and disconnected region that had missed the rising tide of global development—had been made vulnerable by the predations of outside interests. Worse, the very lives that were most at risk were written off as dispensable, meaning that the battle was both philosophical as well as material, moral as well as medical.

Foregrounding powerful patient narratives, its primary themes highlight the actual history of the relationship between West Africa and the colonizing world (illustrating one final time what we will see as Farmer's signature emphasis on being "historically deep" and "geographically broad"). While the specific microbe may be a new one under Farmer's sociopolitical microscope—his previous work focused primarily on tuberculosis and HIV—he details how the same forces of inequality, colonialism, and violence fuel the Ebola epidemic as well. Against any temptation towards "therapeutic nihilism" or the colonial "control-over-care" paradigm, Farmer's emphasis on pragmatic solidarity means that he approaches Ebola no differently than other diseases: "we have to stop telling ... horror stories about an unstoppable mutant virus,

---

[5] Paul Farmer, *Fevers, Feuds, and Diamonds: Ebola and the Ravages of History* (New York: Farrar, Straus and Giroux, 2020).

because those stories often legitimate our inaction."⁶ The necessary changes, however, are only possible if those lives are considered worth saving.

Jennie Weiss Block notes that the Ebola period was a time of personal (and religious) intensity for him, and his sorrow and close retellings of the tragic stories contained in *Fever, Feuds, and Diamonds* reflect his intense attention and acute affective connection with their suffering.⁷ The threads of personal storytelling, historical contextualizing, solidarity, and fighting nihilism are ones which run throughout his scholarly career. Unlike many of his other works, he does not explicitly discuss liberation theology in this book, but emphases on structural violence and accompaniment pervade it.

In the Company of the Poor: Conversations between Dr. Paul Farmer and Fr. Gustavo Gutiérrez (2013)

During his formative college years, Farmer discovered liberation theology through Gustavo Gutiérrez' 1971 *A Theology of Liberation*.⁸ The two most important books for those interested in Farmer's relationship with (liberation) theology were published in the last decade of his life.⁹ The only book not written by Farmer included in this review is Jennie Weiss Block, OP's exquisitely sensitive spiritual biography, *Paul Farmer: Servant to the Poor* (2018).¹⁰ Written by his chief advisor at PIH, his personal spiritual advisor—or as he liked to joke, his "interior decorator"¹¹–and a theologian in her own right, Block's book focuses directly on Farmer's spiritual life. Shorter than Tracy Kidder's biography, *Mountains Beyond Mountains*,¹²

---

⁶ Farmer, *Fevers, Feuds, and Diamonds*, 442.
⁷ Jennie Weiss Block in discussion with the author, July 22, 2022.
⁸ Gustavo Gutiérrez, *A Theology of Liberation: History, Politics, and Salvation* (Maryknoll, NY: Orbis Books, 1988 [1971]).
⁹ A number of representative public lectures from this time are available on YouTube.
¹⁰ Jennie Weiss Block, *Paul Farmer: Servant to the Poor* (Collegeville, Minnesota: Liturgical Press, 2018).
¹¹ Block, *Servant to the Poor*, 8.
¹² Tracy Kidder, *Mountains Beyond Mountains: The Quest of Dr. Paul Farmer, A Man Who Would Cure the World* (NY: Random House, 2003).

Paul Farmer: Servant to the Poor helpfully includes an abbreviated time line of the major events of his life and work, PIH's evolution, and his major publications. For a religiously-inclined audience, it is particularly valuable for its religious literacy and sensitivity: who else would note that at their first meeting, the book he had been reading was Meister Eckhart?[13] The compelling writing and intimate point of view makes this book valuable even beyond its indispensable content.

The second book, based on a series of conversations at the University of Notre Dame and published in 2013, is *In the Company of the Poor: Conversations between Dr. Paul Farmer and Fr. Gustavo Gutiérrez*.[14] Here we find Farmer at his most theologically explicit. Featuring transcripts of conversations between Farmer and Gutiérrez, repackaged versions of previous writings, and new essays where the two friends interact with each other's work, *In the Company of the Poor* is a rich trove of storytelling, friendship, and theological and sociopolitical analysis. The introduction by editors Jennie Weiss Block and Michael Griffin touches on a number of themes that begin to theologize Farmer's work in Gutiérrez's key. His lifetime of working with the poor for their liberation can be read as the work of the "kingdom of God";[15] friendship with the poor despite the certainty of the "long defeat" (a line from J.R.R. Tolkien) is "accompaniment"; and shaking the gates of the world system involves standing as a "prophetic voice" in the public square. Farmer's theological debts and unique contribution are on display, as is Fr. Gutiérrez' full-throated theological affirmation of PIH's work as medically embodying

---

[13] Block, *Servant to the Poor*, 8.
[14] Paul Farmer and Gustavo Gutiérrez, *In the Company of the Poor: Conversations between Dr. Paul Farmer and Fr. Gustavo Gutiérrez*, ed. Michael P. Griffin and Jennie Weiss Block (Maryknoll, New York: Orbis Books, 2013).
[15] Farmer and Gutiérrez, *In the Company of the Poor*; Block, *Servant to the Poor*, 10. Their overlap in interests is perhaps more fortuitous than expected; Fr. Gutiérrez studied medicine for some time before seeking ordination.

the meaning of liberation theology—and even more broadly "the message of the gospel."[16]

These volumes are well-paired with a 2014 article in the progressive Christian magazine *Sojourners*, "Sacred Medicine: How Liberation Theology Can Inform Public Health."[17] Here, Farmer firsts offers homage to "two of my greatest teachers," two "Latin American men, both ordained as Catholic priests" (Romero and Gutiérrez—though he slips in his enthusiasm for a third Latin American priest, the new Pope Francis). He describes how the "slender, frayed thread of my own faith, which I had believed cut, came back into view" through his Haitian hosts and Catholic activists both lay and religious ("most of the most inspiring activists were women"). He draws three crucial lessons from liberation theology that he finds applicable to public health: the preferential option for the poor (which diseases also make), structural violence ("structural sin"), and accompaniment. This article may be used as a short and accessible introduction to arguments made at greater length elsewhere.

To Repair the World: Paul Farmer Speaks to the Next Generation (2013)

Continuing in reverse-chronological order, in 2013 Farmer collected a number of public speeches into *To Repair the World: Paul Farmer Speaks to the Next Generation*.[18] Its title—*tikkun olam* in Hebrew—gestures to the essays' religious texture. The most important address is entitled "Epiphany, Metanoia, and Praxis," a graduation speech which

---

[16] Farmer and Gutiérrez, *In the Company of the Poor*, 14–16. While Farmer's use of liberation theology is fairly nuanced in its application in the world, he does not spend much time parsing the differences between writers or eras, but often amalgamates them into one voice. His use of liberation theology also almost exclusively uses the 'classic' Latin American authors and seldom cites the other (Black, feminist, queer, womanist, minjung, Indigenous, ecological) branches of the tradition.

[17] Paul Farmer, "Sacred Medicine: How Liberation Theology Can Inform Public Health," *Sojourners Magazine*, January 2014, sojo.net/magazine/january-2014/sacred-medicine.

[18] Paul Farmer, *To Repair the World: Paul Farmer Speaks to the Next Generation*, ed. Jonathan Weigel (Berkeley: University of California Press, 2013).

apologetically emphasizes "how important, how life changing, these three lousy Greek words can be."[19] To those interested in medical ethics, specifically formulations of professional identity, "Medicine as a Vocation" offers its self-explanatory emphasis via the traditional religious language of *vocatio*. Medicine is for service to the sick (which most often means the poor): "What's it going to be," he spars, "medicine as a force for good or just another business?"[20] The can't-miss and conceptually inventive speech is "Accompaniment as Policy."[21] Here Farmer attempts to shift the development framework away from aid towards accompaniment both in its existential and practical meanings. Accompaniment is both abstract and immediate: it can include everything from theology (he cites Roberto Goizueta's classic *Caminemos con Jesús: Toward a Hispanic/Latino Theology of Accompaniment*[22]), while exposing the pretenses of philanthrocapitalism and championing community health workers (*accompagnateurs*) and a program for locally-made enriched peanut butter to fight malnutrition.[23] Touching on diverse topics, the book makes clear moral claims—he especially critiques those who comfortably minister from "safe enclosures."[24]

As a whole, *To Repair the World* exemplifies Farmer's religious eye (and tongue). A speech in New Orleans references his apocalyptically-minded taxi driver who had been predicting a biblical flood for years, "John the prophet I'll call him. St. John in a world-class, seer-sucker suit."[25] To this Tulane class of 2008, he stresses with prophetic sensitivity the

---

[19] Farmer, *To Repair the World*, 22.
[20] Farmer, *To Repair the World*, 91. Cf. Farmer, *Partner to the Poor*, 309n41, 323n44–5.
[21] Paul Farmer, "Accompaniment as Policy," in *To Repair the World*, 233–248.
[22] Roberto S. Goizueta, *Caminemos Con Jesús: Toward a Hispanic/Latino Theology of Accompaniment* (Maryknoll, NY: Orbis Books, 1995).
[23] Farmer, "Accompaniment as Policy," 242. Though accompaniment is a well-known concept in liberation theology, Farmer remarks that he heard it first from Haitians who taught him the term. See *To Repair the World*, 235. Farmer had worked on a book project about accompaniment which was never finished.
[24] Farmer, *To Repair the World*, 245.
[25] Farmer, *To Repair the World*, 158.

meaning behind disasters; they have lived through "difficult times," but they "must also be *revelatory* times."[26] Continuing the prophetic vein, the scriptural triplet of the widow, orphan, and stranger (that Israel neglects to its detriment) is expanded to include the rest of medicine's "natural constituency: the sick, the poor, the frail, the hungry, the homeless."[27] Finally, his familiarity with religious themes is evident in his swords-into-plowshares 2004 pun about "Weapons of Mass Salvation," as well as more numerous cultural-religious figures of speech than might be expected in a contemporary scholar-activist's *oeuvre* (e.g., "Jeremiads," "imprimatur," references to Egypt-the Wilderness-the Promised land, or titling chapters "A Plague on All Our Houses").

Reimagining Global Health: An Introduction (2013)

2013 also finds *Reimagining Global Health: An Introduction,* a co-authored global health textbook that attempts to move global health in the direction of social medicine.[28] Chapters treat such topics as the colonial history of global health, successful models of rural health care in Rwanda and Haiti, and the complex role of foreign aid. While addressing some similar topics as Farmer's single-authored works, it does provide a broader analysis of global health as a whole and a more textbook-style survey of topics.

In *Reimagining Global Health*, Farmer traces the roots of imperial Christianity back to the Constantinian legacy, not merely to modern colonialism. The sections that specifically discuss religion and ethics, however, were not written by Farmer but were a repackaged piece by (Farmer's mentor) Arthur Kleinman and Bridget Hanna.[29] They helpfully

---

[26] Farmer, *To Repair the World*, 158–159.
[27] Farmer, *To Repair the World*, 159.
[28] Paul Farmer, Jim Yong Kim, Arthur Kleinman, and Matthew Basilico, *Reimagining Global Health: An Introduction* (Berkeley and Los Angeles: University of California Press, 2013).
[29] This chapter originally appeared as Arthur Kleinman and Bridget Hanna, "Religious Values and Global Health," in *Ecologies of Human Flourishing*, ed. Donald K. Swearer and Susan Lloyd McGarry (Cambridge, MA.: Harvard University Press, 2011).

review the "mixed legacy" of missionary and humanitarian movements, succinctly naming the high points connecting Christianity and global health, while never forgetting the "atrocities perpetrated in the name of God" and "links between Christianity and state [and] imperial power ... during the colonial and postcolonial eras."[30]

"Personal Efficacy and Moral Engagement in Global Health" (2011)

To the original version of what became Kleinman and Hanna's chapter in *Reimagining Global Health* mentioned above, Farmer wrote a beautiful, personal—and otherwise overlooked—response. Both pieces are found in the edited volume *Ecologies of Human Flourishing*.[31] Entitled "Personal Efficacy and Moral Engagement in Global Health," this essay offers one of the clearest and most self-reflective encapsulations of his relationship with faith and how it has influenced his work. With respect to the corporal works of mercy, after which PIH's activities were almost directly modeled, he writes:

> Although I am not always proud to have a Catholic background, there are times when Christian theology brings me helpful clarity....I find the corporal works of mercy among the most compelling Catholic social teachings. Most of the seven corporal works of mercy are intuitive: feed the hungry, clothe the naked, and so on. Two, however, became clear to me only later in life: visiting the prisoners and burying the dead. "Visit the prisoners" led me again and again into prisons around the world, in Haiti, Russia, Kazakhstan, Azerbaijan, and, most recently, in Rwanda.[32]

---

[30] Paul Farmer, Jim Yong Kim, Arthur Kleinman, and Matthew Basilico, *Reimagining Global Health*, 279.
[31] Paul Farmer, "Personal Efficacy and Moral Engagement in Global Health," in *Ecologies of Human Flourishing*, ed. Donald K. Swearer and Susan Lloyd McGarry (Cambridge, MA: Harvard University Press, 2011), 91–99.
[32] Farmer, "Personal Efficacy and Moral Engagement in Global Health," 94.

It was in these prisons where PIH began to address the Multidrug Resistant Tuberculosis (MDR-TB). And it was in Guatemala that he learned about the need to bury the dead. In Guatemala, community health workers led efforts to disinter the mass graves and properly rebury the victims of (para)military violence: "Why? Because the victims had been 'buried with their eyes wide open.' And neither they nor their kin would know peace until they were buried properly. 'So that their eyes may close,'" explained their leader.[33]

In this short chapter, Farmer addresses his own reticence in talking about faith and how his knowledge of the dynamics of Christian history emerged through his work in Haiti.

> Let me say a few words about my own timidity in writing about religion. First, the Enlightenment tradition of critique bars religion from medical schools and elsewhere in the academy because it appears neither scientific nor rational. In college, my mentors in anthropology were stoutly anti-religious....I myself had at least a mild hostility to Catholicism as an undergraduate fascinated by the intersection of medicine and social science. However, as a doctoral student in anthropology, specializing in Haiti, I was expected to learn everything about the cosmology of my [very religious] hosts. Haiti made me start thinking more deeply about Catholicism vis-a-vis voodoo and liberation theology. My reservations about religious roots also rise from ambivalence about Christianity's connection to state power, especially imperial power, starting in the fourth century and continuing since .... Yet radical undercurrents always resist and enliven religious orthodoxies. Dogma begets internal critique. For example, liberation theology illuminates the unnecessary suffering and structural violence that grew out of Catholicism's co-infection with doctrinal orthodoxy and secular ambition.[34]

---

[33] Paul Farmer, *Pathologies of Power: Health, Human Rights, and the New War on the Poor* (Berkeley: University of California Press, 2003), 4.
[34] Farmer, "Personal Efficacy and Moral Engagement in Global Health," 95–96. It is interesting to note that Farmer indicates the crucial moment taking place during his time in Haiti, not during college (with Sr. Julianna de Wolf and the murder of Romero).

This brief chapter also exemplifies Farmer's seamless ability to switch registers, connecting one of Jesus's most pointed parables to the deadly subtleties of international finance.

> The radical posing of that question in four short words—"Who is my neighbor?"—expresses the imperative of engaging with others, especially with those who are unfamiliar and different. The scripture commands us to return to first principles, which is difficult for people of privilege. For example, it takes great courage for First World Catholics to subject the reigning system of global trade—one that is fundamentally unjust and perpetuates the suffering of billions in the developing world—to scrutiny and critique because they derive daily benefits from these very arrangements.[35]

Of course, this implies an active seeking of the neighbor, for "my neighbor [is] the one I must go out to look for, on the highways and byways," according to Gustavo Gutiérrez; neighbor love also reveals that "the poverty of the poor is not a call to generous relief action, but a demand that we go and build a different social order."[36]

Haiti After the Earthquake (2011)

In January 2010, a catastrophic 7.0 Mw earthquake devastated the Haitian capital of Port-au-Prince, obliterating its infrastructure, killing an estimated 316,000 people, and drawing the attention of the world. A year later, Farmer published *Haiti after the Earthquake*.[37] After recounting the

---

[35] Farmer, "Personal Efficacy and Moral Engagement in Global Health," 92–93.

[36] Gustavo Gutiérrez, *The Power of the Poor in History: Selected Writings*, trans. Robert R. Barr (Maryknoll, NY: Orbis Books, 1983), 44–45, and cited in the epigraph to Farmer, "Health, Healing, and Social Justice: Insights from Liberation Theology," in *Pathologies of Power: Health, Human Rights, and the New War on the Poor* (Berkeley: University of California Press, 2003), 139.

[37] Paul Farmer, *Haiti after the Earthquake*, ed. Abbey M. Gardner and Cassia van der Hoof Holstein (New York: PublicAffairs, 2011).

pre-earthquake history of Haiti, the rest of the book itself is a close recounting of the events of the earthquake and the sleepless days and months of the aftermath. The substantial last section of the book is made up of twelve reflections and stories by Haitian and international co-laborers.

While not featuring theology heavily in the content of the book, this book is notable for its humanism and inclusion of the other voices. However, there are moments of where his religious imagination breaks through: the epigraph to the book as a whole comes from Matthew 27, where Jesus breaths his last and the earth quakes. Farmer also insists on accompaniment, which he writes about as "the only way to create durable and transformative change."[38] Furthermore, in the introduction (entitled "Writing about Suffering"), he speaks of a "truncated project"—an unfinished book entitled "*Swords of Sorrow*, from a Gospel line (Luke 2:35): Mary learns that her soul will be pierced by a 'sword of sorrow' because she is willing to be a vessel of grace."[39]

Yet, as is often the case, Farmer's stories in *Haiti After the Earthquake* reveal his proximity to religious life and churches. Checking in on Fr. Fritz Lafontant, an Episcopal priest who had first invited the young Farmer to Cange thirty years earlier, and his wife Mamito after the earthquake, Farmer writes that "the entire church had become a post-op ward...from lintel to altar lay row upon row of mattresses. Above the altar, a black Christ (a beautiful batik from Uganda) presided over a scene of expert

---

[38] Farmer, *Haiti after the Earthquake*, 249.

[39] Farmer, *Haiti after the Earthquake*, 1. The book was going to be based on his remarks from his 2004 Lewis Henry Morgan lectures at the University of Rochester, "Swords of Sorrow: On Violence and Modernity." While the full transcripts are unavailable, the titles of his talks at least point to their content: "Structural Violence and Human Rights," "Witnessing Health Care," and "Making Medicine Matter: Rethinking Health and Human Rights." A transcript of the first is available, where Farmer remarks that just like Mary was pierced with sorrow, "so are all those who seek to understand and combat violence, including the violence born of poverty and disease in the modern world." Special thanks to Donna Mero at the University of Rochester for supplying the text.

mercy."[40] Redolent with Haitian religiosity, Farmer's account also highlights the ways that religious ritual punctuate their work—the burials conducted by Fr. Eddy Eustache (PIH/Zanmi Lasante mental health leader and a Catholic priest) after the earthquake, the benediction of the new PIH academic hospital, and more.[41] He mentions that his famous refrain, "Tout Moun Se Moun" (every person is a person) was the "earliest motto" of the revered priest-politician Fr. Jean-Bertrand Aristide, as well as, of course, being "the favored motto of the poor."[42] These references to mercy, religious (re)burials by NGO employees (either in Haiti or Honduras), and the Black Christ are not exactly *au courant* in the medical or development literature; they lift the corner of the rug to indicate the religious imagination which motivates him and through which he reads the world.

Partner to the Poor: A Paul Farmer Reader (2010)

The 2010 *Partner to the Poor: A Paul Farmer Reader* compiles works stretching back to his earliest anthropological writing in 1988, brought together by his first-week-of-college friend and longtime editor Haun Saussy.[43] It offers a broad selection of the themes of his work and displays the landscape of his interests. The book is divided into four sections, each of which focuses thematically on political economy and history, anthropology, structural violence, human rights, and medical ethics. Yet his interest is never merely descriptive or academic, and thus the book 'lands' with a political and ethical program centered around (especially economic and social) rights—the rights to the very requirements of life and the material prerequisite for civil and political rights. Farmer critiques

---

[40] Farmer, *Haiti after the Earthquake*, 107.

[41] Farmer, *Haiti after the Earthquake*, 108, 186. The hospital, built with generous donor contributions after the earthquake, is called Hôpital Universitaire de Mirebalais/Mirebalais University Hospital (HUM).

[42] Farmer, *Haiti after the Earthquake*, 136. This is often expanded into Farmer's refrain that "the idea that some lives matter less is the root of all that is wrong with the world."

[43] Paul Farmer, *Partner to the Poor: A Paul Farmer Reader* (Berkeley and Los Angeles: University of California Press, 2010), 577.

medical ethics for not making this topic (and poverty) central; as Saussy writes in the introduction, "The right to claim rights, it seems, is what 'structural violence' denies the poor."[44]

Most relevant for our purposes are his writings on structural violence. This concept, "an abiding interest ... (possibly an obsession ...)" of his, refers to "the ways in which epic poverty and inequality, with their deep histories, become *embodied* and experienced as violence."[45] This nexus of interests—the ways in which social, political, environmental, and even religious meanings are incarnated in suffering bodies—resonates distinctly with the prophetic tradition and incarnational theology. Farmer always cites the conceptual coinage of structural violence in the works of Norwegian peace researcher Johan Galtung and the Latin liberation theologians in the 1960's.[46] Here, they appear in an important chapter entitled "Structural Violence and Clinical Medicine." Accessible to even nonmedical readers, this chapter demonstrates how Farmer uses the concept of structural violence, liberation theology as an analytic tool, and the rich tradition of social medicine to address 'real world' medical problems. Social medicine, an underdog in mainstream American medical history but with strong followings in Latin America and Europe, emphasizes how structural and social factors determine the majority of human health—a perspective it shares with public health—but trades public health's affiliation with industry and the state for a radical obligation to the oppressed and a critical view towards the status quo. With Farmer, it holds that analyses must be 'historically deep and geographically broad': the "press for *comprehensiveness* is the task of social medicine."[47] While a full history of social medicine is beyond the scope of this essay, it is a tradition that stretches back to Rudolf Virchow in the nineteenth

---

[44] Haun Saussy, "Introduction: The Right to Claim Rights," in *Partner to the Poor: A Paul Farmer Reader* (Berkeley: University of California Press), 20.
[45] Farmer, *Partner to the Poor*, 293, emphasis in the original.
[46] Johan Galtung, "Violence, Peace, and Peace Research," *Journal of Peace Research* 6, no. 3 (1969): 167–191.
[47] Farmer, *To Repair the World*, 70, emphasis altered.

century and one which Farmer has helped to revive as a vital discipline in the twentieth and twenty-first.[48]

Readers may also note in *Partner to the Poor* Farmer's subtle appreciation of the importance of emotions. Certainly, empathy pervades his writings, but he forwards

> other sentiments, too: solidarity (perhaps the noblest of human sentiments); commitment; pity and mercy (sentiments not to be scorned in this age); curiosity…; the desire to be effective as a clinician and teacher (or student); and even love (of learning, of using the tools that science gives us, of others).[49]

One might add anger, too, and sorrow. The chapter "Never Again? Reflections on Human Values and Human Rights" is guided by Levinas's ethics and "cast[s] light on ways of generating empathy [and] the salutary aspects of humble service to the poor."[50] Nevertheless, Farmer does not display the depth of his own feeling here: "The one thing that scarcely appears in this book is the deep emotion that accompanies the work of solidarity." But reflecting both his deep love and his chosen trauma, his daughter notices his "sorrow bordering on obsession"—and its mirror, holy anger—after the 2011 earthquake, chafing at the way it takes over their holiday dinners.[51]

Global Health in Times of Violence (2009)

The co-edited 2009 volume *Global Health in Times of Violence* emerged from a scholarly seminar and attempts to bring anthropology to bear on

---

[48] Leon Eisenberg, "Rudolf Ludwig Karl Virchow, Where Are You Now That We Need You?," *The American Journal of Medicine* 77, no. 3 (1984): 524–532, doi.org/10.1016/0002-9343(84)90114-1.
[49] Farmer, *Partner to the Poor*, 431, cf. 492.
[50] Farmer, *Partner to the Poor*, 432.
[51] Farmer, *Haiti after the Earthquake*, 207.

questions of violence.[52] Attempting to counter the social tendencies towards silence on such questions, this book is essentially an in-depth anthropological roundtable about the intersection of violence and health. Attempting to better theorize this intersection in order to fight said violence, contributors wrote on topics such as medicine in the Holocaust, refugees and reproductive rights, and landmines and amputations.

Farmer's contribution is important for tracking his emphasis on the "anthropology of structural violence."[53] Farmer's work attempts to go beyond "event violence" towards its roots, seeing in a story of two boys picking up a landmine a whole history of arms sales and structural adjustment programs, and attempting to describe the ways that macro violence is written on micro bodies. We also learn much about Farmer from H.K. Heggenhougen's fascinating chapter; Farmer certainly would share Heggenhougen sentiment that anthropology must engage beyond its studied neutrality for the purposes of justice and human rights.[54] Heggenhougen focuses on a martyred Guatemalan community health worker (CHW), Francisco Curruchiche, a figure Farmer encouraged him to "resurrect."[55] This chapter describes this liberation theology-inspired CHW and the Berhorst Health Program's CHW program in Chimaltenango, Guatemala.[56] These and other liberation-inspired

---

[52] Barbara Rylko-Bauer, Linda M. Whiteford, and Paul Farmer, eds., *Global Health in Times of Violence* (Santa Fe, NM: School for Advanced Research Press, 2009).

[53] See, for example, Farmer, *Pathologies of Power*, 28.

[54] H.K. Heggenhougen, "Planting 'Seeds of Health' in the Fields of Structural Violence: The Life and Death of Francisco Curruchiche," in *Global Health in Times of Violence*, ed. Barbara Rylko-Bauer, Linda M. Whiteford, and Paul Farmer (Santa Fe: School for Advanced Research Press, 2009), 181–200.

[55] Heggenhougen, "Planting 'Seeds of Health' in the Fields of Structural Violence," 197.

[56] This program was featured in a World Council of Churches (WCC) documentary, *Seeds of Health* (1981), produced for World Health Organization's (WHO) important 1978 Primary Health Care Conference in Alma Ata. Dr. Carroll Berhorst was a Lutheran medical missionary. In the WCC documentary, Francisco says to his fellow villagers: "Wherever people cease to accept their miserable situation, there is resurrection. Wherever they struggle with hope, there is resurrection. Wherever unity is achieved for the good of our neighbor and people

movements for health and justice form some of the background and context for PIH's work, especially in Latin America.

Pathologies of Power: Health, Human Rights, and the New War on the Poor (2004)

If a reader is looking to acquire only one do-it-all book by Farmer, it is *Pathologies of Power: Health, Human Rights, and the New War on the Poor*—the best tour through his intellectual project as a whole, and a powerful and "plaintive book ... [which] issues plaints and sides with the plaintiffs."[57] Opening with an introduction by development theorist Amartya Sen, it also includes in the acknowledgements a martyrological list of fallen social medicine comrades.[58] Here, Farmer at his most fiery and passionate—raging against the "terrorism of money" or "US genocide in....officially blessed slaughter" on one page and confessing his "complicity," "indignation ... humility and penitence"[59] on the next—though the fire never quite outpaces the analytical rigor.

As it is his most comprehensive work, I review *Pathologies of Power* in more detail than his other works. Chapter 1, "On Suffering and Structural Violence: Social and Economic Rights in the Global Era," presents the basic themes of the book and provides a key example of his powerful combination of anthropology, medicine, and narrative. He argues that the social determinants of health also are the social determinants of the assaults on human dignity. Equity, in his view, is the "central challenge" for the future of medicine and public health, especially in light of the "outcome gap" between rich and poor which grows with each new advance in medical technology. To protect the dignity of the poor, economic and social rights will need rehabilitation, and they are vindicated at higher

---

have the courage to crucify prestige thinking and individualism, there will be resurrection." Heggenhougen, "Planting 'Seeds of Health' in the Field of Structural Violence," 181.

[57] Farmer, *Pathologies of Power*, 255.

[58] Farmer, *Pathologies of Power*, xxxv-xxxvi. The devastating litany of losses on pp. 254–255 is one of the most personally grieved and powerful passages of the book.

[59] Farmer, *Pathologies of Power*, 4, 11, 157, 258.

levels—certainly transnational, perhaps divine—than the borders of the nation state. Moreover, this chapter is wonderful for its anthropological storytelling, telling the death-stories of Acéphie and Chouchou—whom I discuss further below—due to a combination of violences.

In Chapter 3, "Lessons from Chiapas," Farmer introduces readers to the fascinating tumult of left politics, religion, and indigenous resistance in Mesoamerica, specifically after the Zapatista rebellion and the ongoing struggle for independence, health, and the end of violence (including neoliberalism and neocolonialism). Chapter 5, "Health, Healing, and Social Justice: Insights from Liberation Theology," is perhaps the most important chapter for religious readers. It charts Farmer's own relationship with liberation theology, gleans from it analytic tools that are applicable to medicine, and compares three common approaches (charity, development, and social justice) to remedying global inequality, landing firmly on the latter. This chapter calls health care workers and academics to "adopt a moral stance that would seek to expose and prevent pathologies of power."[60]

Chapter 6, "Listening for Prophetic Voices," contrasts the market-commodity ethos of health care delivery with a rights-focused ethos, warning that justice for the poor is impossible if their basic needs are left to the open market. It also bemoans conventional medical ethics for its focus on the "quandary ethics of the individual" (mostly due to its practitioners' social location) which myopically neglects the more pressing ethical problems of the world. Chapters 8 and 9, "New Malaise: Medical Ethics and Social Rights in the Global Era" and "Rethinking Health and Human Rights: Time for a Paradigm Shift," further criticize the blind spots of medical ethics for its neglect of the structural violence which continues to reap its "grim harvest." These chapters draw on Brazilian Marcio Fabri dos Anjos's pioneering liberation theology critique of

---

[60] Farmer, *Pathologies of Power*, 21.

mainstream medical ethics from the mid-1990s.[61] "Rethinking Health and Human Rights" is a helpful programmatic essay for those who wish to follow where he believed the field should head. All three are helpful for reiterating his insistence upon "pragmatic solidarity" as the ultimate goal of ethical reflection and the aim of one's efforts: "If solidarity is among the most noble of human sentiments, then surely its more tangible forms are better still."[62]

The afterward is unmatched in its poignancy. It depicts Farmer wrestling with his scholarly engagement, for in Haiti, "I will never be asked to write [or] reflect overmuch on what is described in these pages ... [here,] I am asked to do only one thing: to be a doctor, to serve the destitute sick." He ends the book, I believe, like Jacob, wounded and wrestling with God:

> Most of these essays were written in Boston, on planes, or in hotels; it is hard to write here in Haiti. But I wanted to finish it here, with the sound of bamboo scratching on a tin roof, in order to ask a question. Is it really useless to complain? For my own amusement, perhaps, I ask the question out loud. The bamboo gives no answer. I hear only the faint sound of someone singing; a hoe striking the stony earth; a finch ... . I contemplate my own loss of innocence with resentful, sometimes even tearful, silence. From whom can I demand it back? ... Everybody knows that things that go away never return.[63]

Beyond the excellent individual chapters, readers will find Farmer's key themes. Shedding anthropology's cultural relativism, he begins to articulate an "anthropology of structural violence" and calls for a locally-unique but universal real social category: the poor. If the analytical category of "the poor"—not merely euphemisms like the "socioeconomically disadvantaged," "the marginalized," "resource-poor,"

---

[61] Marcio Fabri Dos Anjos, "Medical Ethics in the Developing World: A Liberation Theology Perspective," *Journal of Medicine and Philosophy* 21, no. 6 (1996): 629–637. See Farmer, *Pathologies of Power*, 308, n. 37.
[62] Farmer, *Pathologies of Power*, 230.
[63] Farmer, *Pathologies of Power*, 255–256.

or the "Majority World," let alone "the developing world"[64]—is not robustly retained, politeness or nefarious politics, hiding behind relativism or a kumbaya universalism, can continue to protect deadly oppression.[65] Our epistemology follows our ethical commitments.[66]

Throughout *Pathologies of Power*, we find a second key theme: that while civil and political rights (CPR) are important and deeply linked to economic, social, and cultural rights (ESCR), the former are only possible when the latter are met.[67] This explains the wariness of much of the world's poor when they hear rights-language in the mouths of the powerful, and underlies Farmer's discomfort with mainstream liberalism.[68] Indeed, emerging from what I call his liberationist "realism of the poor," the Church is a frequent target of Farmer's critique when it interferes with the uplift of the oppressed, and the language of rights, despite its rhetoric of protecting the vulnerable, must be taken to task if its acceptance does not guarantee the protection of the poor.

Other themes include proximity (to the poor, to the work), which is essential for accurate epistemology—hence his "persistent struggle against the 'immodest claims of causality'" that doom the sick by misrepresenting the source of their suffering.[69] Frequent, too, is his insistence that there are not two disconnected worlds of rich and poor (implying the need for

---

[64] Cf. Farmer, *Partner to the Poor*, 267.

[65] Farmer, *Pathologies of Power*, 12–13, 15, 20, 27. Cf. *Infections and Inequalities*: "Perhaps as a point of order, I'd like to respond to the question, Who are 'the poor'? The objectification of the poor is, of course, a risk run by anyone who employs some sort of class analysis. ... At the same time, I'm not skittish about using the term: striving to understand a commonality of constraint is hardly tantamount to deny the salience of personal experience. I've been impressed, in my work in Haiti and Peru, at how often people use the label 'the poor' to describe themselves" (xli).

[66] Farmer, *Partner to the Poor*, 489: "It was the philosopher Emmanuel Levinas who observed—and I'm just paraphrasing here—that ethics precedes epistemology. Our responsibility to each other precedes and grounds our duty to discover the truth."

[67] Farmer, *Pathologies of Power*, especially Chapters 1 and 9. In addition to the Haitians, he learns this from liberation theologians like the Leonardo and Clodovis Boff (see p. 49).

[68] Farmer, *Pathologies of Power*, 261n12.

[69] Saussy, "Introduction," 3.

charity or development, tossed over the wall) but one world—in fact, the wealth of the rich is dependent upon the poverty of the poor (implying the need for justice).[70] While oppression is analyzed via intersectional lenses, he does maintain a place of privilege for poverty.

In *Pathologies of Power*, religious themes abound. Liberation theology is used throughout "both to explain and to deplore human suffering"[71]—to use a phrase he picked up from a review of an E.P. Thompson book to describe his own writerly aspirations, it seems that for Farmer liberation theology (and the medicine it inspires) is indeed where "the tygers of wrath fraternize with the horses of instruction."[72] He speaks of "Bearing Witness" (a section heading), "solidarity" and "compassion." The whole book is his "effort to 'explain the presence of pain, affliction, and evil,' [and thus] remains an exercise in theodicy."[73] In asking the *why* of such unfair suffering, his opprobrium is reserved not so much for God as for the lords of the earth, though he is equally as angry with those who by ignorance or malevolence hide the true causes of the suffering of the poor.[74]

---

[70] Farmer, *Pathologies of Power*, 50. To back up his one-world claim, Farmer uses world systems theorist Immanuel Wallerstein and theologian Pablo Richard, who warns after the fall of the Berlin Wall that "a wall between the rich and poor is being built, so that poverty does not annoy the powerful."

[71] Farmer, *Pathologies of Power*, 41.

[72] Paul Farmer, *The Uses of Haiti*, 2nd ed. (Monroe, ME: Common Courage Press, 2003), 6. "It is just this sort of mixture that someone who has worked among the Haitian poor—the poor who will never read this book—might strive to concoct. It is the mixture of one who is grateful for victories, but more accustomed to defeats."

[73] Farmer, *Pathologies of Power*, 28.

[74] In addition to the aforementioned writers in this piece, there is a whole thicket of religious figures peeking out among the pages: Wendell Berry, Bartolomé de las Casas, Oscar Romero, Gustavo Gutiérrez, Paulo Freire, Annie Dillard, Bryan Stevenson, Frei Betto, Jon Sobrino, Pablo Richard, Juan Segundo, Rebecca Chopp, Jack Nelson-Pallmeyer, Dostoyevsky, and Cornel West. These are joined by an enormous range of cultural figures which help to intellectually situate him: Sen, Virchow, Pierre Bourdieu, Chomsky, Susan Sontag, Eduardo Galeano, Maurice Merleau-Ponty, Michel Foucault, Immanuel Wallerstein, and (Subcomandante) Marcos are all found here; as are artists like Graham Greene, Fyodor Dostoyevsky, Anton Chekhov, Bertolt Brecht, and Wisława Szymborska. I claim less familiarity with those he reads in anthropology and poetry.

Via Crucis: The Way of the Cross (written 2003, published 2013)

At the same time as he was working on the magisterial *Pathologies of Power*, Farmer was also crafting a contribution to a small book *Via Crucis: The Way of the Cross*.[75] Written during 2003, though only released in 2013 due to publication difficulties, this beautiful, meditative, hand-stitched letterpress book centers artist Paul-Henri Bourgignon's spare and "haunting" depiction of the traditional twelve steps of Christ's road to the cross, accompanied by poetry by Edward Lense.[76]

Farmer's three-page contribution was written from his adopted Haitian hometown Cange.[77] Here he reflects on the theological theme of "theodicy, [which] arises with the crumbling of meaning or loss of faith in order and justice." From his vantage point witnessing human suffering at inhuman scale, "Golgothas stretch as far as the ... eye can see." One is left only to ask "How long is the way of the cross?," knowing how strong is the temptation to turn our faces away. He finds meagre comfort: "Here in Haiti, where the *Via Crucis* stretches as far as the eye can see, the sorrowful dimensions of the 'good news' and Christ's example seem more compelling than do the joyful ones."

This out-of-the-way publication from a midpoint of his career—and a crucial one, for this is from the era of Tracy Kidder's *New Yorker* profile and subsequent biography *Mountains Beyond Mountains* that catapulted him to the limelight—shows that he is already interpreting his work in a theological and spiritual key, though perhaps one that is markedly somber

---

[75] Paul Farmer, *Infections and Inequalities: The Modern Plagues* (Berkeley and Los Angeles: University of California Press, 1999).

[76] The publication delay was due to lack of interest from mainstream publishers (Erica Bourgignon, "Re: Tomorrow!," e-mail message to Paul Farmer and Jane Hoffelt, August 11, 2013). The book also features a foreword by Farmer's mentor Arthur Kleinman. Enormous thanks are due to Jane Hoffelt, executor of the Bourgignon estate, for making available a copy of this volume and supplying scans of the personal correspondence between Farmer and Erica Bourgignon.

[77] Paul Farmer, "Paul-Henri Bourgignon's Way of the Cross" in *Via Crucis* (Worthington, OH: Igloo Letterpress: Worthington, OH, 2013), n.p.

and Lenten in tone. Meditating and reflecting on all these images during Holy Week, he finds it best to sit with Mary, "pierced with sorrow"—only to follow Jon Sobrino in suggesting that the Crucified people must be taken down from the cross. Deeply wounded by the world, he leans on a rich religious vocabulary as the only language sturdy and murky enough to hold all the pain.

Infections and Inequalities: The Modern Plagues (1999)

His preceding publication—*Infections and Inequalities: The Modern Plagues* (1999)—was another work of medical anthropology, but more importantly "an exercise in social medicine."[78] This book moves from anthropological story-telling about AIDS and tuberculosis in Haiti into a broader historical and social analysis of the forces which drive these epidemics, telling patient stories and puncturing myths along the way. One hears familiar themes about "immodest claims of causality," the importance of practice,[79] the brutality of (racial, unrestrained) capitalism,[80] and the refusal to accept claims of "limited resources" or the soulless logic of cost-effectiveness.[81] Similarly, he voices his fear of being one of the "academic Cassandras who prophesy the coming plagues, but do little to avert them."[82]

Here he also articulates a life-long thesis, that it is more accurate to speak of the agency of structures than of the agency of microbes; "thus do *fundamentally social forces and processes come to be embodied as biological events*," a process to which medicine, with its biological reductionism and class position, is too often blind.[83] He situates himself in the social

---

[78] Farmer, *Infections and Inequality*, xlii. See also p. 5 for how he conceptualizes the book: it is both "a protest" and an attempt, via multiple biosocial tools, to reach a level of analysis described as the 'Holy Grail' of epidemiology.

[79] Paul Farmer, *Infections and Inequalities*, 10, cf. 235–240 as well as Chapter 1, "The Vitality of Practice."

[80] Farmer, *Infections and Inequality*, 250.

[81] Farmer, *Infections and Inequalities*, xxiii–xxviii.

[82] Farmer, *Infections and Inequalities*, xxviii.

[83] Farmer, *Infections and Inequality*, 13–14, cf. 182–183. Emphasis in the original.

medicine tradition via his use of Virchow, Thomas McKeown, and Michael Marmot, and builds upon the development and economic critiques of Amartya Sen, Immanuel Wallerstein, and Richard Wilkinson.[84] His familiarity with the Christian radical peace tradition is shown by his use of Daniel Berrigan in an epigraph on his most autobiographical chapter (Ch. 1, "The Vitality of Practice: On Personal Trajectories"). Prominent in this reflection are the traditional categories of vocation and praxis, but here the fire of intensity comes from the immediacy of needs and the resulting vitality of the practice attempting to meet them.[85] Chapter 2 presents the thesis that inequality itself is the pathogenic force. The final chapter, "The Persistent Plagues: Biological Expressions of Social Inequalities," is a warning and plea against entrenching inequality amidst new diseases and new technologies. After running though many chapters about different examples of AIDS and (recrudescent and resistant) tuberculosis, he draws parallels from the early days of social medicine amidst the typhoid epidemic of Upper Silesia: "Again, where are the Virchows of global public health?"[86]

The book is, again, replete with theological language, such as the "misery and miracles" that fill Haiti,[87] describing a section as a prolegomenon,[88] or wrestling with the claim that "the poor will always be with you."[89] He insists on telling multiple patient stories, based on anthropology as well as a religious concern to hear the forgotten voices of the world, a trait that runs through his entire career. He offhandedly remarks that the name of the "placid young man" whose job is to greet

---

[84] McKeown and Marmot are social epidemiologists whose population-scale studies show the immense power of social forces on health outcomes. Sen, Wallerstein, and Wilkinson are figures whose work focuses on the consequences of inequality, conceptualizing the "world system" and its power relations, and a criticism of mainstream development economics.
[85] Farmer, *Infections and Inequality*, 24.
[86] Farmer, *Infections and Inequalities*, 267. To learn more about Virchow, see Eisenberg, "Rudolf Ludwig Karl Virchow, Where Are You Now That We Need You?"
[87] Farmer, *Infections and Inequality*, 151, cf. 28.
[88] Farmer, *Infections and Inequality*, 53.
[89] Farmer, *Infections and Inequality*, 282.

patients at the Clinique Bon Sauveur "fittingly ... is Seraphim,"[90] an appropriate figure to welcome the patients who for him represented the face of God.

Women, Poverty, and AIDS: Sex, Drugs and Structural Violence (1996)

We have arrived at the earliest stratum of his writings.[91] 1996 saw the publication of *Women, Poverty, and AIDS: Sex, Drugs and Structural Violence*.[92] This scholarly collaborative volume is primarily focused on the titular themes, attempting to explicate their intersectionality through chapters on critical appraisals of the medical and social science literature, the mechanisms that make women and the poor increasingly vulnerable to AIDS, and the necessity of solidarity in response. Though his is not the primary voice in this text, it provides a good example of his anthropology in combination with the theses he develops in *Infections and Inequalities*. Again, this "openly partisan yet rigorous" work aims to combat the false

---

[90] Farmer, *Infections and Inequality*, 26.

[91] Between 1991 and 2003, Farmer also published a series of articles in the Jesuit magazine *America*. Some of these evolved into chapters in his later publications. These essays provide accessible introductions to his work: "The Power of the Poor in Haiti," (1991); Paul Farmer, "Greene in Haiti," (1993); "Medicine and Social Justice," (July 15, 1995), www.america magazine.org/issue/100/medicine-and-social-justice; "Listening for Prophetic Voices in Medicine," (1997); "A Visit to Chiapas," (1998); and "Haitian Refugees, Sovereignty and Globalization," (2003). These essays articulate themes that will continue across his career: that poverty (not diseases) has agency; that good analysis leads to joining the poor and sick in solidarity; that rhetoric is just posturing if not for "pragmatic interventions"; and that real change can only really come from small communities of the poor (and their accomplices). "The Power of the Poor in Haiti" gives detailed attention to Haitian church history and court intrigue amidst dictators and social uprisings; the status of the church was a burning question at the time due to the rise of one of Farmer's favorite figures, a young liberationist priest Fr. Jean-Bertrand Aristide leading the Lavalas social and political movement, who was elected as president in a landslide only to be subsequently deposed by the US. In part due to his support for Aristide, Farmer himself was at times a *persona non grata* to Haitian regimes and was unable to return to his work.

[92] Paul Farmer, Margaret Connors, and Janie Simmons, eds., *Women, Poverty, and AIDS: Sex, Drugs, and Structural Violence* (Monroe, ME: Common Courage Press, 1996).

"myths and mystifications" that prevent doctors (and others) from making common cause with the poor and sick—even momentarily "telling the truth is a victory" in a world of lies.[93] His intended audience is health care professionals, activists, and scholars (and those who would combine these roles).[94] He also continues to center stories of his patients, tying together the global and local as he narrates them. This era of work is marked by its discussion of the "New World Order," which is the neoliberal political and financial system which draws all of life into the orbit of the West's post-Cold War economic hegemony, including international financial institutions, with all its constitutive violence towards the vulnerable.[95]

The Uses of Haiti (1994)

In 1994, Farmer published his second book-length monograph, *The Uses of Haiti*.[96] Introduced by Noam Chomsky, this book is best read as a retelling of history to clear Haiti's good name, to expose those who erect a "wall of disinformation," and to call out those who have found many ways to "use" Haiti over the centuries—for profit, exploitation, negative example, and so on. Far from being an isolated and unfortunate island, Farmer narrates in painful detail how Haiti (and its poverty) is deeply tied to the rest of the world.[97]

Though he focuses mostly on Haiti, he also introduces theological themes, such as: liberationists as the accurate interpreters of history, the

---

[93] Farmer, Connors, and Simmons, eds., *Women, Poverty, and AIDS*, xvii–xviii, 28–29, 33, 38.

[94] Farmer, Connors, and Simmons, eds., *Women, Poverty, and AIDS*, xvii–xviii.

[95] Farmer, Connors, and Simmons, eds., *Women, Poverty, and AIDS*, xx. This connects with Jim Kim's work at the time and the book *Dying for Growth*. Jim Yong Kim, John Gershman, Alec Irwin, Joyce V. Millen, eds., *Dying for Growth: Global Inequality and the Health of the Poor* (Monroe, ME: Common Courage Press, 2002). Kim—whose mother was theologically trained at Union in New York City during their famous mid-century era—would go on to later have an ambivalent presidency at the World Bank.

[96] Paul Farmer, *The Uses of Haiti*, 2nd ed. (Monroe, ME: Common Courage Press, 2003).

[97] Farmer, *The Uses of Haiti*, cf. 50, 52, 78. A good example of debunking a narrative is pp. 285–286.

importance of truth-telling and listening to the voices of the poor, and liberation theology/base ecclesial communities as true hope.[98] Here we already see him reading Haiti biblically, using words like calvary, metanoia, and the via crucis.[99] He places his hope in faith and collective action, penitence and the solidarity it engenders, and the "irruption of the poor."[100] The current enemy of these is the "New World Order"—an amalgamation of neoliberal economics, neocolonialism, and continued exploitation of the poor. Its pages contain an interesting insider-outsider view of the events surrounding Aristide during this tumultuous period, with a generally positive reception of him and the movement. Finally, his citations of left intellectuals—E.P. Thompson, Chomsky, C.L.R. James, Scott James, Louis Althusser, Jean Baudrillard, and Antonio Gramsci—hint at his reading interests and the theorists that he brings into conversation with justice-oriented theologians like Gutiérrez, Jack Nelson-Pallmeyer, Diedrich Bonhoeffer, and Pablo Richard.

AIDS and Accusations: Haiti and the Geography of Blame (1992)

We conclude with his first book, *AIDS and Accusations: Haiti and the Geography of Blame*, adapted from his PhD dissertation and published in 1992.[101] "This book," he writes "is an attempt to constitute an interpretive anthropology of affliction based on complementary ethnographic, historical, epidemiologic, and political-economic analysis."[102] Contextually focused on Haiti, the emergence of HIV/AIDS, and the narratives of attribution for this new disease, it is one of his first demonstrations of an analysis that is "geographically broad and historically deep," while also giving the flavor and narrative texture of the suffering society around

---

[98] Farmer, *The Uses of Haiti*, 110, 292.
[99] Farmer, *The Uses of Haiti*, 253, 304, 336.
[100] Farmer, *The Uses of Haiti*, 307, 343, 346.
[101] Paul Farmer, *AIDS and Accusation: Haiti and the Geography of Blame*, Comparative Studies of Health Systems and Medical Care (Berkeley: University of California Press, 1992).
[102] Farmer, *AIDS and Accusation*, 13.

him—an analysis that is global and local simultaneously. As discussed previously, he also sets himself the enormous task of refuting false accusations—those "immodest claims of causality"—which swirl around Haiti during the beginning the global HIV pandemic (for one, the myth that Haitians represent an HIV threat to Americans, showing that in fact Americans spread the disease to Haiti). This is the beginning of the debunking thread of his career. Of particular note in this volume is his close attention to the lives of his patients, patients whose narratives will otherwise be forgotten (or silenced) beyond their immediate community. These threads already present in his first book—of patient narratives and debunking false claims about a disease and who is to blame—continue all the way through his last book, *Fevers, Feuds, and Diamonds*.

The poignant stories found herein are an important aspect of this book—for example, those of Acéphie and Chouchou. In a sign of their power in his own life and scholarship, their narratives continue to resurface in Farmer's books for the next two decades. The anthropologist's eye is also helpful for describing the history of his chosen town of Cange ("Kay"), a dusty village of transplants in the hills around the Peligre dam that displaced them from their old home in that fertile valley. By weaving in the history of the town, the country, and the international financial institutions that created the dam and its refugees, one is able to see Farmer's analytical comprehensiveness that is his social medicine goal.

Finally, of particular note is the description of Fr. Fritz Lafontant ("Jacques Alexis")—the Episcopal priest who first connected Farmer with Cange—as well as the origins of the clinic there. The 'catalyst' Fr. Lafontant, with "great disdain for those ... *diseurs de messe*" ('Mass sayers') who do not implement the philosophies they preach (as well as with the Protestants who buy converts with food and schools), energetically organizes social programs: "medical care, community organizing, small-scale agricultural projects, and above all, school."[103] Chapters 4 and 5

---

[103] Farmer, *AIDS and Accusation*, 34. This focus on education-as-justice would run throughout his life, eventually culminating in the University of Global Health Equity in

beautifully explain the origins and early days of Clinique Bon Sauveur ("Clinique Saint-André") and PIH/Zanmi Lasante (ZL) in Cange. With funds from a sister Episcopal diocese in South Carolina, and local vocational training in construction led by Lafontant, a church, teacher dormitory, bakery, clinic, laboratory, lunchroom, daycare and nutrition center, guesthouse, and pigsties spring up; unsurprisingly, this "efflorescence of new services drew many new families to the area."[104] The community starts to become a livable home for these water refugees, and in the village a nucleus emerges: while there has been "no village center or 'square,' ... the school-church-clinic complex may be taking on this function."[105] Through this, and through the activation of the people, winds of new hope seem to be brewing in this dusty corner of the Central Plateau.

Conclusion: Where "the Tygers of Wrath Fraternize with the Horses of Instruction"

This completes a narrative review of Farmer's written work, with special attention to the threads of religion, theology, and spirituality through a body of work that was primarily medical. Hopefully, this review has introduced new readers to Farmer's written corpus, helped contextualize his religious influences, and provided a map of the territory enabling future readers to better read this subtle writer. While he was always quick to point out that he was not a theologian—true in the sense that he did not formally study theology nor write on most of the traditional theological *loci*—his thinking and writing manifest a deeply theological imagination and understanding of the world. His legacy is one of both religiously inspired work (both scholarly and in praxis) and an example of life lived

---

Rwanda, departments and programs at Harvard and the Brigham and Women's Hospital, and the Mirebalais University Hospital which is operating successfully as a teaching hospital. When asked about the name, given that there was no university there, Farmer would retort "Yet!"

[104] Farmer, *AIDS and Accusation*, 34.
[105] Farmer, *AIDS and Accusation*, 36.

religiously in its broadest sense. Indeed, the final role of theology and religious language in Farmer's life should be seen in light of liberation theologians' focus and definition of *praxis*—action, and reflection on action.

Besides the analytical tools and fire he derived from liberation theology, he makes recourse to religious language in his writing at its margins, too, when the received language of the mainstream moral imagination is not able to shoulder the load. Thus, concepts like structural violence, accompaniment, and the preferential option for the poor are touchstones throughout his written work. They are accompanied, too, by the methodological choices (like unfailingly narrating in-depth patient stories) that reflect both his theological and anthropological influences, and the numerous religious thinkers which appear in the text.

Engaged *praxis* is the engine of any truly vital scholarship that wishes not just to describe the world but to change it. Beyond his medical expertise, theology motivated his action, as reflected in PIH's motto of "the preferential option for the poor in health care," and was also part of his reflection on the action, such when the failures of the TB program were assessed using principles derived from Base Ecclesial Communities (described in other contributions to this volume). Similarly, the activities PIH engaged in were drawn from the works of mercy. As other forthcoming work will show, the practice of accompaniment itself was also a driver for Farmer's own personal spiritual development.

In any case, Farmer's work holds together a powerful practical *use* of theology throughout his writing with an increasingly explicit voice on the subject itself in the last decade of his life. His theological categories for self-understanding, religious imagination, and theologizing about the work itself are future directions for scholars and practitioners to explore; even beyond the writings analyzed here, the wonderful chapters in this volume elucidate multiple perspectives on the religious dimensions of his work and the theological vitality of his practice. Just like the origin of the hospital in fourth century Asia Minor (co-located in St. Basil the Great's 'new city' with a church, monastery, school, and bakery),[106] Paul Farmer's work at PIH continues to teach lessons about the evergreen power of religiously-inspired work in medicine in a way that transcends borders, class, and generations. Yet, we are also familiar with the terrible abuses of religion and medicine; his perpetual admonishment that we must make a preferential option for the poor in a spirit of accompaniment perhaps serves both as guardrail and inspiration. For me, they confirm that the oldest insights are the freshest and ever-applicable, too. Despite all of the world's obfuscations, some help us to have "eyes to see."

D. Brendan Johnson, MTS, MD(c) is a medical student at the University of Minnesota, future psychiatrist, and recent Fellow at Duke Divinity School's Theology, Medicine, and Culture Initiative. His interests lie at the intersection of liberation theology, social medicine, and continental philosophy, and his work seeks to center theological analysis and communities as key elements in the struggle for health equity. He has published and presented on figures such as Ivan Illich and Deleuze and Guattari, and topics such as climate collapse and health, religious roots to the right to health, the influence of liberation theology on the social medicine movement, and post-secular forms of medical education. He was co-convener of the international Liberation Theology and Health Symposium (2021) and cohosts the podcast *Social Medicine On Air*. His artwork can be found in *Christian Century*.

---

[106] Robert Louis Wilken, "The Sick, the Aged, and the Poor: The Birth of Hospitals," in *The First Thousand Years: A Global History of Christianity* (New Haven: Yale University Press, 2012).

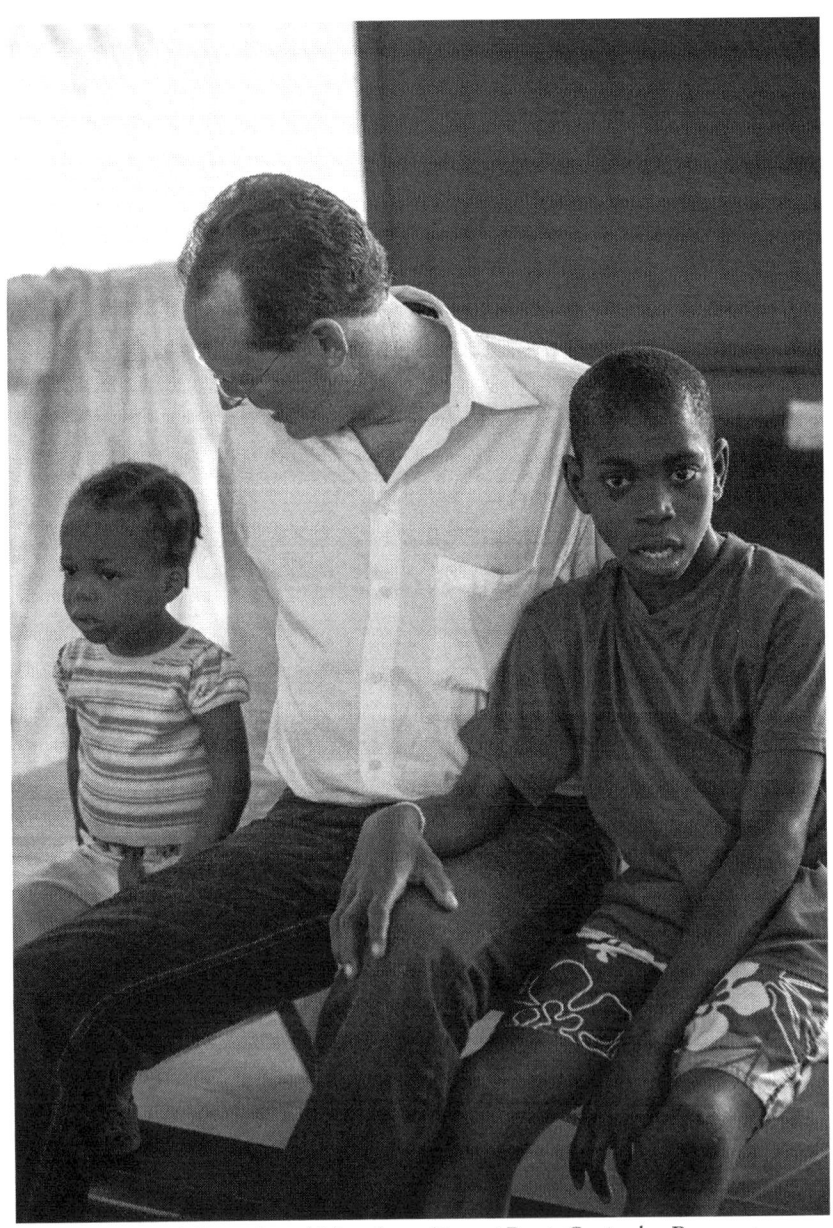

Paul Farmer with Patrick and Natasha at Zanmi Beni, Croix-des-Bouquets, Haiti, 2010 (Photo credit: Behna Gardner)

Afterword: How to Turn the Preferential Option for the Poor into Active Equity

Eddy Eustache

> Go to the people, Live among them. Learn by listening to them.
> Love them. Start with what they know.
> Build on what they have.
> If you are a great leader, when the task is done, when the work is finished, they will say:
> We did it all by ourselves.
> see Dao De Jing, no. 17

> Look how they love one another!
> Tertullian

I met Dr. Paul Edward Farmer for the first time in 2005, when he was in Cange (his "second Alma Mater") for a short stay. Despite the modest size of his house (the smallest in his neighborhood), I expected to find a man full of himself and his growing fame. Instead, he told me that I could call him "Polo," the affectionate nickname given to him by his friends and patients in this small community. Instead of showing off his breadth of knowledge or name-dropping his widening circle of admirers, Paul searched for an affinity that would bring us closer, quickly. He found it in our mutual admiration for Gustavo Gutiérrez, the father of liberation theology and a mentor of Paul. That day, we embarked on a decades-long, shared ministry informed by the central tenet of Fr. Gutiérrez's scholarship and teaching: to provide a preferential option for the poor. I was fortunate, throughout our years together, to benefit from this rare gift of Polo's—his natural affability coupled with his expansive intellect, employed almost-

Afterword

exclusively in efforts toward solidarity with the poor and marginalized. Before meeting Polo, liberation theology was, for me, mostly a theoretical framework for understanding poverty and its vicious mechanisms. My praxis was limited. Upon joining Partners In Health/Zanmi Lasante, I encountered myself amidst the "Anawim of Yahweh." I was asked to locate my own endeavors within the framework of structural violence and systemic poverty. My words were no longer enough; actions had to follow. How many times had I found myself in front of the elderly, or hungry children calling on me for food, shelter, and other basic needs? It was an embarrassing question to ask myself.

From Exclusion to Equity

The poor, I discovered, were not just the people begging on the porches of church buildings, calling on pedestrians to look at them and give them coins. These were the visible poor—the people that political authorities would extract from the streets and hide whenever the need to lie about the misery prevalent in Haiti's cities arose. No, the poor I was about to meet came from all walks of life, and the crisis in which they found themselves could be summarized in one word: exclusion. Polo was not familiar, at first, with this concept of exclusion but came to know it when he first came to Haiti's Central Plateau as a young anthropology student in 1982. There he learned that Haiti is a society split into two social and non-ethnic groups, the urban minority and the excluded, rural majority. Rural Haitians are impacted by more than two centuries of ostracism, prejudice, and limited access to services.

The people that Polo met in the Central Plateau were a generation of peasants expropriated from their land when the Haitian government decided to build a dam to produce electricity for Port-au-Prince, the capital city. The peasants' farmland was flooded and they were forced to migrate to the mountains where their misery compounded. Paul decided to make a quite a radical choice: to stand by them and carry their cause as far as he could. In the late 1980s, when, along with Ophelia Dahl, Jim Kim, Todd McCormack, and Tom White, Paul founded Partners In Health, he

Afterword

made a mission statement of liberation theology's "preferential option for the poor," and swore an oath to do whatever it took to turn this association of dedicated and devoted people into an antidote to despair.[1]

Toward a Model of Promoting Equity

How did Polo accomplish the work that became his legacy? What was his model? Did he have to apply a pre-existing humanitarian protocol and come up with an academic thesis? Of course not. His was a crusader. His talent for outstanding writing helped him to raise awareness among most of his readers (both fans and critics) about well-meaning caregivers' likelihood to "double-victimize" the poor. In *AIDS and Accusation: Haiti and the Geography of Blame*,[2] "blaming the victim" is denounced as a pathology. For years, when I was accompanying HIV+ patients during their post-test counseling, I used what I learned from my reading of Paul's work to help care providers not to blame victims but instead to approach AIDS as a disease with poverty as a direct cause.

Polo was a prolific writer. His books served first as a clarion call for all those who want to help alleviate poverty and those affected by it. There are countless readers who became zealous servants of the cause of the poor after encountering Tracy Kidder's *Mountains Beyond Mountains: The Quest of Dr. Paul Farmer, A Man Who Would Cure the World*.[3] In this bestseller, Kidder presented a detailed, honest portrait of the milieu in which Polo started his mission for the world. He offered sympathetic insight into the mentality of the destitute of rural Haiti, as well as the Harvard doctor who became their ally and advocate. Many who read the book were anxious to meet its fascinating subject and support his vision for health equity.

---

[1] See the mission statement of Partners In Health, www.pih.org.
[2] Paul Farmer, *AIDS and Accusation, Haiti and the Geography of Blame* (Berkeley: University of California Press, 1992).
[3] Tracy Kidder, *Mountains Beyond Mountains: The Quest of Dr. Paul Farmer, A Man Who Would Cure the World* (New York: Random House, 2003).

Afterword

In 2010, after *Mountains Beyond Mountains* had elevated Polo's profile to that of a global celebrity, he gave me a copy of his own collected works inscribed with the following dedication (he was fluent in Haitian Creole): *Pou Pè Eddy, frè-m, kòleg mwen, egzanp pou mwen. Pa bliye kijan nou te komanse travay sa ansanm (li tout nan liv sa), epi pa bliye ke nap travay ansanm pou tout tan gen tan. Love, Polo.* ["To Père Eddy, a brother, a colleague, a model to me. Do not forget how we began that work together (read all of that in this book), and also do not forget that we are working together forever. Love, Polo."]

Polo was more a model to me than I could ever pretend to be to him. *Partner to the Poor: A Paul Farmer Reader* is, to me and to many others, an endless source of inspiration.[4] In it, Paul not only advocates for health equity with arguments informed by anthropological and socio-political scholarship but also offers readers new pathways for making common cause with the poor. His attitude toward his patients went beyond respect; it was one of genuine affection. He saw, in the poor, his partners, his "real bosses."

When I lecture to young doctors and nurses in social medicine, I often ask them to imagine ministering to patients in resource-poor settings. Then, using a Socratic line of questioning, I engage them further about their beliefs and prejudices regarding this patient population. At the end of the session, when I sense that my audience has been sufficiently disabused of their preconceived notions about poor patients, I encourage them to read Paul Farmer's work for an accurate portrayal of health care practice among the poor and excluded.

Accompaniment versus Assistance

This commitment to true partnership and solidarity was evident again during the 2013–2016 Ebola outbreak in West Africa, when Partners In Health was asked by local ministries and governments to assist in

---

[4] Haun Saussy, ed., *Partner to the Poor: A Paul Farmer Reader* (Berkeley: University of California Press, 2010).

responding to the crisis. Often in such scenarios, NGOs arrive on the scene and quickly take action. Their interventions are time-limited, and, while they are certainly effective in addressing the acute crisis, their impact tends not to be transformative in the long term. The populations served are often left in the same state of poverty and despair until the next disaster.

As Chief Strategist at Partners In Health, Polo always preferred a long-term commitment model. He understood the Ebola epidemic as symptomatic of larger structural failures and compounding historical injustices in the region. It was for these reasons, he understood, that Ebola was able to wipe out entire families and even small neighborhoods so easily. When the crisis subsided, it was always Partners In Health's plan to stay for a long-term commitment in West Africa. Today, Partners In Health is present in Sierra Leone and Liberia, leading health programs with easy access to the most in-need patients. During my first visit to that part of the globe, I was delighted to meet a group of young and dynamic professionals and leaders who embraced the model that Polo proposed, along with the philosophy and the values that guarantee the sustainability of the PIH Mission.

Conclusion

On February 21, 2022, Polo was found dead in his room, struck down by a massive heart attack. This loss was felt like an earthquake all over the world, from the halls of Harvard to the huts of rural Haiti. Memorials were held in all the countries that had been made better by his life and work. At Paul's funeral mass in Miami, a fellow Catholic priest recalled the chants of the people during the funeral of Pope John Paul II: *"Santo subito! Santo subito!"* (*"Sainthood now! Sainthood now!"*). He remarked that the same sentiment is universally felt, now, for our beloved Dr. Paul Farmer. I know this sort of praise would have embarrassed Polo, but I also know that he strived to live as Jesus commanded, modeling for us a modern, vital sainthood in a globalized society.

Afterword

> Play your part creatively in all the struggles of men of your time,
> Thereby helping, with the seriousness of study and cheerfulness of knowledge
> To turn the struggle into common experience,
> And justice into passion.
> Bertolt Brecht, Speech to Danish Working Class on the Art of Observation (1934)

Pére Eddy Eustache, **MA**, is a Roman Catholic priest of the Diocese of Cap-Haïtien, Haiti. With an MA in Psychology from St. Paul University in Ottawa, Canada, he serves as the Director of Staff Wellness for Partners In Health, responding to psycho-social support needs of those members of the PIH staff ministering to the destitute poor. Since he joined PIH in 2005, he has led the effort to build a comprehensive mental health program across the PIH sites in Haiti, and he has traveled widely to develop and support mental health programs in PIH sites around the world. Dedicated to the mental health and well-being of those he serves, many refer to Père Eddy as "Haiti's patron saint of mental health."

Paul Farmer: Selected Works

At the time of this writing, Paul Farmer's *curriculum vitae* runs to 107 pages. In addition to the thirteen books listed below, it itemizes 186 peer-reviewed journal articles, eighty-five non-peer-reviewed journal articles, forty-six reviews, chapters, monographs and editorials, eighty 'monographs in other media,' and presentations and lectures too many to count. We invite those interested in reading Dr. Farmer's primary sources to start with the following, many of which are discussed in Brendan Johnson's review in Chapter Fifteen.

Books

Fevers, Feuds, and Diamonds: Ebola and the Ravages of History. New York: Farrar, Straus and Giroux, 2020.

In the Company of the Poor: Conversations with Dr. Paul Farmer and Fr. Gustavo Gutiérrez. Edited by Michael Griffin and Jennie Weiss Block. Maryknoll, NY: Orbis Books, 2013.

Reimagining Global Health: An Introduction. Edited by Paul Farmer, Jim Yong Kim, Arthur Kleinman, and Matthew Basilico. Berkeley, CA: University of California Press, 2013.

To Repair the World: Paul Farmer Speaks to the Next Generation. Edited by Paul Farmer and Jonathan L. Weigel. Berkeley, CA: University of California Press, 2013.

Haiti After the Earthquake. New York: PublicAffairs, 2011.

Selected Works

Partner to the Poor: A Paul Farmer Reader. Edited by Haun Saussy. Berkeley, CA: University of California Press, 2010.

Global Health in Times of Violence. Edited by Barbara Rylko-Bauer, Linda Whiteford, and Paul Farmer. Santa Fe, NM: SAR Press, 2009.

Getting Haiti Right This Time: The US and the Coup. Edited by Noam Chomsky, Paul Farmer, and Amy Goodman. Monroe, ME: Common Courage Press, 2004.

Pathologies of Power: Health, Human Rights, and the New War on the Poor. Berkeley, CA: University of California Press, 2003, 2005.

Infections and Inequalities: The Modern Plagues. Berkeley, CA: University of California Press, 1999, 2001.
French translation: *Fléaux Contemporains: Des Infections et des Inégalité*s. Paris: Economica, 2006.

Women, Poverty, and AIDS: Sex, Drugs, and Structural Violence. Edited by Paul Farmer, Margaret Connors, and Janie Simmons. Monroe, ME: Common Courage Press, 1996, 2010.

The Uses of Haiti. Monroe, ME: Common Courage Press, 1994, 2003, 2006.
Spanish translation: *¿Haití para qué?* Hondarribia, Spain: HIRU Argitaletxea, 1994, 2002.

AIDS and Accusation: Haiti and the Geography of Blame. Berkeley, CA: University of California Press, 1992, 2006.
French translation: *Sida en Haïti: La victime accusée.* Paris: Editions Karthala, 1996.

Selected Works

Biographies and Documentaries

For those who wish to learn more about Paul Farmer's work and life, we recommend the two biographies of his life as well as the award-winning documentary about his work with Partners In Health. Supplementing these are the many videos of Dr. Farmer's lectures available on YouTube.

Jennie Weiss Block, *Paul Farmer: Servant to the Poor*. Collegeville, MN: Liturgical Press, 2018.

Partners In Health, *Bending the Arc* (2017): https://bendingthearcfilm.com/.

Tracy Kidder, *Mountains Beyond Mountains: The Quest of Dr. Paul Farmer, a Man Who Would Cure the World*. New York: Random House, 2003.

Photographs

Paul in Miami, Florida, 2008 xxvii

Paul and Co-Workers in Cange, Haiti 21

Paul and Fr. Gustavo Gutiérrez, OP, Miami, Florida, 2012 109

Paul, Jennie Block, and Patient, Hôpital Universitaire
    de Mirebalais, Mirebalais, Haiti, 2014 198

Paul with Jeff, Zanmi Beni, Croix-des-Bouquets, Haiti, 2011 268

Paul with the Berggruen Prize for Philosophy
    and Culture, Miami, Florida, 2021 303

Paul Farmer with Patrick and Natash,
    Zanmi Beni, Croix-des-Bouquets, Haiti, 2010 365